OXFORD MONOGRAPHS IN
INTERNATIONAL LAW

GENERAL EDITOR: PROFESSOR IAN BROWNLIE CBE, QC, FBA
Chichele Professor of Public International Law in the University of
Oxford and Fellow of All Souls College, Oxford.

SELF-DETERMINATION AND
NATIONAL MINORITIES

OXFORD MONOGRAPHS IN
INTERNATIONAL LAW

The aim of this series of monographs is to publish important and original pieces of research on all aspects of public international law. Topics which are given particular prominence are those which, while of interest to the academic lawyer, also have important bearing on issues which touch the actual conduct of international relations. None the less the series is wide in scope and includes monographs on the history and philosophical foundations of international law.

RECENT TITLES IN THIS SERIES

Land-Locked and Geographically Disadvantaged
States in the International Law of the Sea

S. C. VASCIANNIE

Surrender, Occupation, and Private
Property in International Law

NISUKE ANDO

The Human Rights Committee: Its Role in
the Development of the International Covenant
on Civil and Political Rights

DOMINIC McGOLDRICK

Human Rights in States of Emergency
in International Law

JAIME ORAÁ

China's Practice in the Law
of the Sea

JEANETTE GREENFIELD

The International Law of
Maritime Boundaries and the
Practice of States in the
Mediterranean Sea

FARAJ ABDULLAH AHNISH

Human Rights in the Private Sphere

ANDREW CLAPHAM

Self-Determination and National Minorities

THOMAS D. MUSGRAVE

CLARENDON PRESS · OXFORD
1997

Oxford University Press, Great Clarendon Street, Oxford OX2 6DP

Oxford New York

Athens Auckland Bangkok Bogota Bombay
Buenos Aires Calcutta Cape Town Dar es Salaam
Delhi Florence Hong Kong Istanbul Karachi
Kuala Lumpur Madras Madrid Melbourne
Mexico City Nairobi Paris Singapore
Taipei Tokyo Toronto
and associated companies in
Berlin Ibadan

Oxford is a trade mark of Oxford University Press

Published in the United States by
Oxford University Press Inc., New York

British Library Cataloguing in Publication Data
Data available

Library of Congress Cataloging in Publication Data
Musgrave, Thomas D.
Self-determination and national minorities / Thomas D. Musgrave.
p. cm.—(Oxford monographs in international law)
Includes bibliographical references and index.
1. Self-determination, National. 2. Minorities—Legal status,
laws, etc. I. Title. II. Series.
JX4054.M877 1997 96-40030

ISBN 0-19-826058-X

1 3 5 7 9 10 8 6 4 2

Typeset by Best-set Typesetter Ltd., Hong Kong
Printed in Great Britain
on acid-free paper by
Bookcraft Ltd., Midsomer Norton, Somerset

To my parents

Acknowledgements

This book began as a Ph.D. thesis at the University of Sydney, where I was privileged to have Professor James Crawford as my supervisor. I wish to express my sincere thanks and deep gratitude to Professor James Crawford for his guidance and advice. I also wish to thank the librarians and staff of the Law Library at the University of Sydney, and in particular Margaret McAleese, Sarah Bishop, and Caroline Dwyer, for their assistance. Ray Penn, the Government Publications librarian at the University of Sydney's Fisher Library, Con Sarantis and Toni Smith, the librarians at the United Nations Information Centre, Sydney, Peter Gilbert, the librarian at the US Information Service, Sydney, and my research assistant, Natalie Gray were also very helpful. Finally, I owe a debt of gratitude to Michele Lambert for typing numerous drafts of the thesis and the book.

T.D.M.

Contents

Abbreviations

AC	Appeal Cases, United Kingdom
AD	Annual Digest of Public International Law Cases
ALR	Australian Law Reports
ATS	Australian Treaty Series
BGBI	Bundesgesetzblatt, Federal Republic of Germany
BVerfGE	Entscheidungen des Bundesverfassungsgerichts (Judgments of the Federal Constitutional Court, Federal Republic of Germany)
CTS	Consolidated Treaty Series
GAOR	General Assembly Official Records
ICJ	International Court of Justice
ILM	International Legal Materials
ILO	International Labour Organization
ILR	International Law Reports
JSC	Judgments of the Supreme Court of Cyprus
LNOJ	League of Nations Official Journal
LNTS	League of Nations Treaty Series
LSI	Laws of the State of Israel
OASTS	Organization of American States Treaty Series
OAU	Organization of African Unity
PCIJ	Permanent Court of International Justice
PD	Piskei Din (Judgments, Supreme Court of Israel)
QB	Queen's Bench, United Kingdom
RIAA	Reports of International Arbitral Awards
RSC	Revised Statutes of Canada
S.Ct.	Supreme Court Reporter, United States
SCOR	Security Council Official Records
UNCIO	United Nations Conference on International Organization
UNTS	United Nations Treaty Series
US	United States Reports
WLR	Weekly Law Reports, United Kingdom

Table of Cases

Table of Treaties

Table of Legislation

Introduction

Throughout the nineteenth and twentieth centuries the concept of self-determination has exerted an enormous impact on the international community. It has been an important factor in the unification and dissolution of many states in Europe and elsewehere. It has been a primary force behind the dismantling of colonial regimes and the emergence of many new states on the international plane. It continues to be the goal of many ethnic, linguistic, religious, and indigenous groups throughout the world. That such groups seek to attain self-determination for themselves shows that a close relationship exists between self-determination and minorities, and historical antecedents reveal in a majority of cases that when self-determination is in issue, the status or rights of minority groups will also be in issue.

The relationship between self-determination and minorities, however, is complicated by the fact that in international law the nature and scope of self-determination remains to a large extent unclear. In the eighteenth and nineteenth centuries various political notions of self-determination evolved which were quite different from each other in orientation and focus. When self-determination became a part of international law in the twentieth century, the nature and extent of its transformation from political concept to legal precept were not set out in international instruments, nor were they clearly established by subsequent state practice. This has had important ramifications for minorities at international law.

This book examines the various political theories of self-determination which have developed, the extent to which self-determination has become a legal right, and the complex relationship between self-determination and minorities. The historical development of self-determination and minority rights and their relationship to each other are considered in Chapters 1, 2, and 3. In Chapters 4, 5, and 6 the current status of self-determination and minority rights in international law are examined. The final four chapters address a number of problems which arise from the uncertain ambit of self-determination in international law, and its intrinsic relationship to minorities. This will involve consideration of four issues fundamental both to self-determination and to minorities, namely the definition of a people, secession, irredentism, and territorial claims based on historical title.

1

The Origins of National Consciousness

1. INTRODUCTION

The concept of self-determination originally developed throughout Europe and the United States in the eighteenth and nineteenth centuries. In essence, self-determination is understood to occur whenever a people freely determines its own political status. In Western Europe and the United States the notion of self-determination drew its inspiration primarily from Enlightenment ideas of popular sovereignty and representative government. In Central and Eastern Europe, on the other hand, the notion of self-determination was based primarily on the nineteenth-century phenomenon of nationalism. This meant that in Western Europe and the United States the concept had a political orientation which generally did not take ethnic considerations into account, whereas in Central and Eastern Europe the concept was much more strongly linked to ethnic and cultural factors. In this Chapter the development of these two concepts of self-determination, and the impact of that development on minority groups, are examined.

2. POPULAR SOVEREIGNTY AND REPRESENTATIVE GOVERNMENT

By the eighteenth century in the United Kingdom and France political and administrative power had become highly concentrated. This political cohesiveness had produced a sense of national identity which included all the inhabitants within the boundaries of the existing state. Political debate in the United Kingdom and in France during the eighteenth century focused largely on the issues of political sovereignty, liberty, constitutionalism, and the notion of a society of free citizens based on laws.[1] The issue of political sovereignty became important in England following the Revolution of 1688, when one royal dynasty was replaced by another. John Locke provided a justification for this transfer of sovereignty in his work *Two Treatises of Government*, published in 1690. Locke maintained that political sovereignty ultimately resided in the nation, which was able to transfer it

[1] Louis L. Snyder *The Meaning of Nationalism* (1954) 119.

from one sovereign to another.[2] Locke had asserted as early as 1667 that the people were supreme and that government was fiduciary. In his *Essay Concerning Toleration* he declared that the authority of magistrates was to be exercised only for the 'good, preservation and peace of men in that society', and that their conduct must in consequence be governed by this standard alone.[3] The importance of civil liberty, natural rights, and popular sovereignty was also emphasized by other English political philosophers of this period, including James Harrington, Algernon Sidney, and John Milton. Milton, in *The Tenure of Kings and Magistrates*, noted that the 'power of kings and magistrates is nothing else, but what is only derivative, transferred and committed to them in trust from the people, to the common good of them all, in whom the power yet remains fundamentally, and cannot be taken from them without a violation of their natural birthright.'[4] Harrington wrote in a similar vein. In his work *Oceana* he sought to envisage a model commonwealth. He emphasized that civil liberty would be absolutely fundamental to such a commonwealth, and that its laws would derive from reason, and receive the consent of all. Liberty and equality would be guaranteed by the fundamental law or constitution.[5]

These concepts of liberty and sovereignty exerted considerable influence in France. The philosophy of Locke and his contemporaries inspired the philosophers of the French Enlightenment, and an admiration for English government became the basis of French liberalism.[6] Montesquieu, for example, wrote extensively about English representative government, which he considered to be a model of political liberty. In his book *De l'Esprit des Lois* Montesquieu described the separation of the legislative, executive, and judicial powers in England, and asserted that such separation of powers fostered liberty.[7] Voltaire also held up England as a model for emulation, noting with admiration the freedom of discussion and publication which was permitted there.[8] Jean-Jacques Rousseau redefined the notion of political sovereignty in his celebrated work *Du Contrat Social*. True acts of sovereignty, according to Rousseau, occurred through the expression of what he referred to as the 'General Will' of the people.[9] The ideas of these Enlightenment philosophers found expression in the French Revolution,

---

[2] John Locke 'Of Civil Government' (The Second Treatise) *Two Treatises of Government* (1970) 384, 385. See also pp. 390, 430, 431.
[3] Hans Kohn *The Idea of Nationalism* (1961) 181.
[4] Frank Allen Patterson (ed.) *The Works of John Milton* (1932) Vol. 5 10.
[5] Yehoshua Arieli *Individualism and Nationalism in American Ideology* (1964) 54, 55.
[6] Hans Kohn *Prophets and Peoples* (1952) 461.
[7] *Id.*, 471.
[8] *Id.*, 473.
[9] Jean-Jacques Rousseau *The Social Contract and Discourse on the Origin of Inequality* (1974) 34.

and were explicitly incorporated into the French Declaration of Rights of 1789.[10]

The concepts of liberty, representative government, and popular sovereignty also influenced American thinkers during the eighteenth century. The leaders of the American Revolution drew their inspiration largely from the English and French political philosophers of this period, and the ideals of individual liberty and representative government were set out in the American Declaration of Independence.[11] Thomas Jefferson declared that the principles of the American government were based on the 'freest principles of the English constitution, with others derived from natural right and natural reason'.[12] According to de Tocqueville, the American people overwhelmingly subscribed to these principles: 'What strikes me is that the immense majority of spirits join together in certain common opinions . . . The great majority understand republican principles in the most democratic sense . . . It is an opinion so general and so little disputed . . . that one might almost call it a faith.'[13]

In the United States, the United Kingdom, and France the concept of self-determination thus developed from the notions of popular sovereignty, individual liberty, and representative government. Because it was based upon these principles, self-determination in the Western European context was democratic, ongoing, and universal in character.

3. THE GROWTH OF NATIONALISM

In Central and Eastern Europe the concept of self-determination did not develop from notions of popular sovereignty, individual liberty, and repre-

---

[10] 'All men are born and remain free and equal in rights; social disinctions cannot be founded except in common utility' (Art. 1); 'The principle of all sovereignty resides essentially in the nation. No body of men, no individual can exercise authority that does not emanate expressly from that source' (Art. 3), quoted in C. A. Macartney *National States and National Minorities* (1934) 47. The French Constitution of 1958 also reflects this understanding of self-determination. The Consitution of 1958 was adopted only after its approval by a majority of the French electorate in a referendum. Art. 1 referred to this procedure as an 'act of self-determination'. Art. 1 declares, *inter alia*, that 'The Republic and the peoples of the Overseas Territories who, by an act of self-determination, adopt this Constitution, hereby form a Community': Henry P. de Vries and Nina G. Galston (eds.) *Materials for the French Legal System* (1969) 7.

[11] 'We hold these truths to be self-evident, that all men are created equal, that they are endowed by their Creator with certain inalienable rights, that among these, are life, liberty, and the pursuit of happiness. That, to secure these rights, governments are instituted among men, deriving their just powers from the consent of the governed, that, whenever any form of government becomes destructive of those ends, it is the right of the people to alter or to abolish it, and to institute a new government, laying its foundation on such principles, and organising its power in such form, as to them shall seem most likely to effect their safety and happiness': American Declaration of Independence, para. 2, reproduced in Edward Conrad Smith (ed.) *The Constitution of the United States* (1979) 24.

[12] Paul Leicester Ford (ed.) *The Works of Thomas Jefferson* (1904) Vol. 3 487.

[13] Arieli, 184.

sentative government, but was based on the phenomenon of nationalism. In the United Kingdom and France there existed a politically unified state and a relatively homogeneous culture which facilitated the pursuit of political ideals such as popular sovereignty and representative government. In Central and Eastern Europe this was not the case. There was no correlation in Central and Eastern Europe between states and ethnic groups. There was, for example, no single state in the early nineteenth century within which all ethnic Germans or Italians resided. On the other hand, in the Austro-Hungarian and Russian Empires there were many diverse ethnic groups within a single state. In such circumstances identity became an issue of primary importance.

In the early nineteenth century a number of German writers began to stress the importance of ethnic, cultural, and linguistic factors in determining identity. One of the earliest writers to express such ideas was Johann Gottfried von Herder, whose *Ideen zur Philosophie der Geschichte der Menschheit* was published in the late eighteenth century. Herder developed the idea of the *Volk*, translated into English as the 'people' or the 'nation'. According to Herder, a *Volk* was a community bound together by blood-ties and characterized by a particular language, culture, religion, and set of customs.[14] Like the family of which it was simply a wider extension, the *Volk* was supposedly a 'natural unit'. Every *Volk* had the right to develop its own political institutions uninfluenced and unimpeded by others, and thus to express in the political realm its own unique national character. Each *Volk* therefore must possess its own separate state. The 'most natural state', in Herder's opinion, was 'a community with its own national character'. Multinational states were 'artificial contrivances, patched-up fragile contractions . . . devoid of inner life'.[15]

Herder's theory became very popular amongst Germans. At a time when ethnic Germans were divided amongst a number of states, Herder's concept of the *Volk* provided an identity for all Germans based on their common culture, and thereby gave them a sense of unity in spite of their political divisions. Herder's theory, moreover, provided Germans with a rationale for belonging to a single state, on the basis of their specific ethnic characteristics.[16] A relationship was thus established between the state as a political unit and the nation as a cultural one.[17] Until the nineteenth century, the ethnic composition of a state had been of little or no importance. Some states were composed of diverse cultural elements, and others were culturally homogeneous, but the matter had never been considered of any importance. Now, however, it was asserted that there was an essential relationship between the two. This led to the formulation of the concept of the 'nation-

[14] Macartney, 97; K. R. Minogue *Nationalism* (1967) 57, 59.
[15] Macartney, 62.
[16] *Id.*, 98.
[17] Alfred Cobban, *The Nation State and National Self-Determination* (1969) 35.

state', whereby the boundaries of the state must coincide with those of the nation. No longer could the state be considered simply a juristic and territorial unit.[18]

Herder's theory was taken up by other German writers, such as Johann Gottlieb Fichte, Ernst Arndt, Friedrich von Schlegel, and Friedrich Jahn. The most influential of these writers was Fichte. In his work *Reden an die deutsche Nation*, Fichte emphasized the importance of language as the unifying and distinguishing factor amongst nations. Each distinct linguistic group, or nation, had the right to rule itself.[19] 'True' nations possessed an inherent 'national character' and had a specific 'mission' to perform.[20] The role of the state was simply to promote the nation and thereby enable it to accomplish its mission.[21] Individuals must subsume their own individual character into that of the national character, which would be perpetuated through the fulfilment of its mission.[22]

The idea that nations should be defined by ethnic and linguistic criteria, and that each such nation should govern itself in a separate nation-state, spread throughout Central and Eastern Europe in the nineteenth century. Herder took a special interest in the development of the Slav peoples, whom he considered to be new and 'uncorrupted' nations destined to a great future, and his writings aroused a sense of national consciousness amongst Slavic peoples of Central and Eastern Europe.[23] In Italy the foremost exponent of the nation-state was Giuseppe Mazzini, who spent his life in the pursuit of Italian unification. Like Fichte, Mazzini believed that each nation had a particular mission to accomplish, which would further human progress. This mission could only be accomplished through the instrumentality of the nation-state. It was therefore of the utmost importance that nations achieve political unity. In the Italian context this meant that there was a duty incumbent on all Italians to strive for the liberation and unification of the various Italian states.[24]

Because the concept of self-determination in Italy and in Central and Eastern Europe developed from the phenomenon of nationalism, it may be characterized in this context as being exclusive and particularist in nature, and attaching primary importance to the group rather than to the individual. It was thus very different in nature from self-determination as understood in Western Europe and the United States.

[18] Minogue, 12; Cobban, 35.
[19] Fichte's emphasis on language led to its being adopted as the determining criterion of nationality in Germany and the countries influenced by German thought: Macartney, 99.
[20] Frederick Hertz *Nationality in History and Politics* (1944) 342.
[21] Boyd C. Shafer *Faces of Nationalism* (1972) 126.
[22] Hertz, 342.
[23] Kohn (1961) 437, 438.
[24] E. H. Carr (Chairman) *Nationalism* (A Report of a Study Group of Members of the Royal Institute of International Affairs) (1939) 90; Georges Weill *L'Eveil des Nationalités* (1930) 416.

4. THE CREATION OF NATION-STATES

The growth of national consciousness throughout Central and Eastern Europe found expression in the revolutions of 1848–9. These revolutions occurred throughout Austria, the Italian peninsula, the various German states, and the territories inhabited by Poles. They did not succeed in creating independent nation-states but they did provide the impetus for the subsequent creation of the nation-states of Italy, Germany, and Hungary.

Italy was the first of these nation-states to emerge. In the early nineteenth century the Italian Peninsula was comprised of a number of separate political entities. Austria dominated the Peninsula, and was sovereign in Lombardy-Venetia. Only Piedmont had an Italian ruler and was free from Austrian influence. In 1848 Piedmont, attempting to capitalize on nationalist revolts throughout the Peninsula, declared war on Austria. However, Piedmont was defeated and the nationalist revolts throughout the Peninsula were put down. In 1859 Piedmont again provoked a war with Austria, this time after securing an alliance with France. The Franco-Piedmont alliance brought France into this second war against Austria. Combined French and Piedmontese forces defeated the Austrians, and Austria ceded Lombardy to Piedmont. In 1860 all the remaining Italian states united with Piedmont, and in 1861 Piedmont's king, Victor Emmanual II, became the king of a united Italy. Rome and Venice initially remained outside the new Italian nation-state, but both were added within a decade.[25]

Italian unification was followed ten years later by that of the German states. The unification of the Italian Peninsula had been relatively straightforward because of the ethnic homogeneity of the Italian states. The unification of the various German states was much less straightforward due to the multinational character of Austria. There were two contending notions of the ideal German nation-state, the *Grossdeutsch* and the *Kleindeutsch* concepts. German nationalists who advocated the *Grossdeutsch* concept sought to include Austria within a unified German state. The problem with this proposal was that a majority of Austrian subjects were not ethnic Germans. The new German state, if it were to be a true nation-state unifying ethnic Germans, could not include within it millions of non-Germans. Those who advocated the *Kleindeutsch* concept sought to avoid this problem by excluding Austria from the German nation-state. But if Austria were excluded, the German nation-state would not encompass the entire German people, and would therefore not wholly fulfill its proper role. Austria itself opposed any unification of the German states in which it did not form a part, but opposed equally any breakup of the Habsburg Empire.

---

[25] Carr *et al.*, 87; Louis L. Snyder *Varieties of Nationalism: A Comparative Study* (1976) 100.

Prussia also initially opposed the idea of German unification, fearing that it would be subsumed within a larger state. By mid-century, however, Prussian leaders had become convinced that Prussia could dominate a unified German state from which Austria was excluded. Prussia therefore began to advocate the *Kleindeutsch* approach to German unification and, under the leadership of Bismarck, actively promoted German unification. As a result, all the German states, other than Austria, were unified into the first German nation-state in 1871, with the king of Prussia, Wilhelm I, becoming emperor. However, without the German Austrians it remained in the eyes of many German nationalists an 'imperfect' nation-state.[26]

The growth of nationalism amongst Germans and Italians had led to the unification of the various German and Italian states into the nation-states of Germany and Italy. Nationalism had in these two instances led to unification. But it was equally capable of leading to political disunity, as occurred in Austria. The Austrian Empire was peopled by many diverse ethnic groups, intermingled in the same territory, and ruled by a common sovereign. Twelve ethnic groups lived within the territory of the Austrian Empire: Germans, Hungarians, Czechs, Slovaks, Poles, Ukrainians, Serbs, Croats, Slovenes, Romanians, Italians, and Jews.[27] Up to the mid-nineteenth century the German element within Austria had dominated the state. Then in 1848 the Hungarians revolted, and in April 1849 declared the independence of Hungary. A combination of Austrian and Russian forces suppressed the revolt, and the Hungarian territories were reintegrated into the Austrian Empire. Hungarians, however, continued to press for national recognition. This eventually led to the *Ausgleich* of 1867, which transformed the Austrian Empire into the Dual Monarchy of Austria-Hungary. Under this agreement the Empire was divided into the two distinct states of Austria and Hungary. It provided for a common monarch and three ministers in common with control of the army, foreign affairs, and finance. In all other matters each state exercised exclusive jurisdiction. Each had its own prime minister and its own legislative assembly. A body known as the Delegations, made up of sixty members from each parliament, was summoned annually by the Emperor-King and met alternatively at Vienna and Budapest. There was a common currency and free trade between the two states. The general direction of the economy was regulated by agreements which were renegotiated every ten years.[28]

---

[26] A. J. P. Taylor *The Course of German History* (1961) 107–26.

[27] According to the 1910 census, Germans made up 24% of the population (12 million), Hungarians 19% (10 million), Western and Southern Slavs together 46% (23.5 million), Romanians 6% (3 million), and others 5%, principally Italians and Jews (2.5 million): Franjo Tudjman *Nationalism in Contemporary Europe* (1981) 14.

[28] Snyder (1976) 112.

The *Ausgleich* gave the Hungarians exclusive control over virtually all areas of jurisdiction within their kingdom, yet at the same time allowed them to retain the benefits of great power. Their success encouraged other ethnic groups within Austria-Hungary to seek similar advantages for themselves. The Czechs, who formed a majority in Bohemia and Moravia, began to agitate for a similar arrangement. The Emperor was in favour of according a much wider measure of autonomy to the Czechs and of putting the German and Czech languages onto an equal footing, but these proposals were opposed by the Germans. Germans formed the single largest minority in Bohemia and Moravia, and were the most powerful socio-economic group. They feared that any grant of autonomy to the Czechs would result in a loss of their power. German opposition to the autonomy proposal was supported by the Hungarians, who feared that its implementation would encourage ethnic groups within Hungary to press for greater autonomy. The opposition of the two largest peoples in the realm forced the Emperor to abandon the scheme, which created great bitterness amongst the Czechs.

Ethnic Hungarians were equally reluctant to share power with other ethnic groups, even though such groups made up more than half the population of Hungary.[29] The Hungarian Government pursued a policy of assimilation, on the basis that this would strengthen the Hungarian nation and thereby make it more difficult to alter the structure of the Dual Monarchy. But the other ethnic groups within Hungary vigorously resisted Hungarian attempts to assimilate them. As a result the relationship between ethnic Hungarians and the other ethnic groups in Hungary also became one of bitterness and resentment. This souring of relationships amongst the various ethnic groups in Austria and Hungary created significant internal tensions within Austro-Hungary during the latter half of the nineteenth century.[30]

5. NATIONAL MINORITIES

Early nationalist writers such as Herder and Mazzini imagined that world peace would prevail once every ethnic group had attained its own nation-state.[31] This proved not to be the case. Instead, as national consciousness grew amongst the various peoples of Europe, so too did ethnic conflict.

The nation-state was conceived as the ultimate political expression of a particular people. Its first duty, as the German historian Treitschke said,

---

[29] In 1880 ethnic Hungarians formed 41.2% of the population of Hungary: Victor L. Tapié *The Rise and Fall of the Habsburg Monarchy* (1971) 344.
[30] Macartney, 143.
[31] Minogue, 55.

was 'to develop the national character . . . to permeate the peoples united in it with the like speech and culture'.[32] The concept of the nation-state presupposed an exact correlation in the boundaries of the nation and the state; in reality this seldom occurred. Whenever it did not occur, so that some other ethnic group was also encompassed within the state, tension arose between the majority and minority groups, because the minority was *ipso facto* an alien element. The minority could not join in building the national character and culture of the dominant people, nor could its own national aspirations be satisfied. Minority peoples were anomalies within the nation-state, and were perceived as elements which weakened and divided it. It was thought that such minorities must be assimilated, so that the entire population of the nation-state might belong to one culture and speak one language.

As a result intensive efforts were made to assimilate minorities in the late nineteenth and early twentieth centuries. In Germany various measures were adopted by the German Parliament in 1886 to 'germanize' the Poles, who constituted the largest ethnic minority.[33] Public use of the Polish language was prohibited, including use in the courts, the school system, and all administrative processes.[34] Polish estates were purchased by a Colonization Commission which settled on them German farmers who pledged 'to remain German and, above all, to marry German wives'.[35] Similar policies were adopted towards the Danes in Schleswig and the French in Alsace-Lorraine.

Russia also attempted to assimilate its ethnic minorities with its programme of 'russification'. This sought to force ethnic minorities to adopt Russian Orthodoxy as their religion and Russian as their language. The most vigorous efforts at assimilation were directed against the Poles after the Polish insurrection of 1863. Russian Poland was deprived of its autonomous status within the Empire. Poles were not permitted to hold public office, were obliged to speak Russian in the schools and law courts, and could sell their land only to Russians.[36] Other ethnic minorities also suffered in various ways from the effects of russification. In Byelorussia and Lithuania Russian Orthodoxy was forced on the Catholic populations, as it was on the Protestant majority in Estonia and Latvia. Russian was declared the official language in the Baltic provinces. In the Ukraine the use of the Ukrainian language was prohibited. Finland, which had enjoyed a measure of autonomy within the Empire, was deprived of its special status.

---

[32] Macartney, 103.
[33] Poland had been dismembered by Prussia, Austria, and Russia in the three partitions of 1772, 1793, and 1795. In the final partition the state of Poland ceased to exist. There were approximately 3 million ethnic Poles in Germany in 1886.
[34] Macartney, 128.
[35] Carlton J. H. Hayes *Nationalism: A Religion* (1960) 110.
[36] *Id.*, 111.

These efforts at forcible assimilation were for the most part unsuccessful and even counter-productive. Attempts to assimilate particular ethnic groups often aroused the national consciousness of those groups, so that they became more resistant to the threat to their national identity. Such groups would then develop their own nationalist aspirations, which could be satisfied only through the creation of a separate nation-state.

Another problem which developed as a result of the rise of nationalism involved those national minorities known as 'irredenta', by which is meant sections of an ethnic group which remained outside their nation-state upon its creation.[37] Because the nation-state was based on the idea that a nation must form its own state, nationalists believed that as long as a portion of the nation remained outside the state the nation-state remained incomplete. They also believed that the irredenta would not achieve the same level of fulfilment unless it joined the nation-state. This was the basis on which Treitschke, for example, justified the annexation of Alsace even though the German-speaking Alsatians themselves opposed incorporation into Germany. Treitschke declared:

These territories are ours by the right of the sword, and we shall dispose of them in virtue of a proper right—the right of the German nation, which will not permit its children to remain strangers to the German Empire. We Germans, who know Germany and France, know better than these unfortunates themselves what is good for the people of Alsace, who have remained under the misleading influence of their French connexion outside the sympathies of new Germany. We shall restore them to their true selves against their will.[38]

Most nation-states, however, remained 'incomplete'. After the unifications of Italy and Germany large numbers of Italians and Germans remained outside their respective nation-states. Trieste, Istria, and the Trentino remained Austrian. Nice and Corsica belonged to France, and Ticino to Switzerland. Millions of Germans living in Austro-Hungary, Switzerland, the Netherlands, and the Baltic region were not included in the German nation-state. The continued existence of these irredenta was a constant source of aggravation to nationalists and a destabilizing influence in inter-state relations. The situation was further complicated by the fact that irredenta were often found in areas of mixed population. In areas where several ethnic groups coexisted, there could be competing irredentist claims by several nation-states. Because of the mixed nature of the population, such competing claims were necessarily incompatible.

In Western Europe the position and treatment of national minorities was

---

[37] The word 'irredenta' was first used in the context '*Italia irredenta*', meaning 'unredeemed Italy'. The term was used by Mazzini to describe ethnic Italians inhabiting territories outside the Italian nation-state.

[38] Macartney, 100. Treitschke's comments should be compared to those of Napoleon who, when asked about the nationality of the Alsatians, replied that they 'felt French': *Id.*, 111.

very different. In the nineteenth century national minorities in Western Europe lived for the most part 'on reasonably pleasant terms with the majorities to which they were politically attached, and did not aspire to political independence'.[39] Self-determination in Western Europe was not defined in terms of ethnic groups and nation-states, but rather in terms of popular sovereignty and representative government. The role of the state was to ensure liberty and representative government to all of its inhabitants rather than to foster the well-being of a particular nation. This meant that minorities were accommodated more readily within the state and distinctions were not drawn on the basis of ethnic origin.[40] During the French Revolution there was no discussion amongst the revolutionary leaders of the position of minorities such as the Bretons, Alsatians, or Flemings within the new French Republic. Rather the 'establishment of the same treatment for all appeared to them to meet the whole case'.[41] The same attitude prevailed in the United Kingdom. Zimmern declared that the term 'British' was 'nationally colourless', and maintained that the 'English are the people who have most completely solved the problem of nationality, because they have most completely divorced it from politics'.[42]

Because national consciousness in Western Europe was focused upon the political ideals of individual liberty and representative government, rather than upon ethnic considerations, integration into the state was potentially available to all, whatever their cultural identity or affiliation. In the United States this was evident as early as 1782:

What then is an American, this new man? He is either an European, or the descendant of an European, hence that strange mixture of blood, which you will find in no other country. I could point out to you a man, whose grandfather was an Englishman, whose wife was Dutch, whose son married a French woman, and whose present four sons have now four wives of different nations. He is an American, who, leaving behind him all his ancient prejudices, and manners, receives new ones from

---

[39] Macartney, 152. This was the case even in Belgium. At the time of Belgian independence in 1830, 'there was no significant regional consciousness based on linguistic criteria' and socially mobile Flemish speakers tended to assimilate into the French-speaking group. Flemish nationalism did not develop until the twentieth century: Alexander B. Murphy 'Evoking Regionalism in Linguistically Divided Belgium' in David B. Knight and Elinore Kofman (eds.) *Nationalism, Self-Determination and Political Geography* (1988) 140: William Petersen 'On the Subnations of Western Europe' in Nathan Glazer and Daniel P. Moynihan (eds.) *Ethnicity* (1975) 177. The Irish, on the other hand, were the most significant exception to this state of affairs: Macartney, 152.

[40] The universalism of Western European self-determination thus tended to preclude any special treatment for minorities: Allen Buchanan 'Self-Determination and the Right to Secede' (1991) 45 *Journal of International Affairs* 347, 350, 351.

[41] Macartney, 47. In this regard the French National Assembly in 1791 admitted Jews to complete equality with other French citizens: *id.*, 47.

[42] A. Zimmern *The Third British Empire* (1934) 180, 186.

the new mode of life he has embraced, the new government he obeys, and the new rank he holds. He becomes an American by being received in the broad lap of our great Alma Mater. Here individuals of all nations are melted into a new race of men, whose labours and posterity will one day cause great changes in the world.[43]

As the Western European tradition of self-determination did not involve ethnic considerations, individuals were able to participate as equal members in the political processes of the state whatever their ethnic origins, and minorities coexisted much more easily within the wider population.

6. CONCLUSION

The notion that a people should be able freely to determine its own political status had by the beginning of the twentieth century become a widely held conviction throughout Europe and the United States. The underlying basis for this conviction, however, differed enormously in Western Europe and the United States, on one hand, and in Central and Eastern Europe, on the other.

The Western European tradition of self-determination was based on the concepts of popular sovereignty, individual freedom, and representative government. Self-determination occurred whenever an exercise of popular sovereignty resulted in a representative government. It occurred within the pre-existing boundaries of the state, and was exercisable by all citizens of the state, whatever their ethnic or linguistic attributes. The fact that the boundaries of the state might encompass different ethnic groups was thought to be of no consequence.

In Central and Eastern Europe the concept of self-determination grew out of the phenomenon of nationalism. The 'nation' was generally defined as comprising those who shared the same ethnic, linguistic, and religious attributes. Self-determination in the Central and Eastern European tradition occurred whenever a particular nation was able to create its own nation-state, i.e. a state whose political boundaries corresponded to the geographical distribution of the nation or ethnic group. Self-determination in this context was exercisable only by those who belonged to a particular group, and its aim was the creation of a new state.

Because Central and Eastern Europe contained a large number of ethnic groups intermingled together, the nation-states which were created invariably included national minorities, i.e. those who belonged to ethnic groups other than the predominant one. These national minorities were seen to be

---

[43] J. Hector St. John (Michel Guillaume St. Jean de Crèvecoeur) *Letters From An American Farmer* (1963) 63, 64.

anomalies within the nation-state, which led to ongoing tension between national majorities and minorities within such states. In Western Europe and the United States such tensions were far less significant because self-determination in the Western Europen context was inclusive rather than exclusive in nature.

2

Self-Determination and the First World War

1. INTRODUCTION

By the beginning of the twentieth century the problem of disaffected ethnic groups had dominated the political situation in Central and Eastern Europe for some fifty years. Upon the outbreak of the First World War in 1914 many of the smaller ethnic groups began to press for self-determination. These groups sought to capitalize on the upheaval and dislocation of the War in order to attain independence. As a result the question of self-determination became an important issue during the War and in the subsequent Peace Conference. In this Chapter the various promises of the Allies and the Central Powers to disaffected ethnic groups are considered, followed by an examination of the policies of the Bolsheviks and of Woodrow Wilson with regard to self-determination. The influence of self-determination on the Paris Peace Conference is also examined.

2. PROMISES MADE BY THE BELLIGERENTS DURING THE WAR

At the outset of the War both the Allies and the Central Powers were well aware of the potential for sowing discord in enemy ranks by appealing to the nationalist sentiment of disaffected ethnic groups. However, both sides also recognized that such appeals could be made to their own disaffected ethnic groups. Consequently such tactics were initially assayed with some caution.

The Germans were the first to exploit the nationalism of their opponents' subject nationalities, giving assistance to Sinn Fein and encouraging Flemish separatists. They organized a 'Congress of Nationalities' which met at Lausanne in June 1916, comprised of representatives of the various subject nationalities of Russia.[1] When the Germans occupied Lithuania in 1915 and the Baltic provinces in 1916, they encouraged those peoples to separate from Russia. Similarly, the Germans supported the Finns' desire for independence.

The United Kingdom and France found that their association with Russia

[1] C. A. Macartney *National States and National Minorities* (1934) 183.

prevented them from appealing to the subject nationalities of the Central Powers. As imperial Russia had no intention of granting independence to any of its various nationalities, the United Kingdom and France could not very well advocate a policy of national self-determination for the various minority ethnic groups of Germany and Austro-Hungary without causing problems for their Russian ally. A tentative statement on self-determination was issued by the British Foreign Office in 1916. This memorandum declared:

His Majesty's Government have announced that one of their chief objects in the present war is to ensure that all the states of Europe, great and small, shall in the future be in a position to achieve their national development in freedom and security. It is clear, moreover, that no peace can be satisfactory to this country unless it promises to be durable, and an essential condition of such a peace is that it should give full scope to national aspirations as far as practicable. The principle of nationality should therefore be one of the governing factors in the consideration of territorial arrangements after the war.[2]

Even this modest declaration was qualified in a subsequent paragraph: 'In giving effect to the above principles, however, we are limited in the first place by the pledges already given to our Allies which may, as for instance in the case of Italy, be difficult to reconcile with the claims of nationalities.'[3] It was this qualification which actually represented the policy of the Allies in the early part of the war. The Allies had not hesitated to promise territorial concessions to potential allies such as Italy in return for military assistance. In some cases this amounted to an indirect application of the principle of self-determination, because the promised territorial concessions would result in a closer approximation of political and ethnographic boundaries. However, in other cases territorial promises worked against the principle of self-determination because the inhabitants of the promised territories were not of the same ethnic origin. The Allies persuaded Italy to join their cause by promising Italy all of those territories inhabited by an Italian irredenta, even though most inhabitants of those territories were non-Italians. Likewise, the Allied treaty with Romania promised additional territory far exceeding the ethnic Romanian frontiers. The Central Powers also made similar promises. Bulgaria, for example, was promised territory which extended beyond the regions inhabited by ethnic Bulgarians.[4]

Both sides sought the support of the Poles by promising them some form of resurrected state. However, because Poland was divided amongst Germany, Austro-Hungary, and Russia it was difficult for either side to promise anything which would not threaten their own territorial integrity. Russia

---

[2] David Lloyd George *The Truth About the Peace Treaties* (1938), Vol. 1, 31, 32.
[3] *Id.*, 32.
[4] Macartney, 182.

proposed to unite all three parts of Poland into a single autonomous region, with its own national intitutions, but ultimately remaining subject to Russian sovereignty.[5] In response, Austro-Hungary proposed to establish an independent Polish state comprising all Polish territories. Germany initially proposed independence for Russian Poland only, but by November 1916 it also decided that an independent Poland made up of all Polish territories should be created. This encouraged the Polish leader, Josef Pilsudski, to support the Central Powers against the Russians. The Central Powers thus managed to turn the Poles against the Russians, but Russia succeeded in destabilizing the Austro-Hungarian Army by promising to support the demands of Austro-Hungarian Slavs for independence. This resulted in the desertion of several entire Czech regiments in 1915.[6] Still, neither side was actually prepared to declare itself unequivocally in favour of self-determination', and appeals to self-determination were made only in self-interest.

3. SELF-DETERMINATION AND THE BOLSHEVIKS

In March 1917 the Tsarist regime was overthrown and replaced by the Provisional Government of Alexander Kerensky. There was an immediate change of policy towards the subject nationalities, evidenced by the declaration of the Provisional Government on 29 March 1917. The Provisional Government declared that it repudiated any intention on the part of 'free Russia' either to dominate or to conquer other nations, that it sought to attain 'a durable peace on the basis of the right of nations to decide their own destinies', and that it would voluntarily remove, 'in the name of the higher principles of equality, the chains which weighed down the Polish nation'.[7] This policy of toleration towards the subject nationalities was a marked change from the oppression of the Tsarist regime and did much to encourage nationalist aspirations. The new policy led to declarations of autonomy from several ethnic groups. The peoples of the Northern Caucasus established a separate union in May 1917, and the Ukrainians declared their Parliament at Kiev autonomous in June 1917. The Finns declared the autonomy of their Diet in July 1917, while continuing to press, like the Poles, for complete political independence.

Although it had adopted a policy of toleration towards the non-Russian nationalities, the Provisional Government also wanted to pursue the war effort and to honour the secret treaties which Russia had made with the Allies. It therefore had to keep the various parts of the former empire

---

[5] *Id.*, 183.
[6] Victor-L. Tapié *The Rise and Fall of the Habsburg Monarchy* (1971) 374.
[7] Macartney, 186, 187.

under strict control, and consequently did not welcome these moves by the non-Russian nationalities. As Poland was at this time wholly occupied by Germany, the Provisional Government was forced to match Germany's promise of independence to Poland, but with respect to Finnish demands it remained noncommittal. It was also unresponsive to the small but fervent group of Ukrainian nationalists who were agitating for Ukrainian self-determination.[8]

Unlike the Provisional Government, the Bolsheviks came out strongly in favour of self-determination, and even supported secession if desired by the ethnic group in question. They advocated the independence, not only of Poland, but of Finland and the Ukraine as well. In a conference held in April 1917, the Bolsheviks adopted a resolution which recognized the right 'of all the nations forming part of Russia to freely secede and form independent states'.[9] This resolution reaffirmed the longstanding position of the Bolsheviks with regard to self-determination.[10]

Not all Bolsheviks agreed that self-determination was the proper policy with regard to the nationalities question. Rosa Luxemburg, in a thesis which subsequently became known as the 'Polish heresy', denigrated the idea that nationalities should have the right of self-determination and be entitled to establish their own states. The notion of national independence was a bourgeois concern, in which the proletariat, being essentially international, could have no interest.[11] Luxemburg rejected the idea of independence for Poland, arguing that Poland was tied to the Russian Empire by economic bonds and therefore Polish independence would be retrogressive. The true interests of the Polish proletariat were to be found in the 'universal class strivings of the proletariat', which meant that the Polish proletariat should seek no more than autonomy within a democratized Russian state.[12] Many Bolshevik leaders viewed with considerable unease the impending dissolution of the former Russian Empire, which they saw as the inevitable consequence of self-determination, and yet which seemed to them to be so utterly contrary to the principles of internationalism and the solidarity of the proletariat.[13]

Lenin was the prime advocate of self-determination, for which he argued

---

[8] Samad Shaheen *The Communist Theory of National Self-Determination* (1956) 135; Edward Hallett Carr *The Bolshevik Revolution 1917–1923* (1960) 287.

[9] Joseph Stalin *Marxism and the National and Colonial Question* (1936) 269, 270.

[10] The right to self-determination had originally been adopted by the Second International at the London International Conference in 1896: V. I. Lenin *Selected Works* (1947) Vol. 1, 591, 592. In 1903, at the Second Congress of the Russian Social-Democratic Labour Party, the 'national problem' had been addressed in the Party Programme. Article 9 specifically granted the right of self-determination to all nations in the state: Shaheen, 25, 26.

[11] Carr, 422.

[12] Rosa Luxemburg *The National Question* (1976) 85, 86.

[13] Such as Bukharin, Radek, and Piatakov: Alfred D. Low *Lenin on the Question of Nationality* (1958) 70.

vigorously in a number of pamphlets. He brushed aside the fears of other Bolsheviks regarding the disintegration of the former Russian Empire by drawing an analogy between self-determination and liberal divorce laws:

To accuse the supporters of freedom of self-determination, i.e. freedom to secede, of encouraging separatism, is as foolish and as hypocritical as accusing the advocates of freedom of divorce of encouraging the destruction of family ties . . . They believe that in actual fact freedom of divorce will not cause the disintegration of family ties but, on the contrary, will strengthen them on a democratic basis, which is the only possible and durable basis in civilized society.[14]

Lenin realized that the resentment of the various nationalities against Tsarist Russia which had arisen as a result of the oppressive policy of 'russification' could be used to facilitate the overthrow of the Tsarist regime, and at the same time to elicit support from these peoples for the Bolsheviks. The inclusion of a right of self-determination signalled clearly to the various nationalities that the Russian Marxists were opposed to all forms of discrimination or oppression of one nation by another.[15] Unity would be maintained, Lenin believed, by voluntary agreement: forced unions would not endure, whereas voluntary unions were much more likely to last. Secession would thus occur only in the most intolerable circumstances. By acknowledging the right to secede, the state was in effect declaring to its component nationalities that it would not permit conditions to become intolerable. Moreover, because many economic benefits accrued to small nationalities as a result of their belonging to a large state, the negative economic consequences of secession would provide a strong inducement to avoid such a step. Even if a small nationality did initially secede, it would in all probability be drawn back into the economic orbit of the larger state and eventually rejoin it.[16]

Although Lenin advocated the right of self-determination, he believed, in common with other Marxists, that nationalism was a phenomenon of the capitalist era and would disappear with capitalism itself.[17] However, he also believed that the establishment of nation-states was a vital step in the historical evolution towards a socialist society.[18] In Western Europe and the United States the creation of nation-states had led to the triumph of bourgeois democracy over feudal autocracy. This, in Lenin's opinion, constituted progress. Nationalism was a progressive force insofar as it led feudal societies to evolve into capitalist societies. Once capitalism had become fully developed, however, as it was in the West, nationalism ceased to be a progressive force and became instead an oppressive force. In such fully

---

[14] V. I. Lenin *The Right of Nations to Self-Determination* (1950) 54.
[15] Shaheen, 26.
[16] Buchheit, Lee C. *Secession* (1978) 122.
[17] Richard Pipes *The Formation of the Soviet Union* (1964) 42.
[18] Lenin (1950) 9, 10.

developed capitalist states the dominant nationality within the state oppressed the other nationalities of that state as well as the peoples of its
colonies. The role of the proletariat in such states was therefore to work for
the overthrow of the bourgeois state in order to establish a socialist one.[19]
Eastern Europe, on the other hand, where the process of capitalist development was only in the formative stage, and in the colonial and semi-colonial
areas of the world where capitalism had not yet penetrated at all, the
situation was totally different.[20] Here the necessary capitalist phase had first
to be achieved before the goals of the proletariat could be attained. The
proletariat should therefore co-operate with bourgeois elements in such
countries in order to create a nation-state, since this was a necessary precur-
sor of the socialist state.[21] Nationalism was thus regarded in communist
theory as a retrogressive movement in Western Europe and the United
States, but a progressive movement in the Third World.[22]

The Bolsheviks came to power in October 1917 and immediately began
to implement their policies of self-determination. On 15 November 1917
they issued the Declaration of the Rights of Peoples of Russia. This guaranteed 'the right to self-determination up to and including separation and the
formation of an independent state, the abolition of all national privileges
and restrictions, and freedom of national minorities to develop'.[23] To show
their good faith, the Bolsheviks immediately recognized the independence
of Finland. Recognition of the right of self-determination did much to assist
the Bolsheviks during the civil war which followed their takeover. Fighting
between the Bolsheviks and their opponents took place mostly in areas
of Russia peopled by non-Russians. As a result of the policy of self-
determination, these non-Russian peoples were often persuaded to support
the Bolsheviks.[24]

In December 1917 the Bolsheviks entered into peace negotiations with
the Central Powers at Brest-Litovsk. The principle of self-determination

[19]   Carr, 260. Although Lenin recognized the primacy of language in the formation of nation-
states, he viewed this primacy solely in economic terms, and failed to see that it had a bearing
on the distinctive nature of nationalities. 'Only the clericals and the bourgeoisie,' he wrote,
'can talk of national culture. The toilers can talk only of an international culture of the
universal worker movement.' He believed that what was usually referred to as a 'national
culture' was in reality the culture of the ruling bourgeoisie, which was squarely opposed to the
democratic, socialistic culture of the oppressed classes: Pipes, 35. In this respect Lenin rejected
completely the ideas of Herder and Fichte, who considered language to be the determining
factor both of nationality itself and of that nationality's culture.
[20]   Pipes, 42. For a Marxist critique of Pipes' work, and that of other contemporary American
historians, see I. Zenushkina *Soviet Nationalities Policy and Bourgeois Historians* (1975).
[21]   Carr, 260.
[22]   Elie Kedourie *Nationalism* (1960) 91. Lenin failed to recognize, however, that the 'nation-
states' of Western Europe and United States had not been created as a result of of nationalism.
[23]   G. I. Tunkin *Theory of International Law* (1974) 10. These principles were confirmed in
the first Soviet Constitution of 1918: *id.*, 10.
[24]   Carr, 259.

figured prominently in those negotiations. In the first plenary session, on 22 December 1917, Adolf Joffe, the head of the Bolshevik delegation, proposed that there be no forcible annexation of occupied territories and that all nationalities be given the opportunity to determine their own political status by means of referendum. He further proposed that the rights of minorities be protected by special provisions in those areas where there was more than one nationality.[25] The Central Powers, well aware of the appeal of self-determination to the peoples of this region, made certain that the Treaty of Brest-Litovsk incorporated the principle of self-determination.[26] The treaty, signed on 3 March 1918, imposed extremely severe conditions upon the Bolsheviks, forcing them to surrender large tracts of territory. In each instance of Russian surrender of territory, the Central Powers invoked the principle of self-determination. Thus Article 3, dealing with Poland, Courland, and Lithuania, declared that 'Germany and Austria-Hungary purpose to determine the future status of these territories in agreement with their populations'.[27] Article 4 stated that the Sanjaks of Ardahan, Kars, and Batum (the Russian territory south of the Caucacus) were to determine their own future status 'in agreement with the neighbouring states, especially Turkey'.[28] Article 6 guaranteed the independence of the Ukraine by forcing the Bolsheviks to recognize the separate treaty which the Ukraine had concluded with the Central Powers.[29]

In spite of these references to self-determination, the Germans refused to withdraw their troops from any of the territories where referenda were to be held, and in fact reduced those territories to virtual dependencies of the German Empire.[30] The Ukraine, for example, was occupied by German troops, ostensibly to safeguard Ukrainian independence but in reality to ensure an effective exploitation by the Central Powers of the region's vast grain resources. The references to self-determination in the Treaty of Brest-Litovsk amounted to little more than lip service by the Central Powers. The Treaty actually resulted in the exploitation of the peoples of Eastern Europe, who realized that real self-determination would be achieved only if Germany, Austria-Hungary, and Turkey were defeated.

With Russia out of the war, the United Kingdom and France were no

---

[25] John W. Wheeler-Bennett *Brest-Litovsk: The Forgotten Peace, March 1918* (1966) 11, 118; Judah L. Magnes *Russia and Germany at Brest-Litovsk* (1919) 25; Derek Heater *National Self-Determination* (1994) 35.

[26] 223 CTS 80.

[27] 223 CTS 80, 81. Similar wording was contained in the Supplementary Treaty of Berlin with respect to Estonia and Livonia: Article 7, 224 CTS 66, 68, 69.

[28] 223 CTS 80, 82.

[29] The peace treaty between the Central Powers and the Ukraine, signed at Brest-Litovsk on 9 Feb. 1918, is reproduced at 223 CTS 43.

[30] Umozurike, O. *Self-Determination in International Law* (1972) 16.

longer constrained by the requirement to respect the multinational character of their Russian ally, and could therefore begin to make much more
vigorous declarations in favour of self-determination. This they proceeded
to do, in order both to weaken the Central Powers and to counteract the
appeal to self-determination being made by the Bolsheviks.

4. SELF-DETERMINATION AND WOODROW WILSON

The attitude of the Bolsheviks did much to legitimize self-determination.
The concept was further enhanced by the influence of Woodrow Wilson.
After the entry of the United States into the War in 1917, Wilson's ideas
about self-determination played a central role.

Wilson's ideas initially reflected the Western European understanding of
self-determination. He did not then concern himself with the Central European notion that nations must establish their own states, but concentrated
on the Western European ideal that those within a certain state should have
the right to determine their own government: 'self-government' had long
been a favourite concept of his. By 'self-government' he meant the right of
a population to choose its own form of government; this right was ongoing
and was therefore synonymous with democratic government.[31] Only under
a democratic government could a people choose their own government,
control the actions of that government, and ensure that it did not infringe
the rights of the people.[32] This belief in the fundamental importance of
democratic government inevitably influenced Wilson's attitude towards the
belligerents, so that he saw the war as 'a battle between the forces of
democracy and autocracy.'[33] Consequently, his sympathies were whole-
heartedly with the Allies.

At the end of 1916 Wilson asked the two sides to declare their war aims.
The Central Powers demanded not only the preservation of the territorial
integrity of Austro-Hungary, but also the cession of territory from Russia,
Romania, and Serbia. The Allies, on the other hand, sought the restoration
of sovereignty to Belgium, Serbia, and Montenegro and the evacuation of
enemy troops from French, Russian, and Romanian territory. They went on
to call for:

the reorganization of Europe, guaranteed by a stable regime and based at once on
respect for nationalities and on the right to full security and liberty of economic
development possessed by all peoples small and great . . . ; the restitution of prov-

[31] Michla Pomerance 'The United States and Self-Determination: Perspectives on the
Wilsonian Conception' (1976) 17; Antonio Cassese *Self-Determination of Peoples* (1995)
19.
[32] Kedourie, 131.
[33] Pomerance, 19.

inces formerly torn from the Allies by force or against the wishes of their inhabitants; the liberation of the Italians, as also of the Slavs, Roumanians and Czecho-Slovaks from foreign domination; the setting free of the populations subject to the bloody tyranny of the Turks and the turning out of Europe of the Ottoman Empire as decidedly foreign to Western civilization.[34]

This statement confirmed Wilson in his sympathy for the Allied cause. In an address to Congress on 22 January 1917 he declared that there could be no lasting peace which did not recognize the principle that governments 'derive all their just powers from the consent of the governed, and that no right anywhere exists to hand peoples about from sovereignty to sovereignty as though they were property.'[35] Less than three months later, on 5 April 1917, the United States declared war on Germany.

In a message to Russia dated 9 June 1917 Wilson set out the war aims of the United States. He declared that the United States had entered the war in order to fight 'for liberty, the self-government, and the undictated development of all peoples' because no people should 'be forced under sovereignty under which it does not wish to live.'[36] He also indicated subsequently that the United States would not be bound by the secret treaties entered into by the Allies, and that its policies would be governed by morality rather than expediency.

Wilson's statements regarding the consent of the governed carried great weight with the subject nationalities, and came to be regarded by them as the legal basis for the forthcoming peace negotiations.[37] The subject nationalities did not interpret Wilson's statements in terms of representative government, but in terms of their own concept of self-determination, namely that each ethnic group should form its own nation-state. Wilson himself, as he became more aware of the nature of the demands being made by the various subject nationalities, began to modify his original message of self-government to include the notion of national self-determination. This shift in thinking took place gradually. When he presented his Fourteen Points to a joint sitting of Congress on 8 January 1918 he was certainly thinking in terms of self-determination for some subject nationalities. This is evident from Article XIII, in which he called for an independent Polish state, to be created from 'those territories inhabited by indisputably Polish

---

[34] Macartney, 184. The statement of the Allies was not intended to countenance the creation of new nation-states, as it seemed to imply. The original draft had read 'Italians, Southern Slavs and Roumanians,' and had been intended to refer merely to the territories promised to Italy, Romania, and Serbia in the secret treaties, rather than to the total dismemberment of the Austro-Hungarian Empire. The reference to the 'Czecho-Slovaks' had been added to please Czech *émigré* leaders, with no real thought as to its import: *id.*, 184, 185; Cobban, 53.

[35] Ray Stannard Baker and William E. Dodd (eds.) *The Public Papers of Woodrow Wilson: The New Democracy, 1913–1917* (1970) Vol. 2, 411.

[36] Buchheit, 63.

[37] H. W. V. Temperley *A History of the Peace Conference of Paris* (1920) Vol. 3, 173.

populations'.[38] At this point, however, Wilson had not yet concluded that every people should be entitled to its own independent nation-state. This is borne out by Articles X and XI of the Fourteen Points. In these he addressed the problem of the various ethnic groups of Austro-Hungary and the Ottoman Empire, but proposed no more than 'autonomous development' for them.[39]

Only a month later, Wilson's thoughts on the nationality question had evolved considerably. In his speech to Congress on 11 February 1918 he said:

Peoples are not to be handed about from one sovereignty to another by an international conference or an understanding between rivals and antagonists. National aspirations must be respected; peoples may now be dominated and governed by their own consent. Self-determination is not a mere phrase, it is an imperative principle of action which statesmen will henceforth ignore at their peril.[40]

Wilson was here clearly acknowledging the importance, not only of his original concept of self-government, but also of that of national self-determination for all 'well-defined national elements'.

Wilson's growing acceptance of the concept of national self-determination can perhaps best be seen from his changing attitude towards Austro-Hungary. When the United States declared war on Austro-Hungary on 4 December 1917, Wilson emphasized that the United States sought neither the dismemberment nor the reorganization of the Habsburg monarchy.[41] By the following year, however, Wilson had come to the conclusion that the dismemberment of Austro-Hungary was inevitable. On 18 October 1918 he rejected an Austrian proposal of autonomy for the nationalities of Austro-Hungary. It was, he said, for the various nationalities themselves to decide 'what action on the part of the Austro-Hungarian Government will satisfy their aspirations and their conception of their rights and destiny as members of the family of nations'.[42] By the time of the Peace Conference, Wilson had accepted that all nationalities were entitled to self-determination.

5. THE DISINTEGRATION OF AUSTRO-HUNGARY

When war first broke out between the Allies and the Central Powers, the Allies had no thought of destroying Austro-Hungary as a political unit. Even as the War progressed, and centrifugal nationalist pressures on

---

[38] H. W. V. Temperley, 161.
[39] *Id.*, 160; Heater, 36–46.
[40] Temperley, 180.
[41] *Id.*, 132.
[42] *Id.*, 282.

Austro-Hungary increased in intensity, the Allies were not prepared to seek its dismemberment. As late as January 1918, Lloyd George was insisting that the destruction of Austro-Hungary was not one of the war aims of the United Kingdom.[43] This was in line with statements made by Wilson at the time. France also favoured the continued existence of Austro-Hungary, fearing that its German-speaking areas would otherwise seek to unite with Germany.

The preservation of Austro-Hungary was in the interests of the Allies because it acted as a bulwark against German and Bolshevik expansion. It was also a natural economic unit and gave a measure of strength to the small ethnic groups which they could never have in their own right. All that was necessary to resolve the problem of the Austro-Hungarian nationalities, the Allies believed, was a reorganization of the Austro-Hungarian Empire, in which greater autonomy was granted to the various peoples within the Empire. However, nationalism amongst the various ethnic groups of Austro-Hungary had become far too strong for them to be satisfied merely with an increase in autonomy.

The Allies made various attempts to separate Austro-Hungary from its alliance with Germany, entering into secret negotiations with a view to obtaining a separate peace. These efforts all ended in failure. Since an agreement with Austro-Hungary could not be reached, the idea of bringing about its destruction gradually began to gain support amongst the Allies, particularly after Brest-Litovsk. By mid-1918 the internal situation of Austro-Hungary had deteriorated badly: nationalist and communist groups were making trouble in almost every part of the country, and it became clear to the Allies that the collapse of the Habsburg Monarchy was both imminent and inevitable.[44]

In the latter part of 1918 the Empire rapidly began to disintegrate. On 28 October 1918 the Czechoslovak Committee in Prague issued a declaration severing all constitutional links with Austria. Two days later the Slovak Council severed all constitutional links with Hungary. The Republic of Czechoslovakia was proclaimed on 11 November 1918.[45] An independent state of the Slovenes, Croats, and Serbs was established on 31 October 1918; this united with the states of Serbia and Montenegro on 1 December 1918 to form the Kingdom of the Serbs, Croats, and Slovenes.[46] The Italians, Romanians, and Poles of Austro-Hungary sought to join themselves to the countries of their respective nationalities, Italy, Romania, and the newly emerging Poland. The Austrian Germans established a Council of State for the German-speaking areas of Austria on 21 October 1918. Hungary pro-

[43] Franjo Tudjman *Nationalism in Comtemporary Europe* (1981) 22.
[44] *Id.*, 23; Tapié, 385, 386.
[45] Tudjman, 24, 25.
[46] *Id.*, 25. The Kingdom of the Serbs, Croats, and Slovenes became Yugoslavia in 1929.

claimed its independence on 1 November 1918. The Emperor renounced all
exercise of his authority on 11 November 1918. On the following day the
Provisional Assembly of German Austria proclaimed the Republic of German Austria.[47] The Austro-Hungarian Empire had ceased to exist.

6. THE PEACE CONFERENCE

By the end of the War the Allies had declared that self-determination
would be the guiding principle of the Peace Conference. The various statements made by President Wilson to this effect were affirmed in October
1918 by an Inter-Allied Parliamentary Commission of British, French, Belgian, and Italian representatives. As a result it was widely believed that the
political boundaries of Europe would be restructured to create nation-
states throughout Central and Eastern Europe, and that the ongoing problem of frustrated nationalism would be resolved.

Although the United Kingdom, France, and Italy had declared their
support for Wilson's position on self-determination, however, they could
scarcely have done otherwise once that position became widely publicized
throughout Europe. Wilson had in effect forced the Allies to endorse the
principle. Their real commitment to self-determination was much more
tenuous, particularly on the part of France and Italy. The principle of self-
determination did not sit at all well with Italy, which was determined to
obtain all territories promised to it under the secret Treaty of London,[48]
regardless of ethnic considerations or the wishes of the populations concerned.[49] France was primarily concerned with maintaining its supremacy in
Europe. This could only be done by keeping Germany weak. The real
purpose behind French support for the creation of new nation-states was to
establish a *cordon sanitaire* of client states which would 'provide a counter
weight in the east to a potential German resurgence and at the same time
form a dam against Soviet expansion into Europe'.[50] Whenever the principle of self-determination seemed likely to strengthen Germany, France
opposed its implementation. When German Austria sought to unite with
Germany, France not only prevented it from doing so, but also forced it to
drop the prefix 'German' from its name.

The British were generally more inclined than either the French or the
Italians to apply the principle of self-determination in a thorough-going and
even-handed manner to the peoples of Europe. The British, however, were

[47] Tapié, 387.
[48] 221 CTS 56.
[49] Cobban, 80.
[50] Tudjman, 29. Clemenceau was reported to have told Lloyd George that 'he did not
believe in the principle of self-determination, which allowed a man to clutch at your throat the
first time it was convenient to him . . .': Lloyd George, (1938) Vol. 1, 286.

reluctant to admit that the principle was one of general application, fearing that this would create problems for them with their own subject nationalities. A memorandum of the British Foreign Office, in November 1918, reflects this concern:

It would clearly be inadvisable to go even the smallest distance in the direction of admitting the claim of the American negroes, or the Southern Irish, or the Flemings, or Catalans, to appeal to an Inter-State Conference over the head of their own government. Yet if a right of appeal is granted to the Macedonians or the German Bohemians it will be difficult to refuse it in the case of other nationalist movements.[51]

Quite apart from the other conflicting interests of the Allies, it soon became apparent that there were numerous problems inherent in any implementation of the principle of self-determination. Wilson arrived at the Peace Conference with little real understanding of the complexity of the nationalities problem in Central Europe. He discovered that it was not simply a question of drawing political boundaries to conform to the ethnic distribution of particular populations, because in many instances the populations involved were inextricably mixed together.[52] Even with resort to plebiscites in some areas[53] it proved impossible to avoid creating ethnic minorities in the new nation-states, however the boundaries were drawn.[54]

Moreover, considerations other than that of self-determination had to be taken into account when establishing the new nation-states, which had to be economically viable and militarily defensible. This meant that Czechoslovakia required the industry and mines of German North Bohemia for economic and strategic reasons. Likewise Poland, which had been promised an outlet to the sea, could acquire such access only by incorporating German territory. Wilson had spoken of self-determination as though it were an absolute right; but in fact its application was necessarily tempered by competing interests. This, of course, did not lessen the disappointment of those who were made minorities in an alien nation-state.

Besides determining the disposition of territories in Central and Eastern Europe, the Allies also had to decide what to do with those territories

---

[51] A. Zimmern *The League of Nations and the Rule of Law, 1918–1935* (1936) 199, 200.

[52] Wilson's surprise and dismay at the complexity of the nationalities problem is reflected in a statement he made to the Committee of Foreign Relations of the Senate: 'When I gave utterance to those words [i.e. that all nations had a right to self-determination] I said them without the knowledge that nationalities existed, which are coming to us day after day . . . You do not know and cannot appreciate the anxieties that I have experienced as a result of many millions of people having their hopes raised by what I have said': Temperley (1921) Vol. 4, 429.

[53] See Sarah Wambaugh *Plebiscites Since the World War* (1933) Vol. 1, 3–45; Cobban, 70–5.

[54] The new states themselves made claims based on self-determination only insofar as it suited their purposes; but they also laid claim to territory on grounds other than that of self-determination. Poland, for example, made extensive claims to territories not inhabited by ethnic Poles on the basis that these territories had belonged to Poland prior to the First Partition of 1772.

outside Europe which had come into their hands during the course of the war. These consisted of the Allied occupied provinces of the former Ottoman Empire which were inhabited by peoples who were not ethnic Turks, and all the German colonies which had been captured by the Allies during the course of the war. The Allies had resolved that none of these territories would be returned to their former owners. However, that decision created a dilemma for them: they did not believe that the peoples of those territories possessed sufficient political maturity to govern themselves, but their repeated declarations that the peace treaty would be one of no annexations made it impolitic to incorporate them into the Allied colonial empires. Wilson favoured some form of trusteeship over the territories: as early as October 1918 he indicated to Sir William Wiseman, the British Ambassador to the United States, that he favoured administration of the German colonies by individual states 'in trust'. 'In trust for whom?' Wiseman asked. 'Well, for the League of Nations, for instance', Wilson replied.[55]

The idea of an international trusteeship for the captured non-European territories was not well received by France, Italy, or Japan. These favoured outright annexation, however impolitic it might be. They were supported by the British Dominions of Australia, New Zealand, and South Africa, who were adamant that they would not give up any of the German colonies they had captured. The United States, on the other hand, was equally adamant that there would be no annexations of any kind. Wilson was particularly opposed, for security reasons, to the proposed Japanese annexation of the former German island colonies in the Central Pacific.[56] American opposition to annexations was supported by the United Kingdom. The United Kingdom position was that 'the British Empire was big enough'. It was therefore prepared to allow the former German colonies to be administered through trusteeship.

A compromise was eventually reached with the adoption of the 'Mandate System'. The proposal for such a system originated with General Jan Smuts of South Africa, in a pamphlet entitled *The League of Nations: A Practical Suggestion*. Smuts' original proposal had not included the German colonies, which were, in his words, 'inhabited by barbarians',[57] and he assumed that they would be absorbed into the Dominions which had conquered them. Smuts directed his attention instead to the disintegrating Empires of Austro-Hungary, Russia, and Turkey. He declared that the newly formed League of Nations 'must be the reversionary, in the broadest sense', of the peoples and territories formerly belonging to these disintegrating empires.[58] The new League of Nations should possess the ultimate right of disposal of

---

[55] Solomon Slonim *South West Africa and the United Nations: An International Mandate in Dispute* (1973) 14.

[56] T. D. Gill *South West Africa and the Sacred Trust* (1984) 6.

[57] J. C. Smuts *The League of Nations* (1918) 15.　　　　[58] *Id.*, 11.

these peoples and territories in accordance with two fundamental principles, namely those of 'no annexations' and the 'self-determination of peoples'.[59] However, because these various peoples would be at different stages of political development, they might not be prepared for immediate self-government in an independent state of their own. In such cases the affairs of such peoples would be administered by a 'mandatory' until such time as the peoples so governed had matured sufficiently to govern themselves.[60] There would be a scheme of graded mandates to fit each individual people's level of political maturity.[61]

Wilson adopted Smuts' proposal as a means of resolving the conflict between the United States and the British Dominions. He deleted Smuts' references to Russia and Austro-Hungary and applied the mandate scheme instead to the German colonies and the non-Turkish areas of the former Ottoman Empire. After long and sometimes acrimonious debate, the Dominions eventually agreed that the German colonies which they wanted to annex should instead come under the mandates system.[62] Wilson in return agreed to graduate the mandates so that the territories in dispute, South West Africa, New Guinea, Nauru, and Samoa, would be governed as though they were integral parts of the mandatory state. In addition, it was agreed that there would be no explicit reference to the principle of self-determination, nor would the League be named as the ultimate reversionary.[63]

The mandate system was set out in Article 22 of the Covenant of the League of Nations. There were three categories of mandates, which came to be known informally as A, B, and C mandates.[64] The first category comprised those provinces detached from the Ottoman Empire, which were administered by the United Kingdom and France.[65] The second comprised the former German colonies of Central Africa. The third category com-

---

[59] *Id.*, 12, 15.

[60] For a discussion of the private law meaning of mandate, tutelage and trust see Quincy Wright *Mandates Under the League of Nations* (1930) 375–90.

[61] Smuts, 21, 22.

[62] At one particularly tense moment, Wilson said to the Australian Prime Minister, 'Mr. Hughes, am I to understand that if the whole civilized world asks Australia to agree to a mandate in respect of these islands, Australia is prepared still to defy the appeal of the whole civilized world?' to which Hughes replied, 'That's about the size of it.': Lloyd George, (1938) Vol. 1, 542.

[63] Slonim, 28.

[64] Wright, 47.

[65] The British and French mandates in the Middle East corresponded very closely to the Sykes-Picot Agreement of 16 May 1916, by which the United Kingdom and France had agreed to partition these areas into British and French zones: R. N. Chowdhuri *International Mandates and Trusteeship Systems* (1955) 46. The United States was offered a mandate over the territory of Armenia but refused to accept, with the result that a part of the territory of Armenia became a Soviet Republic, and the remainder was forcibly reincorporated into the Turkish Republic: Philip Marshall Brown 'The Mandate Over Armenia' (1920) 396 *et seq*.

prised those territories which had been in dispute: South West Africa and the islands of the Pacific. The level of administrative control within each of these three categories of mandate appeared simply to correspond to the level of political maturity of the people concerned. In fact, the three categories actually reflected the political agenda of the mandatory states. Those mandatories which had originally wanted to annex their respective mandates were granted a maximum degree of administrative authority and control and a minimal degree of international accountability.[66] Although Wilson had been forced to compromise in this regard, he did achieve his essential goal that all mandates, of whatever category, were subject to international supervision. Thus, Article 22 provided for an annual report to be made by the mandatory to the Council of the League of Nations and further provided for the establishment of a permanent commission to examine the annual reports and to advise the council on all matters relating to the observance of the mandates.[67]

7. THE ATTEMPT TO INCLUDE SELF-DETERMINATION IN THE LEAGUE OF NATIONS COVENANT

Although the declared intention of the Allies was to make self-determination the guiding principle of the Peace Conference, it had never been their intention to apply this principle to their own peoples and territories. This became patently clear when Wilson attempted to include in the Covenant of the League of Nations an article dealing with self-determination. Wilson's proposal was contained in draft Article 3: this specified that the principle of self-determination would be the basis for making any further territorial adjustments as might become necessary as a result of changes in social or political relationships.[68] The Allies, however, were resolutely opposed to the inclusion of such a provision in the Covenant. Even some members of Wilson's own delegation did not support this proposal. David Hunter Miller, Wilson's legal adviser, criticized the President's draft article in the following terms: 'That the territorial adjustments made by the Conference will not satisfy all claims, is the only thing now certain about them. Such general provisions as above will make that dissatisfaction permanent, will compel every Power to engage in propaganda and will legalize irredentist agitation in at least all of Eastern Europe.'[69]

Robert Lansing, Wilson's Secretary of State, was even more outspoken in his criticism. He predicted that self-determination would become a source of political instability and domestic disorder, and a cause of rebellion. The

[66] Gill, 7, 8.   [67] Isaak I. Dore *The International Mandate System and Namibia* (1985) 7.
[68] David Hunter Miller *The Drafting of the Covenant* (1928) Vol. 2 12.
[69] *Id.* 71, fn. 58.

principle of self-determination, in Lansing's opinion, was a phrase 'loaded with dynamite. It will raise hopes which can never be realized. It will, I fear, cost thousands of lives. In the end it is bound to be discredited, to be called the dream of an idealist, who failed to realize the danger until too late'.[70]

The proposed article was redrafted several times: all references to self-determination were eventually deleted. In its final form draft Article 3, which was renumbered Article 10, made no mention of territorial adjustments at all, but emphasized respect for the territorial integrity and existing political independence of the Members of the League.

8. CONCLUSION

By 1920 the map of Europe had been substantially redrawn. Ethnic groups, given the opportunities presented to them by the First World War and the Bolshevik Revolution, had succeeded in dismantling the multi-ethnic empires of pre-war Europe and in replacing them with nation-states. Most of these nation-states were already in existence by the time the Paris Peace Conference convened, so that the Conference had only to recognize them as independent states and to delineate their respective borders.

Although the delegates at the Peace Conference had emphasized the decisive role self-determination would play in their deliberations, it quickly became apparent that the implementation of self-determination was subject to certain fundamental limitations. The principle simply could not be applied in any absolute sense, not only because many territories had mixed populations, but also because the creation of viable states depended upon economic, geographic, and strategic considerations which often ran counter to ethnic considerations. As a result, sizable minorities continued to exist within the new nation-states.

Moreover, self-determination was applied only to the territories of the defeated powers: the Allies were careful to exclude their own territory. They excluded the principle from the Covenant of the League of Nations as a general proposition of international law, and recognized it as a legal concept only insofar as it was incorporated into Article 22 of the Covenant of the League of Nations. Such incorporation was only implicit: the language of Article 22 made no express reference to the principle of self-determination. Apart from Article 22, self-determination continued in all other respects an essentially political, rather than legal, concept.

[70] Robert Lansing 'Self-Determination' *Saturday Evening Post* 9 Apr. 1921, 6, 101.

3

The Inter-War Years:
The Minorities Treaties Regime

1. INTRODUCTION

At the Paris Peace Conference the Allies had attempted to resolve the
ethnic problems of Europe through the creation of new nation-states. The
Allies hoped that a restructuring of the political boundaries of Europe on
an ethnic basis would satisfy the nationalist aspirations of most ethnic
groups, and thereby ensure that there would be no further demands of this
sort. The creation of new nation-states did indeed satisfy the nationalist
aspirations of many, but did not eliminate the ethnic minorities, nor the
desire of such groups for a further readjustment of boundaries so that they
also might achieve ethnic self-determination. The Peace Conference attempted to address this problem through the establishment of the 'minorities treaties regime'. This Chapter examines the position of ethnic
minorities in the years between the First and Second World Wars.

2. THE AALAND ISLANDS DISPUTE

The Aaland Islands dispute was the first case in which the League of
Nations had to consider an appeal to the principle of self-determination. It
is of considerable importance because it demonstrated the attitude of the
League towards self-determination, as well as testing its status in international law.

The Aaland Islands are located at the mouth of the Gulf of Bothnia,
which separates Sweden from Finland. In 1920 the population of these
islands was approximately 25,000, of whom some 97 per cent were Swedish.[1]
The Islands had been part of Sweden until 1809 when they were ceded to
Russia, together with Finland. Thereafter they became a part of the Grand
Duchy of Finland and remained under Russian rule until 1917.

When the Provisional Government fell in October 1917 Finnish nationalists seized the opportunity to proclaim the independence of Finland, which

---

[1] Philip Marshall Brown 'The Aaland Islands Question' (1921) 268; Charles Noble Gregory
'The Neutralisation of the Aaland Islands' (1923) 66.

was recognized by the Bolsheviks on 4 January 1918. The new Finnish Government was overthrown on 18 January 1918 by Finnish Communists with the support of Soviet troops. In the ensuing civil war the Finnish 'whites', with the help of German troops, in turn overthrew the Communists and re-established themselves in government.

When Finnish nationalists declared the independence of Finland, the Aaland Islanders simultaneously declared their desire for union with Sweden, based on the principle of self-determination.[2] Several unofficial plebiscites indicated that an overwhelming majority of the Islanders desired union with Sweden.[3] Finland, meanwhile, declared the Aaland Islands a province on 8 March 1918. The Islanders responded by appealing not only to the Finnish Senate, but to the King of Sweden and to the Emperor of Germany. They argued that they should decide their own political status and demanded an official plebiscite, claiming that their case was a classic instance of self-determination as proclaimed by Woodrow Wilson. However, the Finnish Senate declared that no action hostile to the integrity of the national territory would be tolerated.[4] When Sweden submitted a formal request to Finland for a plebiscite Finland refused, pointing out that even when the islands had belonged to Sweden they had still been administered as a part of Finland.[5]

The Islanders continued to press vigorously for union with Sweden. Petitions were sent to the King of Sweden and appeals made to the United States, the United Kingdom, France, and Italy. A delegation was sent to the Peace Conference and another to the Council of the League of Nations. The Baltic Affairs Commission of the Peace Conference recommended that the League of Nations, rather than the Peace Conference, resolve the matter.[6]

In the spring of 1920 the Finnish Diet itself attempted to resolve the matter by granting autonomy to the Aaland Islands. This autonomy, however, was rejected by the Islanders, who instead sent yet another delegation to Sweden appealing for help.[7] At this point Finland arrested several of the Aaland Islands leaders and charged them with treason, a move which caused a serious deterioration in diplomatic relations between Sweden and Finland. This led the United Kingdom to exercise its 'friendly right' under Article 11(2) of the League Covenant and formally draw the matter of the Aaland Islands to the attention of the League Council.[7a]

---

[2] James Barros *The Aland Islands Question* (1968) 244.
[3] Arnold J. Toynbee 'Self-Determination' (1925) 336.
[4] Gregory, 68.
[5] Norman J. Padelford and K. Gosta A. Andersson 'The Aaland Islands Question' (1939) 472.
[6] Gregory, 68; Padelford *et al.*, 473.
[7] Padelford *et al.*, 473; Toynbee, 337.
[7a] Art. 11(2) provided as follows: 'It is also declared to be the friendly right of each Member of the League to bring to the attention of the Assembly or of the Council any circumstance

Sweden submitted to the Council that sovereignty over the Aaland Islands was an issue which should be decided by the inhabitants of the islands by means of a plebiscite. Sweden pointed out that the Aaland Islanders' demand for self-determination coincided with that of the Finns. As soon as Finland had separated itself from Russia, the Aaland Islanders 'had claimed the right to decide their own destiny'.[8] Finland argued that the Council had no jurisdiction to make a recommendation on the Aaland Islands question as it was a purely domestic matter under Article 15(8) of the Covenant.[9] Finland's submission led the Council to appoint a Commission of Jurists to determine whether the issue was indeed a domestic one.[10]

The Commission of Jurists found that the Aaland Islands dispute was not solely within the domestic jurisdiction of Finland, which meant that the Council was competent under Article 15(4) to make whatever recommendation it deemed 'just and proper'.[11] The Commission arrived at this finding even though it held that the principle of self-determination was not, in normal circumstances, a part of international law:

Although the principle of self-determination of peoples plays an important part in modern political thought, especially since the Great War, it must be pointed out that there is no mention of it in the Covenant of the League of Nations. The recognition of this principle in a certain number of international treaties cannot be considered as sufficient to put it upon the same footing as a positive rule of the Law of Nations.

On the contrary, in the absence of express provisions in international treaties, the right of disposing of national territory is essentially an attribute of the sovereignty of every State. Positive International Law does not recognise the right of national groups, as such, to separate themselves from the State of which they form part by the simple expression of a wish, any more than it recognises the right of other States to claim such a separation.[12]

---

whatever affecting international relations which threatens to disturb international peace or the good understanding between nations upon which peace depends.'

[8] League of Nations, Procès-Verbal of the Seventh Session of the Council, London, 9–12 July 1920, 11.

[9] Art. 15(8) provided as follows: 'If the dispute between the parties is claimed by one of them, and is found by the Council, to arise out of a matter which by international law is solely within the domestic jurisdiction of that party, the Council shall so report, and shall make no recommendation as to its settlement.'

[10] Finland's position in this regard was not entirely consistent. When the autonomy of ethnic Finns in the Soviet Union was at issue, Finland was assiduous in pressing the matter before the League of Nations and the Permanent Court of International Justice, in spite of the objections of the Soviet Union that Finland's actions constituted interference in its internal affairs. See *Status of Eastern Carelia* Reply of the Court to Request for Advisory Opinion (1923) PCIJ Reports, Series B, No. 5, 7.

[11] Art. 15(4) provided as follows: 'If the dispute is not thus settled, the Council, either unanimously or by a majority vote, shall make and publish a report containing a statement of the facts of the dispute and the recommendations which are deemed just and proper in regard thereto.'

[12] *Report of the International Commission of Jurists* (1920) LNOJ Spec. Supp. 3, 5.

In abnormal circumstances the situation would be different, and the Commission went on to qualify the above statement by adding that it:

only applies to a nation which is definitively constituted as a sovereign State, and an independent member of the international community, and so long as it continues to possess these characteristics. From the point of view of both domestic and international law, the formation, transformation and dismemberment of States as a result of revolutions and wars creates situations of fact which, to a large extent, cannot be met by the application of the normal rules of positive law . . . Under such circumstances, the principle of self-determination of peoples may be called into play.[13]

It was this abnormal situation which pertained to the Aaland Islands dispute. In the opinion of the Commission of Jurists, Finland was not at the time of the request from the Aaland Islanders 'definitively constituted as a sovereign State' but was rather a *de facto* revolutionary entity. This meant that the principle of self-determination would have a role to play in the resolution of the dispute.[14]

The Commission of Jurists submitted its report to the Council on 20 September 1920, and the Council appointed a Commission of Rapporteurs to study the problem and make recommendations for its solution. Their report was completed and submitted to the Council on 16 April 1921. The Commission recognized that the issue of self-determination was at the heart of the dispute. Like the report of the Commission of Jurists, it concluded that self-determination was not a part of international law, and should not normally play a role in the determination of sovereignty over certain territory. The Commission declared that self-determination 'is not, properly speaking, a rule of international law and the League of Nations has not entered it into its Covenant'.[15] Self-determination was no more than 'a principle of justice and liberty, expressed by a vague and general formula which has given rise to the most varied interpretations and differences of opinion'.[16]

Unlike the Commission of Jurists, however, the Commission of Rapporteurs found that Finland was 'definitively constituted', thereby disallowing any role for self-determination. The new state of Finland, according to the Commission of Rapporteurs, was simply the continuation of the autonomous Territory of Finland which had always included the Aaland Islands. The Commission noted that Sweden had recognized Finland without making any reservations in its text as to the boundaries of the new state, and concluded that the 'right of sovereignty of the Finnish State over the

---

[13] *Id.*, 5, 6.

[14] James Crawford *The Creation of States in International Law* (1979) 85, 86.

[15] *The Aaland Island Question: Report Submitted to the Council of the League of Nations by the Commission of Rapporteurs* (1921) League Doc. B7.21/68/106, 27.

[16] *Id.*, 27.

Aaland Islands is incontestable and their present legal status is that they form part of Finland'.[17] The Commission decided that the Aaland Islanders, unlike the Finns, were not a 'people', but simply a 'minority'. Minorities, the Commission declared, could not be treated 'in the same manner or on the same footing as a people as a whole',[18] and in particular they were not entitled to claim any right to self-determination:

Is it possible to admit as an absolute rule that a minority of the population of a State, which is definitely constituted and perfectly capable of fulfilling its duties as such, has the right of separating itself from her in order to be incorporated in another State or to declare its independence? The answer can only be in the negative. To concede to minorities, either of language or of religion, or to any fractions of a population the right of withdrawing from the community to which they belong, because it is their wish or their good pleasure, would be to destroy order and stability within States and to inaugurate anarchy in international life, it would be to uphold a theory incompatible with the very idea of the State as a territorial and political entity.[19]

Another important consideration for the Commission was the fact that the Aaland Islanders, unlike the Finns, had not suffered oppression. The issue of oppression had originally been raised by the Commission of Jurists, which declined to offer an opinion 'as to whether a manifest and continued abuse of sovereign power, to the detriment of the population of a State, would . . . give to an international dispute . . . such a character that its object should be considered as one . . . which is not confined to the domestic jurisdiction of the State concerned'.[20] The Commission of Rapporteurs concluded that oppression would be a factor in allowing a minority to separate itself from one state and seek union with another state. However, such action was to be considered only as a 'last resort when the state lacks either the will or the power to enact and apply just and effective guarantees' of religious, linguistic, and social freedom.[21] This was not the case in the Aaland Islands dispute.

The Commission noted that Finland had already offered guarantees of a very substantial nature in the form of the Law of Autonomy of 7 May 1920, in order to assuage the fears of the Aaland Islanders concerning 'Finnish domination' and their own 'gradual denationalisation'.[22] There was thus no need for the Aaland Islanders to separate from Finland in order to preserve their cultural heritage as Finland itself was prepared to guarantee its preservation. The Commission proposed a number of recommendations to be included in the Finnish Law of Autonomy. These recommendations dealt with the exclusive teaching of Swedish within the school system, the exclusive ownership of property by the inhabitants, the regulation of immigra-

---

[17] *The Aaland Island Question*, 25.   [18] *Id.*, 28.   [19] *Id.*, 28.
[20] *Report of the Commission of Jurists*, 5.
[21] *Report of the Commission of Rapporteurs*, 28.   [22] *Id.*, 26.

tion to the Islands by means of the franchise, and appointment of a Governor only after approval by the local General Council. The guarantees were to take precedence over any Finnish law and could be altered only with the consent of the Aaland Islands General Council.[23] The Council of the League would be empowered to supervise the observance of the guarantees. Any complaint or claim which the Aalanders might have about the application of the guarantees could be submitted, through the Finnish Government, to the Council for its consideration, and the Council in turn was entitled to seek an advisory opinion from the Permanent Court of International Justice on any matter of a legal nature.[24] In addition, Finland was not to build any fortifications upon the Islands. Finland and Sweden then concluded an agreement based on the recommendations of the Commission.[25]

The Commission presented its report to the Council on 27 June 1921. The report was accepted by the Council and annexed to its resolution of 24 June 1921, which recognized Finland's sovereignty over the Islands, and called for guarantees for the Islanders and for an arrangement for the neutralization of the Islands.[26] Finland entered into an international obligation to the Council of the League of Nations on 27 June 1921 to respect the guarantees to which it had agreed.[27] Finland also signed a treaty on 20 October 1921, which neutralized the Aaland Islands.[28]

3. BACKGROUND TO THE MINORITIES TREATIES REGIME

The resolution of the Aaland Islands dispute was a good example of the general policy pursued by the Allies at the Peace Conference and subsequently by the League of Nations with respect to those groups of peoples left over once the principle of self-determination had initially been applied. The Peace Conference had attempted to resolve the nationalities problem once and for all by adopting self-determination as its guiding principle.

---

[23] Gregory, 75; Tore Modeen 'The Situation of the Finland-Swedish Population in the Light of International, Constitutional and Administrative Law' (1970) 125.

[24] Modeen, 125.

[25] Agreement between Sweden and Finland regarding the Aaland Islands, placed on record 27 June 1921 (1921) 2 LNOJ 701.

[26] Resolution Adopted by the Council at its Thirteenth Session (1921) LNOJ, Supp. 5, 24–6.

[27] League of Nations Doc. C.L.110., 1927, I, annex, 16.

[28] Convention Relating to the Non-Fortification and Neutralization of the Aaland Islands, Signed at Geneva, 20 Oct. 1921 (1922) 9 LNTS 213. Following the Second World War, a UN Special Commission on Minority Treaties held in 1950 that the Agreement between Sweden and Finland regarding the Aaland Islands remained valid, but that with the dissolution of the League of Nations its provisions were no longer enforceable by an international body: *Study of the Legal Validity of the Undertakings Concerning Minorities* UN Doc. E/LN. 4/367 (1950).

However, the formation of nation-states in which ethnic and state boundaries corresponded exactly was found to be simply not possible, not only because the various peoples of Central and Eastern Europe were so intermingled, but also because of economic and defence considerations. The states which emerged from the Peace Conference reflected this fact. Czechoslovakia had minorities amounting to 34.7 per cent of its population. Minorities in Poland made up 30 per cent, and in Romania 25 per cent of the population.[29]

The national minorities in the new nation-states were for the most part subgroups of larger peoples, separated from their nations as a result of the political settlements at the Peace Conference. The Allies had in effect punished the defeated powers at the Peace Conference by repeatedly deciding against German and Hungarian claims when establishing state boundaries in areas of mixed population. As a result there were large German and Hungarian minorities in virtually all of the newly created nation-states.

In the classic theory of national self-determination the nation comprised all those who shared the same linguistic and cultural attributes. If any part of this nation found itself outside the nation-state, then both the nation-state and that part of the nation remained incomplete until union was achieved. However, this theory of national self-determination threatened the stability of the new order created at the Peace Conference. If that order were to be maintained, the idea of union between a nation-state and its irredenta had to be denied. Some alternative had to be found which would prohibit national minorities from seeking union with their respective nation-states, but which would nevertheless affirm that complete cultural development of such groups was still possible. This led to the idea that if the linguistic, cultural, and religious attributes of national minorities were adequately protected, their union with their respective nation-state would no longer be necessary. The initial purpose of creating nation-states had been simply to provide a framework for such protection, but the framework could be achieved by other means. That both national self-determination and the protection of minority rights had the same ultimate purpose was put forward in the *Aaland Islands* case by the Commission of Jurists:

The principle recognising the rights of peoples to determine their political fate may be applied in various ways; the most important of these are, on the one hand the formation of an independent State, and on the other hand the right of choice between two existing States. This principle, however, must be brought into line with that of the protection of minorities; both have a common object—to assure to some

---

[29] Alfred Cobban *The National State and National Self-Determination* (1969) 86.

national group the maintenance and free development of its social, ethical or religious characteristics.[30]

The subgroups of people left over from the Peace Conference were thus not to be defined as parts of larger nations, but rather as national minorities. Groups so defined were not entitled to self-determination, and therefore had no right to seek union with their own people within its nation-state; as national minorities they were, however, entitled to maintain their separate ethnic identities through guarantees of certain linguistic, cultural, and religious rights.

The idea of guaranteeing some rights to minorities was not a new one in international law, but had been excercised in European peace treaties and peace conferences for over three hundred years.[31] One of the earliest examples occurred in the Vienna Peace Treaty of 1606 between Emperor Rudolf II and Stephen Bockay, Prince of Transylvania, which provided for the protection of religious minorities.[32] Throughout the seventeenth and eighteenth centuries protection of minorities generally focused on religious guarantees. The Christian minorities within the Ottoman Empire received particular attention in this regard, as a number of European states took it upon themselves to protect various denominations: Russia assumed the protection of Orthodox Christians, France that of Catholics, and Prussia that of Protestants.

In the nineteenth century treaty provisions expanded the concept of minority protection. In the Final Act of the Congress of Vienna,[33] signed on 9 June 1815, Russia, Prussia, and Austria agreed to grant 'national representation to the Poles living within their boundaries, and the establishment of national institutions'.[34] When Greece became independent in 1830 it promised in a Protocol to guarantee the civil and political liberties of all its subjects regardless of their religious beliefs.[35] At the Peace of Paris,[36] signed on 30 March 1856, all citizens of the Ottoman Empire were guaranteed equality of race and religion.[37] At the Congress of Berlin in 1878 the principle was established that any state which sought admission to the comity of European nations must first affirm its commitment to the principles of equality and non-discrimination upon which the comity of European na-

---

[30] *Report of the Commission of Jurists*, 6.
[31] Jacob Robinson 'From Protection of Minorities to Promotion of Human Rights' (1948) 115.
[32] *Id.*, 116.
[33] 64 CTS 453.
[34] *Id.*, Art. 1, 457.
[35] Art. 5, 80 CTS 327, 329, 330.
[36] 114 CTS 409.
[37] *Id.*, Art. 9, 414.

tions was based.[38] As a result, in the Treaty of Berlin[39] the states of Bulgaria, Montenegro, Romania, Serbia, and Turkey were required to guarantee the individual rights and freedoms of all their subjects without discrimination based on race or religion.[40]

Given these precedents, it was not surprising that the Allies should seek to supplement the principle of self-determination with an international regime for the protection of national minorities in those cases where self-determination was either not possible or not wanted.[41] The Austrian Government recognized this fact when it declared, in a letter dated 9 April 1929: 'Minority rights, as such, are simply part of and not inconsistent with the so-called right of self-determination of peoples; they constitute a form of compensation offered to the minority by reason of the fact that the latter could not or has not been granted the right of self-determination.'[42]

At the Peace Conference Wilson proposed initially that national minorities be protected by the provisions of the Covenant of the League of Nations. An article to this effect was contained in his draft proposals. However, Wilson's attempts to incorporate into the Covenant articles protecting national minorities and religious freedoms were unsuccessful. Amongst others, the British opposed their inclusion on the ground that the diversity of minority demands would make an adequate general provision difficult to formulate. With regard to religious freedoms, they expressed a reluctance to extend to themselves obligations which had traditionally been limited to a small number of states.[43] It was finally decided that the protec-

---

[38] Helmer Rosting 'Protection of Minorities By the League of Nations' (1923) 645.
[39] 153 CTS 171.
[40] *Id.* 175, 176 (Art. 4); 176 (Art. 5); 180 (Art. 20); 182 (Art. 27); 184 (Art. 35); 187 (Art. 44); and 189, 190 (Art. 62).
[41] Josef L. Kunz 'The Present Status of the International Law for the Protection of Minorities' (1954) 282. The alternative to establishing an international regime for the protection of national minorities was the expulsion of such minorities from the state in which they resided. This occurred in a number of cases. The Convention Concerning the Exchange of Greek and Turkish Populations (1923) 32 LNTS 76 provided in Art. 1 for the 'compulsory exchange of Turkish nationals of the Greek Orthodox religion established in Turkish territory, and of Greek nationals of the Muslim religion established in Greek territory.' This resulted in the forcible transfer of 355,635 Muslims from Greece to Turkey, and of 189,916 Greek Orthodox from Turkey to Greece: C. A. Macartney *National States and National Minorities* (1934) 445. In the Convention Between Greece and Bulgaria Respecting Reciprocal Emigration (1920) 1 LNTS 67 a voluntary exchange of populations was agreed upon. This resulted in the exchange of 101,800 Bulgarians and 52,891 Greeks. Although the exchange was purportedly voluntary, many of those who left were actually deported or coerced into doing so: *id.*, 439–41. For a comprehensive review of the population transfers which occurred after the First World War see Stephen P. Ladas *The Exchange of Minorities* (1932). See also the Advisory Opinion of the Permanent Court of International Justice in the *Exchange of Greek and Turkish Populations Case* (1925) PCIJ Reports, Series B No. 10, 20.
[42] (1929) LNOJ, Spec. Supp. 73, 65.
[43] Patrick Thornberry 'Is There a Phoenix in the Ashes?: International Law and Minority Rights' (1980) 429. See also Patrick Thornberry *International Law and the Rights of Minorities* (1991) 40.

tion of national minorities would best be served through international treaties, the provisions of which would be guaranteed by the League of Nations. When the new states in question complained that this arrangement would be an infringement of their sovereignty, Wilson replied by linking the grant of sovereignty to them with the protection of their minorities:

Nothing, I venture to say, is more likely to disturb the peace of the world than the treatment which might in certain circumstances be meted out to the minorities . . . If this Conference is going to recognize these various powers as new sovereignties within definite territories, the chief guarantors are entitled to be satisfied that their territorial settlements are of a character to be permanent, and that the guarantees given are to insure the peace of the world. It is not, therefore, the interventions of those who would interfere, but the actions of those who would help.[44]

Wilson's soothing words failed to placate those new states which were forced to accept minority obligations. Poland, Romania, and Yugoslavia were from the very beginning loud in their opposition to the minority obligations imposed upon them, arguing that such obligations not only infringed their sovereignty but also violated the principle of equality among states, and were an imputation on their good faith. Their resentment was heightened by the fact that neither the Allies themselves nor Germany and Italy were required to assume these minority obligations. Nevertheless, the new states did eventually accept the minority obligations imposed upon them in order to achieve recognition by the international community.[45]

4. PROVISIONS OF THE MINORITIES TREATIES

The treaty provisions protecting minorities which emerged from the Peace Conference were of two types. With respect to the enemy states of Austria, Hungary, Bulgaria, and Turkey the provisions were contained in the peace treaties signed by those states.[46] With respect to those states created or enlarged by the Peace Conference, the provisions protecting minorities were contained in separate minorities treaties. Poland, Czechoslovakia, Romania, Yugoslavia, Greece, and Danzig signed such treaties.[47] Other

[44] L. C. Green 'Protection of Minorities in the League of Nations and in the United Nations' in Allan Gottlieb (ed.) *Human Rights, Federalism and Minorities* (1970) 188.
[45] Mary Gardiner Jones 'National Minorities: A Case Study in International Protection' (1949) 605.
[46] Austria: the Treaty of St Germain-en-Laye, 10 Sep. 1919, 226 CTS 8; Hungary: the Treaty of Trianon, 4 June 1920, (1921) 6 LNTS 187; Bulgaria: the Treaty of Neuilly-sur-Seine, 27 Nov. 1919, 226 CTS 435; Turkey: the Treaty of Lausanne, 14 July 1923, (1924) 28 LNTS 11.
[47] Poland: the Treaty of Versailles, 28 June 1919, 225 CTS 412; Czechoslovakia: the Treaty of St Germain-en-Laye, 10 Sep. 1919, 226 CTS 170; Romania: the Treaty of Versailles, 9 Dec. 1919, (1921) 5 LNTS 335; Yugoslavia: the Treaty of St Germain-en-Laye, 10 Sep. 1919, 226 CTS 182; Greece: the Treaty of Sevrès, 10 Aug. 1920, (1924) 28 LNTS 244; Danzig: the Convention of Paris, 9 Nov. 1920, (1921) 6 LNTS 189. A minorities treaty with Armenia became irrelevant when Armenia became a Soviet Republic.

states subsequently made arrangements with the League of Nations for the protection of their minorities as a condition of their admission into the League of Nations. Thus, in addition to the agreement of 27 June 1921 between Sweden and Finland with regard to the Aaland Islands,[48] declarations concerning minority rights were made by Albania, Lithuania, Latvia, Estonia, and Iraq before the Council of the League of Nations.[49] Minorities in Memel were protected by the Convention of Paris, signed on 9 May 1924.[50]

The first minorities treaty, the Treaty of Versailles, was signed by Poland on 28 June 1919. Poland was considered by the Peace Conference to require immediate attention because it had been created from territories comprising various ethnic groups. In addition to the Polish majority, the population of Poland included four large minorities, Ukrainians, Jews, Germans, and Byelorussians, as well as smaller minorities.[51] Such a diverse and volatile mix made it essential to establish guidelines for the treatment of minorities quickly. The provisions of the Polish minorities treaty served as a model for the other treaties and formed the basis of the minorities regime.

The minorities treaties attempted not only to protect national minorities but, above and beyond this goal, to assure the maintenance of certain basic rights for all inhabitants of the state, whatever their citizenship or ethnic status. The treaties therefore guaranteed full and complete protection of life and liberty to all inhabitants of the states parties without distinction of birth, nationality, language, race, or religion. Moreover, all inhabitants of the states parties were to be entitled to exercise their religion freely, subject only to the constraints of public order and public morals. Those guarantees were intended to establish within the states parties a general climate of political liberalism, in the belief that rights for minorities would only be secure within such a setting.[52]

Citizenship was considered an essential *quid pro quo* for entitlement to minority rights. Those unable to accept citizenship of the new states were permitted by the treaties to opt for another nationality, and were then required to move to the state of their chosen nationality within twelve months.[53] It was hoped that this option would remove the most intractable

---

[48] See pp. 36–7 *supra*.

[49] On 2 Oct. 1921, 12 May 1922, 7 July 1923, and 11 May 1932 respectively. Alan Renouf 'The Present Force of the Minorities Treaties' (1950) 806.

[50] (1924) 29 LNTS 85.

[51] According to the 1921 census of Poland's 27.1m. inhabitants, about 18.8m. were ethnic Poles, or 69.2%; 3,900,000 were Ukrainians, or 14.3%; 2,100,000 Jews, or 7.8%; 1m. Byelorussians, or 3.9%, and 1m. Germans, or 3.9%. There were smaller numbers of Lithuanians, Russians, and Czechs, who together made up 0.9% of Poland's population: Franjo Tudjman *Nationalism in Contemporary Europe* (1981) 30.

[52] Inis L. Claude, Jr. *National Minorities* (1955) 18.

[53] Theodore S. Woolsey 'The Rights of Minorities Under the Treaty with Poland' (1920) 393, 394. Provisions in the treaties regulated the liquidation of property and the status of minors in such cases.

of minority nationalists from the new states and thereby facilitate relations between the majority and the minority.[54]

The actual rights of the minorities were then set out. Articles 7, 8, and 9 of the treaty signed by Poland exemplify the rights granted. Article 7 guaranteed equality before the law to every citizen of the state, regardless of race, language, or religion. It prohibited discrimination on the basis of religion in matters concerning civil and political rights. It also prohibited restrictions on the use of languages other than Polish, and provided guarantees for the use before the courts of languages other than Polish. Article 8 guaranteed citizens belonging to 'racial, religious or linguistic minorities' the same treatment in law and in fact as other Polish citizens. Such minorities were permitted to maintain their own charitable, religious, social, and educational institutions. Article 9 obliged the state to provide primary school education in the language of a minority which constituted a 'considerable proportion' of the population of an area. It further obliged the state to provide an 'equitable share' of public funds to the minority, again when the minority constituted a considerable proportion of the population in a particular area, for educational, religious, or charitable purposes.[55] These articles did not simply protect minorities from persecution or discrimination. Their purpose was more expansive: they sought to create a legal framework which enabled the minorities to pursue and promote their own language and culture, thereby ensuring that they would not be assimilated by the majority but would survive as a separate entity within the state.

In addition to the general provisions granting rights to minorities, which appeared word for word in virtually all of the minorities treaties, there were special provisions in individual treaties dealing with the particular problems of specified minorities. The treaties with Poland and Romania, for example, contained special provisions with respect to Jews. Similarly, the treaty with Yugoslavia contained provisions with respect to Muslims. The treaty with Czechoslovakia contained a provision which specified autonomy for the Ruthenians (i.e. Ukrainians) south of the Carpathians. Various other treaty provisions provided for the requirements of individual minorities.[56]

The League guaranteed all the rights enumerated. On the domestic level, the obligated state undertook to elevate the treaty provisions to the status of fundamental law, so that all other laws, regulations, or official action which conflicted with them, whether relating to minorities or to the population as a whole, would be declared invalid. On the international level, the rights set out in the minorities treaties were recognized as obligations of international concern, and as such were placed under the

---

[54] Claude, 18.

[55] See 225 CTS 412, 417, 418.

[56] Ifor L. Evans 'The Protection of Minorities' (1923–24) 109; Rosting, 649; Thornbery (1991) 43, 44.

guarantee of the League of Nations. This external guarantee, however, applied only to persons belonging to racial, religious, or linguistic minorities.[57]

The rights contained in the minorities treaties were conferred, not on the minority groups as corporate bodies, but on the individuals belonging to the minorities. It was the individuals who benefited from the treaties, which did not in general recognize minority groups as possessing legal personality.[58] In practice the League did permit minority groups as well as individual members of minorities the right of petition, but as this right of petition did not confer *locus standi* on the petitioner it cannot be said that it amounted to the recognition of group rights.[59]

Those states which were bound by the minorities treaties resented the inequality of treatment and encroachment of sovereignty which the treaties imposed on them. The treaty provisions further angered them because they were perceived to be unfairly weighted in favour of the minorities. The issue of the loyalty of a minority to its new state was a sore point, as this was nowhere specified in the treaties, although it was arguably implied within the citizenship provisions. In an attempt to rectify this situation, the League of Nations adopted a resolution on 21 September 1923 which required members of minorities to co-operate as loyal citizens with the state to which they belonged.[60] Loyalty, however, was a quality which could not be legislated into existence.

5. PROCEDURE UNDER THE MINORITIES TREATIES

The manner in which minority rights were to be guaranteed by the League was set out only very briefly in the minorities treaties. Consequently the League was forced to develop its own procedural rules as minority problems arose. By 1921 a procedure had been established whereby members of minorities, minority organizations, and states not members of the League Council could submit petitions to the Council concerning minority questions. This procedure was not set out in the minorities treaties, and its legality was challenged by the states subject to those treaties. But the Permanent Court of International Justice ruled that the Council had the right to establish its own procedure.[61]

---

[57] Thornberry (1980) 433.

[58] Louis Calvaré *Le Droit International Public Positif* (1951) Vol. 1, 251.

[59] Louis B. Sohn 'The Rights of Minorities' in Louis Henkin (ed.) *The International Bill of Rights* (1981) 274.

[60] André Mandelstam 'La Protection des Minorités' (1923) 445.

[61] *German Settlers in Poland* (1923) PCIJ Reports, Series B No. 6, 6. At p. 22 the Court declared: 'So far as concerns the procedure of the Council in minority matters, it is for the Council to regulate it.'

The minorities did not possess *locus standi* before the Council. Petitions submitted on their behalf, whether by individual minority members, minority organizations, or interested states, did not have the effect of making either the minority or the particular petitioner party to the proceedings before the Council. A petition merely brought to the attention of the Council certain information concerning the treatment of a minority; it was for the Council to decide whether or not to pursue the matter. The League had decided not to permit minorities to appear before the Council or the Permanent Court in order to avoid confrontation between states and their minorities. Granting *locus standi* to the minorities, it was thought, would create the appearance of a state within a state, and would only exacerbate the minority states' sense of grievance regarding their sovereignty. However, as the minorities were the parties most affected by any infringement of the minorities treaties, the League's decision to deny them standing made them feel that their rights had been effectively eviscerated by the procedure adopted by the Council.

The first step in the process of considering a problem arising from a minorities treaty was to submit a petition to the Council; this was examined by the League Secretariat for receivability. The petition had to satisfy five requirements: 1) that it deal with an issue within the ambit of the minorities treaties; 2) that it not raise facts which had already been the subject of a petition; 3) that it not emanate from an anonymous or unauthenticated source; 4) that it not contain violent language; and 5) that it not advocate the severance of political relations between the minority and the state to which it belonged.[62] If the petition was found to meet the standards of receivability, it was sent to the minority state for its response.[63] The petition and any response from the minority state were then circulated to the members of the Council, for purely informational purposes. They were also circulated to a special investigating committee, composed of the President of the Council and two other members chosen by the President.[64] This 'Committee of Three', in conjunction with the Minorities Section of the League Secretariat, would investigate the complaint contained in the petition. The Committee could dispose of the matter at this stage by declaring the complaint unfounded. If the Committee decided that there was some basis to the complaint, it would attempt to resolve the matter by initiating informal negotiations with the minority state in question. If this proved unsuccessful, the Committee would place the matter on the Council agenda by formal recommendation and the case would be handled by the Council as one brought before it by a

---

[62] Mandelstam, 461.

[63] A total of 521 petitions were received during the period from 1929 to 1939, of which 225 were declared non-receivable: Jones, 614.

[64] Claude, 24.

member.[65] Article 4, paragraph 5 of the League Covenant required the
Council to examine the petition in the presence of a representative from the
minority state.[66] The Council therefore could not reach a decision without
the concurring vote of the minority state, which meant that settlement could
only be achieved through an agreed solution.[67]

Recourse to the Permanent Court of International Justice was permitted
under the minorities treaties to resolve questions of a legal nature. This
aspect of the procedure was set out in the minorities treaties in some detail.[68]
Granting jurisdiction to the Permanent Court was an entirely novel idea,
and was considered to be of paramount importance for the protection of
minorities. This was emphasized at the Peace Conference in the Report
of the Committee on New States. The Report stressed the importance of
giving jurisdiction in questions concerning minorities to a Court of Justice,
and went so far as to declare this 'the foundation of the system of protection
to be undertaken by the League'.[69] The Report further stated that: 'The
establishment of the League of Nations of which Poland is a part, moreover,
removes as a consequence all interference of a foreign Power in her
internal affairs, for it assures to her the guarantee of an impartial examination by the Court of Justice of the League of Nations, i.e. by an assembly
which is judicial and not political.'[70] This had been one of the great
weaknesses in earlier attempts to protect minorities. Previously minority
protection had always been based on the threat of intervention by a protector state in the event of breach of a minority provision by a minority state.
Protection on that basis was open to abuse or neglect on the part of the
protector state. The continued existence of protector states, it was thought,
would become unnecessary when a third party tribunal was in place to
adjudicate disputes involving minorities; the threat of intervention would
thereby be greatly reduced. Moreover, recourse to a third-party tribunal
ensured that the minorities treaties would be interpreted in an impartial
manner, which had not previously been possible when protector states had
been involved.

6. THE GERMAN-POLISH CONVENTION RELATING TO UPPER SILESIA

In addition to the minorities treaties promulgated at the Peace Conference,
a number of bilateral treaties, or clauses in bilateral treaties, were con-

[65] Thornberry (1980) 434.

[66] Art. 4(5) provided as follows: 'Any Member of the League not represented on the
Council shall be invited to send a Representative to sit as a member at any meeting of the
Council during a consideration of matters specially affecting the interests of that Member of
the League.'

[67] Claude, 24.

[68] See e.g. Art. 12 of the Treaty with Poland: 225 CTS 412, 419.

[69] Julius Stone *International Guarantees of Minority Rights* (1932) 9.   [70] *Id.*, 9.

cluded between neighbouring states which had as their object the protection of minorities. These treaties differed from the minorities treaties of the Peace Conference in that they were reciprocal in nature and their provisions were not guaranteed by the League of Nations.[71]

The most important of these was the treaty concluded between Germany and Poland with regard to Upper Silesia. Article 88 of the Treaty of Versailles had specified that a plebiscite was to be held in Upper Silesia to determine whether the territory would belong to Germany or Poland. Paragraph 5 of the Annex to Article 88 further stipulated that the territory was to be divided between the two states on the basis of the majority vote within each commune, rather than on the basis of the total vote cast. This resulted in the division of Upper Silesia into two parts, German Upper Silesia and Polish Upper Silesia. Each part contained a sizable ethnic minority of the neighbouring state. The League recommended that an agreement be drawn up between Germany and Poland in order to preserve the economic unity of the region and to protect the respective minorities in each section. With regard to the minorities the League proposed that the provisions of the Polish minorities treaty apply to Polish Upper Silesia and that the same provisions apply to German Upper Silesia for a minimum period of fifteen years. The League also proposed that the provisions concerning minority rights be placed under the guarantee of the League in the same manner as those of the Polish minorities treaty.[72] On the basis of these proposals, Germany and Poland concluded the Geneva Convention of 15 May 1922, otherwise known as the German–Polish Convention Relating to Upper Silesia.[73]

The Convention was divided into three sections. Section I set out the obligations which Poland was bound to observe under its minorities treaty, with parallel obligations agreed to by Germany. Section II contained extremely detailed provisions for minority rights relating to civil and political rights, religion, private education, secondary and higher education, the official language of the administration, and the language to be employed in the courts of law.[74] Section III dealt with procedural matters. The Convention provided for a Mixed Commission, consisting of two Polish members, two German members, and a President of some other nationality. The Commission would first attempt to right a minority grievance through conciliatory means. If this failed, the President would render a decision on the case, providing a reasoned opinion for his finding. The minority state was not bound to carry out the President's decision.[75] If it did not do so, the

---

[71] Jacob Robinson 'International Protection of Minorities: A Global View' (1971) 61, 73. At p. 74 Robinson lists 22 such treaties.

[72] (1921) LNOJ, 2nd Year, No. 10–12, 1230.

[73] The treaty is reprinted in its entirety in Georges Kaeckenbeeck *The International Experiment in Upper Silesia* (1942) pp. 567–822. Excerpts of the principal articles of the treaty are also reprinted in Julius Stone *Regional Guarantees of Minority Rights* (1933) pp. 213–68.

[74] Rosting, 652.   [75] Stone (1933) 93.

petitioner was entitled to petition the League Council, with recourse to the Permanent Court on issues of a legal nature. Unlike other bilateral minority treaties, the provisions of the German–Polish Convention were guaranteed by the League of Nations. Moreover, unlike the other minority treaties guaranteed by the League of Nations, petitions made under the Convention constituted the first legal step in initiating the decision-making process by the Council which was binding on the minority state in question. In other words, under the German–Polish Convention petitioners possessed *locus standi* before the Council.[76]

One of the most interesting cases arising out of the German–Polish Convention was that of *Bernheim*.[77] The provisions of the German–Polish Convention had referred to 'members of a minority' without specifying the ethnic nature of that minority. Up to 1933 petitions had been presented only by the German and Polish minorities. On 12 May 1933 Franz Bernheim presented the first petition on behalf of the Jewish minority in German Upper Silesia. Bernheim's petition alleged violations of the Convention by legislation and decrees of the Third Reich directed against the Jewish minority, and relied, *inter alia*, on Article 67(1). This provided that all German nationals 'shall be equal before the law and shall enjoy the same civil and political rights without distinction as to race, language or religion'.[78] The petition requested that the Council declare the said laws and decrees null and void, and ensure reinstatement and compensation to the injured persons. A report presented to the Council on 30 May 1933 noted that the laws complained of did indeed violate the Convention. The German Government thereupon made a declaration affirming its commitment to its international obligations.[79]

7. DECISIONS OF THE PERMANENT COURT OF INTERNATIONAL JUSTICE

The Permanent Court of International Justice dealt with eight cases involving the minorities treaties. As a result the Court was able to address a number of important issues pertaining to the treaties, including their purpose, the acquisition of nationality, the definition of a minority, and the notion of equality between the majority and the minority.

The Court first had occasion to clarify the purpose of the treaties in the case of *German Settlers in Poland*.[80] It stated that the purpose of the treaty

[76] Tore Modeen *The International Protection of National Minorities in Europe* (1969) 61.
[77] (1933) LNOJ 930.
[78] Kaeckenbeeck, 602, 603; Stone (1933) 218.
[79] Stone (1933) 35; Robinson (1971) 74.
[80] (1923) PCIJ Reports, Series B, No. 6, 6.

with Poland was 'to assure respect for the rights of the minorities and to prevent discrimination against them by any act whatsoever of the Polish state'.[81] This purpose was again set out by the Court in the case of *Minority Schools in Albania*:

The idea underlying the treaties for the protection of minorities is to secure for certain elements incorporated in a State, the population of which differs from them in race, language or religion, the possibility of living peaceably alongside that population and co-operating amicably with it, while at the same time preserving the characteristics which distinguish them from the majority, and satisfying the ensuing special needs.[82]

This interpretation of the purpose underlying the minorities treaties coincided with the aims of the Peace Conference in establishing the minorities treaties in the first place: both intended to satisfy and protect the cultural, religious, and linguistic attributes of national minorities within the existing state structure, and thus to eliminate further need for self-determination on the part of such minorities.

In another extremely important decision, *Acquisition of Polish Nationality*,[83] the Court interpreted the provisions relating to the acquisition of nationality. Since the minorities treaties linked the granting of minority rights to citizenship, only those members of the minority who were nationals of the minority state could avail themselves of those rights. Those who were not nationals were entitled only to the protection offered to 'inhabitants' of the minority state, namely protection of life, liberty, and the free exercise of religion.[84] Pre-war Prussian laws had granted favourable terms to Germans who settled in the German provinces of West Prussia or Posen. German settlement here was encouraged to strengthen the German population in relation to the Polish population. When these territories became a part of Poland in 1919, the Polish Government set out to rid the area of the German settlers. They were informed that they would have to vacate their farms pursuant to a law adopted on 14 July 1920. The settlers successfully impugned this law in *German Settlers in Poland*.[85] The Permanent Court held that the eviction of the settlers from their farms was contrary to the principle of equality specified by Articles 7 and 8 of the minority treaty.[86] Poland pursued the matter in the *Acquisition of Polish Nationality* case,[87] arguing that the law of 14 July 1920 should not be declared null because the settlers were not Polish nationals and were therefore not entitled to the rights guaranteed to minorities in Articles 7 and 8 of the Treaty. Poland

---

[81] *Id.*, 25.   [82] (1935) PCIJ Reports, Series AB, No. 64.
[83] (1923) PCIJ Reports, Series B, No. 7, 6.
[84] See p. 42 *supra*.
[85] (1923) PCIJ Reports, Series B, No. 6, 6.
[86] *Id.*, 36, 37.
[87] (1923) PCIJ Reports, Series B, No. 7, 6.

submitted that the settlers were not Polish nationals because their parents had not been habitually resident in the territory, as required by Article 4 of the Treaty.[88] The Court did not accept this submission; proper construction of Article 4 made it clear that the German settlers were currently Polish nationals, and thus an existing minority:

The Court's task is clearly defined. Having before it a clause which leaves little to be desired in the nature of clearness, it is bound to apply this clause as it stands, without considering whether other provisions might with advantage have been added to or substituted for it. The Minorities Treaty (Article 4, paragraph 1) admits and declares to be Polish nationals, *ipso facto*, persons who were born in the new State 'of parents habitually resident there'. These words refer to residence of the parents at the time of the birth of the child and at this time only . . . To impose an additional condition for the acquisition of Polish nationality, a condition not provided for in the Treaty of June 28, 1919, would be equivalent, not to interpreting the Treaty, but to reconstructing it.[89]

The Court declared that it would not countenance any interpretation of a minorities treaty which would deprive it 'of a great part of its value'.[90] It would not admit interpretations which allowed minority states to deprive their minorities of citizenship, an abuse which the provisions of the minorities treaties were specifically designed to prevent.

The importance of the link between citizenship and minority rights was again emphasized in *Treatment of Polish Nationals and Other Persons of Polish Origin or Speech in the Danzig Territory*.[91] In this case Poland attempted to claim rights for Polish nationals and other persons of Polish origin or speech living in the Free City of Danzig, by virtue of Article 104(5) of the Peace Treaty of Versailles[92] and Article 33 of the Convention of Paris.[93] Article 104(5) provided:

The Principal Allied and Associated Powers undertake to negotiate a treaty between the Polish Government and the Free City of Danzig, which shall come into force at the same time as the establishment of the said Free City, with the following objects:

5) to provide against any discrimination within the Free City of Danzig to the detriment of citizens of Poland and other persons of Polish origin or speech.[94]

Article 33 provided:

---

[88] Art. 4 provided as follows: 'Poland admits and declares to be Polish nationals *ipso facto* and without the requirement of any formality persons of German, Austrian, Hungarian or Russian nationality who were born in the said territory of parents habitually resident there, even if at the date of the coming into force of the present treaty they are not themselves habitually resident there': 225 CTS 412, 416, 417.

[89] (1923) PCIJ Reports, Series B, No. 7, 6, 20.

[90] *Id.*, 17.

[91] (1932) PCIJ Reports, Series A/B, No. 44, 4.

[92] 225 CTS 188.   [93] (1921) 6 LNTS 189.   [94] 225 CTS 188, 248.

The Free City of Danzig undertakes to apply to racial, religious and linguistic minorities provisions identical with those which are applied by Poland on Polish territory, in execution of Chapter I of the Treaty concluded at Versailles on June 28th, 1919, between Poland and the Principal Allied and Associated Powers, with a view, in particular, to ensuring the application of the provisions laid down in Article 104, paragraph 5, of the Treaty of Versailles with Germany.[95]

On the basis of these provisions Poland argued that Polish nationals in Danzig, although not entitled to political rights, were otherwise entitled to enjoy full and entire equality of rights in every domain of public and private law. In particular, they were entitled to their 'free national development', which included the use of Polish in education, in internal administration, and in the administration of justice.

The Court rejected the Polish claim. Poland was not seeking equal treatment for members of the Polish minority who were citizens of Danzig, but for Poles who were citizens of another state, namely Poland. Citizenship was crucial to the rights which could be claimed by members of the minority:

It will be seen that, so far as the treatment of minorities is concerned, a distinction is drawn in the Treaty between minorities in the broad sense and minorities in the narrow sense. Article 2 refers to 'all inhabitants', which also included minorities consisting of non-citizens of the State. This interpretation is in conformity with the practice of the Council and with the Court's Advisory Opinion No. 7 on the question concerning the acquisition of Polish nationality. The members of minorities who are not citizens of the State enjoy protection—guaranteed by the League of Nations—of life and liberty and the free exercise of their religion, while minorities in the narrow sense, that is, minorities the members of which are citizens of the State, enjoy—under the same guarantee—amongst other rights, equality of rights in civil and political matters, and in matters relating to primary instruction . . . [I]t must be observed that the distinction between citizens and non-citizens obtains to a greater or less extent in almost all countries, and is the standard adopted in all the Minorities treaties . . .[96]

Article 104 was designed to prevent unfavourable treatment of Polish nationals in Danzig, but not to obtain privileged treatment for them.[97]

Another important issue arising from the minorities treaties was the definition of a minority and the question of who was entitled to claim membership in it. In the case *Greco-Bulgarian Communities*[98] the Court defined a minority. The Greco-Bulgarian Convention of 27 November 1919[99] provided for voluntary and reciprocal emigration of Greek and Bul-

---

[95] (1921) 6 LNTS 189, 203, 205.
[96] (1932) PCIJ Reports, Series A/B, No. 44, 4, 39.
[97] Calvaré, Vol. 1, 252.
[98] (1930) PCIJ Reports, Series B, No. 17, 4.
[99] (1920) 1 LNTS 67. See p. 40, fn. 41 *supra*.

garian minorities. The Convention referred to such minorities as 'communities',[100] and the Court was called upon to define a 'community'. Noting that
the concept of a 'community' had an 'exclusively minority character', the
Court declared that:

the 'community' is a group of persons living in a given country or locality, having a
race, religion, language and traditions in a sentiment of solidarity, with a view to
preserving their traditions, maintaining their form of worship, ensuring the instruction and upbringing of their children in accordance with the spirit and traditions of
their race and rendering mutual assistance to each other.[101]

It then became necessary for the Court to determine who belonged to a
minority. Was membership of a minority determined solely by the presence
of certain objective elements, such as race, religion, and language, or did it
also involve the subjective element of the individual's will? This issue arose
in the case *Rights of Minorities in Upper Silesia (Minority Schools)*.[102] In
Polish Upper Silesia the Polish authorities had annulled the enrolment of
several thousand children in the German minority school system on the
ground that those children did not speak the language of the minority. The
German Government challenged Poland's action, submitting that the test
of membership in a minority must be primarily subjective. According to the
German argument, it was the right of individuals to declare of their own
free will whether they belonged to the minority. In support of this contention, the German Government relied, *inter alia*, on Articles 74 and 131 of
the German–Polish Convention Relating to Upper Silesia.[103] Article 74
provided that: 'The question whether a person does or does not belong to
a racial, linguistic or religious minority may not be verified or disputed by
the authorities.'[104] Article 131 provided that:

1) In order to determine the language of a pupil or child, account shall be taken of
the verbal or written statement of the person legally responsible for the education of
the pupil or child. This statement may not be verified or disputed by the educational
authorities.
2) Similarly, the educational authorities must abstain from exercising any pressure,
however slight, with a view to obtaining the withdrawal of requests for the establishment of minority educational institutions.[105]

Poland submitted that the test to be applied was an objective one. Minority
status was a question of fact, not of intention. Declarations of minority

[100] *Id.*, Art. 7, 70.
[101] (1932) PCIJ Reports, Series A/B, No. 44, 4, 21.
[102] (1928) PCIJ Reports, Series A, No. 15, 4.
[103] Kaeckenbeeck, 567; Stone (1933) 213.
[104] *Id.*, 610, 224.
[105] *Id.*, 634, 244. (1928) PCIJ Reports, Series A, No. 15, 4, 46.

status under Articles 74 and 131 had therefore to be in accordance with the facts.

The Court upheld the Polish argument, holding that, although the declarations of individuals under Articles 74 and 131 could not be disputed, the declaration had to set out the true position with regard to the facts, and did not constitute an unrestricted right to choose either the language of instruction or the corresponding school.[106] In other words, the test of minority status had to be an objective one. An emphatic dissent to this ruling was registered by Judge Nyholm:

There appears here to be a contradiction in terms. A declaration which cannot be disputed or verified is entirely unimpeachable. Such a declaration cannot be limited by rules of law. The requirement according to which the declaration must correspond to the facts is only a pious wish and any limitations as regards its sincerity come solely within a moral sphere. Since the declaration cannot be examined and since all objections or disputes in regard to it are excluded, the declarer is not subject to a legal obligation and the declaration must be taken as it stands. Consequently, the maker of the declaration may of his own free will make a declaration without considering whether it corresponds to the actual state of affairs.[107]

The issue of enrolment in minority schools remained unsettled in spite of the Court's decision in the *Minority Schools* case, and eventually the matter came before the Court again in the case *German Minority Schools in Polish Upper Silesia*.[108] Language tests had been established 'to ascertain whether children could profitably attend schools in which literary German was the language of instruction'.[109] These tests were challenged by the *Deutscher Volksbund* as being contrary to Articles 74 and 131 of the German–Polish Convention. The assertion of Judge Nyholm that 'the declarer is not subject to a legal obligation and the declaration must be taken as it stands'[110] proved prescient. The Court held that, although a declaration must be in accordance with the facts, the declarations were conclusive and could neither be disputed nor verified. Evidence could not be adduced against such declarations as this was prohibited by the Convention.[111] Thus in effect the Court resiled from its decision in the *Minority Schools* case.

Another important issue on which the Court had to rule concerned the concept of equality. The minorities treaties had specified that the minorities

---

[106] The subjective test put forward by the Weimar Republic turned out to be much more humane than the policy subsequently adopted by the Nazis, who maintained that race was recognizable by certain objective elements. The objective theory had been rejected by the Weimar Government as being '*peu sur*': Calvaré, Vol. 1, 251, fn. 105.

[107] (1928) PCIJ Reports, Series A, No. 15, 4, 63. Judges Huber and Negulesco also dissented, at pp. 48 and 67 respectively.

[108] (1931) PCIJ Reports, Series A/B, No. 40, 4.

[109] *Id.*, 18.

[110] (1928) PCIJ Reports, Series A, No. 15, 4, 63.

[111] (1931) PCIJ Reports, Series A/B, No. 40, 19.

were to be treated equally 'in law and in fact'. The issue of what 'in fact' constituted equal treatment occupied the Court in a number of cases. In *German Settlers in Poland*[112] the Court declared that there 'must be equality in fact as well as ostensible legal equality in the sense of the absence of discrimination in the words of the law'.[113] The Court found that the law evicting the German settlers had not 'in fact' treated them equally, Although the law contained no reference to the German settlers as a specific category of persons, and although it was applicable in a few cases to non-German Polish nationals, it had been designed in order to evict German settlers. It was therefore contrary to the principle of equality set out in the treaty in that it subjected the German settlers to discriminatory treatment.[114]

The Court reiterated the importance of equality in fact in the *Treatment of Polish Nationals in Danzig* case.[115] The Court declared in this case that a prohibition against discrimination, to be effective, had 'to ensure the absence of discrimination in fact as well as in law'.[116] The Court pointed out that a law of apparently general application which in fact adversely affected a particular ethnic group would constitute a violation of the prohibition.[117]

The most interesting application by the Court of the principle of equality in fact involved the *Minority Schools in Albania* case.[118] The Albanian Government had attempted to close down all private schools within the state. When the Greek minority protested against this measure, the Albanian Government replied that the closure of private schools in Albania was a general measure applicable to all Albanians, whether of the majority or of the minority, and was therefore not a violation of the provision guaranteeing equality of treatment in law and in fact. The Court was faced with the dilemma of having to choose between a position which appeared to grant the minority a privileged position within the state, and one which would deprive it of one of its most important cultural institutions.[119] The Court held that the law abolishing all private schools, in spite of its non-discriminatory character, nevertheless violated the principle of equality in fact. In the Court's opinion, equality in law 'precludes discrimination of any kind', but equality in fact 'may involve the necessity of different treatment in order to attain a result which establishes an equilibrium between different situations'.[120] The maintenance of private schools for the minority did

---

[112] (1923) PCIJ Reports, Series B, No. 6, 6.   [113] *Id.*, 24.
[114] *Id.*, 36.
[115] (1932) PCIJ Reports, Series A/B, No. 44, 4.
[116] *Id.*, 28.
[117] *Id.*, 28.
[118] (1935) PCIJ Reports, Series A/B, No. 64, 4.
[119] Jones, 617.   [120] (1935) PCIJ Reports, Series A/B, No. 64, 19.

not place it in a favoured position *vis-à-vis* the majority but, on the contrary, simply enabled it to maintain a position of equality with the majority.[121]

The case of *Polish Agrarian Reform and the German Minority*[122] raised another interesting question concerning the principle of equality of treatment in fact. Certain members of the German minority in Poland possessed extensive landholdings. It was alleged that Poland's efforts to introduce measures for agrarian reform affected these landholders disproportionately, and thus constituted a violation of the principle of equality of treatment in fact. Unfortunately, this case was never argued to conclusion, having been withdrawn by the German Government before the Court arrived at a decision.

8. BREAKDOWN OF THE MINORITIES TREATIES REGIME

In 1930–1 the League received 204 petitions concerning minority problems. By 1938–9 the number of petitions received had fallen to four, of which three were rejected for non-receivability. This decline in petitions reflected the decline of the minorities treaties regime itself. By the end of the decade it had virtually ceased to exist.[123]

The collapse of the minorities treaties regime was the result of a number of factors. In spite of its extensive guarantees to minorities and its elaborate procedure designed to respect the sensibilities of minority states, the regime nevertheless failed to satisfy any of the parties involved. The minority states never reconciled themselves to the limitations imposed by the minorities treaties. The treaties were seen not only to constitute an infringement of the minority states' sovereignty, but also to violate the principle of equality of states, since they were not universally applied. This was deeply resented by the minority states.[124] Moreover, the minority states feared that the continued separate existence of the minorities, which was guaranteed by the treaties, posed a threat to their internal stability.[125] They constantly demanded revision of the system, calling for its adoption by all states or its abolition. They were uncooperative in implementing the treaties and tended to treat their minorities badly.[126] This mistreatment was expressed in

---

[121] PCIJ Reports, 20. For an interesting discussion of this case see Nathaniel Berman 'A Perilous Ambivalence: Nationalist Desire, Legal Autonomy, and the Limits of the Interwar Framework' (1992) 353.

[122] (1933) PCIJ Reports, Series C, No. 71, 7.

[123] Macartney, 338; Thornberry (1980) 436.

[124] Thornberry (1991) 47.

[125] Thornberry (1980) 437.

[126] Czechoslovakia was the outstanding exception in this regard, treating its minorites fairly and co-operating fully with the League system. Estonia also treated its minorities well: Claude, 40.

various ways, ranging from officially tolerated violence against the minorities to refusals to implement the economic, political, or cultural rights of the minorities.[127] In those cases where the minority possessed wealth or property, efforts were frequently made to reduce their standing. The minorities were often persecuted on the grounds of 'disloyalty', which caused greater disaffection. This mistreatment of the minorities was not surprising, given that the governments of the new minority states were strongly nationalist in orientation, and were in many cases motivated by 'a heady and triumphant reaction against previous oppression'.[128]

The minorities also acted to undermine the system. Several of the largest minority groups, such as the Germans and Hungarians, had been members of the ruling class prior to the creation of the minority states. They were accustomed to privilege and elevated social standing, and found it very difficult to accept their new status as national minorities in an alien state, governed by peoples whom they considered culturally and intellectually inferior to themselves.[129] Their relationship with the majority was characterized by an attitude of superiority and disdain, which did nothing to foster harmonious coexistence. They often attempted to utilize the minorities treaties to maintain the privileged position which they had previously enjoyed, and presented petitions of a trivial and pettifogging nature.[130] The minorities constantly demanded revision of the system, so that they might obtain *locus standi* before the Council, and an ever greater degree of autonomy from their respective minority states.[131]

Ironically, the very states which originally constructed the minorities treaties regime at the Peace Conference also contributed to its demise. The major powers refused to include themselves within the minorities treaties regime, even though Italy proved to be one of the worst offenders against its own minorities.[132] France was quite willing to overlook abuses of the minorities treaties in order to gain allies amongst the minority states. The United Kingdom unwisely adopted the policy towards the minorities that, as many of the minorities were German, Germany was the proper state to look after their interests.[133] As a result, minority problems increasingly developed into disputes between states, which in turn enflamed irredentist sentiment amongst the minorities.

Matters came to a head on 13 September 1934 when Poland's Foreign

---

[127] Claude, 41.   [128] Macartney, 387.   [129] Claude, 43.

[130] For example, a petition was submitted under the German–Polish Convention concerning a dispute between a policeman and a woman who had been reprimanded for throwing dirty water and refuse into the street: P. de Azcarate *The League of Nations and National Minorities* (1945) 152.

[131] Thornberry (1980) 437.

[132] Oppression in Italy 'extended even to dead Germans, whose names on tombstones were Italianized, so that, for example, von Sterenbach was posthumously renamed Lago di Stelle': Robinson (1971) 65.   [133] Macartney, 376.

Minister, Colonel Josef Beck, repudiated the Polish Minorities Treaty at the League of Nations. Beck informed the League that Poland would no longer co-operate with the League on minority protection unless the minorities treaties regime was accepted by all states. The United Kingdom, France, and Italy protested that a unilateral declaration of this nature could not release Poland from a multinational treaty, but otherwise took no action. The League's failure to react effectively brought the working of the minorities treaties regime to a standstill, and led eventually to the complete disappearance of the Minorities Section of the League Secretariat.[134]

9. SELF-DETERMINATION IN THE INTER-WAR YEARS

The breakdown of the minorities treaties regime can only be understood in the context of the wider issue of self-determination in the inter-war years. The Peace Conference had proclaimed that the new order which it was establishing was based on the principle of self-determination. However, a number of states were convinced that self-determination had been denied to them at the Peace Conference. This group included Germany, Austria, Hungary, and Bulgaria, i.e. those defeated in the war. These states claimed, with considerable justification, that large numbers of their nationals had been separated from them because the Peace Conference, in establishing frontiers in areas of mixed population, had repeatedly made decisions against them.[135] Italy was also dissatisfied, feeling that it had not been sufficiently rewarded by the Allies at the Peace Conference.[136]

Germany never accepted the provisions of the Treaty of Versailles as either just or permanent. The separation of millions of Germans from the German nation-state was seen as a gross abuse of the principle of self-determination, which had been forced upon Germany by the Allies. The loss of German territory to Poland was particularly resented. The German minority in Poland in the inter-war years numbered approximately one million, and was grouped mainly in the Polish Corridor and in Polish Upper Silesia.[137] Recovery of this territory was a major aim of German foreign policy, and was supported by Germans of all political persuasions. Gustav

---

[134] Josef L. Kunz 'The Future of the International Law for the Protection of Minorities' (1945) 90.

[135] There were in inter-war Europe sizable German-speaking minorites in Belgium, France, Denmark, Italy, Poland, Czechoslovakia, Hungary, Romania, Yugoslavia, Lithuania, Latvia, and Estonia. Likewise there were sizable Hungarian minorities in Romania, Yugoslavia, and Czechoslovakia and a sizable Bulgarian minority in Yugoslavia: Baron Heyking 'The International Protection of Minorites: the Achilles' Heel of the League of Nations' (1927) 32; Macartney, 518–36.

[136] Tudjman, 38.

[137] De Azcarate, 29.

Stresemann, the German Foreign Minister from 1923 to 1929, noted that the Polish frontier was 'a gross violation of the principle of self-determination'.[138] The socialist Prime Minister of Prussia, Otto Braun, declared in 1931 that 'the eastern frontiers of Germany were unjust and unnatural and never to be recognised as equitable'.[139]

As well as the question of the Polish frontier, there was also the issue of the enforced separation of Germany and Austria. In November 1918 the Provisional Assembly of German Austria had declared German Austria to be a constituent part of the German Republic, and this declaration was repeated by the Constituent Assembly in March, 1919.[140] However, at the Peace Conference the Allies prohibited union between Germany and Austria. Article 88 of the Treaty of St Germain declared that Austria's independence was inalienable except with the consent of the Council.[141] That self-determination was denied to the German-speaking people of Austria when it had been declared to be the underlying principle of the Peace Conference was regarded in Germany as one of the worst injustices perpetrated by the Allies against the German people. Stresemann described it as 'a piece of unexampled cynicism'[142] and Hitler, at his trial in 1924, remarked bitterly: 'Self-determination, but self-determination for every negro tribe, and Germany does not count as a negro tribe.'[143] The decision of the Permanent Court in 1931, by eight votes to seven, to prohibit a proposed customs union between Germany and Austria on the basis that it was illegal,[144] was widely perceived to be based on political rather than judicial considerations, and added further to the bitterness felt in Germany.[145]

The creation of various Slav nation-states out of the non-national Habsburg Empire also promoted the growth of pan-Germanism amongst German communities throughout Central and Eastern Europe. While they had been part of the ruling class within the Habsburg Empire, these German communities had not felt so keenly their ethnic and cultural bonds to the German nation-state, but now that they were isolated minorities in states dominated by Slavs, they looked more and more to Germany for support, and became increasingly irredentist in orientation.[146] A Sudeten German senator declared in 1929 that the Germans of Czechoslovakia were

---

[138] Eric Sutton (ed. and trans.) *Gustav Streseman: His Dairies, Letters and Papers* (1935) Vol. 2, 112–13.

[139] Ian F. D. Morrow *The Peace Settlement in the German Polish Borderlands* (1936) 191.

[140] Cobban, 92.

[141] 226 CTS 8, 36.

[142] Sutton (ed.) Vol. 2, 159.

[143] Cobban, 94. See also Derek Heater *National Self-Determination* (1994) 124.

[144] *Customs Regime Between Austria and Germany* (1931) PCIJ Reports, Series A/B, No. 41, 37.

[145] M. Margaret Ball *Post-War German–Austrian Relations* (1937) 154–6; Malcolm Muggeridge *The Thirties* (1967) 113.

[146] Cobban, 93.

'not an ethnological minority in the territory occupied by the Czechs but a part of the totality of the German people, thrust beyond the present State frontiers'.[147]

Within Germany, it was the National Socialist party which most encouraged the *Auslandsdeutsche* to identify their interests with those of the German nation-state. The first article in the programme of the National Socialist Party proclaimed that the Party sought 'the unification of all Germans to form a Great Germany on the basis of the right of self-determination enjoyed by nations'.[148] Hitler declared on the first page of *Mein Kampf* that: 'German-Austria must return to the great German mother country, and not because of any economic considerations. No, and no again: even if such a union were unimportant from an economic point of view; yes, even if it were harmful, it must nevertheless take place. One blood demands one Reich.'[149]

When the National Socialists came to power in 1933 they moved to accomplish these ends. By February 1938 Hitler was openly declaring that 'Germany would no longer suffer ten million German people to be outraged beyond the frontiers'.[150] The *Anschluss* with Austria in March 1938, the incorporation of the Sudetenland in September 1938, and the invasion of Poland in September 1939 followed.

Hungary was also deeply aggrieved by the order established by the Peace Conference. The Treaty of Trianon[151] had deprived Hungary of more than two-thirds of its territory and over thirteen million inhabitants, of whom three million were ethnic Hungarians.[152] Hungary constantly demanded revision of this treaty on the basis of self-determination. The Hungarian minorities in Romania, Yugoslavia, and Czechoslovakia never became reconciled to their new status, and remained intensely irredentist in attitude. Together with the German minorities, they were the most assiduous petitioners of the Council, and were actively encouraged by Hungary to be uncooperative and intransigent. Hungary, like Germany, regarded the disruptive activities of its own ethnic minorities in other states as one of the most effective ways of obtaining a revision of the Versailles order.[153]

In Yugoslavia the attempt to create a united state comprising the three principal Slav peoples of the region, the Serbs, the Croats, and the Slovenes, foundered when the Serbs seized power and proceeded to establish a Ser-

---

[147] Thornberry (1980) 436, fn. 67. See also Ronald M. Smelser *The Sudeten Problem, 1933–1938* (1975).

[148] Cobban, 93.

[149] Adolf Hitler (trans. Ralph Mannheim) *Mein Kampf* (1943) 3.

[150] Eliezer Yapou 'The Autonomy That Never Was' in Yoram Dinstein (ed.) *Models of Autonomy* (1981) 98.

[151] (1921) 6 LNTS 187.

[152] Tudjman, 36.

[153] Thornberry (1980) 435.

bian hegemony over the entire state. The resulting tension between the Serbs, on one hand, and the Croats and Slovenes on the other, was exacerbated by the existence of other large and discontented ethnic minorities. The kin-states of these minorities fostered their grievances as a way of maintaining instability in Yugoslavia. Germany and Hungary encouraged their respective minorities to continual protest. Italy and Bulgaria both lent support to the Macedonian insurrection.

In addition, those ethnic groups which had not become a part of their particular nation-state when it was created, such as the 80,000 Poles of Czechoslovakia, or who had not been able to found a nation-state at all, such as the four million Ukrainians in Poland, experienced profound disappointment, particularly after their hopes had been raised high by the declarations concerning self-determination at the time of the Peace Conference. These groups were now expected to act as loyal citizens of states which regarded them as aliens and misfits.

Given the intensity of nationalism amongst the peoples of Central and Eastern Europe during the inter-war years, and the desire which was engendered for self-determination, it was not surprising that the minorities treaties regime did not survive.

10. CONCLUSION

The conflicting demographic, economic, strategic, and political considerations which arose at the Paris Peace Conference made it impossible for the Allies to accommodate the demands of all ethnic groups for self-determination. As a result it had been necessary to establish an international regime to protect those minorities which had not been able to achieve self-determination for themselves. The Allies hoped that the establishment of a regime which provided international guarantees of minority rights would adequately protect and satisfy ethnic groups which found themselves within the nation-state of another people. Such a regime, it was thought, would also eliminate any further recourse to the fissiparous principle of ethnic self-determination.

In the *Aaland Islands* case ethnic self-determination was not a part of international law, except in cases of oppression.[154] The Aaland Islanders, unlike the Finns, were not a people, but rather a minority; hence they were not entitled to self-determination. However, the distinction drawn in the *Aaland Islands* case between peoples and minorities did not take into account the fact that a minority within one state was frequently a part of the

---

[154] *Report of the International Commission of Jurists* (1920) LNOJ Spec. Supp. 3; *The Aaland Island Question: Report Submitted to the Council of the League of Nations by the Commission of Rapporteurs* (1921) League Doc. B7.21/68/106, 27.

dominant ethnic group of another state. Ethnic, or national, minorities defined themselves in exactly the same manner as 'nations', namely by reference to attributes of language, culture, and religion. It was precisely this perception of themselves as a component part of a larger nation which prompted minorities to seek ethnic self-determination.

It was natural that such minorities would seek to join the nation with which they were ethnically related, or to form a nation-state of their own, because there was no place for them in another nation-state. The role of the nation-state was to promote the national identity and well-being of the nation it embodied. As a result the nation-state demanded ethnic homogeneity of its population. Those who did not belong to the dominant nation could not reflect the 'national personality' of the nation-state, nor could they share the ideals and aspirations of the majority.[155] In such a state the minority was a discordant and unwelcome anomaly, out of step simply by virtue of being ethnically different. An ethnic minority was seen to be an alien element, and therefore suspect. The logical solution to the existence of a minority within a nation-state, from the majority's point of view, was assimilation, expulsion, or extermination. The minorities treaties regime ensured that such minorities would not be assimilated, expelled, or exterminated, but would continue to exist as a separate element within the nation-state. That regime therefore acted as a goad which further aggravated the pre-existing tensions between majorities and minorities. Rampant nationalism on all sides was the ultimate cause of the failure of the minorities treaties regime.[156]

[155] Macartney, 17.   [156] Robert Redslob 'Le Principe des Nationalités' (1931) 67.

4

Self-Determination in Modern International Law: International Instruments and Judicial Decisions

1. INTRODUCTION

Until the Second World War the principle of self-determination remained essentially a political concept. Although self-determination provided the underlying rationale for Article 22 of the Covenant of the League of Nations, the principle itself did not appear anywhere in the Covenant as a general proposition of international law. In the *Aaland Islands* case[1] self-determination was held not to be a part of international law, except in cases of oppression.

In the post-war period the status of self-determination changed dramatically. The principle of self-determination was included in a number of important international instruments, including the Charter of the United Nations and the two International Human Rights Covenants.[2] It has also been the subject of many General Assembly resolutions and figured in numerous cases before the International Court of Justice. Self-determination has therefore developed since 1945 from an essentially political concept into a legal right. In this Chapter the development of self-determination into a legal right, and the problems associated with that development, are examined with reference to the major post-war international instruments, General Assembly resolutions, and decisions of the International Court of Justice.

2. THE UNITED NATIONS CHARTER

The first attempt by the Allies to formulate a charter for a post-war international organization took place at the Dumbarton Oaks Conference in 1944. The Conference produced a number of proposals which the Allies tentatively agreed should be included in the Charter. The United Nations Con-

[1] *Report of the International Commission of Jurists* (1920) LNOJ Spec. Supp. 3, 5. *The Aaland Islands Question: Report Submitted to the Council of the League of Nations by the Commission of Rapporteurs* (1921) League Doc. B7.21/68/106, 27. See Ch. 3, pp. 32–7.
[2] International Covenant on Economic, Social and Cultural Rights (1976) 993 UNTS 3; International Covenant on Civil and Political Rights (1976) 999 UNTS 171.

ference on International Organization was held at San Francisco in 1945; from this conference the Charter of the United Nations emerged in its final form. At both Dumbarton Oaks and San Francisco great emphasis was placed on human rights: it was thought that a new international order based on a universal respect for human rights could be created. This was reflected in the provisions of the Charter, which contain numerous references to human rights.[3] In particular, the Charter declared that one of the purposes of thc Unitcd Nations was to promote and encourage 'respect for human rights, and for fundamental freedoms for all, without distinction as to race, sex, language, or religion'.[4]

The principle of self-determination was initially ignored in the discussions regarding the Charter. There was no reference in the Dumbarton Oaks proposals to self-determination. However, at San Francisco the Soviet Union proposed that references to the 'self-determination of peoples' be included.[5] Despite initial misgivings, the Soviet proposal was eventually accepted by the United States, the United Kingdom, and France. The proposal was adopted as an amendment by the Four Sponsoring Governments on 4 May 1945.[6] As a result the words 'based on respect for the principle of equal rights and self-determination of peoples' were added to Articles 1(2) and 55.

Article 1 of the Charter sets out the purposes of the United Nations. Article 1(2) provides that one of those purposes is—'To develop friendly relations among the nations, based on the respect for the principle of equal rights and self-determination of peoples, and to take other appropriate measures to strengthen universal peace'.

Article 55 is contained in Chapter IX of the Charter, which deals with economic and social co-operation. Article 55 provides as follows:

With a view to the creation of conditions of stability and well-being necessary for peaceful and friendly relations among the nations, based on respect for the principle of equal rights and the self-determination of peoples, the United Nations shall promote higher standards of living, full employment, and conditions of economic and social progress and development, solutions of international, economic, social, health, and related problems, and international, cultural, educational co-operation, and universal respect for the observance of human rights and fundamental freedoms for all, without distinction of race, sex, language, or religion.

The *travaux préparatoires* do not explain why the sponsoring governments thought it necessary to amend Articles 1(2) and 55 to include the reference

---

[3] See Preamble and Arts. 1(3), 13, 55, 62, 68, and 76.

[4] Art. 1(3).

[5] M. K. Nawaz 'The Meaning and Range of the Principle of Self-Determination' (1965) 89.

[6] Satpul Kaur 'Self-Determination in International Law' (1970) 483; A. Rigo Sureda *The Evolution of the Right of Self-Determination* (1973) 97.

to self-determination, nor what the phrase was intended to mean. The Committee which initially discussed self-determination noted that amongst the sponsoring governments there were two views on self-determination. The expansive view was that the 'principle corresponded closely to the will and desires of peoples everywhere and should be clearly enunciated in the Charter'; the narrow view was that 'the principle conformed to the purposes of the Charter only insofar as it implied the right of self-government of peoples and not the right of secession'.[7] The Full Committee, which adopted the amended articles unchanged, also provided little clarification of the meaning or import of self-determination: it indicated that the principle of equal rights and the self-determination of peoples were 'two complementary parts of one standard of conduct' and that 'an essential element' of the principle was 'a free and genuine expression of the will of the people'.[8] The only forthright statement concerning the amendment came from the Soviet Foreign Minister, Molotov. Molotov declared that the Soviet Union 'attached first-rate importance' to the amendment. 'We must first of all see to it,' he stated, 'that dependent countries are enabled as soon as possible to take the path of national independence.' He went on to stress that the United Nations should act to promote this goal by facilitating 'the realization of the principles of equality and self-determination of nations'.[9]

The issue of 'dependent countries', i.e. non-self-governing and trust territories, was specifically dealt with in Chapters XI, XII, and XIII of the Charter. The Trusteeship System, governed by Chapters XII and XIII, replaced the Mandate System set up by the League of Nations. The Trusteeship System was designed to cover a much wider range of territories than the Mandate System, which had applied only to specific territories detached from the Ottoman Empire and to Germany's colonies. Under Article 77 the Trusteeship System was to apply to territories held under mandate, territories which had been detached from enemy states as a result of the Second World War, and territories voluntarily placed under the system by states responsible for their administration. As it turned out, only one territory detached from an enemy state, Italian Somaliland, became a trust territory, and no territories were voluntarily placed under the Trusteeship System. Thus the Trusteeship System was restricted, with one exception, to the former mandated territories. Between 1946 and 1950 eleven trusteeships were established.[10]

The objectives of the Trusteeship System were set out in Article 76; paragraph (b) specifies that the Trusteeship System shall:

---

[7] (1945) 6 UNCIO 296.   [8] *Id.*, 455.

[9] Ruth B. Russell *A History of the United Nations Charter* (1958) 811.

[10] Leland M. Goodrich, Edvard Hambro, and Anne Patricia Simons *Charter of the United Nations* (3rd edn.) (1969) 480. All trust territories have now attained self-government of one form or another.

Promote the political, economic, social and educational advancement of inhabitants of the trust territories and their progressive development toward self-government, or independence, as may be appropriate to the particular circumstances of each territory and its peoples, and the freely expressed wishes of the peoples concerned, and as may be provided by the terms of each trusteeship agreement.

Article 81 provided that the obligations and responsibilities of states administering territories under the Trusteeship System were to be set out in individual trusteeship agreements. These agreements tended to follow the same general pattern, and contained only minor variations to take into account the special circumstances of particular territories.[11]

Non-self-governing territories other than trust territories were dealt with in Chapter XI of the Charter. Articles 73 and 74, which comprise Chapter XI, constituted a compromise between those states which sought to apply the Trusteeship System to all colonial territories and those which opposed that proposal.[12] Article 73 set out the responsibilities of states administering non-self-governing territories. The most important part of Article 73 was paragraph (b), which obliged member states administering non-self-governing territories to develop self-government in those territories. The provisions of Chapter XI did not empower the United Nations to supervise the attainment of self-government in non-self-governing territories, but Article 73(e) did oblige administering states to transmit regularly to the Secretary-General certain information relating to the economic, social, and educational conditions in the territories.[13]

Chapters XI, XII, and XIII contained no explicit reference to the principle of self-determination. The Soviet Union sought to include such a reference by proposing an amendment to Article 76(b).[14] But the United Kingdom and France opposed the amendment, and it was eventually rejected on the grounds that reference to self-determination would create more problems than it would resolve, particularly in Palestine where it was feared that too much emphasis on self-determination might lead to civil war.[15] The Soviet Union, however, argued that as one of the purposes of the United Nations included the 'self-determination of peoples', the principle could hardly be omitted from the provisions of the Trusteeship System.[16] Consequently, Article 76 was amended to provide that the basic objectives of the Trusteeship System were 'in accordance with the Purposes of the United Nations', introducing an oblique reference to self-determination.[17]

---

[11] *Id.*, 502. [12] James Crawford *The Creation of States in International Law* (1979) 92.

[13] Michla Pomerance *Self-Determination in Law and Practice* (1982) 10.

[14] See (1945) 3 UNCIO 618 for the wording of the proposed amendment.

[15] Russell, 831; Umozurike O. Umozurike *Self-Determination in International Law* (1972) 97.

[16] (1945) 10 UNCIO 441. [17] Umozurike, 97.

Although no explicit reference to self-determination had been included in the provisions relating to the Trusteeship System, the Soviet Union, with the support of China, sought to insure that independence was the ultimate goal both of trust territories and of non-self-governing territories.[18] The Soviet proposal to include independence as one of the objectives of Articles 73 and 76 was also opposed by the United Kingdom and France. Although the United States tended to favour the inclusion of 'independence' as reflecting the American tradition of anti-colonialism, it did not want to give offence to its allies or to be accused of interfering in the internal affairs of other states.[19] In the end another compromise was negotiated, whereby it was agreed that there would be no reference to independence in Article 73, regarding non-self-governing territories, but that it would be included amongst the objectives of Article 76, with respect to trust territories.[20]

The Charter of the United Nations thus contains an unusual mix of explicit and implicit references to self-determination. Articles 1(2) and 55, which contain the explicit references to self-determination, do not primarily address the issue of self-determination at all, but refer to self-determination only in subordinate clauses added to the two articles as amendments. On the other hand, there is no explicit reference to self-determination in Chapters XII and XIII, with regard to the establishment and regulation of the Trusteeship System. Yet the principle of self-determination was undoubtedly embodied in Chapters XII and XIII, because self-determination had been the motivating principle behind the creation of the Mandate System, which the Trusteeship System replaced. Whether Chapter XI, dealing with non-self-governing territories other than trust territories, also embodied the principle of self-determination, was much less certain. Self-determination was not referred to in the provisions of Chapter XI, nor was there any reference in the provisions of the Chapter to such territories eventually attaining independence. Chapter XI was to prove one of the major areas of contention with regard to the proper interpretation and application of self-determination.

3. THE INTERNATIONAL HUMAN RIGHTS COVENANTS

The desire to create a new post-war international order based on universal human rights also found expression in the promulgation of an 'international bill of rights', first suggested during the Second World War. In 1946 the Economic and Social Council of the United Nations established the Com-

---

[18] G. I. Tunkin *Theory of International Law* (1974) 63.
[19] Russell, 817.
[20] Goodrich *et al.*, 451.

mission on Human Rights to investigate, amongst other things, the formulation of such a bill.[21] There was considerable debate as to whether a declaration or a covenant was the more appropriate way of proceeding: with either method there were advantages and disadvantages. A declaration of the General Assembly, although an expression of collective opinion, would be no more than an instrument of moral or political suasion, without binding effect in international law. A covenant would bind its signatories in international law and place on them a duty to adapt their laws and practices to conform to international obligations, but would not possess the same universality as a declaration. In the end it was decided to adopt both a declaration and a covenant.[22]

The Universal Declaration of Human Rights, which the General Assembly proclaimed 'as a common standard of achievement for all peoples and all nations', was adopted by the United Nations in General Assembly Resolution 217A(III) on 10 December 1948. A Soviet proposal to include self-determination was rejected, and as a result there is no reference to self-determination in the Universal Declaration on Human Rights.[23]

Meanwhile, work was proceeding on the drafting of an international covenant. In 1952 it was decided that two covenants would be required, one dealing with civil and political rights, and the other with economic, social, and cultural rights.[24] The two covenants would be prepared and opened for signature simultaneously. The Soviet Union again proposed that an article on self-determination be included in the covenants.[25] Those states with colonial possessions, such as the United Kingdom, France, and Belgium, opposed the introduction of such an article. They argued that self-determination was not a legal right but rather a vague political principle, usually attained through extra-legal processes, and often involving secession. Despite this opposition the Soviet proposal received the support of African, Asian, and Latin American states. On 4 December 1950 the General Assembly adopted Resolution 421D(V), the sixth paragraph of which called upon the Economic and Social Council to request the Commission on Human Rights 'to study ways and means which would ensure the right of peoples and nations to self-determination, and to prepare recommendations for consideration by the General Assembly at its sixth session'.

---

[21] Umozurike, 47.

[22] Vratislav Pechota 'The Development of the Covenant on Civil and Political Rights' (1981) 35.

[23] Tunkin, 64. The vote on Resolution 217A(III) was 48–0–8. The Soviet Union, Byelorussian SSR, the Ukrainian SSR, Poland, Czechoslovakia, Yugoslavia, South Africa, and Saudi Arabia abstained.

[24] General Assembly Resolution 543(VI) of 5 Feb. 1952.

[25] This proposal was first made in 1949: Antonio Cassese 'The Self-Determination of Peoples' in Louis Henkin (ed.) *The International Bill of Rights* (1981) 92.

Resolution 421D(V) was followed in 1952 by Resolution 545(VI). The General Assembly noted in Resolution 545(VI) that it had 'recognized the right of peoples and nations to self-determination as a fundamental human right' in Resolution 421D(V), and went on to declare that the international covenants on human rights should therefore include an article on self-determination. Resolution 545(VI) even set out in part the wording of the proposed article to be included. In response to Resolutions 421D(V) and 545(VI) the Commission on Human Rights spent much of its 1952 session discussing the issue of self-determination, and the terms in which an article on self-determination should be drafted.[26]

Most Western states were opposed to any reference to self-determination in the covenants. When it became apparent that an article on self-determination would be included, Western states which had originally opposed its inclusion then sought to widen the terms of the article so that it would apply not only to peoples in colonial situations, but also to peoples in sovereign and independent states. Unlike other major Western powers, the United States had not initially opposed the inclusion of an article referring to self-determination, but the American attitude changed when Chile proposed that a paragraph be added declaring the right of all peoples to dispose of their natural wealth and resources. The United States opposed this proposal on the basis that it would threaten foreign investment. The inclusion of this paragraph caused the United States to oppose the article.[27] When debate on the issue ended in 1955, and a vote was taken on whether to include the draft article in the covenants, Third World and communist states voted overwhelmingly in favour, whereas most Western states voted against. The vote was thirty-three in favour to twelve against, with thirteen abstentions.[28]

In its final form, the provision on self-determination appeared in language identical to that of Article 1 of the International Covenant on Civil and Political Rights[29] and Article 1 of the International Covenant on Economic, Social and Cultural Rights.[30] Article 1 provided:

1. All peoples have the right of self-determination. By virtue of that right they freely determine their political status and freely pursue their economic, social and cultural development.

2. All peoples may, for their own ends, freely dispose of their natural wealth and resources without prejudice to any obligations arising out of international economic co-operation, based upon the principle of mutual benefit, and international law. In no case may a people be deprived of its own means of subsistence.

[26] Lee C. Buchheit *Secession* (1978) 77.
[27] Cassese, 92, 93.
[28] Vernon van Dyke 'Self-Determination and Minority Rights' (1969) 223–5. The United States, the United Kingdom, and France voted against inclusion of the article.
[29] (1976) 999 UNTS 171, 173.
[30] (1976) 993 UNTS 3, 5.

3. The States Parties to the present Covenant, including those having responsibility for the administration of Non-Self-Governing and Trust Territories, shall promote the realization of the right of self-determination, and shall respect that right, in conformity with the provisions of the Charter of the United Nations.

The International Human Rights Covenants were declared open for signature and ratification on 19 December 1966. The International Covenant on Economic, Social and Cultural Rights entered into force on 3 January 1976, in accordance with Article 27, which required the ratification or accession of thirty-five states. The International Covenant on Civil and Political Rights entered into force on 23 March 1976, in accordance with Article 49, which also required the ratification or accession of thirty-five states. The United States, the United Kingdom, France, and indeed virtually all of those states which had opposed inclusion of an article on self-determination, have now ratified or acceded to both covenants.[31]

4. GENERAL ASSEMBLY RESOLUTIONS

General Assembly resolutions dealing with self-determination have for the most part linked the concept of self-determination to that of decolonization. This connection reflected the orientation of the majority of member states in the General Assembly in the post-war period. These states, comprised largely from the Third World and the Communist bloc, sought to dismantle as quickly as possible the colonial empires of the Western powers. They referred to this process as self-determination. The association of self-determination with decolonization was evident, for example, in Resolution 637 (VII) of 16 December 1952, which called upon members of the United Nations to 'recognise and promote the realisation of the right of self-determination of the peoples of non-self-governing and trust territories who are under their administration'.

As part of their goal to decolonize non-self-governing and trust territories as quickly as possible, Third World and Communist states sought to assert greater control over the administration of such territories. This was done by resort to Article 73(e) of the Charter, which required members of the United Nations which administered non-self-governing territories to transmit information to the Secretary-General 'relating to economic, social and educational conditions in the territories for which they are respectively responsible'. The Charter had not defined when a territory would be consid-

---

[31] Australia, Belgium, Canada, Luxembourg, the Netherlands, New Zealand, Norway, Sweden, and Turkey also voted against inclusion: UN Doc. A/C.3/SR.676 para. 27 (1955). Only Turkey has not yet ratified or acceded to either Convention: *Multilateral Treaties Deposited With the Secretary-General: Status as at 31 December 1994* New York: United Nations (1995) 108, 118.

ered non-self-governing, nor when it would cease to be non-self-governing. Although this determination had originally been left to the member states themselves, the General Assembly quickly moved to assert control over the criteria used to determine whether a particular territory was non-self-governing. Thus, in Resolution 334(IV) of 2 December 1949 the General Assembly declared that: 'it is within the responsibility of the General Assembly to express its opinion on the principles which have guided or which may in future guide the Members concerned in enumerating the territories for which the obligation exists to transmit information under Article 73e of the Charter.' Resolutions 567(VI) of 18 January 1952, 648(VII) of 10 December 1952, and 742(VIII) of 27 November 1953 set out the factors which were to be taken into account in deciding whether or not a territory was one whose people had attained full self-government. Resolution 648 further noted that the factors enumerated were to serve as a guide with regard to obligations under Article 73(e), and should not be used to hinder in any way the attainment of self-government by non-self-governing territories. This provision was reaffirmed in Resolution 742(VIII), which went on to emphasize that independence was the primary means by which a non-self-governing territory attained full self-government.

Subsequent resolutions of the General Assembly increasingly insisted on the need to promote self-determination in non-self-governing territories.[32] On 14 December 1960 the General Assembly adopted Resolution 1514(XV), entitled 'The Declaration on the Granting of Independence to Colonial Countries and Peoples'. Resolution 1514(XV) was the most important General Assembly resolution to associate the concepts of self-determination and decolonization, and it has become the definitive statement of the General Assembly with regard to colonial situations. Paragraph 2 of the Resolution declared that all peoples have the right to self-determination, and reiterated word for word the principle of self-determination as set out in Article 1, paragraph 1 of the International Human Rights Covenants.[33] In its Preamble the Resolution proclaimed 'the necessity of bringing to a speedy and unconditional end colonialism in all its forms and manifestations', and declared in paragraph 1 that the subjection of peoples to alien subjugation, domination, and exploitation was a denial of fundamental human rights, contrary to the Charter of the United Nations, and an impediment to the promotion of world peace and co-operation. Such situations could only be righted, as indicated in paragraph 5, by the immediate transfer of 'all powers to the peoples of those territories, without any conditions or reservations, in accordance with their

---

[32] See, for example, Resolution 1188(XII) of 11 Dec. 1957.
[33] See p. 68 *supra*.

freely expressed will and desire, without any distinction as to race, creed or colour, in order to enable them to enjoy complete independence and free-dom'. This grant of independence to non-self-governing territories was not to be delayed, according to paragraph 3, by any inadequacy of political, economic, social, or educational preparedness.[34] Paragraph 4 proscribed the use of 'armed action' or 'repressive measures of all kinds' to prevent de-pendent peoples from exercising 'peacefully and freely their right to com-plete independence'. The transition from colonial status to independence was not to affect the territorial composition of the new states, a point which was emphatically made in paragraph 6: 'Any attempt aimed at the partial or total disruption of the national unity and the territorial integrity of a coun-try is incompatible with the purposes and principles of the Charter of the United Nations.' Finally, paragraph 7 stated that all states were to observe the provisions of the Charter of the United Nations, the Universal Declara-tion of Human Rights, and the present Declaration 'on the basis of equality, non-interference in the internal affairs of all States, and respect for the sovereign rights of all peoples and their territorial integrity'. This final paragraph, as Crawford points out, sought to place Resolution 1514(XV) 'on a par with the Universal Declaration of Human Rights and the Charter itself'.[35]

The day after the adoption of Resolution 1514(XV), the General Assem-bly adopted another very important resolution on self-determination: Resolution 1541(XV) of 15 December 1960. The purpose of this Resolution was to enumerate a definitive list of factors, known as 'principles', to guide members in determining whether an obligation existed to transmit informa-tion under Article 73(e) of the Charter. Like Resolution 1514(XV), the language of Resolution 1541(XV) was resolutely anti-colonial in nature. Principle I specified that Chapter XI of the Charter was to apply to territo-ries 'known to be of the colonial type', and Principle II observed that such territories were in a 'dynamic state of evolution and progress towards a "full

[34] Resolution 35/118 of 11 Dec. 1980 subsequently enlarged the list of factors which could not be raised in order to delay the granting of independence to a non-self-governing territory. Resolution 35/118 was entitled 'Plan of Action for the Full Implementation of the Declaration on the Granting of Independence to Colonial Countries and Peoples'. Para. 17 of the Annex to Resolution 35/118 declared: 'Questions of territorial size, geographical isolation and limited resources should in no way delay the implementation of the Declaration.'

[35] Crawford, 357. The attempt to equate Resolution 1514(XV) with the Charter occurred notwithstanding some rather significant inconsistencies between the provisions of the two instruments. Resolution 1514(XV) called for a 'speedy and unconditional' dismantling of colonialism 'in all its form and manifestations', whereas the Charter, in Arts. 73 and 76, called for a gradual and progressive development towards increased self-government, 'taking into account the particular circumstances of each territory' (Art. 73(b)). Moreover, Resolution 1514(XV) asserted that self-determination must work so as to maintain territorial integrity, whereas the provisions of the Charter do not protect the territorial integrity of colonies: Pomerance, 11.

measure of self-government"'. Principle III declared that the obligation to transmit information was an international one, which must continue, according to Principle II, until a 'full measure of self-government is attained'.[36] The crucial element of the definition, the basic definition of a non-self-governing territory, was set out in Principle IV: '*Prima facie* there is an obligation to transmit information in respect of a territory which is geographically separate and is ethnically and/or culturally distinct from the country administering it.' A number of additional factors were then enumerated which were also to be taken into account when determining whether a territory was non-self-governing. These were set out in Principle V, and were broadly enumerated as elements 'of an administrative, political, juridical, economic or historical nature'. If, taking such elements into account, it was found that they affected the relationship between the metropolitan state and the territory so as to place arbitrarily the territory 'in a position or status of subordination', then such elements could be used to support the presumption that the territory was non-self-governing, and therefore that there was an obligation to transmit information under Article 73(e). Principle VI set out the ways in which a non-self-governing territory could achieve a full measure of self-government. Principle VI listed three alternatives: independence, free association with an independent state, or integration with an independent state. Previous resolutions had emphasized that independence was the normal and expected way in which a full measure of self-government would be achieved. As independence was considered to be the usual outcome in the process of self-determination, Resolution 1541(XV) did not place any conditions on the attainment of independence by non-self-governing territories. It was otherwise, however, with respect to free association and integration. Principle VII, addressing the alternative of free association, stipulated that free association 'should be the result of a free and voluntary choice by the peoples of the territory concerned expressed through informed and democratic processes'. Principle VII went on to specify that the individuality and cultural characteristics of the territory and its peoples must be respected, as well as the ability to modify their status and the right to determine its internal constitution without outside interference. Principles VIII and IX dealt with the alternative of integration. As integration was considered an irreversible procedure, very stringent conditions were placed on it. Principle VIII stipulated that

---

[36] The role of the General Assembly in this regard was subsequently extended by Resolution 2870(XXVI) of 20 Dec. 1971. The General Assembly declared, in para. 4, that 'in the absence of a decision by the General Assembly itself that a Non-Self-Governing Territory has attained a full measure of self-government', an administering state must continue to transmit information under Art. 73(e). In the previous year, the General Assembly, in Resolution 2701(XXV) of 14 Dec. 1970, had instructed the United Kingdom to continue transmitting information with respect to certain territories under its administration in the absence of a decision of the General Assembly to the contrary.

integration be 'on the basis of complete equality'. According to Principle IX, it could occur only after the integrating territory had attained 'an advanced stage of self-government with free political institutions', based on 'the freely expressed wishes of the territory's peoples acting with full knowledge of the change in their status, their wishes having been expressed through informed and democratic processes, impartially conducted and based on universal adult suffrage'. Integration was thus discouraged in all but the most politically advanced of territories, i.e. those which would be the least likely to adopt this alternative. The final three principles of Resolution 1541(XV), Principles X, XI, and XII, dealt with security and constitutional limitations to the transmission of information under Article 73(e). They set out the nature and extent of such limitations and specified that such limitations could not relieve an administering member of its obligations under Chapter XI.

Both Resolution 1514(XV) and Resolution 1541 (XV) placed great emphasis on the attainment of independence. Resolution 1514(XV) had declared independence to be the only method of achieving self-determination for non-self-governing territories. Resolution 1541(XV), although it provided for two other alternatives, nevertheless emphasized that independence was to be regarded as the normal outcome for non-self-governing territories. This emphasis on independence was repeated again and again in subsequent resolutions on self-determination, the wording of which invariably linked the terms 'self-determination' and 'independence'.

Paragraph 4 of Resolution 1514(XV) declared that armed action or repressive measures of any kind were not to be used against colonial peoples to prevent them from exercising 'peacefully and freely their right to complete independence'. This principle was expanded considerably by the General Assembly in subsequent resolutions, and eventually evolved into the quite different notion of condoning armed action by colonial peoples seeking to achieve independence. Resolution 2621(XXV) of 20 December 1970 declared, in paragraph 1, that the continuation of colonialism was a 'crime', and reaffirmed, in paragraph 2 'the inherent right of colonial peoples to struggle by all necessary means at their disposal against colonial Powers which suppress their aspiration for freedom and independence'. The wording of Resolution 33/24 of 29 November 1978 went even further, stressing in paragraph 2 the primacy of armed struggle. It declared that the General Assembly reaffirmed 'the legitimacy of the struggle of peoples for independence, territorial integrity, national unity and liberation from colonial and foreign domination and foreign occupation by all available means, particularly armed struggle'.

A corollary of this legitimization of armed struggle by colonial peoples was the notion that states were not merely permitted, but encouraged to assist these colonial peoples in their struggle for self-determination. Such exhortations to third-party states were frequently repeated in General Assembly resolutions. General Assembly Resolution 2105(XX) of 20 December 1965, for example, recognized in paragraph 10 'the legitimacy of the struggle by the peoples under colonial rule to exercise their right to self-determination and independence', and went on to invite 'all States to provide material and moral assistance to the national liberation movements in colonial Territories'. Another example is Resolution 3314(XXIX) of 14 December 1974, which provided a definition of aggression. Paragraph 7 provided that the struggle for self-determination of peoples 'under colonial and racist regimes or other forms of alien domination' would not constitute aggression. Paragraph 7 also recognized the right of such peoples 'to seek and receive support' in their struggle for self-determination.

States were not only encouraged to support peoples in their struggles for self-determination, but were also discouraged from acting in any way which would inhibit the attainment of self-determination. In this regard Resolution 2131(XX) of 21 December 1965 declared in paragraph 6 that the right of self-determination should be freely exercised 'without any foreign pressure'. Similarly, Resolution 2160(XXI) of 30 November 1966 declared in paragraph 1(b) that: 'Any forcible action, direct or indirect, which deprives people under foreign domination of their right to self-determination and freedom and independence and of their right to determine their economic, social and cultural development constitutes a violation of the Charter of the United Nations.'

Such resolutions were adopted by the General Assembly as a result of efforts by the Third World, with the support of the Soviet Union and the Communist bloc states. Western states opposed virtually all the resolutions on self-determination. The resolutions of the General Assembly on self-determination therefore represented for the most part the views of the Third World and the Soviet bloc, but not those of the West.

One notable exception was Resolution 2625(XXV) of 24 October 1970. This resolution was entitled 'The Declaration on Principles of International Law concerning Friendly Relations and Co-operation among States in accordance with the Charter of the United Nations'. In 1962 the General Assembly had agreed to undertake a study of the fundamental principles of the Charter and the duties deriving therefrom.[37] The principle of equal rights and self-determination of peoples was one of the fundamental principles to be examined. In 1963 the General Assembly established a Special Committee to study these principles.[38] After seven years' work the Special Committee completed the Declaration on Friendly Relations, which was then adopted by the General Assembly by a consensus vote. Resolution

---

[37] See General Assembly Resolution 1815(XVII) of 18 Dec. 1962.
[38] See General Assembly Resolution 1966(XVIII) of 16 Dec. 1963.

2625(XXV) thus incorporated within its provisions not only the views of the Third World and the Soviet bloc, but also those of the West.

Resolution 2625(XXV) dealt with self-determination in eight paragraphs. Unlike most other General Assembly resolutions relating to self-determination, it made no reference to Resolution 1514(XV). Had Third World states insisted on this, agreement from Western states would not have been forthcoming, and consensus would not have been possible.[39] Although Resolution 2625(XXV) did not refer to Resolution 1514(XV), however, it did make clear in its provisions that decolonization was a very important aspect of self-determination. Paragraph 2 declared that every state had a duty to promote self-determination in order, *inter alia*, to bring 'a speedy end to colonialism, having due regard to the freely expressed will of the people concerned'. It went on to note that the 'subjection of peoples to alien subjugation, domination and exploitation' was a violation of the principle of self-determination, as well as a denial of fundamental human rights, and was contrary to the Charter. Paragraph 6 ensured that the peoples of colonies and other non-self-governing territories would be entitled to exercise their right of self-determination by specifying that the status of a colony or other non-self-governing territory would remain separate and distinct from that of the administering state until the people of that territory had exercised their right to self-determination.

However, Resolution 2625(XXV) did not limit self-determination to decolonization. Self-determination had a wider meaning, as indicated by paragraphs 1 and 2. Paragraph 1 provided:

By virtue of the principle of equal rights and self-determination of peoples enshrined in the Charter of the United Nations, all peoples have the right freely to determine, without external interference, their political status and to pursue their economic, social and cultural development, and every State has the duty to respect this right in accordance with the provisions of the Charter.

Paragraph 2 reiterated the duty of every state to promote the 'realization of the principle of equal rights and self-determination of peoples', and linked this duty to the general goal of promoting friendly relations and co-operation among states, as well as to the specific goal of ending colonialism. The use of the phrase 'all peoples' in paragraph 1, coupled with the reference in paragraphs 1 and 2 to 'all States', and the enumeration of a goal which did not necessarily refer to colonial situations, were evidence of the Western desire to extend the principle of self-determination beyond the colonial context, and to make it universal in application. Paragraph 7, moreover, linked self-determination to representative government and

[39] Robert Rosenstock 'The Declaration of Principles of International Law Concerning Friendly Relations: A Survey' (1971) 730, 731.

made territorial integrity subject to the maintenance of representative government. Paragraph 7 provided:

Nothing in the foregoing paragraphs shall be construed as authorizing or encouraging any action which would dismember or impair, totally or in part, the territorial integrity or political unity of sovereign and independent States conducting themselves in compliance with the principle of equal rights and self-determination of peoples as described above and thus possessed of a government representing the whole people belonging to the territory without distinction as to race, creed or colour.

The fact that territorial integrity was predicated upon representative government implied that self-determination would be an ongoing process. If a government was not representative of 'the whole people belonging to the territory', that portion of the people not represented in the government would not be obliged to respect the territorial integrity of the state. In such circumstances secession would be permissible. The injunction in paragraph 8 not to undertake 'any action aimed at the total or partial disruption of the national unity and territorial integrity of any other State or country' applied only to states, and not to peoples excluded from government. This was very different from the position set out in Resolution 1514(XV), which specified that self-determination could not be achieved in a manner which affected territorial integrity.

Resolutions 1514(XV) and 1541(XV) placed particular emphasis on the attainment of independence as the normal outcome of self-determination. Paragraph 4 of Resolution 2625(XXV), however, presented independence as only one of several equally legitimate alternatives, declaring that the right of self-determination could be implemented by the establishment of an independent state, association, or integration with an independent state, or 'the emergence into any other political status freely determined by a people'. The option of 'any other political status freely determined by a people' was an innovation; it permitted the recognition of political arrangements other than those enumerated in Resolution 1541(XV) to be considered as legitimate expressions of self-determination.[40]

Resolution 1514(XV) had specified in paragraph 4 that armed action or other repressive measures were not to be employed against colonial peoples peacefully exercising their right to independence. Paragraph 5 of Resolution 2625(XXV) similarly called upon states to refrain from any forcible action which would deprive peoples of their right to self-determination. Paragraph 5, however, sanctioned neither armed struggle nor the supply of material by third-party states in support of such

[40] M. G. Kaladharan Nayar 'Self-Determination Beyond the Colonial Context' (1975) 335, 336.

struggle.[41] It did state that peoples seeking self-determination were 'entitled to seek and to receive support', but it was arguable that this meant only moral, and not material, support.[42] The orientation of Resolution 2625(XXV) to self-determination was thus different in many respects from that of its predecessors.

5. DECISIONS OF THE INTERNATIONAL COURT OF JUSTICE

The principle of self-determination has figured in a number of decisions of the International Court of Justice. The first was the *Case Concerning the Right of Passage Over Indian Territory (Portugal v. India)*.[43] This involved the status of two Portuguese enclaves within Indian territory. In July and August of 1954 an insurrection occurred in the enclaves, whereupon India prohibited any further access to the enclaves by Portuguese authorities. Portugal sought a declaration from the Court that it possessed a right of passage to the two enclaves. Both Portugal and India raised the issue of self-determination in their pleadings before the Court. Portugal referred to a declaration made on 6 September 1955 by Indian Prime Minister Nehru that India would not 'tolerate the presence of the Portuguese in Goa even if the Goans want them to be there'.[44] Portugal submitted that this statement constituted 'the very negation of the right of self-determination of peoples'.[45] India, on the other hand, argued that its conduct was justified on the basis that it was merely assisting the populations of the Portuguese enclaves to exercise their right of self-determination.[46] In response, Portugal requested that the Court hold India's argument to be 'without foundation'.[47]

In its judgment the Court did not address any of the submissions relating to self-determination. Judge Spiropoulos was the only member of the Court to make any reference to self-determination, although he did not explicitly use the term. Judge Spiropoulos noted:

It is a fact that after the departure of the Portuguese authorities, the population of the enclaves set up a new autonomous authority based upon the will of the popula-

---

[41] Para. 7, Resolution 3314(XXIX) of 14 Dec. 1974 legitimized the struggle of peoples for self-determination, but predicated this struggle upon conformity to the provisions relating to self-determination set out in Resolution 2625(XXV).

[42] For an analysis of the legal effects of General Assembly resolutions see Blaine Sloan 'General Assembly Revisited (Forty Years Later)' (1987) 39.

[43] Merits, ICJ Reports 1960, p. 6.

[44] ICJ Pleadings Vol. IV, 589. Nehru's statement should be compared to that of Treitschke: see Chapter 1, p. 11.

[45] ICJ Reports 1960, pp. 6, 16.

[46] *Id.*, pp. 6, 25. ICJ Pleadings, Vol. IV, 857–60.   [47] ICJ Reports 1960, pp. 6, 31.

tion. Since the right of passage assumes the continuance of the administration of the enclaves by the Portuguese, the establishment of a new power in the enclaves must be regarded as having *ipso facto* put an end to the right of passage.[48]

The decision of the Court as a whole focused only on the questions of sovereignty and right of passage in the year 1954, and the Court did not concern itself with the outcome of events thereafter. Consequently it was able to find that in view of the tension prevailing in the Indian territory between the Portuguese colonies and the coast, India's refusal of passage could not be held to be action contrary to its obligation resulting from Portugal's right of passage.[49]

The question of self-determination was also implicit in the *Case Concerning the Northern Cameroons (Cameroon v. United Kingdom).*[50] One of the issues which arose in this case concerned the legal effects of the termination of trusteeship under Chapter XII of the Charter. The German protectorate of Kamerun had been placed under the Mandates System of the League of Nations in 1919. The territory was divided into two mandates, one of which was administered by France and the other by the United Kingdom. These two mandates had both become trust territories in 1946. In order to accommodate the ethnic divisions within the territory, the northern part of the British Cameroons trust territory was administered separately from the southern half. The northern half had no administrative identity of its own, but was administered as part of the two northern provinces of Nigeria.[51]

In 1958 a United Nations Special Mission was sent to the British Cameroons to investigate how best to ascertain the views of the population concerning their political future. It concluded, on the basis of the ethnic and linguistic differences existing between the northern and southern parts of the territory, that the wishes of the northern and southern parts should be determined separately.[52] The General Assembly thereupon adopted Resolution 1350(XIII) of 13 March 1959, which recommended that separate plebiscites be held in the northern and southern parts of the British Cameroons. Meanwhile, the French Cameroons trust territory had become independent as the Republic of Cameroon on 1 June 1960.

In the plebiscite held on 11 and 12 February 1961 in the northern part of the British Cameroons, the people were asked whether they wished to achieve independence by joining either the Federation of Nigeria or the Republic of Cameroon. The majority were in favour of joining Nigeria. On 1 October 1961 a plebiscite was held in the southern part of the trust territory, in which the same question was put. The majority there favoured

---

[48] ICJ Reports 1960, 53.   [49] *Id.*, 45.
[50] Preliminary Objections, Judgment of 2 Dec. 1963, ICJ Reports 1963, p. 15.
[51] Rigo Sureda, 163–4.   [52] *Id.*, 164–5.

union with the Republic of Cameroon. The total combined vote in favour of joining the Republic of Cameroon in the two regions was 331,230, whereas the total combined vote in favour of joining Nigeria was only 244,037. Had a single plebiscite been held for the whole trust territory, the entire territory would have become part of the Republic of Cameroon.[53] On 21 April 1961 the General Assembly adopted Resolution 1608(XV), which endorsed the results of the plebiscites. This was in spite of a petition by the Republic of Cameroon to have the plebiscite in the northern part declared null and void. The northern part of the trust territory became a province of Nigeria, while the southern half was incorporated into the Republic of Cameroon.

The Republic of Cameroon then brought an action against the United Kingdom before the International Court of Justice. Cameroon alleged that the joint administration by the United Kingdom of the northern part of the British Cameroons with the two northern provinces of Nigeria constituted a breach of its Trusteeship Agreement. The United Kingdom had failed to lead the people of Northern Cameroon to self-government in accordance with Article 76(b) of the Charter.[54]

The Court held the action to be inadmissible, as no question of actual legal rights was involved.[55] The Court stated that even if it were to find that there had been a violation of the Trusteeship Agreement, this 'would not establish a causal connection between that violation and the result of the plebiscite'.[56] The Court also noted that:

It was not to this Court but to the General Assembly of the United Nations that the Republic of Cameroon directed the argument and the plea for a declaration that the plebiscite was null and void. In paragraphs numbered 2 and 3 of resolution 1608(XV), the General Assembly rejected the Cameroon plea. Whatever the motivation of the General Assembly in reaching the conclusions contained in those paragraphs, whether or not it was acting wholly on the political plane and without the Court finding it necessary to consider here whether or not the General Assembly based its action on a correct interpretation of the Trusteeship Agreement, there is no doubt—and indeed no controversy—that the resolution had definitive legal effect.[57]

In this passage the Court clearly indicated that, in terminating a Trusteeship Agreement, a resolution of the General Assembly had more than simply a recommendatory effect, and in fact had 'executive' authority. This flowed from the fact that the role of the General Assembly in such cases was a determinative one, i.e. it was designated by the provisions of Chapter XII

---

[53] *Id.*, 166–7.   [54] Crawford, 342.
[55] ICJ Reports 1963, pp. 15, 37.   [56] *Id.*, 33.
[57] *Id.*, 32. This finding was briefly distinguished by the Court in *Case Concerning Certain Phosphate Lands in Nauru (Nauru v. Australia)*, Preliminary Objections, Judgment, ILJ Reports 1992, p. 240 at 251.

'to decide particular matters of political fact, applying principles of self-determination implicit in the Trusteeship Agreements'.[58]

Reference to self-determination was made by Judge Ammoun in his separate opinion in *Barcelona Traction, Light and Power Company Limited*.[59] In a wide-ranging discussion of new developments in international law, Judge Ammoun postulated that such developments were in large measure due to the participation of the Third World, whose quest for freedom and justice had led to the infusion of higher ideals as principles of international law.[60] He declared that self-determination was one of these higher ideals of international law, and traced its development from the nineteenth century to its inclusion in the Charter of the United Nations and various General Assembly resolutions, most notably Resolution 1514(XV).[61] He concluded by stating that 'the law-making nature of such declarations and resolutions could not be denied,' given that 'they reflect well-nigh universal public feeling'.[62] These musings did not appear in the judgment of the Court, nor were they referred to by any other judge.

The first case in which the Court as a whole actually pronounced on the issue of self-determination was in its 1971 Advisory Opinion on the status of Namibia, *Legal Consequences for States of the Continued Presence of South Africa in Namibia* (*South West Africa*) *notwithstanding Security Council Resolution 276* (*1970*).[63] The status of Namibia (formerly South West Africa)[64] had involved South Africa in a protracted dispute with the United Nations, producing in the process four Advisory Opinions and two Judgments from the International Court.

South West Africa was a German colony which was captured during the First World War by South African troops. By virtue of Article 22 of the League of Nations it was subsequently placed under mandate, with South Africa as the administering power. When the League was dissolved in 1946, South Africa took the position that the United Nations possessed no successor supervisory role and that South Africa was under no obligation to place South West Africa under the United Nations Trusteeship System. In South Africa's opinion, the mandate over South West Africa had expired, and it was consequently at liberty to annex the territory.[65]

The position of South Africa prompted the General Assembly to seek the

---

[58] Crawford, 343, 344.   [59] Judgment, ICJ Reports 1970, p. 3.   [60] *Id.*, 310.

[61] Citing various 19th C. examples of self-determination, Judge Ammoun made particular reference to the attempted secession of the Confederate states: Judgment, ICJ Reports 1970, 311. This was hardly a perspicacious choice to illustrate the emergence of self-determination.

[62] Judgment, ICJ Reports 1970, 311.

[63] Advisory Opinion, ICJ Reports 1971, p. 16.

[64] The name 'South West Africa' was replaced by that of 'Namibia' by virtue of General Assembly Resolution 2372(XXII) of 12 June 1968. Para. 1 proclaimed that 'in accordance with the desires of its people, South West Africa shall henceforth be known as "Namibia"'.

[65] T. D. Gill *South West Africa and the Sacred Trust* (1984) 25.

advice of the International Court on the status of South West Africa. In 1950 the Court handed down its Advisory Opinion in *International Status of South West Africa*.[66] The Court found that the mandate over South West Africa had not lapsed, as South Africa alleged, and that the dissolution of the League of Nations had not brought to an end South Africa's obligations as administering power with regard to South West Africa. The Court rejected South Africa's claim that it was at liberty to annex South West Africa, noting that the creation of the mandate 'did not involve any cession of territory or transfer of sovereignty to the Union of South Africa'.[67] When the mandate system was first established, the Court pointed out, two principles had been of paramount importance: 'the principle of non-annexation and the principle that the well-being and development of such peoples form "a sacred trust of civilization"'.[68] The Court reasoned that the principle of the 'sacred trust of civilization' in fact preserved the regime of the mandate after the League had ceased to exist. Under Article 22 of the Covenant and Articles 2 to 5 of the Mandate Agreement, South Africa had undertaken certain obligations 'to promote to the utmost the material and moral well-being and the social progress of the inhabitants'.[69] However, the Court also found that Articles 75 and 77 of the Charter, which governed the conversion of mandated territories into trust territories, were permissive in nature, as indicated by the wording 'as may be placed thereunder'.[70] Moreover, both articles made reference to the 'agreements' which would place the territories in question under the Trusteeship System. The Court observed that the word 'agreement' implied consent. Consequently a mandatory power could not be compelled by the United Nations to accept the terms of the proposed agreement. Thus South Africa was not obligated to place the South West Africa mandate under the United Nations Trusteeship System. This did not mean that South Africa was not subject to the supervisory power of the United Nations. Certain mandate obligations regarding the 'machinery of implementation' had survived the dissolution of the League. In this respect the obligation on South Africa to submit to supervision had continued, and the General Assembly, by virtue of Article 10 of the Charter, was competent to exercise such supervision.[71] The Court specified that

[66] ICJ Reports 1950, p. 128.   [67] *Id.*, 132.   [68] *Id.*, 131.   [69] *Id.*, 133.

[70] *Id.*, 139. Art. 75 provides as follows: 'The United Nations shall establish under its authority an international trusteeship system for the administration and supervision of such territories as may be placed thereunder by subsequent individual agreements. These territories are hereinafter referred to as trust territories.' Art. 77 provides, *inter alia*: '(1) The trusteeship system shall apply to such territories in the following categories as may be placed thereunder by means of trusteeship agreements: (a) territories now held under mandate; . . .'

[71] Art. 10 provides: 'The General Assembly may discuss any questions or any matters within the scope of the present Charter or relating to the powers and functions of any organs provided for in the present Charter, and, except as provided in Article 12, may make recommendations to the Members of the United Nations or to the Security Council or to both on any such questions or matters.'

the degree of supervision to be exercised by the General Assembly was not to exceed that which applied under the Mandates System.[72] In addition, the Court held that South Africa was under an obligation to accept the compulsory jurisdiction of the Court, by virtue of Article 7 of the Mandate Agreement, in conjunction with Article 37 of the Statute of the International Court of Justice and Article 80(1) of the United Nations Charter.[73] The Court concluded by stating that 'competence to determine and modify the international status of South West Africa rests with the Union of South Africa acting with the consent of the United Nations'.[74] Pursuant to this finding, the Court rendered two subsequent Advisory Opinions, in 1955 and 1956, which established the proper procedure to be used by the General Assembly when exercising its supervisory functions.[75]

In spite of these Advisory Opinions, South Africa continued to deny the ongoing existence of the mandate in South West Africa, and refused to co-operate with the United Nations. Article 7 of the Mandate Agreement had specified, *inter alia*, that:

if any dispute whatever should arise between the Mandatory and another Member of the League of Nations relating to the interpretation or the application of the provisions of the Mandate, such dispute, if it cannot be settled by negotiation, shall be submitted to the Permanent Court of International Justice provided for by Article 14 of the Covenant of the League of Nations.

In an attempt to bind South Africa by a judgment of the International Court, Ethiopia and Liberia undertook contentious proceedings against South Africa in 1960.[76] Amongst other things, Ethiopia and Liberia alleged that South Africa had violated the terms of the Mandate by introducing apartheid into South West Africa. South Africa responded by challenging the jurisdiction of the Court to try the matter, and the Court was thus forced to deliver a preliminary judgment dealing with the objections raised by South Africa. This it did in 1962 in the *South West Africa Cases* (*Ethiopia* v. *South Africa; Liberia* v. *South Africa*).[77] South Africa's primary objection was that the conflict between itself and Ethiopia and Liberia was not a 'dispute' within the meaning of Article 7 of the Mandate Agreement, in that no material interests of either Ethiopia or Liberia were involved.[78] The Court rejected this line of argument, holding that Article 7 gave the member states of the League a 'legal right of interest' in ensuring that a mandatory power fulfil its obligations 'both towards the inhabitants

[72] ICJ Reports 1950, pp. 128, 138.   [73] *Id.*, 138.   [74] *Id.*, 143.
[75] *Voting Procedure on Questions Relating to Reports and Petitions Concerning the Territory of South West Africa*, Advisory Opinion, ICJ Reports 1955, p. 67; *Admissibility of Hearings of Petitioners by the Committee on South West Africa*, Advisory Opinion, ICJ Reports 1956, p. 23.
[76] Both Ethiopia and Liberia had been original members of the League of Nations.
[77] Preliminary Objections, ICJ Reports 1962, p. 319.
[78] *Id.*, 327.

of the mandated territory, and towards the League of Nations and its members'.[79]

The Court then considered the merits of the case in its 1966 decision, the *South West Africa Cases* (*Ethiopia* v. *South Africa; Liberia* v. *South Africa*), Second Phase.[80] Ethiopia and Liberia had included in their submissions the allegation that South Africa's policy of apartheid in South West Africa had 'impeded opportunities for self-determination by the inhabitants of the Territory'.[81] This submission was not addressed in the majority judgment, but it was taken up by Judge *ad hoc* van Wyck in his separate opinion. Judge *ad hoc* van Wyck noted that Article 73 of the Charter referred to 'territories whose peoples have not yet attained a full measure of self-government', prescribed 'due respect for the cultures of the peoples concerned', and declared that 'due account should be taken of the political aspirations of the peoples concerned', who should be assisted in the development of their 'free political institutions according to the particular circumstances of each Territory and its peoples and its varying stages of advancement'. The fact that Article 73 referred to 'territory' in the singular form and 'peoples' in the plural form meant, in Judge *ad hoc* van Wyck's opinion, that more than one people could inhabit a particular trust territory. Moreover, the wording of Article 73 did not 'support the existence of a general prohibition of the allotment of rights, burdens, privileges, etc. on the basis of group, class or race'.[82] This led Judge *ad hoc* van Wyck to conclude that South Africa, far from impeding opportunities for self-determination, had actually pursued 'a policy aimed at separate self-determination for the various population groups of South West Africa'.[83]

Judge Tanaka, dissenting, responded to the arguments put forward by Judge *ad hoc* van Wyck. Judge Tanaka noted that the case involved the question of the legal standards regarding non-discrimination. This in turn was 'intimately related to the essence and nature of fundamental human rights', in which the 'principle of equality before the law' occupied 'the most important part'.[84] Different treatment was an exception to the principle of equality, and as such it was incumbent on those who advocated different treatment to show its *raison d'être* and to demonstrate its reasonableness.[85] Different treatment was reasonable in certain circumstances because the 'mechanical application' of equal treatment could lead to injustice if it did not take into account the 'concrete circumstances of individual cases'.[86] However, the criteria used to distinguish one race from another did 'not constitute in themselves relevant factors as the basis for different political or legal treatment'.[87] South Africa's policy of apartheid, which established

---

[79] *Id.*, 343. [80] ICJ Reports 1966, p. 4. [81] *Id.*, 15.
[82] *Id.*, 166. [83] *Id.*, 196.
[84] *Id.*, 287. [85] *Id.*, 309.
[86] *Id.*, 308. [87] *Id.*, 308.

status, rights, and duties solely on the basis of membership in a group or race, was therefore nothing more than the 'justification or official recognition of racial prejudice or sentiment of racial superiority on the part of the White population which does harm to the dignity of man'.[88]

The majority judgment did not consider any of these issues. It confined itself to the finding that South Africa's obligations with respect to the treatment of the inhabitants of South West Africa were owed to the League alone, and not to individual members of the League. The cases brought by Ethiopia and Liberia against South Africa were therefore dismissed.[89]

The General Assembly reacted to the Court's decision by adopting Resolution 2145(XXI) on 27 October 1966. Paragraph 3 noted that 'South Africa has failed to fulfil its obligations in respect of the administration of the Mandated Territory and to ensure the moral and material well-being and security of the indigenous inhabitants of South West Africa and has, in fact, disavowed the Mandate.' Paragraph 4 declared that the mandate conferred on South Africa was terminated, and that henceforth South West Africa would come 'under the direct responsibility of the United Nations'. The provisions of General Assembly Resolution 2145(XXI) were reiterated in several subsequent Security Council resolutions. Security Council Resolution 264 (1969), for example, recognized the termination of the mandate and the illegality of the continued presence of South Africa in Namibia, as it was now known.[90] Security Council Resolution 269 (1969) called upon South Africa to withdraw from Namibia. Security Council Resolution 276 (1970) reaffirmed in its Preamble General Assembly Resolution 2145(XXI), and declared in paragraph 2 that the continued presence of South Africa in Namibia was illegal.

Faced with South Africa's continued intransigence on the issue, the Security Council requested an Advisory Opinion from the Court concerning the legal consequences of South Africa's continued presence in Namibia, contrary to Security Council Resolution 276 (1970).[91] The Court responded with its Advisory Opinion of 1971, *Legal Consequences for States of the Continued Presence of South Africa in Namibia (South West Africa) notwithstanding Security Council Resolution 276 (1970)*.[92] The Court confirmed again that the mandate had continued in spite of the dissolution of the League, and that the General Assembly had inherited the supervisory powers of the League. It found that South Africa had not fulfilled its obligations under the Mandate Agreement and consequently was not entitled to retain its rights as mandatory under that Agreement. The General

---

[88] ICJ Reports 1966, p. 312.

[89] Michael Akehurst *A Modern Introduction to International Law* (1984) 249.

[90] See p. 80, fn. 64 *supra* concerning the change of name from 'South West Africa' to 'Namibia'.

[91] Security Council Resolution 284 (1970).   [92] ICJ Reports 1971, p. 16.

Assembly, in the Court's opinion, had the capacity to terminate the Mandate and had lawfully done so. The Court indicated that in this regard the General Assembly had simply applied the general principle of law that a power of termination must form a part of all agreements in the event of breach, even if such power of termination is not expressly set out in the agreement itself.[93] South Africa was thus under a duty, the Court concluded, to withdraw from Namibia.

In this decision the Court explicitly addressed the issue of self-determination for the first time. In its 1950 Advisory Opinion the Court had declared the principle of the 'sacred trust' to be of paramount importance with respect to the mandate. In its 1971 Advisory Opinion the Court held that the 'sacred trust', as a result of developments in international law, now extended 'to "all territories whose peoples have not yet attained a full measure of self-government" (Article 73)'.[94] The Court went on to declare that 'the ultimate objective of the sacred trust was the self-determination and independence of the peoples concerned'.[95] The Court noted that 'the subsequent development of international law in regard to non-self-governing territories, as enshrined in the Charter of the United Nations, made the principle of self-determination applicable to all of them'.[96]

The principle of self-determination was again specifically addressed by the Court in its 1975 Advisory Opinion on the *Western Sahara*.[97] The Western Sahara had been a colony of Spain since 1884, and was formerly known as the Spanish Sahara. In 1966 the General Assembly adopted Resolution 2229(XXI) which reaffirmed in paragraph 1 'the inalienable rights of the peoples of Ifni and Spanish Sahara to self-determination in accordance with General Assembly resolution 1514(XV)'. In paragraph 4 the General Assembly directed Spain to hold a referendum in the Western Sahara in order to allow the indigenous population to exercise its right to self-determination. Spain eventually agreed to hold a referendum in 1975. But before this occurred, Morocco and Mauritania objected. These two states both claimed the territory of the Western Sahara on the basis of historic title predating Spain's colonization. The General Assembly then sought, at the instigation of Morocco and Mauritania, an Advisory Opinion from the International Court as to 1) whether the Western Sahara was *terra nullius* prior to Spain's colonization, and 2) in the event that it was not, what legal ties existed at this time between the Western Sahara and Morocco, on one

[93] ICJ Reports 1971, pp. 16, 48. The Court's reasoning on this point has been criticized on the basis that the United Nations was 'not the contractual successor of the League in respect of Mandates *qua* treaties. It was on the ground of status, as distinct from contract, that the Court in 1950 held the General Assembly entitled to exercise supervisory powers': Crawford, 351.

[94] ICJ Reports 1971, pp. 16, 31.

[95] *Id.*, 31.   [96] *Id.*, 31.   [97] ICJ Reports 1975, p. 12.

hand, and Mauritania on the other.[98] In response to the first question, the Court found that the territory in question was not *terra nullius* because the territory, when first colonized, had been inhabited by nomadic peoples who were socially and politically organized. With respect to the second question the Court found that, although some Saharan tribes had had ties of personal allegiance to Morocco, there was no evidence which demonstrated political authority amounting to sovereignty, on the part of either Morocco or Mauritania. The Court concluded that there were no legal ties which might prevent or otherwise affect the expression of self-determination, as set out in Resolution 1514(XV), by the people of the Western Sahara.[99]

The Court then addressed the issue of self-determination. The Court reiterated the position it had set out in the *Namibia* case in 1971, to the effect that self-determination was applicable to all non-self-governing territories. In this regard the Court linked the explicit references to self-determination contained in Articles 1 and 55 of the Charter to Chapter XI, stating that those explicit references to self-determination had 'direct and particular relevance for non-self-governing territories'.[100] The Court also discussed Resolution 1514(XV), noting that it had 'provided the basis for the process of decolonization which has resulted since 1960 in the creation of many States which are today Members of the United Nations'.[101] After referring to certain key provisions of Resolutions 1514(XV), 1541(XV), and 2625(XXV), the Court concluded that it was necessary, in the process of self-determination, 'to pay regard to the freely expressed will of the peoples'.[102]

The Court next dealt with the issue of self-determination in its 1986 decision, *Military and Paramilitary Activities in and against Nicaragua (Nicaragua v. United States of America)*.[103] Although there was no specific reference by the Court to the principle of self-determination, its decision nevertheless had important consequences for the meaning and scope of the principle. In the *Namibia* and *Western Sahara* cases the Court had discussed self-determination only in the context of non-self-governing territories. In the *Nicaragua* decision, however, the Court specifically pointed out that it was not 'concerned with the process of decolonization'.[104]

After determining that it had jurisdiction to try the matter,[105] the Court found that the United States had breached customary international law by

---

[98] General Assembly Resolution 3292(XXIX) of 13 Dec. 1974.
[99] ICJ Reports 1975, pp. 12, 68.
[100] *Id.*, 31.
[101] *Id.*, 32.
[102] *Id.*, 33.
[103] Merits, Judgment, ICJ Reports 1986, p. 14.
[104] *Id.*, 108.
[105] *Military and Paramilitary Activities in and against Nicaragua (Nicaragua v. United States of America)*, Jurisdiction and Admissibility, Judgment, ICJ Reports 1984, p. 392.

using force against another state, by violating the sovereignty of another state, and by intervening in the affairs of another state. The Court declared that states were obliged to respect the principle of non-intervention, which involved 'the right of every sovereign State to conduct its affairs without outside interference'.[106] The Court elaborated on the principle of non-intervention in the following terms:

the principle forbids all States or groups of States to intervene directly or indirectly in internal or external affairs of other States. A prohibited intervention must accordingly be one bearing on matters in which each State is permitted, by the principle of State sovereignty, to decide freely. One of these is the choice of a political, economic, social and cultural system, and the formation of foreign policy. Intervention is wrongful when it uses methods of coercion in regard to such choices, which must remain free ones.[107]

By referring to a right to decide freely on a political, economic, social, and cultural system, the Court was in effect paraphrasing Article 1(1) of the International Human Rights Covenants and paragraph 1 of Resolution 1514(XV).[108] Moreover, because the *Nicaragua* decision did not involve the process of decolonization, the Court affirmed in this case that the right to freely choose a political, economic, social, and cultural system was as applicable to independent, sovereign states as it was to non-self-governing territories.[109]

The Court's interpretation of the principle of non-intervention in independent states had another important consequence for the principle of self-determination. There had been attempts prior to the *Nicaragua* case to justify intervention on the basis of self-determination. The Brezhnev

---

[106] ICJ Reports 1986, pp. 14, 106.

[107] *Id.*, 108.

[108] It should be noted, however, that the Court held that it was states which possessed this right, whereas the International Covenants and Resolution 1514(XV) declared that 'peoples' possessed this right.

[109] Judge Schwebel, dissenting, considered that the Court's ruling with respect to non-intervention had 'disturbing implications': *id.*, 350. Although the Court had declared that foreign intervention in the internal affairs of a state was in general prohibited, it had nevertheless intimated that there could be 'a particular right of intervention provided that it is in furtherance of "the process of decolonization"': *id.*, 351. Judge Schwebel noted that in contemporary international law, 'the right of self-determination, freedom and independence of peoples is universally recognized; the right of peoples to struggle to achieve these ends is universally accepted; but what is not universally recognized and what is not universally accepted is any right of such peoples to foreign assistance or support which constitutes intervention. That is to say, it is lawful for a foreign State or movement to give to a people struggling for self-determination moral, political and humanitarian assistance; but it is not lawful for a foreign State or movement to intervene in that struggle with force or to provide arms, supplies and other logistical support in the prosecution of armed rebellion. This is true whether the struggle is or is proclaimed to be in pursuance of the process of decolonization or against colonial domination. Moreover, what entities are susceptible of decolonization is a matter of dispute in many cases. What is a colony, and who is the colonizer, are the subjects of sharply differing views': *id.*, 351.

Doctrine, for example, posited that self-determination would, in the natural course of events, inevitably advance the cause of Communism in Communist states. If it did not do so, other Communist states were entitled to intervene in the affairs of that state in order to preserve the international Communist polity.[110] Certain American writers, such as W. M. Reisman, had argued similarly that intervention by democratic states was justified if such intervention 'enhanced opportunities for on-going self-determination,' i.e. if it 'increased the probability of the free choice of peoples about their government and political structure'.[111] The Court's decision in the *Nicaragua* case, however, clearly repudiated such justifications for intervention.[112]

The issue of self-determination was also raised in the case of *Certain Phosphate Lands in Nauru (Nauru v. Australia).*[113] This involved a claim by Nauru against Australia for compensation for the physical damage done to much of its territory as a result of extensive phosphate mining, which took place when Nauru was a non-self-governing territory jointly administered by Australia, New Zealand, and the United Kingdom. The damage done to the territory mined rendered that territory uninhabitable. Nauru argued, *inter alia*, that this constituted a breach of the principle of self-determination, in that it 'involved the literal disposal of the territorial foundation of the unit of self-determination'.[114] Australia raised preliminary objections concerning the jurisdiction of the Court and the admissability of the claim, but these were rejected by the Court in its Judgment of 26 June 1992, allowing the case to proceed on the merits.[115] The case was settled on 10 August 1993, when Australia agreed to pay Nauru 107 million dollars in compensation, and in return Nauru agreed to release Australia, New Zealand, and the United Kingdom from any further liability.[116]

The issue of self-determination also came before the International Court of Justice in the case of *East Timor (Portugal v. Australia).*[117] In this case Portugal contested the right of Australia to conclude an agreement with Indonesia concerning the delimitation of the sea-bed boundary between northern Australia and East Timor. In 1975 East Timor, a non-

---

[110] See Chapter 5, pp. 106–7.

[111] W. Michael Reisman 'Coercion and Self-Determination: Construing Charter Article 2(4)' (1984) 642–4. For criticism of Reisman's position see Oscar Schachter 'The Legality of Pro-Democratic Invasion' (1984) 645.

[112] See Chapter 8, pp. 191–2, for a discussion of intervention as it relates to self-determination.

[113] Order of 18 July 1989, ICJ Reports 1989, p. 12; Order of 8 February 1991, ICJ Reports 1991, p. 3.

[114] Memorial of the Republic of Nauru, Vol. 1, April 1990, 154, para. 413.

[115] *Idem*, Preliminary Objections, Judgment, ICJ Reports 1992, p. 240.

[116] Agreement Between Australia and the Republic of Nauru for the Settlement of the Case in the International Court of Justice Concerning Certain Phosphate Lands in Nauru (1993) ATS No. 26.

[117] ICJ Reports 1995, p. 1.

self-governing territory administered by Portugal, was invaded and an-nexed by Indonesia. Portugal argued that Indonesia's invasion of East Timor was illegal. This meant that Indonesia's subsequent occupation of East Timor was also illegal. By illegally invading and occupying East Timor, Indonesia had deprived the people of East Timor of their right of self-determination. Portugal further argued that when Australia entered into an agreement with Indonesia which recognized Indonesia's sovereignty over East Timor, it also violated the right of the people of East Timor to self-determination (including the related rights of territorial integrity and permanent sovereignty over its natural wealth and resources), as well as violating the position of Portugal as the administering power over the non-self-governing territory of East Timor.[118] Portugal initiated its claim against Australia rather then Indonesia because Australia, unlike Indonesia, had accepted the jurisdiction of the Court with respect to any other state accept-ing the same obligation, which Portugal had done.[119]

The Court held that it was unable to adjudicate on the case. Although it found, contrary to Australia's assertion, that there was a legal dispute betwen the parties, it concluded that it could not rule upon that dispute without first determining whether Indonesia was entitled to conclude the 1989 Treaty with Australia. This would have required the Court to rule on the lawfulness of Indonesia's conduct towards East Timor. Given that under its Statute the Court could not rule on the rights and obligations of a state without its consent, it was unable to make a ruling on Indonesia's conduct, as Indonesia had not consented to the Court's jurisdiction. With-out being able to rule on Indonesia's conduct, the Court was also precluded from ruling on the dispute between Portugal and Australia.[120]

The Court nevertheless made several pronouncements on self-determination. It declared, at paragraph 29, that the right of peoples to self-determination was 'one of the essential principles of contemporary international law' and that it had an '*erga omnes*' character.[121] It further noted, at paragraph 31, that East Timor remained, with regard both to Portugal and to Australia, a non-self-governing territory and that its people continued to possess the right of self-determination. Moreover, the Court added, the General Assembly continued to regard East Timor as a non-self-governing territory for the purposes of Chapter XI, and the Security

---

[118] Application Instituting Proceedings, filed in the Registry of the Court on 22 Feb. 1991, 15, para. 27.

[119] Art. 36(2), Statute of the International Court of Justice. See C. M. Chinkin 'The Merits of Portugal's Claim Against Australia' (1992) 423, 428–9; Jean-Pierre L. Fonteyne 'The Portu-guese Timor Gap Litigation Before the International Court of Justice: A Brief Appraisal of Australia's Position' (1991) 170; and Antonio Cassese *Self-Determination of Peoples* (1995) 223–30.

[120] Judgment ICJ Reports 1995, p. 90, 105 (para. 34), Judge Weeramantry and Judge *ad hoc* Skubiszewski dissenting.   [121] *Id.*, 102.

Council had called for self-determination for the people of East Timor in two resolutions.[122]

9. CONCLUSION

The principle of self-determination has developed in the post-war period from an essentially political concept into a legal right. It has been incorporated into the most fundamental instrument of modern international law, the Charter of the United Nations, as well as into other important international instruments such as the International Covenant of Civil and Political Rights, and the International Covenant of Economic, Social and Cultural Rights. The references to self-determination in these specific instruments did not delimit in any precise or definitive manner the scope of the principle as a legal right, but this has been done to a certain extent by General Assembly resolutions, most notably by Resolutions 1514(XV), 1541(XV), and 2625(XXV). By virtue of these resolutions self-determination has become closely associated with the process of decolonization, and the International Court of Justice has confirmed that this aspect of self-determination constitutes a part of international law. There are, however, considerable differences between the provisions of Resolutions 1514(XV) and 1541(XV), on one hand, and Resolution 2625(XXV) on the other.

From the wording of various international instruments it appears that the legal right of self-determination extends beyond the colonial context. Article 1 of the two International Human Rights Covenants declared that self-determination was a right of all peoples.[123] Resolution 2625(XXV) declared that self-determination was a right applicable to all peoples and a duty incumbent upon all states. Although the principle of self-determination constitutes a legal right for the peoples of independent states, as well as those of non-self-governing territories, however, the nature and extent of the right with regard to peoples of independent states remains unclear. No definitive demarcation between self-determination as a political concept and self-determination as a legal right can be found in the Charter of the United Nations, the International Human Rights Covenants, General Assembly resolutions, or the decisions of the International Court of Justice. Consequently, the nature and extent of self-determination as a legal right remains a matter of considerable controversy amongst states. A review of state practice may shed some light on the extent to which self-determination is accepted as a legal right.

[122] Judgment ICJ Reports 1995, 102. The question of East Timor is discussed in further detail in Chapter 10, pp. 242, 243.
[123] International Covenant on Civil and Political Rights (1976) 999 UNTS 171, 173; International Covenant on Economic, Social and Cultural Rights (1976) 993 UNTS 3, 5.

5

Self-Determination in Modern International Law: The Practice of States

1. INTRODUCTION

Since the Second World War the principle of self-determination has been transformed from an essentially political concept into an important element of international law. However, the exact parameters of the legal right of self-determination remain unclear. The post-war international instruments which invoke the 'right to self-determination' do not define that term in any detail. Given this absence of precise guidelines in the international instruments, and also given the existence of widely differing theories of self-determination in the political context, the practice of states has become an important means of ascertaining the scope of self-determination at international law. This Chapter therefore examines state practice with regard to self-determination.

2. SELF-DETERMINATION AND DECOLONIZATION

The law relating to self-determination in the post-war era has developed in large measure as a result of the growth of nationalism in the Third World, particularly in the states of Africa and Asia.[1] Most states of the Third World were formerly colonies, and consequently the nationalism which developed in those states had as goals the termination of colonial status and the attainment of independence. The concept of self-determination in such states became associated primarily, if not exclusively, with the process of decolonization.

The linking of self-determination to decolonization has already been noted in Chapter 4 with regard to General Assembly resolutions.[2] As the colonies of Africa and Asia attained independence and became members of the United Nations, they were more and more able, with the support of the states of the Communist bloc and of South America, to set forth in General Assembly resolutions their understanding of self-

---

[1] See K. R. Minogue *Nationalism* (1967); Martin Kilson (ed.) *New States in the Modern World* (1975); Anthony D. Smith *Nationalism in the Twentieth Century* (1979); and John Breuilly *Nationalism and the State* (1982).

[2] See Chapter 4, pp. 69–74.

determination.[3] Resolution 1514 (XV) of 14 December 1960 best exemplifies this trend.[4] Every state in Africa, Asia, and the Middle East voted in favour of Resolution 1514 (XV), as did the entire Communist bloc and all but one of the Latin American states.[5]

Self-determination was also linked to decolonization in many Third World regional international instruments and in individual declarations. The 1963 Charter of the Organization of African States, for example, declares in Article II(1)(d) that one of its purposes is 'to eradicate all forms of colonialism from Africa'.[6] In the 1982 Banjul Charter on Human and Peoples' Rights,[7] the preoccupation of African states with decolonization is evident in Articles 19 and 20, which provide as follows:

Article 19. All peoples shall be equal; they shall enjoy the same respect and shall enjoy the same rights. Nothing shall justify the domination of a people by another.

Article 20(1). All peoples shall have the right to existence. They shall have the unquestionable and inalienable right to self-determination. They shall freely determine their political status and shall pursue their economic and social development according to the policy they have freely chosen.

(2) Colonized or oppressed peoples shall have the right to free themselves from the bonds of domination by resorting to any means recognised by the international community.

(3) All peoples shall have the right to the assistance of the States parties to the present Charter in their liberation struggle against foreign domination, be it political, economic or cultural.[8]

The use of phrases such as 'colonized or oppressed peoples', 'foreign domination', and 'domination of a people by another' indicates that in the Banjul Charter self-determination was meant to be equated with decolonization.

The declaration of India with regard to Article 1 of the International Human Rights Covenants provides another good example of self-determination being equated with decolonization. The Indian declaration

---

[3] The position of the Communist states with regard to self-determination and decolonization is described *infra* at p. 93. The states of South America had attained independence from colonial status in the first half of the nineteenth century, and were generally sympathetic to the decolonization policies of the African and Asian states: Hurst Hannum *Autonomy, Sovereignty and Self-Determination* (1990) 48.

[4] See Chapter 4, pp. 70–1.

[5] Dusan J. Djonovich (ed.) *United Nations Resolutions* Series 1, Resolutions Adopted by the General Assembly, Vol. VIII (1960–62), 38. No state voted against Resolution 1514 (XV), although 9 states abstained: Australia, Belgium, the Dominican Republic, France, Portugal, South Africa, Spain, the United Kingdom, and the United States: *id.*

[6] (1963) 479 UNTS 39, 72.

[7] (1982) 21 ILM 59. The Charter was expressly designed to address African problems and reflect African values: Richard Gittleman 'The African Charter on Human and Peoples' Rights: A Legal Analysis' (1982) 668.

[8] (1982) 21 ILM 59, 62.

stated that: 'With reference to Article 1 . . . the Government of the Republic of India declares that the words "the right to self-determination" appearing in this article apply only to the peoples under foreign domination and that these words do not apply to sovereign independent states or to a section of a people or a nation—which is the essence of national integrity.'[9] By defining self-determination solely in terms of 'foreign domination', the Indian declaration restricts the application of self-determination to colonial situations. Moreover, by denying that self-determination applies either 'to sovereign independent States' or 'to a section of a people or a nation', the Indian declaration explicitly rejects those notions of self-determination whereby the concept is understood to mean a right to representative government or a right of particular ethnic groups to determine their own political status.

The Soviet Union and its Communist allies also placed great emphasis on decolonization in the post-war era. The demise of the capitalist system, according to Communist theory, would be presaged by the collapse of their colonial empires.[10] Consequently, Soviet policy in the post-war period stressed the anti-colonial aspects of self-determination. Tunkin declared that the 'spearhead' of self-determination was 'aimed against the system of colonialism'.[11] Because the position of the Soviet Union and the Communist bloc states largely coincided with that of Third World states, most resolutions of the General Assembly which dealt with self-determination were directed at the question of decolonization, and were adopted by the General Assembly with comfortable majorities.[12]

The anti-colonial stance of Third World and Communist bloc states was in sharp contrast to the position taken by most Western states in the early post-war period. Western states possessing colonial territories refused, for the most part, to acknowledge that there was any connection between self-determination and decolonization, and resisted attempts to apply the principle of self-determination to their colonial possessions. A number of Western states opposed the increasing jurisdiction of the General Assembly over non-self-governing territories, arguing that the determination as to whether a particular territory was non-self-governing under Article 73(e) was a matter of domestic jurisdiction, by virtue of Article

[9] *Multilateral Treaties Deposited With the Secretary General: Status as at 31 Dec. 1994* (1995) New York: United Nations, 109, 121. India's declaration was made on 10 Apr. 1979.

[10] D. B. Levin 'The Principle of Self-Determination of Nations in International Law' (1962) 45; Antonio Cassese *Self-Determination of Peoples* (1995) 45.

[11] G. I. Tunkin *Theory of International Law* (1974) 4. See Chapter 2, pp. 18–20 for a detailed explanation of Lenin's theory in this regard.

[12] Such important anti-colonial resolutions as 334(IV), 1514(XV), 2105(XX) and 3103(XXVII) all received the support of the Soviet Union and its Communist allies: Dusan J. Djonovich (ed.) *United Nations Resolutions* Series I, Resolutions Adopted by the General Assembly, New York: Oceana Publications, Vol. II (1948–49); Vol. VIII (1960–62) 38; Vol. X (1964–65) 51; Vol. XIV (1972–74) 170.

2(7).[13] Various arguments were also put forward by Western states which challenged the applicability of Chapter XI to their colonial possessions. France and Portugal maintained that their colonial possessions were integral parts of the metropolitan state, having been incorporated into the state by virtue of its constitution; consequently, such territories did not qualify as non-self-governing.[14] Belgium argued that as Chapter XI did not specify that non-self-governing territories were limited to colonial possessions, an interpretation of Chapter XI which applied only to colonial possessions would unjustly exclude non-self-governing peoples within independent states. According to Belgium, Chapter XI applied not only to colonial possessions, but to all territories (including the territory of independent states) where part of the state's population differed from the majority in its level of political maturity and where, as a result, it did not participate fully in the political, economic, and cultural life of the state.[15] The United Kingdom, while recognizing that Chapter XI had been designed to apply to colonial territories, argued that this did not necessarily mean that those territories had to become independent states. The provisions of Chapter XI specified only that the administering states were obliged to promote the development of 'self-government' in the non-self-governing territories which they were administering. Chapter XI did not state that independence must be granted to such territories: indeed, there was no reference at all to 'independence' in the Chapter. The United Kingdom therefore maintained that it was possible to satisfy the provisions of Chapter XI by granting self-government to a non-self-governing territory, without granting that territory independence. In other words, a non-self-governing territory could become self-governing without being independent of the United Kingdom.[16]

The attitude of the United States towards decolonization differed from that of other Western states. The United States had itself attained independent statehood from colonial status, and it had no colonial empire. Consequently it tended to support the efforts of colonial peoples to achieve independence.[17] However, because it maintained close relationships with

[13] Josef L. Kunz 'Chapter XI of the United Nations Charter in Action' (1954) 107. Art. 2(7) provides as follows: 'Nothing contained in the present Charter shall authorize the United Nations to intervene in matters which are essentially within the domestic jurisdiction of any State or shall require the Members to submit such matters to settlement under the present Charter; but the principle shall not prejudice the application of enforcement measures under Chapter VII.'

[14] Inis L. Claude, Jr. 'Domestic Jurisdiction and Colonialism' (1975) 129.

[15] Michla Pomerance *Self-Determination in Law and Practice* (1982) 82, fn. 72; Claude, 125, 126; Kunz (see fn. 13 above) 109.

[16] Ruth B. Russell *A History of the United Nations Charter* (1958) 815; Louis B. John: 'Models of Autonomy Within the United Nations Framework' in Yoram Dinstein (ed.) *Models of Autonomy* (1981) 14.

[17] Robert E. Asher *et al. The United Nations and Promotion of the General Welfare* (1957) 825.

major colonial powers such as the United Kingdom and France, the anti-colonial stance of the United States tended to remain muted. Thus, although the United States supported decolonization, it declared that the status of territories under Article 73 was to be determined by the administering state rather than by the General Assembly.[18]

The position of the Western colonial powers was eventually repudiated in the United Nations. In a series of General Assembly resolutions a majority of states decided that the General Assembly did indeed possess jurisdiction to determine whether a territory was non-self-governing and that an administering state must continue to transmit information under Article 73(e) until the General Assembly had declared that that territory was no longer non-self-governing.[19]

Western arguments concerning the intrepretation of Chapter XI were also rejected by a majority of states in the General Assembly, with the adoption of Resolutions 1514(XV) and 1541(XV). By focusing uniquely on colonial situations, Resolution 1514(XV) repudiated the Belgian argument by providing an interpretation of non-self-governing territories which corresponded only with colonial entities.[20] Resolution 1541(XV) was even more explicit in this regard, declaring in Principle I of the Annex that the authors of the Charter 'had in mind that Chapter XI should be applicable to territories which were then known to be of the colonial type'. Resolution 1541(XV) also addressed the question of the relationship of overseas territories to the metropolitan state. Principle IV of Resolution 1541(XV) repudiated the French and Portuguese arguments by declaring that there was an obligation to transmit information in respect of a territory which was 'geographically separate and distinct ethnically and/or culturally from the country administering it'. In this statement the General Assembly indicated that it would no longer accept the proposition that an overseas territory was an integral part of a metropolitan state, but would instead presume that such territories were non-self-governing unless the metropolitan state could prove otherwise. The General Assembly also responded to the argument of the United Kingdom by emphasizing, in Resolutions 742(VIII), 1514(XV), and 1541(XV), that independence was the normal goal of non-self-governing territories. The argument that the concepts of 'self-government' and 'independence' should be differentiated was therefore rejected. Self-determination occurred primarily when such territories attained independence.

The position of the Western colonial powers thus became increasingly untenable. Resolutions 1514(XV) and 1541(XV) were adopted by large

---

[18] Kunz (see fn. 13 above) 108.
[19] See the discussion of Resolutions 334(IV), 567(VI), 648(VII), 742(VIII), 1514(XV), and 2870(XXVI) in Chapter 4, pp. 69–71, 72, fn. 36.
[20] Claude, 126.

majorities in the General Assembly, demonstrating widespread support throughout the international community for the decolonization of all non-self-governing territories.[21] Subsequent resolutions of the General Assembly put increasing pressure on the colonial powers to grant independence to their respective colonies.[22] By 1970 the Western states had come to accept that decolonization was an integral part of self-determination. This they did in Resolution 2625(XXV), which specified that every state had a duty to promote self-determination in order, *inter alia*, to 'bring a speedy end to colonialism, having due regard to the freely expressed will of the people concerned'. The Resolution received the unanimous support of the General Assembly. Given the support of the Western states for this proposition, the International Court of Justice recognized that decolonization had become a part of international law when it declared that 'the subsequent development of international law in regard to non-self-governing territories, as enshrined in the Charter of the United Nations, made the principle of self-determination applicable to all of them'.[23]

3. SELF-DETERMINATION AND REPRESENTATIVE GOVERNMENT

Western states have traditionally associated the principle of self-determination with popular sovereignty and representative government.[24] Such states considered self-determination to be a political concept which was not particularly amenable to legal formulation. This understanding of self-determination was current amongst Western states in the early post-war period, even though the Charter on the United Nations made explicit reference to self-determination in Articles 1(2) and 55.[25] Western states did not acknowledge that the Charter references to self-determination conferred legal status on the concept. Apart from Article 55, self-determination was referred to only in Article 1, which dealt with the purposes of the United Nations. It was not referred to in Article 2, which dealt with its principles. Self-determination was therefore considered

---

[21] The vote with regard to Resolution 1514(XV) was 89–0–9. The vote with regard to Resolution 1541(XV) was 69–2–21; Djonovich (ed.), Vol. VIII (1960–62) 38, 40.

[22] See Chapter 4, pp. 73–4.

[23] *Legal Consequences for States of the Continued Presence of South Africa in Namibia (South West Africa) notwithstanding Security Council Resolution 276 (1970)* Advisory Opinion, ICJ Reports 1971, pp. 16, 31.

[24] See Chapter 1, pp. 2–4.

[25] The European Convention for the Protection of Human Rights and Fundamental Freedoms (1955) 213 UNTS 221, for example, does not recognize the right to self-determination. The Convention was signed on 4 Nov. 1950 and entered into force on 3 Sep. 1953.

to be 'one of the desiderata of the Charter rather than a legal right as such'.[26]

Western states were forced to abandon this understanding of self-determination in the 1960s as the concept became more and more associated with decolonization. In 1966 a new approach to self-determination became imperative when self-determination was recognized as a legal right in Article 1 of the International Human Rights Covenants.[27] Western states responded by seeking to define the legal right of self-determination in terms of their own political traditions of popular sovereignty and representative government. This approach was reflected in the drafts presented by the United States and the United Kingdom to the United Nations Special Committee on Friendly Relations. The American draft proposal provided that: 'The existence of a sovereign and independent State possessing a representative Government, effectively functioning as such to all distinct peoples within its territory, is presumed to satisfy the principle of equal rights and self-determination as regards those peoples.'[28]

The British draft proposal was framed in much the same language. It provided that: 'States enjoying full sovereignty and independence, and possessed of a representative government, effectively functioning as such to all distinct peoples within their territory, shall be considered to be conducting themselves in conformity with this principle ("equal rights and self-determination") as regards those peoples.'[29]

Because the right of self-determination was linked in Western opinion to the notion of representative government, it applied not only to non-self-governing territories, but also to sovereign and independent states. In other words, it was a right of universal application.[30] Thus, when India declared that Article 1 of the International Human Rights Covenants did not apply to 'sovereign independent States',[31] France, the Netherlands, and the Federal Republic of Germany recorded vigorous objections. 'Any attempt to limit this right or to attach conditions not provided for in the relevant

---

[26] Yehuda Z. Blum 'Reflections on the Changing Concept of Self-Determination' (1975) 511. A good example of this approach can be found in Norman Bentwich and Andrew Martin *A Commentary on the Charter of the United Nations* (1950). At p. 7 the authors note that Art. 1(2) is simply 'a declaration of good-will towards peoples which have not yet achieved self-determination in either the legal or political sense'. They go on to add that 'it would be unwarranted to argue that the paragraph is a sufficient basis for immediate claims by not fully self-governing peoples for a change in their status'. It should be noted, however, that the French version of Art. 1(2) does explicitly refer to self-determination as a right: it speaks of respect for the 'principe de l'égalité des droits des peuples et de leur droit à disposer d'eux-mêmes'. See Lee Buchheit *Secession* (1978) 129.

[27] For a discussion of Art. 1 of the International Human Rights Covenants, see Chapter 4, pp. 66–9.

[28] UN Doc. A/AL.125/L.32, 12 Apr. 1966.

[29] UN Doc. A/AL.125/L.44, 19 July 1967.

[30] Antonio Cassese *Self-Determination of Peoples* (1995) 46–7.

[31] See *supra* pp. 92–3 for the text of India's declaration.

instruments', the Government of the Netherlands declared, 'would under-mine the concept of self-determination and seriously weaken its universally acceptable character.'[32] Moreover, because self-determination took place whenever the people of a given state or territory were freely able to elect the government of their choice, it could not take place in Communist states, because there was no opportunity for the governed to consent to their government.[33]

When Western states formally acknowledged in Resolution 2625(XXV) that self-determination did indeed constitute a legal right in international law, they did so on the basis that it was a universally applicable principle which should be defined in terms of representative government. The uni-versal nature of the principle was set out in paragraphs 1 and 2, which declared that 'all peoples' had a right to self-determination, and 'all States' a duty to respect that right. The principle was linked to the notion of representative government in paragraph 7, which declared that those states which complied with the principle would be 'possessed of a government representing the whole people belonging to the territory without distinction as to race, creed or colour'. Although decolonization was recognized in paragraph 2 as constituting self-determination, in the light of paragraphs 1, 2, and 7 it constituted only one aspect of the universal right to representa-tive government. The American delegate to the Third Committee of the General Assembly made clear the American position on self-determination when he declared: 'Freedom of choice is indispensable to the experience of self-determination. For this freedom of choice to be meaningful, there must be corresponding freedom of thought, conscience, expression, movement and association. Self-determination entails legitimate lively dissent and testing at the ballot-box with frequent regularity.'[34] This interpretation of self-determination was based largely on the fact that paragraph 7 referred to 'a government representing the whole people of the territory without distinction as to race, creed or colour'.

The European Community has adopted the same position. On 15 Octo-ber 1986 a representative of the United Kingdom, acting on behalf of the member states of the Community, declared in a speech to the Third Com-mittee of the General Assembly:

In accordance with the principles set out in the Charter, the common first article of both International Covenants proclaims the right of self-determination. It is impor-tant to remember that, under the Covenants, self-determination is a right of peoples.

[32] *Multilateral Treaties Deposited With the Secretary-General: Status as at 31 Dec. 1994* New York: United Nations (1995) 113.
[33] Pomerance, 39; Boris Meissner 'The Right of Self-Determination After Helsinki and Its Significance for the Baltic Nations' (1981) 382.
[34] 'US Urges Self-Determination for Peoples Everywhere' (1972) *Department of State Bul-letin* (25 Dec. 1972) 740, 741.

It applies with equal force to all peoples, without discrimination . . . Self-determination is not a single event—one revolution or one election. The exercise of this right is a continuous process. If peoples are to, in the words of the Covenants, 'freely determine their political status and freely pursue their economic, social and cultural development', they must have regular opportunities to choose their governments and their social systems freely, and to change them when they so wish.[35]

For Western states, self-determination therefore means the ongoing right of all citizens within the state to participate in periodic elections which result in a representative government. This understanding of self-determination is reflected in international instruments to which Western states are party, such as the Final Act of the Conference on Security and Co-operation in Europe (CSCE), otherwise known as the Helsinki Declaration.[36] Self-determination was defined in Principle VIII of the Declaration:

The participating states will respect the equal rights of peoples and their right to self-determination, acting at all times in conformity with the purposes and principles of the Charter of the United Nations and with the relevant norms of international law, including those relating to the territorial integrity of States.

By virtue of the principle of equal rights and self-determination of peoples, all peoples always have the right, in full freedom, to determine, when and as they wish, their internal and external political status, without external interference, and to pursue as they wish their political, economic, social and cultural development.

The participating States reaffirm the universal significance of respect for and effective exercise of equal rights and equal self-determination of peoples for the development of friendly relations among themselves as among all States: they also recall the importance of the elimination of any form of violation of this principle.[37]

This text reflects the basic tenets of the Western view of self-determination. The Declaration refers to self-determination as a right which is 'universal'

---

[35] 'United Kingdom Materials on International Law' (1986) 57 *British Yearbook on International Law* 487, 516. The position of Australia with regard to self-determination corresponds very closely to that of the European Community. On 9 Oct. 1984 Australia's representative to the Third Committee of the General Assembly declared that the right of self-determination was not limited by time or by geographical criteria, nor could it be regarded as being guaranteed once and for all by a process of decolonization or by an act of self-determination leading to independence. 'Self-determination implied the continuing right of all peoples and individuals within each nation to participate fully in the political process by various means, including free and fair elections': Jonathan Brown (ed.) *Australian Practice in International Law 1984–1985* (1987) 25.
[36] (1975) 14 ILM 1293. The Declaration was signed on 1 Aug. 1975 by 33 European states, the United States, and Canada. The following European states were signatories to the Declaration: Austria, Belgium, Bulgaria, Cyprus, Czechoslovakia, Denmark, Finland, France, the German Democratic Republic, the Federal Republic of Germany, Greece, the Holy See, Hungary, Iceland, Ireland, Italy, Leichtenstein, Luxembourg, Malta, Monaco, the Netherlands, Norway, Poland, Portugal, Romania, San Marino, the Soviet Union, Spain, Sweden, Switzerland, Turkey, the United Kingdom and Yugoslavia: Harold S. Russell 'The Helsinki Declaration: Brobdingnag or Lilliput?' (1976) 242, fn. 1.
[37] (1975) 14 ILM 1293, 1295.

and applies to 'all peoples'. Because the signatories to the Declaration were all sovereign and independent states, the reference to self-determination in the Declaration represented an affirmation that the principle applied to the peoples of sovereign and independent states as well as to those of non-self-governing territories. Moreover, by using words such as 'always' and 'when and as they wish', the Declaration indicated that self-determination was a continuing right, requiring the periodic consent of those governed.[38]

Since the signing of the Helsinki Declaration, the signatory states have agreed in a number of conferences to more detailed formulations of the Declaration. On 29 June 1990 they adopted the Copenhagen Document, in which it was declared that 'the will of the people, freely and fairly expressed through periodic and genuine elections, is the basis for authority and legitimacy of all government'.[39] On 21 November 1990 the signatory states adopted the Charter of Paris for a New Europe.[40] The Charter reaffirmed 'the equal rights of peoples and their right to self-determination in conformity with the Charter of the United Nations and with the relevant norms of international law, including those relating to territorial integrity of states'.[41] This must be read in the light of the Charter's Preamble, which stated that the ten principles of the Helsinki Declaration would 'guide' the signatory states to a realization of their 'hopes and expectations', by 'steadfast commitment to democracy based on human rights and fundamental freedoms; prosperity through economic liberty and social justice; and equal security for all our countries'.[42] Moreover, they added a provision to the Charter granting all individuals the right 'to participate in free and fair elections'.[43] These provisions underscored the connection made by Western states between self-determination and representative government.[44]

Third World states generally take a different approach to the relationship between self-determination and representative government. To many Third World states decolonization remains the essential element of self-determination. Such states seek to explain the reference to a representative

[38] Antonio Cassese 'The Helsinki Declaration and Self-Determination' in Thomas Buergenthal (ed.) *Human Rights, International Law and the Helsinki Accord* (1977) 100.

[39] (1990) 29 ILM 1305, 1309.

[40] (1991) 30 ILM 190.   [41] *Id.*, 197.   [42] *Id.*, 193.   [43] *Id.*, 194.

[44] It should be noted that neither the Helsinki Declaration nor the Charter of Paris are legally binding instruments. The Helsinki Declaration provides, in its third last paragraph, that 'The Government of the Republic of Finland is requested to transmit to the Secretary-General of the United Nations the text of this Final Act, which is not eligible for registration under Art. 102 of the Charter of the United Nations . . .': (1975) 14 ILM 1293, 1325. Similarly, the Charter of Paris provides that it was 'not eligible for registration under Art. 102 of the Charter of the United Nations': (1991) 30 ILM 190, 208. For a detailed discussion of the legal nature of the Helsinki Declaration, see P. van Dijk 'The Final Act of Helsinki: Basis for a Pan-European System?' (1980) 106–9. Although neither the Helsinki Declaration nor the Charter of Paris are legally binding instruments, Thomas Franck has argued that the right of self-determination must now be equated to that of representative government, as a result of international practice: 'The Emerging Right to Democratic Governance' (1992) 46.

government in paragraph 7 of Resolution 2625(XXV) by arguing that the phrase 'a government representing the whole people belonging to the territory without distinction as to race, creed or colour' simply means that the government must be non-racist in composition. In other words, it means that no element of the population can be specifically excluded from government, as in an apartheid regime.[45] A variation of this interpretation is provided by Arangio-Ruiz, who argues that the purpose of paragraph 7 was to protect multi-racial states by providing such states with a presumption of compliance to the requirement that they possess 'a government representing the whole people without distinction as to race, creed and colour'.[46]

In practice, Third World states have endorsed the representative government theory of self-determination when it has been clear that the government of a particular state was not representative of the entire people. Thus the General Assembly regularly condemned the apartheid regime in South Africa as being contrary to the principle of self-determination. In Resolution 2396(XXII) of 2 December 1968, for example, the General Assembly reaffirmed 'the urgent necessity of eliminating the policies of apartheid so that the people of South Africa as a whole can exercise their right to self-determination and attain majority rule based on universal suffrage'. Similarly, when the white minority Government of the non-self-governing territory of Rhodesia unilaterally declared its independence on 11 November 1965, the General Assembly responded by adopting Resolution 2024(XX). This Resolution condemned 'the unilateral declaration of independence made by the racialist minority of Southern Rhodesia', and called upon the United Kingdom 'to put an end to the rebellion by the unlawful authorities of Southern Rhodesia'. The following day the Security Council, in Resolution 216, called upon all states 'not to recognise this illegal racist minority regime in Southern Rhodesia and to refrain from rendering any assistance to this illegal regime'. A second resolution of the Security Council, adopted on 20 November 1965, asserted that the declaration of independence had 'no legal validity'.[47] The United Nations refused to recognize the emergence of a non-self-governing territory into independent statehood when it became apparent that its government was not representative of the entire population.[48]

---

[45] Cassese (1977) 90; Pomerance, 39.

[46] 'The Normative Role of the General Assembly of the United Nations and the Declaration of Principles of Friendly Relations' (1972) Vol. 3, 570.

[47] Security Council Resolution 217, para. 3 (1965).

[48] See J. E. S. Fawcett 'Security Council Resolutions on Rhodesia' (1965–66) 112; James Crawford *The Creation of States in International Law* (1979) 103–6. For a more detailed discussion of the Rhodesian situation, see Jericho Nkala *The United Nations, International Law and the Rhodesian Independence Crisis* (1985) and Vera Gowlland-Debbas *Collective Responses to Illegal Aspects in International Law* (1990). In *Madzimbamuto* v. *Lardner-Burke* (1969) 1 AC 645 the Privy Council refused to recognize that Rhodesia had attained any status as an independent state.

4. SELF-DETERMINATION AND ETHNIC GROUPS

Ethnic groups frequently claim to have a right to self-determination on the basis that they are 'peoples', and are therefore entitled to determine their own political status. As seen in Chapter 1, this notion of self-determination originated in Central and Eastern Europe and grew out of the phenomenon of nationalism.[49] The unification of Germany and Italy in the nineteenth century and the creation of nation-states such as Poland and Czechoslovakia after the First World War constituted acts of self-determination consistent with this understanding of the principle.

Although ethnic self-determination was an extremely powerful political force in Europe throughout the nineteenth and early twentieth centuries, theorists assumed that it would inevitably decline in importance, on the basis that nationalism was a transitory phenomenon. Modern technology, communications, and economic interdependence, it was thought, would lead to greater understanding and acceptance amongst ethnic groups, and this in turn would result in their social and political integration into larger and more heterogeneous communities.[50]

However, ethnic self-determination, has not disappeared with the advent of modern technology and greater economic interdependence. Modern technology has in fact had the opposite effect:[51] modern technology enables much greater contact between ethnic groups. This heightens each group's consciousness of its own peculiar identity, because the differences recognized in other groups highlight the criteria which make up the group's identity.[52] Economic interdependence has also contributed to increased ethnic consciousness, because the economic differences which can result from unequal distributions of resources or industries often coincide with ethnic divisions. Economic status can thus become associated with membership of a particular ethnic group.[53]

Modern technology and the increase in economic interdependence throughout the world, far from decreasing nationalism, have stimulated ethnic awareness, which in turn intensifies nationalist sentiment among many ethnic groups. The power of nationalist sentiment has been most clearly evinced in recent times in Central and Eastern Europe, where

---

[49] See Chapter 1, pp. 4–6.

[50] Anthony H. Birch 'Minority Nationalist Movements and Theories of Political Integration' (1977) 327; Harris O. Schoenberg 'Limits of Self-Determination' (1976) 93.

[51] Walker O'Connor 'The Politics of Ethnonationalism' (1973) 3, 4; Richard Pipes 'Nationality Problems in the Soviet Union' in Nathan Glazer and Daniel P. Moynihan (eds.) *Ethnicity* (1975) 454, 455; Wood, 116. See also Dov Ronen *The Quest for Self-Determination* (1979).

[52] John R. Wood 'Secession: A Comparative Analytical Framework' (1981) 116.

[53] René Lemarchand 'The Limits of Self-Determination: The Case of the Katanga Secession' (1962) 415.

nationalism was a primary contributing factor in the dissolution of the Soviet Union, Yugoslavia, and Czechoslovakia.[54]

Nationalism has also become a potent political factor in Western Europe, where minority ethnic groups had traditionally sought simply to preserve their particular cultural, religious, or linguistic attributes. In the 1960s, however, such groups became much more demanding as their sense of nationalism grew.[55] They began to seek increased political autonomy and, in some cases, the creation of independent nation-states. Political parties which were nationalist in orientation grew in popularity. In the United Kingdom there has been a growth of support over the past thirty years for nationalist parties among the Scottish and the Welsh.[56] In France there has been a similar rise in nationalist parties amongst the Bretons, the Corsicans, and the Alsatians[57] and in Spain amongst the Basques and the Catalans.[58] Canada is yet another Western state in which minority ethnic nationalism has grown steadily. In the predominantly French-speaking province of Québec there has been increasing support over the past several decades for the proposal that Québec should secede from Canada and form an independent nation-state.[59]

There has also been an increase in awareness of ethnic differences amongst the populations of many Third World states. During the colonial period, the nationalism which developed amongst the populations of Third World territories was largely anti-colonial in nature. Anti-colonial nationalism was able to create a sense of unity amongst diverse ethnic groups within a colony by focusing opposition on the European imperial power and by emphasizing the common racial character of the colonized population as against that of the colonizer.[60] However, once independence was attained

---

[54] See pp. 108–24 *infra* for a discussion of the role of nationalism in the dissolution of the Soviet Union and Yugoslavia.

[55] Phillip Rawkins 'Living in the House of Power: Welsh Nationalism and the Dilemma of Antisystem Politics' in Edward A. Tiryakian and Ronald Rogowski (eds.) *New Nationalisms of the Developed West* (1985) 308.

[56] *Id.*, 294 *et seq*; Alan Butt Philip *The Welsh Question* (1975); Louis L. Snyder *Varieties of Nationalism* (1976) 152–7; Christopher Harvie *Scotland and Nationalism* (1977); Keith Webb *The Growth of Nationalism in Scotland* (1977); Jack Brand *The National Movement in Scotland* (1978); John Mercer *Scotland: The Devolution of Power* (1978); Franjo Tudjman *Nationalism in Contemporary Europe* (1981) 74–7.

[57] Rawkins, 308; Tudjman, 77–9.

[58] Snyder, 150–2; Rawkins, 308; Tudjman, 79–84; Oriol Pi-Sunyer 'Catalan Nationalism' (1985) 254; Michael S. Carter 'Ethnic Minority Groups and Self-Determination: The Case of the Basques' (1986) 55; Joxerramon Bengoetxea 'Nationalism and Self-Determination: the Basque Case' (1991) 133.

[59] C. Michael MacMillan 'Language Issues and Nationalism in Québec' (1987) 229; Pierre Corbeil and André Montambault 'Secession and Independence for Québec: How Legitimate?' (1990) 181; Cassese (1995) 248–54. For a statement of the Canadian position on self-determination, see 'Canadian Practice in International Law' (1989) 27 *Canadian Yearbook of International Law* 373, 378. Canada does not recognize secession as a part of self-determination: *id.*, 378.

[60] Smith, 104, 105.

the *raison d'être* for this unity disappeared, and ethnic considerations then increasingly formed the basis for identification. As elsewhere, the spread of modern technology increased the opportunities for ethnic groups to make comparisons and observe differences, which in turn resulted in a heightened sense of their own separate identity. Cobbah notes that after two to three decades of independence many African states are 'fraught with ethnic conflicts of all sorts'.[61] Mazrui makes the same point, declaring that 'Africans are far more likely to kill each other because they belong to different ethnic groups than because they belong to different religions'.[62] Asian states have also experienced considerable ethnic conflict in the post-colonial era: in India, for example, there has been ongoing unrest resulting from ethnic, religious, and linguistic differences. The most serious conflicts in India have given rise to secessionist movements which are active in Nagaland, Kashmir, and the Punjab.[63] Disaffected ethnic groups in India have managed to create new states for themselves within the Indian federal system or to alter the boundaries of existing states so that their particular group is concentrated within one state and thus better able to control political events in that state.[64] In addition, there have been serious ethnic problems in China, Indonesia, Malaysia, Burma, and Sri Lanka.[65]

The notion that a particular ethnic group may achieve self-determination raises the issue of secession: a process which conflicts with the principle of the territorial integrity of states. Most states have been very reluctant to recognize secession as a part of self-determination, and therefore deny that ethnic groups have any right to self-determination. According to the Western tradition, self-determination occurs within the established boundaries of the state, not through secession from that state. The United States fought a civil war to prevent its own southern states from seceding, and the US Supreme Court has held that the Union of the American states is 'perpetual' in nature.[66] In 1952 Eleanor Roosevelt, the US representative to the United Nations, explicitly denied that the principle of self-determination included the right to secession:

---

[61] Josiah A. M. Cobbah 'Towards a Geography of Peace in Africa: Redefining Sub-State Self-Determination Rights' in R. L. Johnston, David B. Knight, and Eleanore Kofman (eds.) *Nationalism, Self-Determination and Political Geography* (1988) 70, 71.

[62] Ali M. Mazrui *The African Condition* (1980) 96.

[63] Hannum, 151–76.

[64] Jyotirinda Das Gupta 'Ethnicity, Language Demands, and National Development in India' (1975) 482–6; Hannum, 171–3.

[65] Hannum, 280–307, 420–7, 440–8; Ronald D. Renard 'The Karen Rebellion in Burma' in Ralph R. Premdas, S. W. R. de A. Samarasinghe, and Alan B. Anderson (eds.) *Secessionist Movements in Comparative Perspective* (1990) 93; K. M. de Silva 'Separatism in Sri Lanka: The "Traditional Homelands" of the Tamils' *op. cit.* (1990) 32; S. W. R. de A. Samarasinghe 'The Dynamics of Separatism: The Case of Sri Lanka' *op. cit.* (1990) 48; Nihal Jayawickrama 'The Right of Self-Determination: A Time for Reinvention and Renewal' (1993) 5–10.

[66] *Texas* v. *White* 74 US (7 Wall.) 700, 725 (1869).

Does self-determination mean the right of secession? Does self-determination constitute a right of fragmentation or a justification for the fragmentation of states? Does self-determination mean the right of a people to sever association with another power regardless of the economic effect upon both parties, regardless of the effect upon their internal stability and their external security, regardless of the effect upon their neighbours or the international community? Obviously not.[67]

The United States also opposed the secession of Katanga from the Congo, Biafra from Nigeria, and Bangladesh from Pakistan.[68]

Most Third World states also maintain that self-determination does not include secession or any alteration of a state's boundaries. A newly independent state must retain exactly the same boundaries as the colony from which it emerged. Once independent, the territorial integrity of that state must remain sacrosanct. The OAU Charter declares in its Preamble that member states will 'safeguard and consolidate the hard-won independence as well as the sovereignty and territorial integrity of our States'.[69] Article II declares that one of the purposes of the Organization is 'to defend their sovereignty, their territorial integrity, and independence'.[70] Article III states that members 'solemnly affirm and declare their adherence' to the principles of 'non-interference in the internal affairs of States' and 'respect for the sovereignty and territorial integrity of each State and for its inalienable right to independent existence'.[71] The declarations in the OAU Charter on the inviolability of territorial integrity have been reinforced by the 1964 OAU 'Resolution on Border Disputes'.[72] This affirmed that the borders of African states, on the day of their independence, constituted a 'tangible reality', and declared that member states were pledged to respect those frontiers.[73] This affirmation of territorial integrity regulates not only inter-state conduct, but 'even those territorial changes that may originate from conflicts internal to individual states'.[74] This was made clear by the OAU 'Resolution on the Situation in Nigeria' (1967), in which the membership of the OAU declared its 'condemnation of secession in Member States'.[75]

Unlike most Western and Third World states, the Soviet Union and its Communist allies in Central and Eastern Europe maintained that specific ethnic groups did have a right to self-determination which could be exer-

---

[67] (1952) *Department of State Bulletin* 917, 919.

[68] Buchheit, 118–9. The United States is, however, willing to countenance the division of non-self-governing territories into separate entities, as evidenced by US policy with regard to the transformation of the Trust Territory of Micronesia into a number of separate states. For a discussion of Micronesia see Chapter 8, pp. 186–7.

[69] (1963) 479 UNTS 39, 70.   [70] *Id.*, 72.   [71] *Id.*, 74.

[72] I. Brownlie *Basic Documents in African Affairs* (1971) 360.

[73] *Id.*, 360–1.

[74] Onyeonoro S. Kamenu 'Secession and the Right of Self-Determination: An OAU Dilemma' (1974) 355.

[75] Brownlie, 364.

cised through secession. The Soviet position was first advocated by Lenin. It was adopted in order to placate the national minorities within the Tsarist Empire and to win them over to the Bolshevik cause.[76] In Soviet theory, self-determination was traditionally associated not only with anti-colonialism but also with the desires of ethnic groups. Soviet writers routinely defined a people entitled to self-determination on the basis of ethnic criteria, and asserted that such peoples had a right to secede if they so desired. D. B. Levin, for example, declared a 'people' to be those 'possessing a common territory, and most often a common language, who are united by a community of aims in the struggle for liberation'.[77] This right to self-determination, in his opinion, included the 'freedom of state succession and the formation of an independent state'.[78] The right to secede was even enshrined in the 1977 Soviet Constitution: Article 70 declared the Soviet Union to be 'an integral, federal, multinational state formed on the principle of socialist federalism as a result of the free self-determination of nations and the voluntary association of equal Soviet Socialist Republics'.[79] Article 72 gave each Union Republic within the Soviet Union 'the right freely to secede from the USSR'.[80]

Self-determination, however, was always understood in Communist theory to be subordinate to the right of the working class to consolidate and strengthen its power. The relationship of self-determination to the higher right of the working class was first discussed by Stalin in 1923, when he held the post of People's Commissioner of Nationalities. 'The right of self-determination', Stalin wrote, 'cannot and must not serve as an obstacle to the working class in exercising its right to dictatorship. The former must yield to the latter'.[81] In 1955, at the Geneva Conference of Foreign Minis-

---

[76] See Chapter 2, pp. 18–19.   [77] Levin, 47.   [78] *Id.*, 47.
[79] Albert P. Blaustein and Gisbert H. Flanz (eds.) *Constitutions of the Countries of the World* Binder XVII (1989) 31.
[80] *Id.*, 31. The Chinese Communist Party initially followed the Soviet line on secession, but subsequently departed from it. At the first All-China Soviet Congress in 1931 the Chinese Communist Party declared in the Constitution of the Kiangsi Soviet that it recognized the right of self-determination for the national minorities of China, including their right to separate from China and to form independent states. By 1949, however, when the Communists had assumed control over the entire mainland, they were no longer willing to discuss rights of secession, but rather only the possiblity of creating 'autonomous regions'. In the 1975 Constitution, secession was ruled out as an alternative for China's national minorities. Art. 4 of the Constitution declared that the 'People's Republic of China is a unitary multi-national State. The areas where regional national autonomy is exercised are all inalienable parts of the People's Republic of China': Buchheit, 101, 102; Lucian W. Pye 'China: Ethnic Minorities and National Security' (1975) 494–5; Arthur Rosett 'Legal Structures for Special Treatment of Minorities in the People's Republic of China' (1991) 1510. This was reaffirmed in para. 3 of Art. 4 of the 1982 Constitution, which declares: 'All the national autonomous areas are inalienable parts of the People's Republic of China': Blaustein and Flanz (eds.) *Constitutions of the Countries of the World* Binder IV (1991) 1.
[81] Josef Stalin 'Reply to the Discussion on National Factors in Party and State Affairs' (1953) Vol. 5, 269–70.

ters, Molotov stated that the Soviet Union would not consider any settlement of the German problem which might have the effect of 'jeopardizing the social achievements of the workers in the German Democratic Republic'.[82] The subordinate position of self-determination in relation to the 'right' of the working class meant that in practice the Soviet Union was able to disregard self-determination whenever it was inimical to its interests; as a result the position of the Soviet Union with regard to secession was in reality little different from that of Western and Third World states.

The antipathy of states to secession has been reflected in the practice of the United Nations. Up to the post-cold-war period, the United Nations demonstrated a marked reluctance to permit unilateral secession or to recognize entities which had unilaterally seceded as independent states. In 1960 the United Nations authorized military assistance to the newly independent Congo; this effectively prevented the secession of the province of Katanga from the Congo.[83] In 1968 the United Nations refused to involve itself in the Nigerian conflict and would not permit Biafran authorities to address the General Assembly.[84] In 1983 when Turkish Cypriots seceded from Cyprus and formed the independent Turkish Republic of Northern Cyprus, the United Nations refused to recognize the new state, condemning the secession as illegal.[85] Following the unilateral secession of Bangladesh from Pakistan in 1971, the United Nations did permit Bangladesh to become a member state of the General Assembly in 1974. It was noted by some commentators, however, that the circumstances in which Bangladesh seceded were unique, given that Bangladesh was geographically separate

---

[82] Kazimierz Grzybowski *Soviet Public International Law* (1970) 144. See also Ilya Levkov 'Self-Determination in Soviet Politics' 169. Art. 1 of the 1968 Constitution of the German Democratic Republic basically reiterated Molotov's position: 'The German Democratic Republic is a socialist State of German nationhood. It is the political organization of the working people in town and countryside who, together under the leadership of the working class and its Marxist-Leninist party, make socialism a reality': Blaustein and Flanz (eds.) *Constitutions of the Countries of the World*, Binder V (1989) (1968) 26. The Soviet Union similarly justified its invasion of Czechoslovakia in 1968 on the basis that the events taking place there did not serve to strengthen the working class as represented by the Communist Party and were therefore contrary to the principles of socialist internationalism: 'Sovereignty and International Duties of Socialist Countries' *Pravda*, 25 Sep. 1968, reproduced in (1968) 7 ILM 1323, 1324. The United States, on the other hand, condemned the Soviet invasion of Czechoslovakia as a violation, *inter alia*, of Czechoslovakia's right to self-determination: '... the Soviet-led invasion, occupation, and political control of Czechoslovakia constitute a violation of the principle of equal rights and self-determination of peoples. They constitute a violation of the right of the people of Czechoslovakia to determine their future in conditions of peace and tranquility. The fundamental right of self-determination—and the duty of others to respect it—is a right of all peoples everywhere. That right, too, has been denied the people of Czechoslovakia by the invasion and occupation': (1968) 7 ILM 1317, 1319.

[83] Susan E. Himmer 'The Achievement of Independence in the Baltic States and its Justifications' (1992) 274.

[84] See Chapter 8, pp. 195–9 for a discussion of the attempted secession of Biafra.

[85] In the case of Cyprus there was the additional factor of Turkish intervention. See Chapter 9, pp. 222–9, for a discussion of the situation in Cyprus.

from West Pakistan as well as being ethnically different in the composition of its population. Bangladesh could not therefore be seen as establishing a general precedent for unilateral secession.[86]

Because states have sought to discourage secession and to maintain their territorial integrity, and because nationalism remains such a powerful motivating force amongst many ethnic groups, tension still remains between the desire to maintain the territorial integrity of states, on one hand, and to accommodate the desires of ethnic groups to determine their own political status, on the other.

5. POST COLD-WAR DEVELOPMENTS IN CENTRAL AND EASTERN EUROPE

The most dramatic recent manifestations of nationalism have occurred in Central and Eastern Europe: the Soviet Union, Yugoslavia, and Czechoslovakia have all disintegrated as a result of nationalist pressures.

Nationalism remained a potent and potentially divisive force in the Soviet Union from the time of the Revolution.[87] The population of the Soviet Union consisted of a large number of ethnic groups: according to the 1979 Soviet census, there were ninety-two distinct ethnic groups. Russians comprised the largest group, forming approximately 52 per cent of the population. Ukrainians comprised 16.2 per cent of the population, Uzbeks 4.7 per cent, Byelorussians 3.6 per cent, Kazakhs 2.5 per cent, Tatars 2.4 per cent, and Azerbaijanis 2.1 per cent. Tajiks, Armenians, Moldavians, and Lithuanians accounted for between 1 and 2 per cent each, and the remaining eighty-one groups together constituted less than 1 per cent of the population.[88]

Under the Soviet Constitution, the constituent republics and other autonomous regions were organized on an ethnic basis, within a federal structure, in order to accommodate the largest ethnic groups within the state. Fifteen 'Union Republics' had been established, each of which contained a majority of the members of a particular ethnic group within its territory. Within the boundaries of the Union Republics there were an additional twenty Autonomous Republics and seven Autonomous Provinces, where other ethnic groups formed a majority of the population.[89] The Union Republics, however, exercised very little real power, because the Constitution granted extensive powers to the Central Government.[90] The highly

---

[86] See, for example, James Crawford *The Creation of States in International Law* (1979) 116.
[87] See Chapter 2, pp. 17–22.
[88] Hannum, 96, 97.
[89] Hannum, 361.
[90] The extent of the Central Government's power may be seen from Art. 73 of the 1977 Constitution. This conferred jurisdiction on the Central Government to establish 'general

centralized nature of the state permitted Soviet authorities to suppress expressions of nationalism amongst the various ethnic groups within the country. Nationalism was condemned as a 'bourgeois deviation', and those who advocated secession were imprisoned for anti-state activities.[91] Political unity within the Soviet Union was maintained through the imposition upon all aspects of society of a monolithic ideology, under the direction of a single political party.[92]

The enforced unity produced by this combination of centralization, oppression, and ideological uniformity began to break down after the introduction of the policies of *glasnost* and *perestroika*. With the liberalization of Soviet society, unity could no longer be maintained through oppression. The free speech and proliferation of ideas which resulted from the policy of *glasnost* undermined the dominance of Communist theory as the single, unifying ideology of Soviet society. When the Communist Party decided in February 1990 to abrogate the constitutional guarantees which had made it the sole legal party in the Soviet Union, it weakened its own role as a unifying institution in the country.[93] Many of the new political parties formed subsequently were nationalist in orientation, such as *Sajudis*, the Lithuanian nationalist mass movement, and *Rukh*, the Ukrainian nationalist movement.

Although nationalism in the Soviet Union had been suppressed for decades, it had continued to exist as a powerful, if latent, force amongst ethnic groups. The large-scale migration of Russians into non-Russian territories contributed to nationalist tensions. The non-Russian territories of the Soviet Union had long been 'the homelands of major nationalities, many of

principles for the organization and functioning of republican and local bodies of state authority and administration' (para. 3), to ensure 'uniformity of legislative norms throughout the USSR and establishment of the fundamentals of the legislation of the Union of Soviet Socialist Republics and Union Republics' (para. 4), to pursue 'a uniform social and economic policy' and to direct 'the country's economy' (para. 5), to ensure 'conformity of the Constitutions of the Union Republics to the Constitution of the USSR (para. 11), and the 'settlement of other matters of All-Union importance' (para. 12). Art. 74 declared that in 'the event of a discrepancy between Union Republic law and an All-Union law, the law of the USSR shall prevail': Blaustein and Flanz (eds.) *op. cit.* 'The Union of the Soviet Socialist Republic' 31, 32.

[91] Pipes, 463; Hannum, 365.

[92] The power of the Communist Party and the pervasiveness of Communist ideology within Soviet society can be seen from Art. 6 of the 1977 Constitution: '1. The leading and guiding force of Soviet society and the nucleus of its political system, of all state organizations and public organizations, is the Communist Party of the Soviet Union. The CPSU exists for the people and serves the people. 2. The Communist Party, armed with Marxism-Leninism, determines the general perspectives of the development of society and the course of the home and foreign policy of the USSR, directs the great constructive work of the Soviet people, and imparts a planned, systematic and theoretically substantial character to their struggle for the victory of communism. 3. All party organizations shall function within the framework of the Constitution of the USSR': Blaustein and Flanz (eds.) *op. cit.* 'The Union of the Soviet Socialist Republics' 21.

[93] Richard F. Starr (ed.) *Yearbook on International Communist Affairs 1991* (1991) 361.

them with cultures entirely different from the Russian, some with traditions of statehood reaching back to the pre-Christian era'.[94] The steady migration of Russians into these territories led to bitter conflicts with the local populations over scarce land, housing, and jobs, and this in turn led to the development of deep resentments and animosities on the part of local populations against ethnic Russians.[95] These sentiments found expression in the nationalist parties which proliferated in the era of *glasnost* and *perestroika*. The ultimate goal of the nationalist parties was to secede from the Soviet Union and to transform their particular Union Republics into independent nation-states. Because the nationalist parties operated solely within the confines of their own particular Union Republic, they were often able to command majority support from the local ethnic population, and were therefore able either to assume control of the Union Republic or to exert significant influence on its political direction.

In response to these nationalist movements the Central Government undertook to revise the 1922 Union Treaty which had originally created the Soviet Union.[96] On 24 July 1991 the Central Government announced that the terms of a new union arrangement had been agreed upon with nine of the Union Republics. Under the terms of the new treaty substantial powers would be transferred to the republics. The terms of the proposed treaty were not acceptable to conservative elements within the Communist Party. On 19 August 1991, the day before the new treaty was to be signed, these elements staged a coup to prevent its implementation. The coup collapsed within three days, but the failure to implement the treaty caused thirteen of the fifteen Union Republics to declare independence from the Soviet Union within the following two months.[97]

The international community initially responded to the centrifugal forces of nationalism at work in the Soviet Union by seeking to discourage those forces and to advocate the continued territorial integrity of the Soviet Union. Throughout 1991 the United States pursued a policy which sought to promote some form of unity amongst the constituent republics of the

[94] Pipes, 463.   [95] *Id.*, 463.

[96] Arthur S. Banks (ed.) *Political Handbook of the World 1990* (1990) 668. Following the Russian Revolution, the Bolsheviks established, on 10 July 1918, a state known as the Russian Socialist Federated Soviet Republic (RSFSR). Soviet republics were also established in the Ukraine, Byelorussia, and Transcaucasia. In 1922 the Union of Soviet Socialist Republics was formed through the federation of these four republics: Hannum, 359. The Transcaucasian Republic became the three Union Republics of Armenia, Azerbaijan, and Georgia in 1936: Banks (ed.) 664.

[97] Estonia declared its independence on 20 Aug. 1991; Latvia on 23 Aug.; the Ukraine on 24 Aug.; Byelorussia on 25 Aug.; Azerbaijan on 30 Aug.; Uzbekistan on 31 Aug.; Tadjikistan on 9 Sep.; and Turkmenistan on 27 Oct. Lithuania and Georgia had declared their independence prior to the coup, on 11 Mar. 1990 and 9 Apr. 1991, respectively. Armenia had declared its sovereignty on 23 Aug. 1990, and announced that it would work to full independence over five years: Keesing's *Record of World Events* (1991) Vol. 37, 38372–3, 38538.

Soviet Union; President Bush delivered a speech in Kiev on 1 August 1991 in which he warned against the dangers of 'suicidal nationalism'.[98] When the United States indicated on 2 September 1991 that it would re-establish diplomatic relations with the Baltic states, Secretary of State James Baker made it clear that similar action would not be taken with the remaining twelve republics.[99] Other Western states, such as the United Kingdom, France, Germany, Italy, and the Netherlands also initially demonstrated considerable reluctance in recognizing entities seceding from the Soviet Union as independent states.[100]

Once it became apparent that the dissolution of the Soviet Union was inevitable, there was a significant shift in the position of Western states. They began to call on the various Union Republics to regularize their emergence into independent statehood through a formal agreement. Agreement was considered essential in order to establish that the dissolution had occurred with the consent of all concerned.[101] International law does not prohibit consensual dissolution and there have in fact been many instances of consensual dissolution in the twentieth century.[102]

The consensual dissolution of the Soviet Union depended upon an orderly devolution of power to the successor states: this could only occur if territorial disputes amongst the successor states could be avoided. In order to ensure that such disputes did not arise, the United States and the member states of the European Community insisted that the internal boundaries of the former constituent republics be recognized as the international boundaries of the new successor states. This would also ensure that the process of dissolution would occur only at the level of the constituent republics; but it also meant that ethnic minorities within a particular constituent republic would be unable to unite with the same ethnic group in an adjoining republic. It was therefore necessary to ensure that those ethnic

[98] (1991) 2 *US Department of State Dispatch* (No. 32, 12 Aug. 1991) 597.

[99] (1991) 2 *US Department of State Dispatch* (No. 36, 9 Sep. 1991) 667. The Baltic states had taken the lead throughout 1990 and 1991 in asserting their independence from the Soviet Union. Most Western states were sympathetic to the idea of independence for the Baltic states, but did not consider that such a step would threaten the unity of the Soviet Union because the status of the Baltic states differed from that of the other constituent republics of the Soviet Union. The Baltic states had been illegally incorporated into the Soviet Union in 1940 as a result of the Rippentrop-Molotov Pact, and consequently the United States and most member states of the European Community had never recognized Soviet sovereignty over that territory: Colin Warbrick 'Recognition of States' (1992) 474.

[100] Nicolas Rothwell 'The Yeltsin Challenge' 1991, 26; 'Russia Top Priority as US Plans Links' *Sydney Morning Herald* 26 Dec. 1991, 16; Mary Dejevsky 'Russia "Coming Apart at the Seams"' *The Australian* 2 Jan. 1992, 8.

[101] Marc Weller 'The International Response to the Dissolution of the Socialist Federal Republic of Yugoslavia' (1992) 605.

[102] Examples include the separation of Norway from Sweden (1905), Iceland from Denmark (1944), Senegal from the Mali Federation (1960), Jamaica from the West Indian Federation (1961), and Singapore from Malaysia (1965).

groups which were or would become minorities in the successor states received adequate guarantees for the protection of their rights as minorities. Western states consequently insisted that the rights of minorities be guaranteed within the new states.

This emphasis on the maintenance of internal boundaries and the rights of minorities was reflected in a speech made by US Secretary of State James Baker on 4 September 1991. Baker declared that the policy of the United States with respect to the political changes occurring in the Soviet Union would be governed by five principles: self-determination, respect for borders, support of democracy, safeguarding of human rights, and respect for international law. Baker specified that human rights were to include the 'equal treatment of minorities'.[103] The inviolability of internal frontiers was also insisted upon by the member states of the European Community. In a joint declaration made on 16 December 1991 the member states of the European Community made the inviolability of internal frontiers and the guarantee of minority rights necessary preconditions to formal recognition. The Declaration on the 'Guidelines on the Recognition of New States in Eastern Europe and in the Soviet Union' provided as follows:

The Community and its member States confirm their attachment to the principles of the Helsinki Final Act and the Charter of Paris, in particular the principle of self-determination. They affirm their readiness to recognise, subject to the normal standards of international practice and the political realities in each case, those new States which, following the historic changes in the region, have constituted themselves on a democratic basis, have accepted the appropriate international obligations and have committed themselves in good faith to a peaceful process and to negotiations. Therefore, they adopt a common position on the process of recognition of these new States, which requires:

- respect for the provisions of the Charter of the United Nations and the commitments subscribed to in the Final Act of Helsinki and in the Charter of Paris, especially with regard to the rule of law, democracy and human rights;
- guarantees for the rights of ethnic and national groups and minorities in accordance with the commitments subscribed to in the framework of the CSCE;
- respect for the inviolability of all frontiers which can only be changed by peaceful means and by common agreement;
- acceptance of all relevant commitments with regard to disarmament and nuclear non-proliferation as well as to security and regional stability;
- commitment to settle by agreement, including where appropriate by recourse to arbitration, all questions concerning State succession and regional disputes.

The Community and its member States will not recognise entities which are the result of aggression. They would take account of the effects of recognition on neighbouring States.

---

[103] (1991) 2 *US Department of State Dispatch* (No. 36, 9 Sep. 1991) 667.

The commitment to these principles opens the way to recognition by the Community and its member States to the establishment of diplomatic relations. It could be laid down in agreements.[104]

These requirements for recognition went far beyond the traditional requirements for statehood.[105] However, under the declaratory theory of recognition, it is quite possible for states to lay down additional preconditions for recognition, because recognition is considered to be no more than a political act on the part of a recognizing state which occurs independently of the actual existence of a new state as a subject of international law.[106]

Western efforts to specify parameters for the dissolution of the Soviet Union were successful insofar as eleven of the twelve remaining Union Republics of the Soviet Union agreed to those terms in the Alma Ata Declaration of 16 December 1991.[107] Those states specified in the Declaration that they would recognize 'each other's territorial integrity' and would respect 'human rights and freedoms including the rights of national minorities'.[108] Shortly thereafter the successor states of the Soviet Union received widespread recognition from the international community, and were admitted to the United Nations as member states.[109]

Yugoslavia also disintegrated as a result of conflicting nationalist forces. Like the Soviet Union, Yugoslavia contained a number of distinct ethnic groups. According to the 1981 census Yugoslavia had a population of 22,424,687 persons. Serbs constituted 37 per cent of the population, Croats 20 per cent, Bosnian Muslims 9 per cent, Slovenes and Albanians 8 per cent each, Macedonians 6 per cent, Montenegrins 3 per cent, and Hungarians 2 per cent.[110]

---

[104] (1992) 31 ILM 1486.

[105] Art. 1 of the 1933 Montevideo Convention on Rights and Duties of States lists only 4 qualifications for statehood: (1) a permanent population; (2) a defined territory; (3) government; and (4) capacity to enter into relations with other states: (1936) 165 LNTS 19, 25.

[106] Weller, 588. See Chapter 8, pp. 193–5 for a detailed discussion of the nature and impact of recognition.

[107] (1992) ILM 148. The 11 signatory states were Armenia, Azerbaijan, Byelorussia, Kazakhstan, Kurgystan, Moldova, the Russian Federation, Tajikistan, Turkmenistan, Uzbekistan, and Ukraine. The three Baltic states had already attained independence the previous September and admitted as member states of the United Nations on 17 Sep. 1991.

[108] (1992) ILM 148, 148.

[109] Ukraine and Byelorussia had been members of the United Nations since its inception. Estonia, Latvia, and Lithuania became members of the United Nations on 17 Sep. 1991, pursuant to General Assembly Resolutions 46/4, 46/5 and 46/6, respectively. On 2 Mar. 1992 Moldova, Kazakhstan, Kyrgystan, Uzbekistan, Armenia, Tajikistan, Turkmenistan, and Azerbaijan were admitted to the United Nations pursuant to General Assembly Resolutions 46/223, 46/224, 46/225, 46/226, 46/227, 46/228, 46/229, and 46/230. Georgia was admitted to the United Nations pursuant to General Assembly Resolution 46/241 on 31 July 1992. The Russian Federation assumed the membership of the former Soviet Union, as had been agreed in the Alma Ata Declaration.

[110] Arthur S. Banks (ed.) *Political Handbook of the World: 1990* (1990) 736. The population in 1990 was estimated to be some 23,827,000: *id.*, 736.

Yugoslavia became an independent state on 1 December 1918 as a result of the unification of the states of Serbia and Montenegro and the incorporation of the Austro-Hungarian territories of Croatia, Dalmatia, and Bosnia-Herzegovina.[111] A Communist government assumed power upon the conclusion of the Second World War, and on 29 November 1945 the Federal Peoples' Republic of Yugoslavia was proclaimed. The state was constituted on the basis of equality of the major national groups.[112] To this end six constituent republics were set up within a federal structure. The six constituent republics were Serbia, Croatia, Slovenia, Macedonia, Bosnia-Herzegovina, and Montenegro. The boundaries of the constituent republics corresponded more or less to the territorial distribution of particular ethnic groups, so that each ethnic group inhabited a particular constituent republic. However, some ethnic groups, such as the Serbs, formed significant minorities within constituent republics other than their own. There were also ethnic groups which did not have their own constituent republic, such as the Albanians and Hungarians, who were concentrated respectively in the autonomous provinces of Kosovo and Vojvodina, within Serbia.[113]

The relationship of Yugoslavia's various ethnic groups to each other had long been characterized by hostility and bitterness.[114] In the post-war period ethnic tensions continued to be a major and ongoing source of difficulty. Ethnic tensions had led to the replacement of the 1946 Constitution by the Constitution of 1963, and the replacement of the 1963 Constitution by the Constitution of 1974. Under the 1974 Constitution a Presidential Council directed the affairs of government at the federal level. This Presidential Council amounted to a collective presidency, the chairmanship of which rotated amongst the heads of the constituent republics and autonomous provinces.[115] However, these constitutional revisions failed to resolve ethnic tensions. They also failed to resolve the debate amongst the ethnic groups as to the nature of the federal structure itself. Serbia, Montenegro, and the autonomous province of Vojvodina supported a centralized federal system, whereas Croatia and Slovenia, with some support from Bosnia-Herzegovina, Macedonia, and the autonomous province of Kosovo, were in favour of a loose confederal system.[116]

On 22 January 1990 the Yugoslav Communist Party, emulating the policies of liberalization then being pursued in the Soviet Union, decided to eliminate those provisions in the Constitution which guaranteed it a 'lead-

[111] See Chapter 2, p. 25.

[112] Banks (ed.), 737.

[113] Richard F. Iglar 'The Constitutional Crisis in Yugoslavia and the International Law of Self-Determination: Slovenia's and Croatia's Right to Secede' (1992) 215–6.

[114] See Derek Heater *National Self-Determination* (1994) 167–73 for a discussion of the ethnic conflict in Yugoslavia from 1919 to 1946.

[115] Weller, 569.

[116] Iglar, 216.

ing' political role.[117] Various nationalist parties were formed within the constituent republics. The emergence of these nationalist parties caused a grave deterioration in the constitutional debate, which up to this time had been carried on under the unifying aegis of the Communist Party. In elections held in 1990 the Communist Party lost power in Croatia, Slovenia, Bosnia-Herzegovina and Macedonia. Nationalist parties replaced the Communists. In Serbia and Montenegro, on the other hand, the Communist Party was returned to power. The Communist Party, however, remade itself as a Serbian nationalist party.[118] This meant that every party in power in Yugoslavia in 1990 was essentially nationalist in character. It was thus hardly surprising that the functioning of the Presidential Council became deadlocked in May 1991. The membership refused to appoint the member next in line, a Croat, to the chairmanship; Croatia threatened to secede, prompting the Yugoslav Federal Prime Minister to declare that 'all means available' would be used to prevent secession by any constituent republic. Nevertheless, on 25 June 1991 both Croatia and Slovenia declared their independence. This caused an outbreak of hostilities in Slovenia between Slovenian forces and the Yugoslav Federal Army, which was largely Serbian in composition. Hostilities in Slovenia were short-lived, as the Federal Army decided to withdraw from the region, but hostilities shifted to Croatia. The Croatian declaration of independence had provoked an insurrection amongst Croatia's sizable Serbian population, and the fighting which broke out there involved not only Croatian forces and the Yugoslav Federal Army, but Serbian irregulars from Croatia as well.[119]

Western states responded at first to the crisis in Yugoslavia in much the same way as they had to the crisis in the Soviet Union: by refusing to recognize the dissolution of the state, and attempting instead to preserve its territorial integrity. On 19 June 1991 the Conference on Security and Co-operation in Europe adopted a declaration which expressed support for 'democratic development and territorial integrity in Yugoslavia'. James Baker strongly endorsed this declaration while in Belgrade on 21 June 1991.[120] The United Kingdom, France, and the Netherlands voiced disapproval of the secession of Croatia and Slovenia from Yugoslavia. Hans van den Brock, the Dutch Foreign Minister, declared in August 1991 that 'sepa-

---

[117] Section VIII of the Basic Principles of the 1974 Constitution had declared the Communist Party to be 'the leading organized ideological and political force of the working class and of all working people in the creation of socialism and in the realization of solidarity among the working people and of brotherhood and unity among the nations and nationalities of Yugoslavia': Blaustein and Flanz (eds.) *Constitutions of the Countries of the World*, Supplement 'Yugoslavia' 1991, 42.

[118] Iglar, 217.

[119] Warbrick, 475; Weller, 570. In 1991 ethnic Serbs constituted approximately 11.5% of Croatia's population: Weller, 569.

[120] Weller, 570.

ratism is not the way ahead'. 'The right to self-determination', he continued, 'is not an absolute, unqualified principle—its practical application needs to be squared with other principles.'[121] Early attempts by the European Community to negotiate a ceasefire in Croatia, however, proved unsuccessful, and the fighting there became more widespread and intense. By August 1991 approximately one-third of Croatia had come under the control of Serbian forces.[122]

As the fighting in Croatia worsened and it became increasingly apparent that Yugoslavia would not survive as a single unified state, the policy of the European Community changed. Rather than continuing to call for the preservation of Yugoslavia's territorial integrity, it began to address the issue of Yugoslavia's dissolution into a number of separate states. The policy of the European Community was to obtain the agreement of all parties to the dissolution, and to insist on the maintenance of internal boundaries and the protection of minority rights. On 27 August 1991 the European Community issued a statement in which it resolved 'never to recognize changes of frontiers which have not been brought about by peaceful means and by agreement'. The statement went on to create the European Community Peace Conference on Yugoslavia and established an Arbitration Commission.[123]

The first session of the Peace Conference was held on 7 September 1991. Very little was achieved. The European Community, however, took this opportunity to re-emphasize that the Peace Conference must proceed on the basis that there would be 'no unilateral change of borders by force'.[124] This policy of insisting on the preservation of existing internal borders was also adopted by the Security Council. In Resolution 713 of 25 September 1991 the Security Council declared that no territorial gains or changes brought about by violence would be acceptable.[125]

The situation in Yugoslavia continued to deteriorate. In Croatia fighting continued on a large scale between Croats and Serbs, and repeated attempts to establish a ceasefire were unsuccessful. Fearing domination from Serbia in the absence of a counterbalancing effect from Croatia and Slovenia, Macedonia and Bosnia-Herzegovina also decided to separate from Yugoslavia. On 9 September 1991 74 per cent of the electorate in Macedonia voted in favour of independence.[126] On 15 October 1991 the

---

[121] Nicolas Rothwell 'EC Ready to Broker New Talks on Peace' *The Australian* 14 Aug. 1991, 6.

[122] Keesing's *Record of World Events* (1991) Vol. 37, 38420.

[123] European Political Co-operation (EPC) Declaration of 27 Aug. 1991 (Brussels), EPC Press Release 82/91. The Arbitration Commission came to be known as the Badinter Commission.

[124] Extraordinary EPC Meeting, Declaration on Yugoslavia (The Hague, 3 Sep. 1991), EPC Press Release (4 Sep. 1991).

[125] Weller, 579.   [126] Keesing's *Record of World Events* (1991) Vol. 37, 38420.

Legislature of Bosnia-Herzegovina declared the republic to be a 'sovereign state'. Muslim and Croatian deputies supported the declaration; Serbian deputies did not.[127]

As a result of these developments, the dissolution of Yugoslavia into a number of independent states became inevitable, and the European Community sought to regulate the process of dissolution in as orderly a manner as possible. The preservation of existing internal boundaries, provision for minority rights, and the agreement of all parties involved were considered to be necessary for an orderly dissolution. However, no general agreement to the terms and conditions of Yugoslavia's dissolution was forthcoming. Unlike the situation in the Soviet Union, the dissolution of Yugoslavia proceeded neither peacefully nor with the concurrence of all parties involved. Both the Yugoslav federal authorities (whose membership now comprised representatives from only four of the eight republics and autonomous provinces) and the representatives of Serbia refused to agree to any terms of dissolution.[128] This refusal to acknowledge the dissolution of Yugoslavia, or to enter into any agreement concerning the terms and conditions of the dissolution, prompted the European Community to abandon its policy of seeking to obtain the agreement of all parties to the dissolution, and to adopt instead a position which would permit recognition of the seceding republics without the agreement of all parties to the dissolution. Under the new policy, recognition of the European Community would occur if the entities seeking it agreed to certain conditions laid down by the European Community. The conditions were set out in the joint Declaration of 16 December 1991.[129] The Declaration laid down amongst its conditions for recognition the inviolability of all frontiers and guarantees for the rights of minority groups, as well as specifying that entities which were 'the result of aggression' would not be recognized by the Community.[130] Although the European Community was no longer seeking to obtain the agreement of all parties to the dissolution, it continued to insist on the inviolability of frontiers and safeguarding of minority rights before according recognition to the successor states. Given the intractability of the Yugoslav federal authorities and Serbia, recognition of the constituent republics of Yugoslavia was now seen by the European Community as a means of 'internationalizing' the situation, so that hostilities in Yugoslavia would then be legitimately subject to international security and control, and the boundaries of the new states could not be altered by the actions of the Yugoslav Federal Army.[131]

In addition to the Declaration on Guidelines for Recognition, which

---

[127] *Id.*, 38513.   [128] Weller, 582–3.
[129] Declaration on the 'Guidelines on the Recognition of New States in Eastern Europe and in the Soviet Union (1992) 31 ILM 1486. See pp. 112–13 *supra*. The Declaration, as has already been seen, also applied to the successor states of the Soviet Union: see *supra*, pp. 112–13.
[130] See *supra*, p. 112.   [131] Warbrick, 480.

applied both to the successor states of the Soviet Union and to those of
Yugoslavia, the European Community also issued, on 16 December 1991, a
joint 'Declaration on Yugoslavia',[132] which set out conditions specifically
applicable to the situation in Yugoslavia. The Declaration invited all Yugoslav constituent republics to indicate whether they wished to be recognized
as independent states, and required them to indicate whether they accepted
the conditions set out in the Declaration on Guidelines for Recognition.[133]
In its Declaration on Yugoslavia the European Community further specified that the applications of those constituent republics seeking recognition
as independent states would be submitted to 'the Arbitration Commission
for advice before the implementation date'.[134] The European Community
had created the Arbitration Commission at the same time as it established
its Peace Conference on Yugoslavia, on 27 August 1991. The Commission
was composed of the Presidents of the French Constitutional Council,
the German and Italian Constitutional Courts, the Spanish Constitutional
Tribunal, and the Belgian Court of Arbitration.[135]

Serbia strongly protested against these actions of the European Community, claiming that they constituted 'an aggression against Yugoslavia'.[136]
Slovenia, Croatia, Macedonia, and Bosnia-Herzegovina, on the other hand,
all applied to the European Community for recognition as independent
states. Their applications were submitted to the Arbitration Commission
for its consideration; the Commission dealt with their applications in Opinions 4 to 7, handed down on 11 January 1992.

The Commission found that both Macedonia and Slovenia satisfied the
conditions laid down by the European Community in its Declaration of 16
December 1991 and so qualified for recognition.[137] Croatia was found to
qualify except for the fact that its Constitution of 4 December 1991 did not
make adequate provision for the 'special status' of minorities. The Commission recommended that Croatia amend its Constitution in order to do so.[138]
With regard to Bosnia-Herzegovina, the Commission found that the local
Serb population had not associated itself with the declaration of independence made by the Legislature, nor with constitutional changes subsequently
put forward. The Commission also took note of a declaration made on 10
November 1991 by the 'Serbian people of Bosnia-Herzegovina' that they
wished to remain within Yugoslavia, or, should Bosnia-Herzegovina separate itself from Yugoslavia, to establish a separate Serbian Republic of

---

[132] (1992) 31 ILM 1485.
[133] *Id.*, 1485, 1486.
[134] *Id.*, 1486.
[135] Alain Pellet 'The Opinions of the Badinter Arbitration Committee: A Second Breath for
the Self-Determination of Peoples' (1992) 178.
[136] Weller, 588.
[137] Opinion No. 6 (1992) 31 ILM 1507–12; Opinion No. 7 (1992) 31 ILM 1512–17.
[138] Opinion No. 5 (1992) 31 ILM 1503, 1505.

Bosnia-Herzegovina. Given these findings, the Commission concluded that the will of the peoples of Bosnia-Herzegovina for an independent state had not been fully established. The Commission indicated, however, that this assessment could be reviewed if an internationally supervised referendum were held.

On 15 January 1992 the European Community recognized both Slovenia and Croatia, although Croatia had not altered its Constitution as suggested by the Arbitration Commission,[139] and despite the fact that approximately one-third of Croatia was at that time under the control of the local Serb population, which refused to be a part of an independent Croatia and which had set up a Republic of Serbian Krajina in the areas which it controlled.[140] Macedonia was not recognized by the European Community, even though the Arbitration Commission had indicated that it satisfied the European Community's conditions for recognition. In this regard the Community deferred to the objections of Greece. Greece objected to the recognition of Macedonia on the ground that the name 'Macedonia' had historically been associated with Greeks, rather than with the Slavic people who now inhabited Macedonia. As there was a Greek province known as 'Macedonia', Greece also feared that the state of Macedonia would make territorial claims on its province, even though the Arbitration Commission had found that 'use of the name "Macedonia" could not be taken to imply any territorial claim with respect to another State'.[141] Macedonia remained unrecognized until 8 April 1993, when a compromise solution was found whereby it was admitted to the United Nations under the name of 'the former Yugoslav Republic of Macedonia', pending settlement of its name.[142]

The Arbitration Commission declared in Opinion No. 4 that Bosnia-Herzegovina did not satisfy the European Community's conditions for recognition because popular support for independence had not been sufficiently demonstrated. A referendum on independence was therefore held in Bosnia-Herzegovina on 1 March 1992. Unlike the other constituent republics of Yugoslavia, Bosnia-Herzegovina was not made up of one predominant ethnic group, but was a mixture of Serbs, Croats, and Muslims. Muslims comprised 40 per cent of the population, Serbs 32 per cent, and Croats 18 per cent.[143] The Serbs within Bosnia-Herzegovina had already

---

[139] Weller, 593.

[140] The fighting between Croats and Serbs came to an end in mid-February 1992, when an agreement was reached which permitted the deployment of a United Nations peace-keeping force: Keesing's *Record of World Events* (1992) Vol. 38, 38778–9.

[141] Opinion No. 6 (1992) 31 ILM 1507, 1511.

[142] UN Press Release GA/8474, 8 Apr. 1993. Macedonia was admitted to the UN pursuant to General Assembly Resolution 47/225 of 8 Apr. 1993.

[143] Weller, 569. The Muslims of Bosnia-Herzegovina are the descendants of Slavs who converted to Islam during the Ottoman period. They were categorized in Yugoslavia as a separate ethnic group rather than simply as a religious group.

declared their own Serbian Republic of Bosnia-Herzegovina on 9 January 1992, and many Serbs boycotted the referendum held on 1 March 1992. Nevertheless, of the 63 per cent of the electorate who did vote, an overwhelming majority indicated that they were in favour of independence.[144] As a result, proposals for a new constitution were drafted. These proposals, however, were rejected by Bosnian Serb leaders on 28 March 1992, and intense fighting broke out between Bosnian Serbs, on one hand, and Muslims and Croats on the other. Despite the opposition of the Bosnian Serbs to independence, and despite the widespread fighting which had broken out, Western states nevertheless moved quickly to recognize Bosnia-Herzegovina. The member-states of the European Community and the United States did so on 7 April 1992.[145] Slovenia, Croatia, and Bosnia-Herzegovina were admitted to the United Nations as member states on 22 May 1992.[146]

Fighting in Bosnia-Herzegovina continued largely unabated for the next three years. During this time the Bosnian Serbs gained control over approximately 70 per cent of the territory of Bosnia-Herzegovina. Efforts by the United Nations and the European Community to arrange a political settlement and re-establish peace in the region proved unsuccessful. In a referendum held on 15 May 1993, the Bosnian Serbs overwhelmingly rejected a joint peace plan of the United Nations and the European Community, under which Bosnia-Herzegovina would remain a single, independent state composed of ten autonomous cantons organized on an ethnic basis. Partition of Bosnia-Herzegovina and the establishment of a separate Serbian Republic of Bosnia-Herzegovina was the goal of the Bosnian Serbs.[147]

In August 1995 Croatian forces attacked and overran the Serb held areas of Croatia.[148] In September 1995 Muslim and Croat forces in Bosnia-Herzegovina went on the offensive against Bosnian Serbs. When the offensive came to an end in October 1995, the Bosnian Serbs had lost

---

[144] Weller, 593.

[145] Weller, 597; 'Bush Announces Recognition of Former Yugoslav Republics' *US Information Agency EPF 210*, 7 Apr. 1992. The early recognition of Bosnia-Herzegovina represented a change in US policy, as it had previously cautioned restraint with regard to the recognition of Slovenia and Croatia. In October 1991, Warren Zimmerman, the American ambassador to Yugoslavia, had declared that US recognition of Slovenia and Croatia was 'not on the agenda'. In December 1991 President Bush had described the situation in Yugoslavia as 'fraught with danger' and had indicated that it would be a mistake for the West to act quickly in recognizing Slovenia and Croatia as independent states. The policy of restraint was abandoned with the rapid recognition of Bosnia-Herzegovina. The United States recognized both Slovenia and Croatia at the same time as it recognized Bosnia-Herzegovina.

[146] Slovenia was admitted to the UN pursuant to General Assembly Resolution 46/236; Bosnia-Herzegovina pursuant to General Assembly Resolution 46/237; and Croatia pursuant to General Assembly Resolution 46/238. All 3 resolutions were adopted on 22 May 1992.

[147] Keesing's *Record of World Events* (1993) Vol. 39, 39470.

[148] *Id.*, Vol. 41, 40691–2.

approximately 20 per cent of the territory they had previously occupied.[149] Negotiations for peace were then entered into by the parties, resulting in the signing of a peace agreement by the leaders of Bosnia-Herzegovina, Croatia, and Serbia on 14 December 1995. Under the terms of this agreement, Bosnia-Herzegovina remained a sovereign state within its internationally recognized boundaries. It was, however, divided into two entities: the Muslim-Croat Federation of Bosnia-Herzegovina, which controlled 51 per cent of the territory, and the Serb Republic, which controlled 49 per cent. A federal system was put in place, but the federal government had jurisdiction only in the areas of foreign policy, foreign trade, customs policy, immigration, monetary policy, international and inter-entity transportation, air traffic control, and the financing of government operations and obligations. The two entity governments had jurisdiction over all other matters. Moreover, the entity governments were entitled to enter into special relations with neighbouring states (such as Serbia and Croatia), although such arrangements had to respect the sovereignty and territorial integrity of Bosnia-Herzegovina. The three ethnic groups of Bosnia-Herzegovina were also permitted under the agreement to maintain their own separate armies. The agreement thus preserved the *de jure* sovereignty and territorial integrity of Bosnia-Herzegovina, but effectively created two separate *de facto* entites.[150]

In Yugoslavia itself, the departure of four of the six constituent republics forced the remaining two constituent republics to reconstitute the state. On 27 April 1992 the remaining members of the Yugoslav Federal Parliamentary Assembly, in conjunction with the National Assembly of Serbia and the Assembly of Montenegro, adopted a new constitution, and created the 'Federal Republic of Yugoslavia'. They declared that the Federal Republic of Yugoslavia was the sole successor state to the Socialist Federal Republic of Yugoslavia, on the basis that international legal continuity had been preserved from the Socialist Federal Republic of Yugoslavia to the Federal Republic of Yugoslavia.[151] In response, the European Community requested three additional Opinions from the Arbitration Commission. These were handed down by the Commission on 4 July 1992. In Opinion No. 8 the Arbitration Commission found that the dissolution of the Socialist Federal Republic of Yugoslavia was complete and that that state no longer existed.[152] In Opinion No. 9 the Commission found that no single successor state to the Socialist Federal Republic of Yugoslavia could claim continued membership in any international organization.[153] In Opinion No. 10 the

---

[149] *Id.*, 40735, 40780.

[150] Bosnia and Herzegovina-Croatia-Yugoslavia: General Framework Agreement for Peace in Bosnia and Herzegovina with Annexes (1996) 35 ILM 75, 118–25.

[151] Weller, 595; Yehuda Z. Blum 'UN Membership of the "New" Yugoslavia: Continuity or Break?' (1992) 833.   [152] (1992) 31 ILM 1521–3.   [153] *Id.*, 1523–5.

Commission found that the reconstituted Federal Republic of Yugoslavia was in fact a new state and not a continuation of the former Socialist Federal Republic of Yugoslavia. Consequently, the Federal Republic of Yugoslavia had to obtain recognition from the European Community on the same basis as the other constituent republics of Yugoslavia which had become independent.[154] The European Community refused to acknowledge the Federal Republic of Yugoslavia as the sole successor state to the Socialist Federal Republic of Yugoslavia and demanded instead that it seek recognition from the Community on the basis of the Community's two Declarations of 16 December 1991.

This was also the position adopted by the United Nations. In Resolution 757 of 30 May 1992 the Security Council declared that 'the claim of the Federal Republic of Yugoslavia (Serbia and Montenegro) to continue automatically the membership of the former Socialist Federal Republic of Yugoslavia in the United Nations has not been generally accepted'. In Resolution 777 of 19 September 1992 the Security Council declared that the former Socialist Federal Republic of Yugoslavia had 'ceased to exist'; the new Federal Republic of Yugoslavia could not therefore simply continue the membership of the previous state. The Security Council recommended to the General Assembly that the Federal Republic of Yugoslavia not participate in the work of the General Assembly, but rather 'apply for membership in the United Nations'. The Security Council's recommendation was endorsed by the General Assembly in its Resolution 47/1 of 22 September 1992.[155]

State practice has been very important with regard to the dissolution of the Soviet Union and of Yugoslavia. The emphasis placed by Western states on the preservation of existing internal boundaries and guarantees of minority rights constitutes an attempt to contain the dissolution within certain defined and predictable limits. However, it also represents an attempt by Western states to impose a definition of self-determination which conforms more to the traditional Western view than to an understanding based on ethnic self-determination. Ethnic self-determination focuses on the rights of a particular ethnic group to determine its own political status. When a particular ethnic group claims the right of self-determination for itself, it seeks self-government and political independence solely for that particular group, which usually involves redefining the boundaries of the state. The traditional Western position, by contrast, posits that self-determination occurs within a state which is already territorially defined, and amongst the entire population of that state, regardless of ethnic criteria. Self-determination in the Western tradition does not confer special rights upon any one particular group, but rather allows

---

[154] (1992) 31 ILM, 1525–6.   [155] Blum, 833.

the population as a whole to exercise a right of popular sovereignty and thereby elect a representative government. By insisting on the maintenance of internal frontiers and guarantees of minority rights, Western states were attempting to define the process of self-determination in terms of their own tradition.

Because self-determination in the Western tradition is understood to mean representative government for the entire population of a defined territorial unit, self-determination can only occur through the exercise of popular sovereignty, i.e. in a democratic context. The democratic nature of self-determination was repeatedly emphasized by Western states in their response to the dissolution of the Soviet Union and Yugoslavia. On 4 September 1991, when James Baker set out the policy of the United States with respect to the political changes occurring in the Soviet Union, he linked the concept of self-determination to that of democracy.[156] Similarly, when the European Community issued its Declaration on Guidelines for Recognition on 16 December 1991, the very first condition it set out for recognition was a commitment to democracy.[157] The Arbitration Commission also emphasized the democratic nature of self-determination. In Opinion No. 1 it pointed out that the popular will for independence had been expressed in Slovenia, Croatia, and Macedonia by recourse to a referendum.[158] In Opinion No. 4 it recommended that Bosnia-Herzegovina not be recognized as an independent state until after a referendum had been held there in order to ascertain 'the will of the peoples of Bosnia-Herzegovina'.[159]

Yet despite this emphasis by Western states on those elements which embodied the traditional Western understanding of self-determination, the response of Western states to the dissolution of the Soviet Union and of Yugoslavia represented in many ways a fundamental departure from the traditional Western position. The European Community and the United States considered the exercise of popular sovereignty within the constituent republics of the Soviet Union and of Yugoslavia as amounting to acts of self-determination. However, these exercises of popular sovereignty did not occur within the defined territorial limits of the state as a whole, nor amongst its entire population, but only within particular areas of the state

---

[156] Baker declared that the policy of the United States with respect to the political changes occurring in the Soviet Union would be governed by 5 principles: self-determination, respect of borders, support of democracy, safeguarding of human rights, and respect for international law. Under self-determination Baker stated that it was 'for the Soviet peoples to determine themselves, peacefully and consistent with democratic values and practices and the principles of the Helsinki Final Act': James Baker 'US Approach to Changes in the Soviet Union' (Opening statement from news conference, Washington DC, 4 Sep. 1991) (1991) 2 *US Department of State Dispatch* (No. 36, 9 Sep. 1991) 667.

[157] See the Declaration on Guidelines for Recognition, pp. 112–13 *supra*.

[158] (1992) 31 ILM 1494, 1496.

[159] *Id.*, 1501, 1503.

and amongst particular sections of its total population. Western states were thus no longer continuing to assert, as they had traditionally done, that self-determination must occur within the state as a whole and amongst its entire population. On the contrary, it appeared that Western states had now accepted the proposition that the process of self-determination could legitimately occur within one section of a state's territory and amongst one part of that state's population. This was particularly important with regard to Yugoslavia, where the dissolution of the state occurred without the concurrence of all parties to the process. The response of the European Community and the United States to the situation in Yugoslavia indicated that particular sections of the state's population, within a particular part of that state's territory, could unilaterally create an independent state of their own, which would then be recognized by the international community on the basis that an act of self-determination had occurred.

Moreover, although Western states emphasized that self-determination must occur within the frontiers of a constituent republic and amongst its entire population regardless of ethnic criteria, the exercise of popular sovereignty within the constituent republics of the Soviet Union and of Yugoslavia was in reality an act of self-determination by a particular ethnic group, because the constituent republics had been organized on an ethnic basis. An inevitable result of allowing self-determination to occur within a territorial unit which has been organized on an ethnic basis, and where the population of that unit was imbued with nationalist fervour, was the perception that an act of ethnic self-determination had occurred, which had as its outcome the creation of an independent nation-state for that particular ethnic group.

6. CONCLUSION

In the early post-war period there was considerable dispute between Western states, on one hand, and Communist and Third World states on the other, as to whether self-determination involved the process of decolonization. This uncertainty has been resolved, largely through the practice of the United Nations with regard to non-self-governing territories. It is now accepted throughout the international community that self-determination does indeed include the process of decolonization. The process of self-determination, in the context of decolonization, occurs through the granting of self-government to non-self-governing territories. This grant of self-government usually results in the creation of an independent state.

In addition to this aspect of self-determination, Western states assert that self-determination also involves the periodic exercise of popular sovereignty through democratic elections, resulting in the formation of a representative government. They have repeatedly affirmed this understanding of self-determination in their state practice. International instruments concluded by Western states, such as the Helsinki Declaration, reflect this understanding of self-determination. Moreover, Western states maintain that General Assembly Resolution 2625(XXV) embodies this understanding of self-determination, because it describes self-determination as having application in all states and specifically refers in paragraph 7 to the concept of representative government.

Third World states do not accept that the language contained in Resolution 2625(XXV) imports an obligation on states to ensure that representative governments are elected in a democratic process. The wording of Resolution 2625(XXV), in the opinion of many Third World states, simply requires the state to ensure that its government is not racist in composition. This means that only states which advocate overtly racist policies would fail to satisfy the requirement set out in paragraph 7. Third World states tend to assert that the sovereignty and territorial integrity of the state is paramount in all circumstances. This position is reflected in international instruments concluded by Third World states, such as Charter of the Organization of African Unity.

Claims to self-determination are also put forward by ethnic groups. Such claims often involve secession from an existing state, and consequently have not generally been accepted by members of the international community. Most states in the post-war period, whatever their political motivation, maintained a policy of not recognizing entities which had seceded from independent states. This situation, however, appears to have changed with the dissolution of the Soviet Union and of Yugoslavia into a number of ethnically based nation-states. These successor states have been recognized by the international community and accepted as member states of the United Nations. This response by the international community has been particularly important with regard to Yugoslavia, where the dissolution of the state and the emergence of internationally recognized successor states occurred unilaterally. The response of the international community to the dissolution of the Soviet Union and of Yugoslavia therefore calls into question the extent to which self-determination based on ethnic criteria may now constitute an element of international law, and the circumstances in which it may apply.

6

The Protection of Minorities in Modern International Law

1. INTRODUCTION

As observed in previous chapters, there is a close link between self-determination and minorities. When self-determination takes place it usually affects minorities in one way or another, whether the act of self-determination is an act of decolonization, an exercise of popular sovereignty, or results in the formation of a nation-state. Decolonization affects national minorities because it perpetuates minority status for some ethnic groups; this occurs because the boundaries of a new state must correspond to its pre-existing boundaries as a non-self-governing territory.[1] Therefore, an ethnic group which was a minority within a non-self-governing territory will continue to be a minority within the newly independent state. National minorities are also affected when self-determination occurs in the context of popular sovereignty: the representative government theory of self-determination assumes that any exercise of popular sovereignty will take place within the established boundaries of a particular state and amongst the entire population of that state, whatever its ethnic composition.[2] Thus an ethnic group which is a minority within a particular state cannot alter its status under the representative government theory of self-determination, but must continue to function as a minority within the existing state. National minorities are also fundamentally affected by ethnic self-determination. Minorities are able to change their status through ethnic self-determination. By creating a nation-state of its own, a minority can become a majority. However, even when a minority becomes a majority through the creation of a nation-state, that act usually creates other minorities, because state boundaries can seldom be drawn in a manner which neatly divides one ethnic group from another. The dissolution of the Soviet Union and of Yugoslavia provide good examples of this process. Ethnic Russians and ethnic Serbs comprised the largest ethnic groups within the Soviet Union and Yugoslavia, respectively, but with the dissolution of those states ethnic Russians and ethnic Serbs outside the Russian Federation and Serbia became minorities within the new successor states.

[1] See Chapter 4, p. 71.
[2] See Chapter 1, pp. 11–13 and Chapter 5, pp. 96–100.

Self-determination thus affects national minorities in one way or another. This means that the protection of minorities, as Kunz points out, is a 'strict and logical corollary' of self-determination.[3] In the inter-war years the protection of minorities occurred through the establishment of the minorities treaties regime, which followed the creation of new nation-states in Central and Eastern Europe. By the outbreak of the Second World War the minorities treaties regime had been thoroughly discredited, and in the immediate post-war period the concept of minority rights was replaced by that of human rights. It was then thought that the universal protection offered by human rights would render unnecessary the need for any special protection for minority groups. This proved not to be the case. Minorities did continue to require special protection. In this Chapter the protection which minorities receive from modern international law is examined.

2. TREATMENT OF NATIONAL MINORITIES IN THE IMMEDIATE POST-WAR PERIOD

During the Second World War Germany promoted the transfer of ethnic Germans from isolated communities in Eastern Europe to the Reich. Under various agreements concluded with the Soviet Union, ethnic Germans were 'repatriated' from Soviet-occupied areas in the Baltic, Poland, and Romania. Treaties with Romania and Italy also resulted in the transfer of ethnic Germans from these states. More than 560,000 Germans were transferred to Germany under these agreements. Germany's allies also engaged in population transfers on a large scale: under an agreement signed between Bulgaria and Romania, 63,000 Bulgarians and 110,000 Romanians were repatriated. Over 50,000 Croats were transferred from Serbia and Macedonia and some 13,500 Hungarians from the Bukovina.[4]

The Allies also favoured the idea of population transfers as a means of resolving the problem of national minorities. The minorities treaties regime had proved unworkable, and this had done much to discredit the idea of minority rights in general. The collaboration of ethnic German minorities with the Nazi occupying forces convinced the Allies that German minorities could not be allowed to remain in these regions. Polish and Czech leaders in exile believed that the expulsion of the German minorities from their states was the only way to resolve the minority problem. In the House of Commons on 15 December 1944, Churchill confirmed that the Allies were contemplating the transfer of several million people upon the war's conclusion: 'expulsion is the method which, so far as we have been able to see, will

---

[3] Josef L. Kunz 'Chapter XI of the United Nations Charter in Action' (1954) 282.
[4] Jacob Robinson 'International Protection of Minorities: A Global View' (1971) 81.

be the most satisfactory and lasting. There will be no mixture of populations to cause endless trouble . . . A clean sweep will be made. I am not alarmed by these large transferences, which are more possible in modern conditions than they ever were before.'[5]

In the Potsdam Agreement of 1 August 1945[6] the Allies agreed, *inter alia*, to the expulsion of ethnic Germans from beyond the Oder-Niesse Line. Part XIII of the Potsdam Agreement provided that ethnic Germans living in Poland, Czechoslovakia, and Hungary were to be transferred to Germany.[7] Some 3.5 million Germans were expelled from Poland, 2.5 million from Czechoslovakia, and 500,000 from Hungary.[8] Romania and Yugoslavia also proceeded to expel substantial numbers of Germans from their territory, even though the Potsdam Agreement had not authorized them to do so.[9]

In addition to this massive transfer of ethnic Germans, other transfers of populations also took place. As a result of the Potsdam Agreement, Poland gained territory on its western frontier at the expense of Germany, but had been forced, as had Czechoslovakia, to cede territory on its eastern frontier to the Soviet Union. This led to an exchange of populations between the Soviet Union and Poland, and between the Soviet Union and Czechoslovakia. Poles who found themselves living within the new frontiers of the Soviet Union were forced to return to Poland, while Russians, Byelorussians, and Ukrainians within Poland were moved to the Soviet Union. Czechs and Slovaks living within the annexed area of Carpatho-Ruthenia were transferred to Czechoslovakia. Population transfers also occurred between Poland and Yugoslavia, and between Hungary and Czechoslovakia.[10] Although no official figures of those transferred were released, Robinson estimates that they could number in millions.[11]

These massive and forced transfers of peoples from one state to another were denounced as illegal. It was argued that the minorities treaties, never expressly abolished, were still binding on their signatories. They were therefore not at liberty to effect such transfers. These criticisms prompted the United Nations to commission a study of the status of the minorities treaties. Published in 1950, the *Study of the Legal Validity of the Undertakings Concerning Minorities* concluded that the minorities treaties were in gen-

---

[5] (1944–45) 406 Parliamentary Debates (Hansard), House of Commons 1484.
[6] Protocol of Proceedings of Potsdam Conference (1945) Foreign Relations of the United States, Diplomatic Papers: The Conference of Berlin (Potsdam), Vol. 2, 1477.
[7] *Id.*, 1495.
[8] Jacob Robinson 'From Protection of Minorities to Promotion of Human Rights' (1948) 139.
[9] Inis L. Claude Jr. *National Minorities* (1955) 118.
[10] Robinson (1971) 81.
[11] Robinson (1948) 139. See also Patrick Thornberry *International Law and the Rights of Minorities* (1991) 113–15.

eral no longer in force and that consequently there was no obligation on the United Nations to enforce them.[12] There were two exceptions: the agreement between Sweden and Finland concerning the Aaland Islands[13] and the Greek and Turkish obligations with regard to their respective minorities[14] were found to be still valid. However, after the dissolution of the League there remained no international body empowered to enforce their provisions.[15] The study's conclusion was based on the principle of *clausula rebus sic stantibus*:[16] it took into account the declining role of the minorities treaties regime during the inter-war years, the dissolution of the League, and the changed position of those states affected by the minorities treaties.[17] Of greatest importance, however, was the observation that the protection of minorities in the post-war era was governed by a new philosophy: the promotion of fundamental human rights for all human beings.[18] With regard to special minority rights, the study noted that it was a system which had 'to a large extent been supplanted by another' and which no longer possessed 'the standing that it had immediately after the First World War.'[19] As the minorities treaties were no longer considered to be in force, the minorities of Central and Eastern Europe could not rely on them to prevent their forcible transfer from one state to another.

3. THE UNITED NATIONS CHARTER AND THE UNIVERSAL DECLARATION OF HUMAN RIGHTS

The new approach of promoting universal human rights, rather than special minority rights, was reflected in the discussions held by the Allies at Dumbarton Oaks in 1944. The Dumbarton Oaks Conference was the first attempt by the Allies to formulate a charter for the future United Nations. It produced a number of proposals which the Allies tentatively agreed should

---

[12] UN Doc. E/CN.4/367 (1950).

[13] Agreement between Sweden and Finland regarding the Aaland Islands, placed on record 27 June 1921 (1921) 2 LNOJ 701.

[14] Treaty of Lausanne (1924) 28 LNTS 11.

[15] Patrick Thornberry 'Is There a Phoenix in the Ashes?: International Law and Minority Rights' (1980) 438, 439, fn. 74.

[16] 'Premises for the application of the *rebus sic stantibus* rule are, firstly, the disappearance of circumstances prevalent at the time of the treaty and responsible for its conclusion; secondly, the presence of new circumstances differing substantially from those which existed at the time when the treaty was concluded, and making its application impossible from both a moral and a political point of view': Tore Modeen *The International Protection of National Minorities in Europe* (1969) 68, 69. Cf. Art. 62 of the 1969 Vienna Convention on the Law of Treaties (1969) 8 ILM 679, 702.

[17] Modeen, 69.

[18] Claude, 153; Thornberry (1991) 54.

[19] UN Doc. E/CN.4/367 (1950), 41.

be included in the charter. These proposals made no mention of minority rights, although they did contain a reference to human rights.[20]

The United Nations Conference on International Organization in San Francisco followed Dumbarton Oaks in 1945. From this conference the Charter of the United Nations emerged in its final form. This Charter also made no reference to minorities, but did contain numerous references to human rights:[21] its provisions reflect the shift from special protection of minority rights to universal protection of human rights.

This new emphasis on human rights was also evident in the absence of any provision relating to the protection of minorities in the Universal Declaration of Human Rights.[22] A proposal to include a provision protecting minorities in the Declaration was expressly rejected by the General Assembly, which concluded that it would be too difficult to formulate a provision applicable to all minorities, given their particular circumstances and problems.[23] Consequently, the Declaration does not address the issue of minorities or minority protection, although its Article 2 prohibits discrimination.

4. MULTILATERAL CONVENTIONS

Although there was considerable reluctance in the immediate post-war period to confer rights on minorities, a number of post-war multilateral conventions did grant some protection to minorities, although usually in a non-specific and indirect manner. One of the first to do so was the Convention for the Prevention and Elimination of the Crime of Genocide,[24] which came into force in 1951. Article II of the Convention extends protection from genocide to 'a national, ethnic, racial or religious group'.[25] The protected group could be either the majority or a minority of the population.[26] Article II defined genocide to include any of the following acts when committed 'with intent to destroy in whole or in part [the group] as such': a) killing members of the group; b) causing serious bodily or mental harm to members of the group; c) deliberately inflicting on the group conditions of life calculated to bring about its physical destruction in whole or in part; d) imposing measures intended to prevent births within the group; and e)

---

[20] Dumbarton Oaks Proposals, s. A(1) (1946–47) 1 *Yearbook of the United Nations* 8.
[21] See Preamble and Arts. 1(3), 13, 55, 62, 68, and 76.
[22] GA Resolution 217(III) of 10 Dec. 1948.
[23] Modeen, 104. See Part C of Resolution 217(III).
[24] (1951) 78 UNTS 277.
[25] *Id.*, 280.
[26] John P. Humphrey 'Preventing Discrimination and Positive Protection for Minorities: Aspects of International Law' (1986) 26.

forcibly transferring children of the group to another group.[27] The crime of genocide as set out in Article II was subsequently recognized by the International Court of Justice in *Reservations to the Convention on Genocide* to be a peremptory norm of international law.[28]

However, the Genocide Convention did nothing to protect minorities from measures designed to undermine or destroy their cultural or linguistic attributes.[29] The Ad Hoc Committee which originally drafted the Convention had included 'cultural genocide' as a prohibited category, but the notion of 'cultural genocide' was strongly resisted by the United States and France, and eventually the category was dropped from the list of prohibited acts.[30] Thus, although the Convention guarantees the right of continued existence to *members* of minorities, it does not guarantee the continued existence of a *group* as a discrete entity.[31]

The European Convention for the Protection of Human Rights and Fundamental Freedoms[32] was another early post-war multilateral convention which indirectly provides some protection to minorities. Like the Universal Declaration of Human Rights, the European Convention contains no explicit guarantee of rights to minorities. However, Article 14 of the Convention does include 'association with a national minority' as a prohibited ground for discrimination. Article 14 provides that: 'The enjoyment of rights and freedoms as set forth in this Convention shall be secured without discrimination on any ground such as sex, race, colour, language, religion, political or other opinion, national or social origin, association with a national minority, property, birth or other status.'[33]

National minorities have invoked Article 14 in a number of cases in attempts to obtain rights for themselves under the Convention. This occurred both in the *Belgium Linguistics* Case[34] and in the case of *Mathieu-Mohin and Clerfayt* v. *Belgium*.[35] In both cases the applicants were unsuccessful. In the *Belgium Linguistics* case, French-speaking parents re-

---

[27] (1951) 78 UNTS 277, 280.

[28] Advisory Opinion, ICJ Reports 1951, p. 15, 23.

[29] Thornberry (1980), 444; Thornberry (1991) 72–3.

[30] Joseph B. Kelly 'National Minorities in International Law' (1973) 269.

[31] *Id.*, 269. The ICJ, in the case of *Application of the Convention on the Prevention and Punishment of the Crime of Genocide (Bosnia and Herzegovina* v. *Yugoslavia (Serbia and Montenegro))* Request and Further Requests for the Indication of Provisional Measures (1994) 95 ILR 1, pointed out that the Convention also does not guarantee the continued existence of particular states. The Court noted that the essential characteristic of the definition of genocide was 'the intended destruction of "a national, ethnical, racial or religious group", and not the disappearance of a State as a subject of international law or a change in its constitution or its territory': *id.*, 63.

[32] (1955) 213 UNTS 221.

[33] *Id.*, 232.

[34] *Case Relating to Certain Aspects of the Laws on the Use of Languages in Education in Belgium* Merits, Eur. Ct. HR, Ser. A, No. 6, Judgment of 23 July 1968.

[35] Eur. Ct. HR, Ser. A, No. 113, Judgment of 2 Mar. 1987.

siding in the Flemish unilingual zone of Belgium argued that they were entitled under the Convention to send their children to state French-language schools; this would require the state to provide French-language schools in the Flemish zone on the same basis as Flemish-language schools. The applicants based their contention on Article 2 of Protocol 1 (the right to education), and Article 8 of the Convention (the right to family life), in conjunction with Article 14. With respect to Article 14, the applicants relied on the prohibition against discrimination on the ground of 'language'. Although the applicants did not claim discrimination based on 'association with a national minority', it was clear that they were relying on the right to use their language in their capacity as a national minority.

The Court held that the Convention did not establish 'a right to education as would require (the Contracting Parties) to establish at their own expense, or to subsidise, education of any particular type or at any particular level'.[36] The obligation on the Contracting Parties to provide an education simply required them to guarantee 'to persons subject to the jurisdiction of the Contracting Parties the right, in principle, to avail themselves of the means of instruction existing at a given time'.[37] The Court also held that Article 14 had no independent existence because, under its terms, 'it relates solely to "rights and freedoms set forth in the Convention"'.[38] The applicants' claim therefore failed.

In the case of *Mathieu-Mohin and Clerfayt* v. *Belgium* the applicants relied upon Article 14 in conjunction with Article 3 of Protocol 1. Article 3 of the Protocol guaranteed 'free elections at reasonable intervals by secret ballot', under conditions which would 'ensure the free expression of the opinion of the people in the choice of the legislature'.[39] The applicants alleged that they had been subject to discrimination on grounds of language and membership of a national minority, within the terms of Article 3 of Protocol 1. The applicants were members of the French-speaking minority in the Flemish district of Halle-Vilvoorde, who had been elected to the Belgian Legislature. The applicants took their parliamentary oath in French, and thereby became ineligible for membership of the Flemish Community Council, instead becoming eligible for membership in the French Community Council. However, as Halle-Vilvoorde was a Flemish district, it was the Flemish Community Council which exercised administrative functions in the district. The applicants argued that this situation denied both them and the French-speaking minority in Halle-Vilvoorde rights guaranteed in Article 3 of Protocol 1.

The Court found that there had been no violation either of Article 3 of Protocol 1 taken alone, or of Article 3 of the Protocol in conjunction with Article 14. The Court noted that the 1980 Belgian legislation which created

---

[36] Eur, Ct. HR, 31.　　[37] *Id.*, 31.　　[38] *Id.*, 33.　　[39] (1955) 213 UNTS 221, 264.

this principle of territoriality was 'designed to achieve an equilibrium between the Kingdom's various regions and cultural communities by means of a complex pattern of checks and balances'.[40] The aim of the legislation, the Court found, was 'to diffuse the language disputes in the country by establishing more stable and decentralised organizational structures'.[41] This aim was 'legitimate in itself'.[42] The Court went on to declare that the French-speaking electors in the district of Halle-Vilvoorde enjoyed the same rights to vote and to stand for election as Dutch-speaking electors, and were in no way deprived of these rights simply because they had to choose between candidates who would sit in either the French or the Flemish Community Council depending on the language in which they took their oath.[43] The applicants were therefore unsuccessful in alleging discrimination either on the ground of language or on that of membership of a national minority.[44]

A third early post-war international instrument which dealt with the question of minorities was the 1960 Convention Against Discrimination in Education.[45] This Convention was sponsored by the United Nations Educational, Scientific, and Cultural Organization (UNESCO). Article 5(c) of the Convention provides as follows: 'It is essential to recognize the right of members of national minorities to carry on their own educational activities, including the maintenance of schools and, depending on the educational policy of each State, the use or the teaching of their own language . . .'[46] Article 5 simply affirms the right of minority groups to maintain their culture and language.[47] There is no obligation on states parties to support or to subsidize educational activities, or even to allow the use of the minority's language in minority schools.[48]

5. BILATERAL TREATIES

At the multilateral level there was clearly a reluctance in the early post-war period to grant special rights to minorities. None the less, during the same period a number of bilateral treaties on the subject were concluded.

---

[40] Eur. Ct. HR, Ser. A, No. 113, Judgment of 2 Mar. 1987, 25.   [41] *Id.*, 25.
[42] *Id.*, 25.   [43] *Id.*, 25.
[44] The dissenting opinion found that the Belgian legislation did contravene Belgium's obligations under the Convention. The Belgian electoral system, whereby representatives were elected to two different assemblies as a result of the same election, created limitations which were not general in nature and application, but which applied only to the French-speaking voters and representatives of the district of Halle-Vilvoorde, and 'on the sole basis of the language criterion'. This amounted to discrimination prohibited by the provisions of the Convention: *Id.*, 28.
[45] (1962) 429 UNTS 93.   [46] *Id.*, 100.
[47] Kelly, 267.   [48] Thornberry (1991) 290.

Amongst these are the 1946 Agreement between Italy and Austria, which provided for the protection of the German-speaking minority in the South Tyrol,[49] the 1950 Agreement between Pakistan and India, which made provision for religious minorities in order to end the flow of refugees between the two states,[50] the London Treaty of 1954 Concerning Trieste, which extended protection to Italians and Yugoslavs,[51] the 1955 Declarations of Denmark and the Federal Republic of Germany with regard to their respective minorities,[52] and the 1955 Treaty with Austria protecting minority Slovenes and Croats.[53]

These treaties only provided reciprocal protection to minorities. They did not, unlike the treaties of the minorities regime, contain any provisions which would permit resort to the United Nations for the enforcement of the rights contained in them. The 1946 Treaty between Italy and Austria for the protection of the German-speaking minority of the South Tyrol illustrates this. A dispute arose between Italy and Austria with regard to the implementation of the agreement. Italy appealed to the United Nations to resolve the dispute, but the General Assembly, in Resolutions 1497(XV) of 31 October 1960 and 1661(XVI) of 28 November 1961, responded only by calling on the parties to resolve their dispute through negotiations. Italy then sought to take the matter to the International Court of Justice, as the General Assembly had suggested in Resolution 1497(XV). Austria, however, maintained that the matter was political rather than legal in nature, since it involved a claim for autonomy for the province of Bozen (Bolzano). Eventually the two states resolved the dispute, concluding an agreement on 30 November 1969.[54] An additional agreement was signed between the two states in Rome, which made the International Court of Justice the sole arbiter of any future disputes between them.[55] Italy and Austria had to resolve the matter between themselves. Attempts to resort to the United Nations and the International Court were unsuccessful because there were no provisions in the original treaty permitting such recourse.

The peace treaties concluded with Bulgaria,[56] Hungary,[57] and Romania[58] at the end of the Second World War did not specifically provide for the protection of minorities. However, they did contain provisions prohibiting

---

[49] (1950) 49 UNTS 126 at 184 (Annex IV).   [50] (1952) 131 UNTS 3.
[51] (1956) 235 UNTS 100, at 104 (Annex II).
[52] Report on the Position of National Minorities, Eur. Consult. Ass., 11th Sess., Doc. No. 1002, Appendix IX, (1959).
[53] (1955) 217 UNTS 223.
[54] (1969) 9 *Österreichische Zeitschrift für Außenpolitik* 317.
[55] *Id.*, 345. These two agreements were not treaties, but their provisions were informally approved by the Austrian and Italian Parliaments in Dec. 1969, and an amended Autonomy Statute entered into force in 1972: Law No. 1670 of 31 Aug. 1972, (1972) 1 *Raccolta Ufficiale delle Leggi*. See Hurst Hannum *Autonomy, Sovereignty, and Self-Determination* (1990) pp. 432–40 for a detailed discussion of the South Tyrol arrangements.
[56] (1949) 41 UNTS 21.   [57] (1949) 41 UNTS 135.   [58] (1949) 42 UNTS 3.

discrimination, intended to protect minority groups within these states. Article 3(2) of the Romanian peace treaty provided that Romania undertook not to enact any laws which would: 'either in their content or in their application, discriminate or entail any discrimination between persons of Roumanian nationality on the ground of their race, sex, language or religion, whether in reference to their persons, property, business, professional or financial interests, status, political or civil rights or any other matter.'[59]

This corresponded with Article 2 of the Bulgarian peace treaty[60] and with Article 2(1) of the Hungarian peace treaty.[61] All three treaties also contained express provisions permitting recourse to an outside body, a Commission of three members, in the event of a dispute concerning the interpretation or execution of the treaties.[62] These provisions stated that each side to the agreement should select a representative, who would jointly select a representative from a third state. In the event that the two representatives were unable to agree on a third, the Secretary-General would be requested to appoint one. The decision of the majority of this Commission would be definitive and binding upon the parties.

The three states were subsequently charged by the Allied and Associated Powers with violations of the guarantees against discrimination contained in their respective peace treaties. However, they refused to appoint a representative to their respective Commissions to investigate the allegations. The International Court of Justice was requested to give an advisory opinion on the matter. In the case *Interpretation of Peace Treaties With Bulgaria, Hungary and Romania*[63] the Court found that the three states were in breach of their treaty obligations in failing to appoint a representative, but that in the absence of such representatives no Commission could be formed; the signatories were therefore able to act in defiance of their treaty obligations not to discriminate against particular groups.

6. THE INTERNATIONAL COVENANT ON CIVIL AND POLITICAL RIGHTS

Although most states in the early post-war period were reluctant to recognize minority rights, the General Assembly had indicated, in Resolution 217(III) of 10 December 1948, that it would not 'remain indifferent to the fate of minorities', even though protection of minority rights was not in-

---

[59] *Id.*, 38.   [60] (1949) 41 UNTS 21, 52.   [61] (1949) 41 UNTS 135, 172.
[62] Art. 36 of the Bulgarian peace treaty, (1949) 41 UNTS 21, 84; Art. 40 of the Hungarian peace treaty, (1949) 41 UNTS 135, 210; and Art. 38 of the Romanian peace treaty, (1949) 42 UNTS 3, 72.
[63] Advisory Opinion, ICJ Reports 1950, p. 65.

cluded in the Universal Declaration.[64] In order to give effect to this clause, it was agreed that an article protecting minority rights should be included in the proposed Covenant on Civil and Political Rights. An article was drafted as follows: 'Ethnic, religious and linguistic minorities shall not be denied the right to enjoy their own culture, to profess and practise their own religion, or to use their own language.'[65]

This initial draft was criticized on the basis that it appeared to grant judicial personality to minority groups as such, which was unacceptable to many states because it presented a challenge to state sovereignty. Moreover, if juridical personality were granted to minority groups, the freedom of individuals within a minority group to choose voluntary assimilation rather than preservation of their particular minority attributes could be jeopardized, given that the primary interest of the group would be to preserve its unity and strength, rather than to respect the liberty of the individual, particularly if that individual's choice involved a weakening of the group.[66] The proposed article was therefore amended to read as follows: 'Persons belonging to ethnic, religious or linguistic minorities shall not be denied the right, in community with the other members of their group, to enjoy their own culture, to profess and practise their own religion, or to use their own language.'[67] The amended version was still unacceptable to many states, particularly those which received large numbers of immigrants, such as the United States and the countries of South America. These states opposed the universal application of an article protecting minorities on the ground that it would encourage immigrants to establish separate minority communities and thereby impede the natural and desired process of assimilation.[68] As a result, a qualifying phrase suggested by Chile was added to the draft article in order to exclude immigrant-assimilating states from its application. With this second amendment, the article read as follows: 'In those States in which ethnic, religious or linguistic minorities exist, persons belonging to such minorities shall not be denied the right, in community with the other members of their group, to enjoy their own culture, to profess and practise their own religion, or to use their own language.'[69] This version of the article was approved by the Commission on Human Rights in 1953, and eventually became Article 27 of the Covenant. It is the only article of the Covenant which directly addresses the issue of minorities.

[64] See *supra*, p. 130.

[65] Louis B. Sohn 'The Rights of Minorities' (1981) 273.

[66] Francisco Capotorti *Study on the Rights of Persons Belonging to Ethnic, Religious and Linguistic Minorities* (UN Report E/CN.4/Sub.2/384/Rev.1) (1979) 35.

[67] Sohn, (1981) 273–4.

[68] J. W. Bruegel 'A Neglected Field: The Protection of Minorities' (1971) 432. The 1948 American Declaration of the Rights and Duties of Man contains no provision relating to minorities. The 1948 American Declaration is reproduced in (1949) 43 *American Journal of International Law* (Supplement) 133.

[69] Art. 27, International Covenant on Civil and Political Rights (1976) 999 UNTS 171, 179.

Article 27 refers to 'ethnic, religious and linguistic minorities'. Use of the term 'ethnic' to describe minorities was a departure from the usual phraseology.[70] The inter-war minorities treaties had referred to 'racial, religious or linguistic minorities',[71] and the European Convention spoke of 'national minorities'.[72] The term 'ethnic' was considered more all-embracing than either 'racial' or 'national', because it was said to include all biological, cultural, and historical characteristics, unlike the other two terms which were considered to be more limited in scope. Use of the term 'ethnic' was therefore not meant to exclude racial or national minorities, but rather to subsume them within an even broader category.[73]

Article 27 grants the members of ethnic minorities the right to enjoy, in conjunction with other members of the minority, those cultural, religious, and linguistic attributes which differentiate them from the majority.[74] Article 27 does not, however, 'place governments under any positive duties to promote minority culture, language, or religion'.[75] The obligations contained in Article 27 consist simply of a duty not to interfere with the minority in its enjoyment of its right.

[70] The term 'ethnic' had been used in the Genocide Convention of 1950: see *supra*, p. 130.

[71] See, for example, Arts. 8 and 9 of the Treaty of Versailles 225 CTS 412, 417–8.

[72] See *supra*, p. 131.

[73] Thornberry (1980) 448. The term 'racial' was thought to refer only to 'inherited biological features': *id.*, 448. In *Ealing London Borough Council* v. *Race Relations Board* (1972) AC 342, for example, Lord Kilbrandon held, at p. 366, that 'colour, race, or ethnic or national origins' were characteristics which 'have not been acquired' and 'are not held by people, of their own choice. They are in the nature of inherited features which cannot be changed, as religion, politics, and nationality can be changed . . .' Similarly, Kerr LJ, in the case of *Mandla* v. *Dowell Lee* (1983) 1 QB 1, at p. 19, observed that the above-mentioned words 'clearly refer to human characteristics with which a person is born and which he or she cannot change, any more than the leopard can change his spots'. In the *South West Africa Cases* (*Ethiopia* v. *South Africa*; *Liberia* v. *South Africa*) Second Phase, ICJ Reports 1966, p. 4 at 308, Judge Tanaka, in his dissenting opinion, noted that 'what man considers as a matter of common-sense as criteria to distinguish one race from the other, are the appearance, particularly physical characteristics such as colour, hair, etc., which do not constitute in themselves relevant factors as the basis for different political or legal treatment'. But this limited definition of the term 'racial' contrasts with the definition put forward by Brennan J. in *Commonwealth* v. *Tasmania* (1983) 46 ALR 625, at 793. Brennan J. declared that 'a common history, a common religion or spiritual beliefs and a common culture' were factors which, in addition to the 'biological element' and 'physical similarities', must be considered in determining whether a person was a member of a particular race. The cultural and religious gloss which Brennan J. put on the term 'racial' is a significant departure from the traditional definition of 'race'. For a general discussion of the various possible meanings of the terms 'race' and 'racial' see Robert J. Sadler 'The Federal Parliament's Power To Make Laws "With Respect to . . . the People of Any Race . . ."' (1985) 591; Thornberry (1991) 158–61.

[74] Members of religious minorities are also able to benefit from the guarantees set out in Article 18, providing for the right of every individual to freedom of thought, conscience and religion: International Covenant on Civil and Political Rights (1976) 999 UNTS 171, 178. Article 15 of the International Covenant on Economic, Social and Cultural Rights similarly recognizes the right of every person to participate in cultural life: (1976) 993 UNTS 3, 9.

[75] Thornberry (1980) 449.

The opening clause of Article 27 reads: 'In those States in which ethnic, religious or linguistic minorities exist . . .' Some states have interpreted this clause to mean that they themselves may determine whether or not there exist any minority groups within their borders.[76] That interpretation has been strongly criticized by a number of commentators. Thornberry asserts that the words of the article actually emphasize 'the factual existence of a minority group'. The existence of a minority must therefore be determined by 'objective recognition' rather than by whether or not it is 'legally recognized' by a particular government.[77] Capotorti likewise asserts that the existence of minorities must be determined on 'the basis of objective criteria' and that the state cannot be allowed to have 'discretionary power in the matter'.[78]

Article 27 has been invoked on a number of occasions before the Human Rights Committee of the United Nations. Article 27 was in issue in the 1983 case of *Lovelace* v. *Canada*.[79] Lovelace was a Canadian Indian woman who married a non-Indian. She petitioned the Human Rights Committee following the loss of her Indian status and her right to live on a reservation, pursuant to section 12(1) of the Canadian Indian Act.[80] The Committee held that section 12(1) of the Act did indeed contravene the petitioner's rights under Article 27, by preventing the petitioner from exercising her right to live in her own cultural milieu and to use her own language in community with other members of her group.[81] Following this declaration by the Committee, Canada undertook to amend the Indian Act so as to make it consistent with Canada's international obligations.[82]

Article 27 was again in issue in the 1990 case of *Ominayak and the Lubicon Lake Band* v. *Canada*.[83] A group of Cree Indians, known as the Lubicon Lake Band, alleged violations of Article 1 of the International Covenant on Civil and Political Rights. The band claimed that leases for oil and gas exploration granted by the Canadian Government to the Provincial Government of Alberta would deprive them of their right of self-

---

[76] France, for example, has made a reservation declaring Art. 27 not to be applicable to France by virtue of Art. 2 of the French Constitution: Multilateral Treaties Deposited With the Secretary-General: Status as at 31 Dec. 1994 New York: United Nations (1995) 120. Art. 2 of the French Constitution reads as follows: 'France is a Republic, indivisible, secular, democratic and social. It shall ensure the equality of all citizens before the law, without distinction of origin, race or religion. It shall respect all beliefs . . .': Blaustein and Flanz (eds.) *Constitutions of the Countries of the World* Binder V, 'France' (1988) 22.

[77] Thornberry (1980) 448; Thornberry (1991) 154–8.

[78] Capotorti (1979) 35.

[79] UN Doc. CCPR/C/DR[XII]/R6/24 (31 July 1983).

[80] (1970) RSC c.I-6.

[81] Francesco Capotorti 'Les Développements Possibles de la Protection Internationale des Minorités' (1986) 253.

[82] Jules Deschênes 'Qu'est-ce qu'une Minorité?' (1986) 282. See p. 172 of Chapter 7 for further discussion of the *Lovelace* case.

[83] UN Doc. A/45/40, Vol. II, App. A (1990).

determination. Such exploration, it was argued, would prevent the group from pursuing its traditional aboriginal way of life.[84] The Committee found that the case did not involve a question of self-determination but instead raised issues relating to Article 27.[85] The Committee held that the band's right 'to enjoy their own culture' included 'social and economic activities' which were a 'part of the culture of the community'.[86] The right 'to enjoy their own culture' thus extended to social and economic activities when such activities were necessary for the continued existence of the ethnic minority.[87]

7. THE HELSINKI DECLARATION

Provision has also been made for the protection of minorities in the Final Act of the Conference on Security and Co-operation in Europe (CSCE), otherwise known as the Helsinki Declaration.[88] Paragraph 4 of Principle VII declares that: 'The participating States on whose territory national minorities exist will respect the right of persons belonging to such minorities to equality before the law, will afford them the full opportunity for the actual enjoyment of human rights and fundamental freedoms and will, in this manner, protect their legitimate interests in this sphere.'[89] The paragraph refers to 'national minorities' rather than to the 'ethnic, religious or linguistic minorities' of Article 27. Paragraph 4 does not actually protect in any specific manner the 'national' attributes of national minorities, but simply guarantees to them 'equality before the law' and 'full opportunity for the actual enjoyment of human rights and fundamental freedoms'. The concluding clause implies that the general guarantees set out in the paragraph will be sufficient to protect the 'legitimate interests' of national minorities as members of a national minority.[90]

In meetings subsequent to the Helsinki Declaration, the signatory states considerably extended their undertakings to national minorities. In the 1989 Vienna Concluding Document[91] the signatory states declared that they

---

[84] Dominic McGoldrick 'Canadian Indians, Cultural Rights and the Human Rights Committee' (1991) 661.

[85] The Human Rights Committee had similarly found in *Kitok* v. *Sweden* UN Doc: A/43/40 (1988), at para. 6.3, that alleged violations of Art. 1 actually involved issues under Art. 27. In the *Kitok* case the Committee had to decide whether reindeer husbandry was a cultural activity. The Committee held in this case that there had been no violation of Art. 27. The Committee noted, however, that where an economic activity 'is an essential element in the culture of an ethnic community, its application to an individual may fall under Article 27 of the Covenant': UN Doc. A/43/40 (1988), at para. 9.6.

[86] UN Doc. A/45/40, Vol. II, App. A (1990), at para. 32.2.

[87] McGoldrick, 665.

[88] (1975) 14 ILM 1292. See also Chapter 5, pp. 99–100.

[89] (1975) 14 ILM 1292, 1295.

[90] Thornberry (1991) 253.   [91] (1989) 28 ILM 527.

would 'refrain from any discrimination' against members of national minorities and would 'contribute to the realization of their legitimate interests and aspirations in the field of human rights and fundamental freedoms'.[92] They further declared that they would 'protect and create conditions for the promotion of the ethnic, cultural, linguistic and religious identity of national minorities on their territory'.[93] In the 1990 Charter of Paris[94] the signatory states to the Helsinki Declaration emphasized their commitment to protecting the identity of national minorities. The Charter also called for the convening of a 'meeting of experts on national minorities' to be held in Geneva in July 1991.

This meeting of experts was duly convened and produced a document known as the Report of the CSCE Meeting of Experts on National Minorities.[95] In the Report the signatory states confirmed: 'that persons belonging to national minorities have the right freely to express, preserve and develop their ethnic, cultural or religious identity and to maintain and develop their culture in all its aspects, free of any attempts at assimilation against their will.'[96] Human rights and fundamental freedoms were recognized as the basis for the protection and promotion of rights of persons belonging to national minorities, and questions relating to national minorities could 'only be resolved in a democratic political framework based on the rule of law, with a functioning independent judiciary'.[97] The signatory states undertook to extend the same rights of citizenship to persons belonging to national minorities and to provide such persons with equal opportunities to participate in the public life and economic activities of the state.[98] They declared that they would not hinder the establishment of minority educational, cultural, or religious institutions.[99] With regard to access to the media, they declared that they would not discriminate on ethnic, cultural, linguistic, or religious grounds, nor would they subject members of national minorities to penal or administrative sanctions for having contacts of an ethnic, cultural, linguistic, or religious nature beyond the frontiers of the state.[100] The Report declared that national minorities formed an 'integral part of the society of the States in which they live',[101] but added that issues concerning national minorities were 'matters of legitimate international concern' and consequently did 'not constitute exclusively an internal affair of the respective State'.[102]

---

[92] (1989) 28 ILM, 535.   [93] *Id.*, 535.
[94] (1991) 30 ILM 190. See Chapter 5, p. 100 for a discussion of the Charter of Paris.
[95] (1991) 30 ILM 1692.
[96] *Id.*, 1696.
[97] *Id.*, 1695.
[98] *Id.*, 1697.
[99] *Id.*, 1699.
[100] *Id.*, 1701.
[101] *Id.*, 1694.   [102] *Id.*, 1695, 1696.

8. POST COLD-WAR DEVELOPMENTS

The protection of the rights of minorities assumed greater importance following the dissolution of the Soviet Union and of Yugoslavia, which created many problems with regard to ethnic minorities.

As a result of the dissolution of the Soviet Union, approximately 25 million ethnic Russians were reduced to minority status.[103] This created considerable tension between the Russian Federation and a number of the former Soviet Republics where significant Russian minorities remained. The Russian Federation has indicated on several occasions that it will not remain indifferent to the fate of ethnic Russians in the other successor states. In August 1991 Pavel Voshchanov, Yeltsin's Press Secretary, declared that the Russian Federation must take care of the Russian minorities that live in the other republics and 'not forget that these lands were settled by Russians'.[104] In October 1991 the Russian Federation circulated a document of the Russian State Council which noted that in some areas of the disintegrating Soviet Union there had been 'infringement[s] of the rights of Russians', and declared that the 'rights, lives, honour and dignity of ethnic Russians and others coming from Russia' would be defended by 'all legitimate forms and methods'.[105] In October 1992 Yeltsin declared that Russia would not tolerate the violation of human rights of ethnic Russians.[106] Relationships between the Russian Federation and Latvia and Estonia are particularly strained as a result of the decision by Latvia and Estonia to disenfranchise most of their Russian inhabitants.[107]

However, the treatment of minorities has been far worse in Yugoslavia following its disintegration. The change to minority status for the Serb population of Croatia and Bosnia-Herzegovina was one of the primary contributing factors to the war in those states. In 1991 ethnic Serbs constituted approximately 11.5 per cent of the population of Croatia, and they still comprise approximately 32 per cent of the population of Bosnia-Herzegovina.[108] They refused to accept minority status within the two suc-

---

[103] In 1994 ethnic Russians comprised 35.8% of the population in Kazakhstan; 33.1% in Latvia; 29.0% in Estonia; 22.1% in the Ukraine; 21.5% in Kirghizia; 13.2% in Byelorussia; 13.0% in Moldova; 9.8% in Turkmenistan; 8.5% in Lithuania; 8.3% in Uzbekistan; 7.6% in Tadjikistan; 7.4% in Georgia; 5.6% in Azerbaijan; and 1.5% in Armenia. Within the Russian Federation ethnic Russians comprise 82.6% of the total population of 147 million: *The European World Yearbook* Vols. I and II (1995).

[104] 'Yeltsin "Risks War" Over Territory' *The Australian* 28 Aug. 1991, 10.

[105] Mark Coulton 'Russian Vows to Defend Her Own' *Sydney Morning Herald* 2 Oct. 1991, 10.

[106] Bruce Clark 'Georgia, Russia Brace for Full-Scale War' *The Australian* 8 Oct. 1992, 6.

[107] Andrea J Hanneman 'Independance and Group Rights in the Baltics: A Double Minority Problem' (1995) 509–21; Keesing's *Record of World Events* (1992) Vol. 38, 39155.

[108] Marc Weller 'The International Response to the Dissolution of the Socialist Federal Republic of Yugoslavia' (1992) 569. When Croatia retook the territories previously occupied

cessor states, and instead sought, by force of arms, to secede from Croatia and Bosnia-Herzegovina in order to to join Serbia.

In the ensuing war in Croatia and Bosnia-Herzegovina all ethnic groups were subjected to appalling human rights violations, which included mass executions and forced population transfers. Croats and Muslims engaged actively and extensively in these activities against both the Serbs and each other, but the Serbs were the worst offenders:[109] they pursued a policy which became known as 'ethnic cleansing', whereby they sought to eliminate, in one way or another, all non-Serbs from the territory they controlled. In 1995 the United Nations Commission on Human Rights concluded that the Bosnian Serbs had pursued a 'systematic policy of ethnic cleansing and genocidal acts', which included mass murder, torture, disappearances, and arbitrary executions.[110]

The European Community and the United States had foreseen that the dissolution of the Soviet Union and of Yugoslavia might create problems with regard to minorities, and they had therefore insisted that the emerging successor states guarantee minority rights as a precondition to recognition. The European Community's Declaration on the 'Guidelines on the Recognition of New States in Eastern Europe and in the Soviet Union' required, *inter alia*, 'guarantees for the rights of ethnic and national groups and minorities in accordance with the commitments subscribed to in the framework of the CSCE'.[111] The United States similarly declared that its policy with regard to the political changes occurring in the Soviet Union would be governed, *inter alia*, by the 'safeguarding of human rights', which included 'equal treatment of minorities'.[112] The Badinter Commission reinforced the position of the European Community and the United States in this regard by holding, in Opinion No. 1, that 'respect for the fundamental rights of the individual and the rights of peoples and minorities' were 'binding on all parties to the succession' as 'peremptory norms of general international law'.[113] In Opinion No. 2 it held that the Serb population of Bosnia-Herzegovina was a minority entitled to 'all rights accorded to minorities under international law';[114] it went on to declare that such rights were

---

by Croatian Serbs in its offensive of August 1995, this resulted in a mass exodus of Croatian Serbs to Serbia and Bosnia-Herzegovina, effectively eliminating the Serb minority from Croatia: Keesing's *Record of World Events* (1995) Vol. 41, 40692.

[109] Keesing's *Record of World Events* (1991) Vol. 37, 38560; (1992) Vol. 38, 38704, 38919, 39012, 39035, 39102; (1993) Vol. 39, 39278–9, 39427, 39469, 39605, 39697, 39744; (1994) Vol. 40, 39870, 39926, 39967, 40018, 40072, 40196, 40248; (1995) Vol. 41, 40371, 40466, 40668, 40689, 40692.

[110] Keesing's *Record of World Events* (1995) Vol. 41, 40466.

[111] (1992) 31 ILM 1486, 1487. See Chapter 5, p. 112.

[112] James Baker 'US Approach to Changes in the Soviet Union' (Opening statement from news conference, Washington DC, 4 Sep. 1991) (1991) 2 *US Department of State Dispatch* (No. 36, 9 Sep. 1991) 667. See Chapter 5, p. 112.

[113] Opinion No. 1 (1992) 31 ILM 1494, 1496.

[114] Opinion No. 2 (1992) 31 ILM 1497, 1498.

'peremptory norms' and therefore applied 'to all the Republics *vis-à-vis* the minorities on their territory'.[115]

It is doubtful whether minority rights in fact constitute peremptory norms of international law, as the Badinter Commission asserted. Neither the Charter of the United Nations nor the Universal Declaration of Human Rights refer to minority rights. Although Article 2 of the Declaration prohibits discrimination, the Declaration does not 'make obligatory the adoption of positive policies to safeguard the identity of minorities'.[116] Moreover, Article 27 of the International Covenant on Civil and Political Rights neither embodies pre-existing customary international law nor is accepted by many states as having a universal character.[117] As Thornberry points out, Article 27 appears merely 'to be a right granted by treaty without wider repercussions in customary international law'.[118]

Although overstated, the position taken by the Badinter Commission reflects the growing importance placed on minority rights by the international community. This increased emphasis on minority rights has found expression in Resolution 47/135, adopted by the General Assembly on 18 December 1992, and entitled the 'Declaration on the Rights of Persons Belonging to National or Ethnic, Religious and Linguistic Minorities'. It declares in its Preamble that 'the United Nations has an important role to play regarding the protection of minorities' and recognizes 'the need to ensure even more effective implementation of international instruments with regard to the rights of persons belonging to national or ethnic, religious and linguistic minorities'. Articles 2 and 3 of the Declaration prohibit discrimination against minorities on various grounds. Article 2(1) sets out the rights of minorities in much the same language as Article 27 of the International Covenant on Civil and Political Rights. Unlike Article 27 of the International Covenant, however, the provisions of Article 2(1) are not qualified by a clause restricting the exercise of minority rights to states 'in which ethnic, religious or linguistic minorities exist'. The absence of this qualifying clause means that states cannot themselves determine under Article 2(1) whether minorities exist within their territories.[119]

The most important aspects of the Declaration are contained in Articles 1 and 4(2), which represent a new development in minority rights. Article 1, like the Genocide Convention, requires states to protect the existence of minorities within their territories. Article 1 goes much further than the provisions of the Genocide Convention in that it also requires states to protect 'the national or ethnic, cultural, religious and linguistic identity' of minorities, and to 'adopt appropriate legislative and other measures to achieve those ends'. Article 4 declares that: 'States shall take measures to create favourable conditions to enable persons belonging to minorities to

---

[115] *Id.*, 1498.   [116] Thornberry (1991) 241.
[117] *Id.*, 243–6.   [118] *Id.*, 246.   [119] See *supra*, p. 138.

express their characteristics and to develop their culture, language, religion, traditions and customs, except where specific practices are in violation of national law and contrary to international standards.'

These two provisions differ radically from the provisions of previous international instruments in that they do not simply impose a negative duty on states to permit minorities to enjoy their own culture, practise their own religion, or use their own language; they oblige states actively to promote the identity and welfare of minorities within their territories. This represents a significant change in the approach of the international community to minority rights, since positive duties had not previously been imposed on states by international instruments.[120]

These positive duties of states with regard to minorities must be read in the light of Article 8(4), which provides that nothing in the Declaration 'may be construed as permitting any activity contrary to the purposes and principles of the United Nations, including sovereign equality, territorial integrity and political independence of states'. Article 8(4) ensures that minorities must consider themselves to be integral parts of the state within which they live, and not use the rights they possess under the Declaration to challenge the territorial integrity of the state or otherwise weaken its position as a subject of international law.

A further development in the protection of minorities occurred when the Framework Convention for the Protection of National Minorities, drawn up by the Council of Europe, was opened for signature on 1 February 1995 and entered into force in the same year.[121] The Framework Convention states in its Preamble that its purpose is 'to define the principles to be respected and the obligations which flow from them' in relation to 'the effective protection of national minorities and of the rights and freedoms of persons belonging to those minorities', having regard to the Convention for the Protection of Human Rights and Fundamental Freedoms, the United Nations Conventions and Declarations protecting minorities, and the documents of the Conference on Security and Co-operation in Europe, particularly the Copenhagen Document of 29 June 1990.[122]

Although the Framework Convention does not define a 'national minority', it does set out the 'essential elements' which will make up the identity of persons belonging to national minorities. Article 5(1) lists these as 'their religion, language, traditions and cultural heritage'.[123] Section II of the Framework Convention, which comprises Articles 4 to 19, sets out the rights and freedoms to be granted by the signatory states to persons belong-

---

[120] See *supra*, p. 137.
[121] Art. 28 declared that the Convention would enter into force 3 months after 12 member states of the Council of Europe had expressed their consent. By 31 Mar. 1995, 22 member states had signed the Convention: (1995) 34 ILM 351, 358.
[122] *Id.*, 353.   [123] *Id.*, 354.

ing to national minorities. Article 4(1) grants the right of equality before the law and equal protection of the law. Articles 7, 8, and 9 grant the freedoms of assembly, association, expression, thought, conscience, religion, and media access. Articles 10 and 11 grant rights relating to the use of the language of the national minority. Articles 12, 13, and 14 grant education rights. Article 16 prohibits signatory states from engaging in measures 'which alter the proportions of the population in areas inhabited by persons belonging to national minorities and are aimed at restricting the rights and freedoms flowing from the principles enshrined in the present Framework Convention'. Articles 17 and 18 permit transfrontier contacts and co-operation.[124]

However, the Framework Convention does not simply impose negative duties on states proscribing interference with a national minority's enjoyment of its particular minority attributes. Following the lead taken by General Assembly Resolution 47/135, it places positive duties on states parties to promote the continued existence and development of national minorities. In this regard Article 5(1) provides as follows: 'The Parties undertake to promote the conditions necessary for persons belonging to national minorities to maintain and develop their culture, and to preserve the essential elements of their identity, namely their religion, language, traditions and cultural heritage.'[125]

Article 4(2) places a positive obligation on states parties to adopt adequate measures to promote 'effective equality' between members of a national minority and those of the majority 'in all areas of economic, social, political and cultural life'.[126] Article 4(3) states that measures 'adopted in accordance with paragraph 2 shall not be considered to be an act of discrimination'.[127] (This is reminiscent of the inter-war minority treaty provisions with regard to 'equality in fact'.[128]) States parties must also, by virtue of Article 15, 'create the conditions necessary for the effective participation of persons belonging to national minorities in cultural, social and economic life and in public affairs, in particular those affecting them'.[129] The obligations placed on states parties by the Framework Convention, as well as the rights which members of national minorities are granted by it, must be read in the context of Article 21, which declares that nothing in the Framework Convention may be interpreted as granting any right or justifying any act which would be contrary to the sovereign equality, territorial integrity, or political independence of states.[130]

The Framework Convention, together with other Human Rights Agreements including the European Convention for the Protection of Human Rights and Fundamental Freedoms and the International Covenant on

---

[124] *Id.*, 354–7.   [125] *Id.*, 354.   [126] *Id.*, 354.   [127] *Id.*, 354.
[128] See Chapter 3, pp. 43, 53–5.   [129] (1995) 34 ILM 351, 356.   [130] *Id.*, 357.

Civil and Political Rights, was adopted by Bosnia-Herzegovina and by its two constituent entities in the Peace Agreement on Bosnia-Herzegovina.[131] The Framework Convention will be of particular importance in the context of Bosnia-Herzegovina, given the past actions of the warring parties there.[132]

9. CONCLUSION

In the early post-war period the notion of protecting minorities at international law had been largely abandoned as a result of the failure of the minorities treaties. Instead, a new emphasis was placed on the protection of human rights. This was reflected in the Charter of the United Nations and in the Universal Declaration of Human Rights. These two instruments dealt extensively with the protection of human rights, but made no reference to minorities or minority rights. Treaties which did extend some protection to minorities tended to do so in a general and indirect manner, through provisions which simply prohibited discrimination.

The inclusion of Article 27 in the International Covenant on Civil and Political Rights did provide specific rights to the members of ethnic, linguistic, and religious minorities. Since the appearance of Article 27 in 1966 there has been a gradual acceptance of the notion of special guarantees for minorities. This change of attitude can be seen in the inclusion of a principle regarding minority rights in the Helsinki Declaration. However, states remained reluctant to grant more than the most minimal rights to minorities. The experience of the minorities treaties regime in the inter-war period had demonstrated how destabilizing minority rights could be, and states have since been wary of granting rights to minorities which might allow them to create a state within a state.

The dissolution of the Soviet Union and of Yugoslavia resulted in the creation of many large new minorities in Central and Eastern Europe, which necessitated the introduction of more extensive measures to protect minority rights. This has been reflected in the policies of the European Community and the United States, the adoption of Resolution 47/135 by the General Assembly, and the formulation of the Framework Convention for the Protection of National Minorities.

However, the dissolution of the Soviet Union and of Yugoslavia has also demonstrated the very real threat which ethnic minorities can pose to the continued existence of a multi-ethnic state. The emergence of the new nation-states of Central and Eastern Europe was largely the result of ethnic

[131] Bosnia and Herzegovina-Croatia-Yugoslavia: General Framework Agreement for Peace in Bosnia and Herzegovina with Annexes (1996) 35 ILM 75, 126.
[132] See *supra*, pp. 141–2.

self-determination. The ethnic groups which created these new nation-states had been minorities within a larger multi-ethnic state. The dissolution of the Soviet Union and of Yugoslavia thus reveals a paradoxical situation with regard to minorities: the emergence of new large ethnic minorities means that it is now necessary to establish more extensive guarantees of minority rights; but ethnic minorities have dramatically demonstrated their ability to undermine and destroy the state itself. There is an inherent tension in this situation, reflected in the Report of the CSCE Meeting of Experts on National Minorities. The Report enumerates various minority rights, but then declares that national minorities form 'an integral part of the society of the States in which they live'.[133] The same tension is reflected in Article 8(4) of the Declaration on the Rights of Persons Belonging to National or Ethnic, Religious and Linguistic Minorities, and in Article 21 of the Framework Convention for the Protection of National Minorities, which seek to place the rights of minorities in the context of the sovereign equality, territorial integrity, and political independence of the states to which those minorities belong. By such qualifications states are attempting to ensure that minority rights are defined in a manner which excludes ethnic self-determination, and which thereby removes the threat to the state's continued existence.

[133] (1991) 30 ILM 1692, 1694.

7

Definitions of the Term 'People'

1. INTRODUCTION

In the post-war period international instruments and resolutions relating to self-determination have invariably referred to the 'people' as being entitled to the right of self-determination. The meaning of the term 'people' is therefore vital to the understanding and application of the right of self-determination. Yet this term has never been defined in any comprehensive or satisfactory manner. Sir Ivor Jennings, in his oft-quoted remark, noted that at first glance self-determination seemed pre-eminently simple and reasonable: let the people decide their own fate. The problem, however, was that 'the people cannot decide until someone decides who are the people'.[1] Rupert Emerson pointed out in 1971 that the term 'people' had never attained 'any generally accepted meaning which can be applied to the diverse world of political and social reality'.[2] In 1983 Sir Ian Sinclair, the Legal Adviser to the British Foreign and Commonwealth Office, declared that 'there is no internationally accepted definition of the term "peoples".'[3] This inability to determine a generally accepted meaning for the term 'people' means that the appropriate circumstances in which to apply the right of self-determination often remain in doubt. This Chapter considers the various definitions of the term 'people'.

2. KELSEN'S DEFINITION: THE STATE AS THE PEOPLE

Article 1(2) of the United Nations Charter declares that one of the purposes of the United Nations is to 'develop friendly relations among nations based on respect for the principle of equal rights and self-determination of peoples'. In 1951 Kelsen made an early attempt to define 'people' by equating the word 'peoples' in Article 1(2) with that of 'states'. He noted that Article 1(2) referred to the relations among states. As only states could

---

[1] Sir Ivor Jennings *The Approach to Self-Government* (1956) 55–6.

[2] Rupert Emerson 'Self-Determination' (1971) 462.

[3] Geoffrey Marston (ed.) 'United Kingdom Materials on International Law 1983' (1983) 399. Boratynski, the Polish delegate to the United Nations during its sixth session, maintained that 'the search for definitions was unnecessary as self-determination should be proclaimed for all': Clyde Eagleton 'Self-Determination in the United Nations' (1953) 91.

possess equal rights in general international law, Kelsen concluded that the reference to 'peoples' in the same clause meant 'states'.[4]

The *travaux préparatoires* to the Charter, however, reveal that those who drafted Article 1(2) did not intend the word 'peoples' to signify 'states'. When Article 1(2) was being drafted, the Belgian delegate expressed concern over the use of the word 'peoples' and submitted that the word 'states' would be more appropriate.[5] That proposal was rejected by the drafting committee, which explained that the term 'people' was a separate and distinct concept from that of 'state', and that the word 'peoples' in Article 1(2) did not signify 'states'. The committee explicitly declared that Article 1(2) was intended 'to proclaim the equal rights of peoples as such'. 'Equality of rights', it said, 'extends in the Charter to states, nations and peoples.'[6]

This distinction between a 'people' and a 'state' was clearly confirmed in the subsequent interpretation of Charter principles by Resolution 2625(XXV), which declared in paragraph 1 that 'all peoples' had the right to self-determination and that 'every state' had 'the duty to respect this right'. In the light of the *travaux préparatoires* of the Charter and of paragraph 1 of Resolution 2626(XXV), it is clear that Kelsen's analysis of Article 1(2) was incorrect, and that 'peoples' and 'states' are separate and distinct entities.

3. THE DECOLONIZATION DEFINITION

In the post-war period self-determination became strongly identified with the process of decolonization. Amongst many Third World states decolonization is considered to be the only aspect of self-determination which has attained legal status.[7] This approach to self-determination necessarily means that the term 'people' must be defined solely within the context of decolonization. Within that context the term can only mean the population of a non-self-governing territory. This is the position adopted by Rigo Sureda:

At the present stage of the international community it has only been possible to reach a working consensus on colonies as territories deprived of their right to self-determination. This has been so in spite of solemn declarations whereby all peoples are said to be entitled to self-determination. In practice, all peoples are considered to have exercised self-determination except those falling within the category of colonial peoples.[8]

---

[4] Hans Kelsen *The Law of the United Nations* (1951) 52.   [5] (1945) 6 UNCIO 300.
[6] *Id.*, 704.
[7] See Chapter 5, pp. 91–3.
[8] *The Evolution of the Right of Self-Determination* (1973) 215.

Those who assert that the term 'people' means only 'colonial' or 'dependent' people interpret Article 1(2) of the United Nations Charter by reference to Chapters XI, XII, and XIII, so that the word 'peoples' in Article 1(2) is understood to refer only to peoples in non-self-governing or trust territories. Article 1 of the Human Rights Covenants is interpreted in the same manner.[9]

The decolonization definition is further circumscribed by paragraph 6 of Resolution 1514(XV), which prohibits any impairment of the existing territorial boundaries of non-self-governing entities. This means that the term 'people' is not only limited to colonial populations, but is also limited to a given colonial population within pre-existing boundaries. In other words, the 'people' are defined by the territory of the non-self-governing entity in which they find themselves. The fact that those found within such territories may comprise the most diverse and disparate cultural, linguistic, or religious groups does not make them any less a 'people' under this definition. Such 'peoples', it is asserted, will overcome their differences through a process known as 'nation-building', whereby those differences which exist amongst various groups will be subsumed in an overriding loyalty to the state.[10]

Many difficulties arise in attempting to restrict the meaning of 'people' to 'colonial' or 'dependent' peoples. Article 1(2) does not reveal any express intention to do so, nor do the *travaux préparatoires*.[11] Indeed, the provisions of Resolution 2625(XXV) indicate that the right set out in Article 1(2) was a universal one to which all peoples, whether 'colonial' or not, were entitled.[12] This can be seen not only from the fact that the enumerated purposes of self-determination set out in Resolution 2625(XXV) extend beyond decolonization, but also because the reference to 'a government representing the whole people belonging to the territory' would not be necessary if self-determination applied only to colonial territories.[13] Moreover, the General Assembly has not limited its use of the term 'people' to colonial situations, but has also recognized a right of self-determination for many non-colonial peoples, including 'the people of South Africa' and 'the people of Palestine'.[14]

Difficulties of construction also arise in attempting to apply the decolonization definition of 'people' to Article 1 of the International

[9] See India's declaration with regard to Art. 1 of the International Human Rights Covenants, reproduced at Chapter 5, pp. 92–3.

[10] M. Crawford Young 'Nationalism and Separatism in Africa' in Martin Kilson (ed.) *New States in the Modern World* (1975) 57; J. P. Humphrey 'Preventing Discrimination and Positive Protection for Minorites: Aspects of International Law' (1986) 25.

[11] (1945) 6 UNCIO 703–4.

[12] Robert Rosenstock 'The Declaration of Principles of International Law Concerning Friendly Relations: A Survey' (1971) 731.

[13] James Crawford 'Aboriginal Self-Government in Canada' (1988), 54.

[14] See GA Resolutions 2396(XXII) of 2 Dec. 1968 and 2672C(XXV) of 8 Dec. 1970 respectively.

Human Rights Covenants to colonial situations. Such an interpretation, as Crawford points out, cannot logically be applied to all three paragraphs of Article 1:

Article 1(2) reflects the principle of 'permanent sovereignty over natural resources', and it locates that principle firmly within the matrix of self-determination. Whatever the scope or effect of 'permanent sovereignty over natural resources', the point for present purposes is simple: it could hardly be argued that the words 'all peoples' in Article 1(1) have a different and narrower meaning than the same words in Article 1(2), and it is clear that Article 1(2) is of general application, and is not limited to 'peoples' under colonial rule or foreign occupation. The case for a broad construction of the principle of self-determination in Article 1 is also reinforced by the specific, and merely inclusive, reference to colonial territories in Article 1(3).[15]

Consequently, the term 'people', whether considered from the position of textual analysis or from the position of United Nations practice, cannot be limited to colonial situations, and must have a broader meaning.

4. THE REPRESENTATIVE GOVERNMENT DEFINITION

A much broader definition of the term 'people' is contained in the representative government theory of self-determination. As noted above, the representative government theory posits that self-determination is an ongoing and universal right whereby the population of a given territorial unit exercises popular sovereignty in the choice of its government.[16] In this theory the 'people' is defined as the entire population of a territorial unit, which includes both non-self-governing territories and independent states. Adherents of the representative government theory assert that this understanding of 'peoples' underlay the drafting of Article 1(2) of the Charter, and that the provisions of Resolution 2625(XXV) confirm their position. The provisions of Resolution 2625(XXV) certainly lend support to such an interpretation; paragraph 1 indicates that self-determination is a right of 'all peoples' and a duty incumbent upon 'every State'. Paragraph 7 incorporates a reference to representative government, which would be superfluous if the provisions related only to non-self-governing governments.[17] Moreover, the representative government interpretation of 'peoples' is confirmed by reference to Article 1 of the two International Human Rights Covenants. Article 1 of each Covenant specifically states that 'All peoples have the right to self-determination'; the article does not limit the right to the populations of non-self-governing territories.

[15] Crawford (1988) 52.
[16] For a more detailed discussion of this theory of self-determination, see pp. 2–4 of Chapter 1 and Chapter 5, pp. 96–100.
[17] Crawford (1988) 52.

The representative government definition parallels the decolonization definition by defining a 'people' in terms of prior existing territorial boundaries. Rosalyn Higgins writes that self-determination 'refers to the right of the majority within a generally accepted political unit to the exercise of power. In other words, it is necessary to start with stable boundaries and to permit political change within them.'[18] This means that the term 'peoples' in Article 1(2) of the Charter must be understood within the context of prior existing state boundaries. The 'people' will comprise the entire population of a state. Reference to the *travaux* reveals support for this contention: 'Concerning the principle of self-determination . . . it was stated that the principle conformed to the purposes of the Charter only insofar as it implied the right of self-government of peoples and not the right of secession.'[19]

The representative government definition of a 'people' is therefore characterized by two features: (1) it is universal in scope, applying both to sovereign and independent states and to non-self-governing territories, and (2) the 'people' in question comprise the entire population of the political entity, which means that the 'people' is defined by the territorial limits of the state. These two features of a 'people' under the representative government concept of self-determination help to ensure that its ultimate objective is achieved, namely the periodic exercise of popular sovereignty within a given political unit in order to obtain a representative government.

A good example of the representative government definition of 'peoples' is contained in the Helsinki Declaration.[20] Principle VIII sets out the right of peoples to self-determination. The reference to 'peoples' in Principle VIII must apply to the populations of sovereign and independent states, as the signatories to the Declaration were all sovereign and independent states. However, because Principle VIII also refers to the territorial integrity of states, self-determination must take place within the territorial limits of the state.[21]

The representative government definition, however, fails to take account of the enormous impact of linguistic, cultural, and religious factors on the way in which populations identify themselves.[22] Populations do not in general consider themselves as one 'people' by virtue of the fact that they

[18] *The Development of International Law Through the Political Organs of the United Nations* (1963) 104.

[19] (1945) 6 UNCIO 296.

[20] (1975) 14 ILM 1292. See pp. 99–100 of Chapter 5 and pp. 139–40 of Chapter 6 for more detailed discussion of the provisions of the Helsinki Declaration.

[21] Antonio Cassese 'Political Self-Determination: Old Concepts and New Developments' in Antonio Cassese (ed.) *UN Law Fundamental Rights* (1979) 150.

[22] This same criticism applies to the decolonization definition, which either ignores such factors completely or attempts to minimize their importance with talk of 'nation-building'.

happen to reside within certain established territorial limits. Elements within such populations tend to identify themselves with those who share common attributes such as language, culture, and religion, or to differentiate themselves on the same basis. Language, culture, and religion play a fundamental role in group identification. Although the representative government definition of 'peoples' was formulated in order to promote the goal of self-government through the exercise of popular sovereignty, regardless of the composition of a given population, criteria such as language, culture, and religion cannot be ignored, because differences within a given population based on these factors create considerable problems for the exercise of popular sovereignty and the functioning of representative government. These problems were cogently described by J. S. Mill:

Free institutions are next to impossible in a country made up of different nationalities. Among a people without fellow-feeling, especially if they read and speak different languages, the united public opinion, necessary to the working of representative government, cannot exist. The influences which form opinions and decide political acts are different in the different sections of the country. An altogether different set of leaders have the confidence of one part of the country and of another. The same books, newspapers, pamphlets, speeches, do not reach them. One section does not know what opinions, or what instigations, are circulating in another. The same incidents, the same acts, the same system of government, affect them in different ways . . .[23]

The exercise of popular sovereignty within a multi-ethnic state often produces political representation which is ethnically oriented. Moreover, because ethnic groups consider themselves as distinct units and do not identify with the entire population of the territory, they may not accept that the principle of democracy applies to them simply as one part of a larger population.[24] Such groups do not consider the 'will of the majority' to be that of the population as a whole, but that of their own group. If that group is a minority within the total population, the will of its majority may be constantly thwarted because the majority of that group is outnumbered by other groups in the population. Disputes between ethnic groups within a given territory cannot be resolved through an appeal to the will of the majority, because the will of the majority will simply reflect the position of the most numerous ethnic group within the territory.[25] The inability of a particular ethnic group to control political events which affect it is likely to result in dissatisfaction amongst the members of that group; that dissatisfaction may in some cases be so extreme as to induce the group to secede and

---

[23] *Considerations on Representative Government* (1861) 289.
[24] This is the position, for example, of the Turkish minority in Cyprus. See pp. 224, 228–9 of Chapter 9.
[25] Philip Marshall Brown 'Self-Determination in Central Europe' (1920) 236.

form a nation-state of its own, in which it can control political events.[26] This is what happened in the Soviet Union and in Yugoslavia when a democratic system was introduced. The exercise of popular sovereignty within those multi-ethnic states led to political fragmentation.

5. THE ETHNIC DEFINITION

Ethnic affinity has been a predominant factor in group identification since the rise of nationalism in the nineteenth century.[27] During the nineteenth century ethnic affinity was commonly defined by the concepts of 'nation' or 'nationality'. Since the nineteenth century many definitions of those terms have been put forward, but none has ever received general acceptance; significant exceptions have always been found to every definition proposed.[28] The only feature which most definitions of 'nation' or 'nationality' have in common is a reliance on both objective and subjective criteria. After listing various objective characteristics, most definitions add the qualification that such characteristics are not sufficient to constitute a nation, but that the subjective factor of self-consciousness is also necessary, i.e. the group must be conscious of the fact that it comprises a separate entity by virtue of the enumerated objective characteristics. Moreover, it must possess the will to maintain its distinctiveness on the basis of these characteristics. The subjective factor is essential to the definition, otherwise the objective characteristics have no impact on the group's perception of itself.[29]

Although ethnic affinity was generally associated with the concepts of 'nation' and 'nationality' during the nineteenth and early twentieth centuries, the term 'people' was also used as a synonym of 'nation' or 'nationality', albeit less frequently. In the *Aaland Islands* case, for example, both the Commission of Jurists and the Commission of Rapporteurs made reference to the term 'peoples' in contexts which clearly associated that term with ethnic groups.[30]

The terms 'nation' and 'people' were both included in the final draft of

---

[26] See Chapter 5, pp. 108–24.

[27] See Chapter 1, pp. 4–9.

[28] Alfred Cobban *The Nation-State and National Self-Determination* (1969) 107; W. Ofuatey-Kodjoe *The Principle of Self-Determination in International Law* (1977) 25.

[29] Robert Redslob 'Le Principe des Nationalités' (1931) 15–24; Rupert Emerson *From Empire to Nation* (1962) 102–4; Alfred Cobban *The Nation-State and National Self-Determination* (1969) 107; Benjamin Akzin 'Who is a Jew? A Hard Case' (1970) 260; Dov Ronen *The Quest for Self-Determination* (1979) 128.

[30] *Report of the International Commission of Jurists* (1920) LNOJ Spec. Supp. 3, 5; *The Aaland Islands Question: Report Submitted to the Council of the League of Nations by the Commission of Rapporteurs* (1921) League Doc. B7.21/68/106. See Chapter 3, pp. 32–7.

the Charter of the United Nations.[31] Since these terms had, up to this time, generally been used to refer to ethnic groups, there was considerable discussion about their precise meaning when the Charter was being drafted. The Belgian delegate, for example, maintained that the term 'people' in Article 1(2) referred to 'national groups which do not identify themselves with the population of a state'.[32] The Belgian delegate also sought clarification on the use of the term 'nation' in Article 1(2), querying whether that term meant 'state' or 'national group'.[33] However, his concerns were brushed aside by a response which did little to clarify the meaning of the terms in question.[34]

Further discussion about the meaning of these terms occurred at the Co-ordination Committee stage. On this occasion France raised objections to the inclusion of the term 'nations' in Article 1(2), arguing that its use in conjunction with the term 'peoples' appeared to introduce a right of secession. It was also submitted that international relations were conducted between states, not nations.[35] The United States, on the other hand, defended the use of the term on the basis that 'there would be some parties to the Charter who would not be states in the strict sense of the word'.[36] It was then agreed to ask the Secretariat to define, *inter alia*, the terms 'nations' and 'peoples' in the context of the Charter. The Secretariat reached the following conclusions:

The word 'nation' is broad and general enough to include colonies, mandates, protectorates, and quasi-states as well as states . . . The word 'nations' [in Articles 1(2), 55, and 14] seem[s] preferable in order to emphasize the idea of friendly relations among all types of political entities.

The word 'peoples' [is] used in connection with the phrase 'self-determination of peoples'—this phrase is in such common usage that no other word seems appropriate.[37]

With respect to the use of the terms 'nations' and 'peoples' in Articles 1(2) and 55 the Secretariat found that 'there appears to be no difficulty in this juxtaposition since "nations" is used in the sense of all political entities, states and non-states, whereas "peoples" refers to groups of human beings who may, or may not, comprise states or nations'.[38] These offerings from the Secretariat did little to clarify the meaning of either 'nation' or 'people'. In

---

[31] Apart from the term 'United Nations', the word 'nation' appear in Arts. 1(2), 1(4), 14, and 55. The words 'people' or 'peoples' appear in the Preamble and in Arts 1(2), 55, 73, 76, and 80(1).

[32] (1945) 6 UNCIO 300.

[33] *Id.*, 300.

[34] *Id.*, 704.

[35] *Id.*, 142.

[36] *Id.*, 142.

[37] (1945) 18 UNCIO 657.   [38] *Id.*, 658.

particular, the Secretariat's response failed to resolve the question of whether or not 'peoples' comprised ethnic groups.

Various other comments which appear in the *travaux préparatoires* also do not shed much light on the meaning of these terms. The *travaux* indicate, on two separate occasions, that an 'essential element' of the principle of self-determination 'is a free and genuine expression of the will of the people, which avoids cases of the alleged expression of the popular will, such as those used for their own ends by Germany and Italy in later years'.[39] These references to the pre-war practices of Germany and Italy have led some commentators to conclude that the term 'people' cannot refer to ethnic groups. Ofuatey-Kodjoe, for example, argues that: 'the reference to the interpretation of the principle of self-determination advocated by Germany and Italy is significant. It will be recalled that Germany and Italy advocated the principle of "one nation: one state", which we termed the theory of national determination. In this statement, therefore, the committee explicitly rejected this.'[40] Ofuatey-Kodjoe, however, reads far too much into the *travaux*. It is clear from the comments of the committee that it condemned aggressive expansionism by a state on the basis of ethnic affinity; but this does not necessarily mean that the committee also rejected the notion of a people as an ethnic group. Indeed, the opposite conclusion could be drawn if one reads the comments which immediately follow the reference to Germany and Italy. After referring to the practices of Germany and Italy the committee went on to declare that 'the principle as one whole extends as a general basic conception to a possible amalgamation of nationalities if they so freely choose'.[41] It appears from this statement that the committee understood the principle to apply ordinarily to individual nationalities. If they so desired, such nationalities could amalgamate with other nationalities, and this would also be considered to be a legitimate form of self-determination. The fact that the committee specified that nationalities could amalgamate if they so wished indicates that it considered this form of self-determination to be the exception rather than the rule.

In the final analysis, the Charter *travaux* reveal no definitive interpretation of the term 'people'. That an ethnic interpretation was not ruled out at this time can be seen from the fact that such an interpretation was regularly put forward by various members of the United Nations. The Soviet Union proposed that a paragraph referring to the equal rights of peoples and nationalities within states be included in the Universal Declaration of Hu-

---

[39] (1945) 6 UNCIO 396; see also (1945) 6 UNCIO 704.
[40] Ofuatey-Kodjoe, 109.
[41] (1945) 6 UNCIO 704.

man Rights.[42] During the General Assembly debate in 1958 concerning the right of self-determination for Cyprus, Turkey maintained that the Turkish Cypriots were a separate people.[43] Moreover, the General Assembly itself referred to an ethnic group as a people on a number of occasions. In response to various petitions from the Ewe tribe of West Africa, the Assembly adopted Resolution 441(V) on 2 December 1950, in paragraph 1 of which it recognised 'the great importance of the Ewe problem', and impressed upon the Trusteeship Council and the administering authorities concerned 'the importance of finding an adequate solution as soon as possible and in full accordance with the real wishes and interests of the people concerned'.[44] The General Assembly again referred to an ethnic group as a people in its series of resolutions regarding the Chinese invasion of Tibet. Resolutions 1353(XIV) of 21 October 1959, 1723(XVI) of 20 December 1961, and 2079(XX) of 18 December 1965 all referred either to the 'people of Tibet' or the 'Tibetan people'. Resolution 1723(XVI) went so far as to demand self-determination for the 'Tibetan people', calling in paragraph 2 for 'the cessation of practices which deprive the Tibetan people of their fundamental human rights and freedoms, including their right to self-determination.'

When the General Assembly in its early years used the term 'people' to describe an ethnic group, it was not particularly concerned with the question of territorial integrity. This was because the General Assembly initially adopted a pragmatic approach to the question of territorial integrity with regard to non-self-governing entities. When ethnic differences in such territories seemed to portend future instability, the General Assembly was quite willing to divide those territories into separate political entities along ethnic lines: in 1947, for example, it sanctioned the partition of the Palestine mandate into Jewish and Arab states.[45]

In 1958 the General Assembly decided to divide the trust territory of the British Cameroons into two separate regions in order to ascertain the

---

[42] Official Records of the General Assembly, Third Session, Part I, Annexes, agenda item 58, doc. A/784. The General Assembly ultimately rejected this proposal: Francesco Capotorti *Study on the Rights of Persons Belonging to Ethnic, Religious and Linguistic Minorities* (UN Study E/CN.4/Sub.2/384/rev.1) (1979) 27.

[43] The word 'peoples' in Arts. 73 and 76 of the Charter, the Turkish representative asserted, was always used in the plural, whereas the word 'territory' was used in the singular. This meant that there could be more than one people within a given non-self-governing territory entitled to self-determination: Official Records of the General Assembly, Twelfth Session, 1st Committee, 928th Meeting, Paragraph 5. See pp. 222–9 of Chapter 9 for a more detailed discussion of the situation in Cyprus. The argument put forward by the Turkish representative in 1958 was reiterated by Judge *ad hoc* van Wyck, in his separate opinion in the *South West Africa Cases* Second Phase, ILJ Reports 1966, p. 4 at 66. See Chapter 4, p. 83.

[44] See p. 158, fn. 48 *infra* for details of the Ewe question.

[45] Resolution 181(II) of 29 November 1947.

political wishes of each region separately. This was undertaken on the basis of a report submitted by a Special Mission sent to the British Cameroons by the General Assembly. The Mission had found that: 'On the whole, the natural affinities of these broad groups of peoples in terms of language, customs and social intercourse tend to be stronger with their immediate neighbours in one or the other (depending on the locality) of the adjoining territories of Nigeria and the Cameroons under French administration than between one another.'[46] The separate plebiscites in the two regions resulted in the incorporation of the northern half of the territory into Nigeria, and the southern half into the Republic of the Cameroons.[47]

Again, in 1962, the partition of the trust territory of Ruanda-Urundi was sanctioned by the General Assembly in Resolution 1746(XVI).[48] This partition was also made on an ethnic basis: the regions which became the states of Rwanda and Burundi were respectively dominated by the Hutu and Tutsi tribes.[49] The willingness of the General Assembly to countenance partitions of non-self-governing territories on the basis of ethnic differences amounted in effect to an implicit recognition that at least some ethnic groups were entitled to self-determination, and therefore that they were peoples.

The pragmatic approach of the General Assembly to the question of the territorial integrity of non-self-governing entities was abandoned after the adoption of Resolution 1514(XV) in 1960. Paragraph 6 declared that any attempt to disrupt 'the national unity and the territorial integrity of a country is incompatible with the purposes and principles of the Charter of the United Nations'. Paragraph 6 had important implications for the way in which the term 'people' was to be understood. Paragraph 2 of Resolution 1514(XV) declared that all peoples had the right to self-determination, and that 'by virtue of that right they freely determine their political status'. Ethnic groups within non-self-governing territories, however, could not now be considered as 'peoples' because they were prohibited by paragraph 6 from establishing their own nation-state, and therefore were unable 'freely [to] determine their political status', as 'peoples' were entitled to do under paragraph 2.[50]

---

[46] Rigo Sureda, 164.   [47] *Id.*, 163–8. See Chapter 4, pp. 78–80.
[48] 27 June 1962. In 1955 the General Assembly also demonstrated a willingness to accommodate the desires of the Ewes to establish a separate state. A Special Mission of the General Assembly initially proposed that the trust territory of British Togoland be divided into 4 separate regions, comprising the Ewe and non-Ewe populations respectively, and that the political wishes of each region be separately ascertained by way of plebiscite. However, as a result of the objections of the administering power, the United Kingdom, this plan was abandoned, and eventually a plebiscite was held within the entire, undivided trust territory: Rigo Sureda, 151–63.
[49] Michla Pomerance *Self-Determination in Law and Practice* (1982) 19.
[50] Wilhelm Wengler asserted that the meaning of the term 'people' was resolved as early as 1955, when it was decided not to include the term 'nation' in the wording of the International

With the adoption of Resolution 1514(XV), the United Nations became increasingly unwilling to permit any partition of non-self-governing territories, no matter how different or incompatible their constituent ethnic or religious groups might be. Thus, the Security Council has taken action to condemn the separation of Cyprus into two distinct political entities, in spite of the deep-seated antipathy between Greek and Turkish Cypriots.[51] Likewise the General Assembly has often acted to ensure the continued territorial integrity of non-self-governing territories following independence, whatever the wishes of the various ethnic or religious groups within those territories. When the Netherlands transferred West Irian to Indonesia in 1962 without a plebiscite, the General Assembly approved the transfer,[52] even though the population of West Irian differed significantly from that of Indonesia in terms of race, ethnicity, language, and culture. The General Assembly endorsed the Indonesian argument that such differences were irrelevant, given the fact that West Irian had been a part of the non-self-governing territory of the Netherlands East Indies.[53] The General Assembly also moved to ensure the continued union of Rio Muni and the island of Fernando Po, which together comprised Equatorial Guinea.[54] It insisted that islands contiguous to the Seychelles and Aden should not be separated from those territories upon independence.[55] Since 1976 the General Assem-

Human Rights Covenants. Using the term 'people' rather than 'nation', according to Wengler, signified an intention to identify the notion of a 'people' with the totality of those who were citizens of a state: 'Le Droit de la Libre Disposition des Peuples comme Principe du Droit International' (1957) 29. On the other hand, Resolution 545(VI) of 5 Feb. 1957, which called for the inclusion in the International Human Rights Covenants of an article relating to the right of peoples to self-determination, recognized in both the Preamble and para. 1 that this right was one belonging to 'peoples and nations'. Thus, when the Resolution specified in para. 1 that the article relating to self-determination was to read 'All people shall have the right of self-determination', it is not unreasonable to assume that use of the term 'people' was meant to include 'nations' within its ambit. Johnson confirmed that this was indeed the practice of the United Nations in its early years: 'In the discussions in the United Nations concerning the definition of the terms "people" and "nation" there was a tendency to equate the two. When a distinction was made, it was to indicate that "people" was broader in scope. The significance of the use of this term centered on the desire to be certain that a narrow application of the term "nation" would not prevent the extension of self-determination to dependent peoples who might not yet qualify as nations': Harold S. Johnson *Self-Determination Within the Community of Nations* (1967) 55.

[51] SC Resolution 541 (18 Nov. 1983). It should of course be noted tht the separation of Cyprus into 2 political entities arose from an external use of force. See pp. 222–9 of Chapter 9 for a detailed discussion of the situation in Cyprus.

[52] Resolution 1752(XVII) of 21 Sep. 1962.

[53] J. Robert Maguire 'The Decolonization of Belize: Self-Determination v. Territorial Integrity' (1982) 864, 865, fn. 93.

[54] Resolutions 2230(XXI) of 20 Dec. 1966; 2355(XXII) of 19 Dec. 1967.

[55] Resolutions 2232(XXI) of 20 Dec. 1966; 2357(XXII) of 19 Dec. 1967; 2430(XXIII) of 18 Dec. 1968; (1967) *United Nations Yearbook* 657. This occurred even though, in the case of Aden, the Kuria Muria islanders had indicated by plebiscite a desire to be integrated with Muscat, the state to which they were geographically closest and to which they had belonged before being transferred to the UK in 1854: Maguire, 864, fnn. 91, 92.

bly has annually adopted a resolution calling for the reintegration of the island of Mayotte into the Islamic Republic of the Comoros, even though 99.4 per cent of the island's predominantly Christian population voted in 1976 to remain part of France.[56]

Although the General Assembly has not generally recognized ethnic groups as peoples in the context of non-self-governing territories since the adoption of Resolution 1514(XV), it has continued to recognize some ethnic groups as peoples in other contexts. This has occurred both explicitly and implicitly. For example, in Resolution 2672C(XXV) of 8 December 1970 the General Assembly explicitly recognized 'that the people of Palestine are entitled to equal rights and self-determination, in accordance with the Charter of the United Nations'.[57] The General Assembly implicitly recognized an ethnic group as a people, for example, when Bangladesh was admitted to the United Nations on 17 September 1974 by General Assembly Resolution 3203(XXIX). The great majority of the population of Bangladesh was Bengali; this ethnic group succeeded in separating itself from the larger state to which it had belonged, and established a nation-state of its own.[58] The admission of Bangladesh into the United Nations as a sovereign and independent state constituted implicit recognition by the General Assembly that the Bengalis were a people, since only a people can freely determine its own political status.

Moreover, the principal General Assembly resolutions dealing with self-determination describe 'peoples' in language which appears to refer to ethnic groups. Both Resolutions 1514(XV) and 2625(XXV) declare that 'peoples' have the right not only to determine their political status but also to 'pursue their economic, social and cultural development'. Resolution 1541(XV), in Principle IV, describes the 'people' of a non-self-governing territory as being 'distinct ethnically and/or culturally' from those who administer the territory. A culture, however, can only develop amongst a group whose members share basic common cultural attributes, such as language, religion, historical antecedents, and customs: these attributes define ethnic groups. Therefore, 'cultural development' should logically refer only to ethnic groups.

Apart from the language and practice of the General Assembly, many commentators continue to associate the term 'people' with ethnic groups. Yoram Dinstein asserts that several 'peoples' can exist within one state, and defines 'people' in terms of ethnic criteria:

---

[56] Pomerance, 98, fn. 178. See Chapter 8, pp. 183–6 for a more detailed discussion of the question of Mayotte.

[57] See p. 164 *infra* for a more detailed discussion of the Palestinian identity.

[58] See Chapter 8, pp. 189–92, for a more detailed discussion of the secession of Bangladesh from Pakistan.

Peoplehood must be seen as contingent on two separate elements, one objective and the other subjective. The objective element is that there has to exist an ethnic group linked by common history . . . It is not enough to have an ethnic link in the sense of past genealogy and history. It is essential to have a present ethos or state of mind. A people is both entitled and required to identify itself as such.[59]

Brownlie similarly defines a 'people' largely in terms of ethnic criteria:

the principle (of self-determination) appears to have a core of reasonable certainty. This core consists in the right of a community which has a distinct character to have this character reflected in the institutions of government under which it lives. The concept of distinct character depends on a number of criteria which may appear in combination. Race (or nationality) is one of the more important of the relevant criteria, but the concept of race can only be expressed scientifically in terms of more specific features, in which matters of culture, language, religion and group psychology predominate.[60]

The International Commission of Jurists, set up in 1972 to investigate the events in East Pakistan, also defined 'people' in terms of ethnic criteria. It found that 'by 1970 the population of East Pakistan constituted a separate "people"'.[61] The Commission discussed the meaning of the term in the following passage:

If we look at the human communities recognised as peoples, we find that their members have certain characteristics in common, which act as a bond between them. The nature of the more important of these common features may be:

- historical,
- racial or ethnic,
- cultural or linguistic,
- religious or ideological,
- geographical or territorial,
- economic,
- quantitative.

This list, which is far from exhaustive, suggests that none of the elements concerned is, by itself, either essential or sufficiently conclusive to prove that a particular group constitutes a people . . .
 . . . we have to realise that our composite portrait lacks one essential and indeed indispensable characteristic—a characteristic which is not physical but rather ideo-

---

[59] 'Collective Human Rights of Peoples and Minorites' (1976) 104.

[60] Ian Brownlie 'The Rights of Peoples in Modern International Law' in James Crawford (ed.) *The Rights of Peoples* (1988) 5. Others who equate 'peoples' with ethnic groups include M. G. Kaladharan Nayar 'Self-Determination Beyond the Colonial Context' (1975) 340–1; Jacques Brossard 'Le Droit du Peuple Québecois à l'Autodétermination et à l'Indépendance' (1977) 154; Ved P. Nanda 'Self-Determination Under International Law: Validity of Claims to Secede' (1981) 276; T. W. Bennett, N. S. Peart 'The Ingwavuma Land Deal: A Case Study of Self-Determination' (1986) 27.

[61] International Commission of Jurists 'East Pakistan Staff Study' (1972) 49.

logical and historical: a people begins to exist only when it becomes conscious of its own identity and asserts its will to exist.[62]

With the almost universal elimination of colonialism, some commentators have called for a general recognition of ethnic groups as 'peoples', arguing that the recognition of such groups would provide a new and appropriate role for self-determination in a world of sovereign and independent states, particularly in cases of political oppression.[63]

However, defining 'peoples' as ethnic groups raises serious difficulties. The ethnic group, or 'nation', is a concept which seems to defy precise definition. Although the 'nation' has generally been defined in terms of both objective and subjective criteria, fixing appropriate objective criteria has proven impossible. Significant exceptions have always been found to every list of objective criteria proposed. It is for this reason that no single definition of the 'nation' has ever been agreed.[64]

The Jews represent a striking example of a 'nation' which has proved extraordinarily difficult to define in terms of the usual objective criteria. Stalin denied that the Jews constituted a nation. What sort of a nation, he demanded, 'is a Jewish nation that consists of Georgian, Daghistanian, Russian, American and other Jews, the members of which do not understand each other (since they speak different languages), inhabit different parts of the globe, will never see each other, will never act together'.[65] The Nazis did recognize the Jews as a separate nation, but adopted a purely arbitrary definition of 'Jewishness': a Jew was anyone descended from three Jewish grandparents, or from two if the descendant practised the Jewish religion or was married to a Jew.[66] Amongst Jews themselves, there have been widely divergent views as to what exactly constitutes 'Jewishness'. Because factors such as a common language and common culture have been lacking amongst Jews, the one factor which has traditionally been a feature of Jewishness, adherence to a common religious belief, has led many Jews to describe themselves simply as a religious community rather than as an ethnic group.[67] Yet many Jews believed that there was something more to

---

[62] International Commission of Jurists, 47.

[63] T. Carey 'Self-Determination in the Post-Colonial Era: The Case of Québec' (1977) 56; Nayer, 343–5; Nanda, 263.

[64] For an interesting discussion of the objective and subjective components of a nation see Nathaniel Berman 'Sovereignty in Abeyance: Self-Determination and International Law' (1988) 90–103.

[65] *Marxism and the National and Colonial Question* (1936) 12. Although Stalin refused to recognize the Jews as a distinct nation, this did not prevent him from attributing national characteristics to them. In 1937 he declared that the Jews had 'created one eternally true legend—that of Judas': E. H. Carr (Chairman) *Nationalism* (A Report of a Study Group of Members of The Royal Institute of International Affairs) (1939) 77.

[66] First Ordinance Under the Reich Citizenship Law, 14 Nov. 1935. Reprinted in G. A. Kertesz *Documents in the Political History of the European Continent 1815–1939* (1968) 426. See also Eugene Davidson *The Trial of the Germans* (1966) 269.   [67] Akzin, 261.

being Jewish than simply adhering to a common religion. When asked by a member of the United Nations Special Committee on Palestine whether Jews who had converted to Christianity would still be regarded as Jews, the Chief Rabbi of Palestine replied that even a Jew who had abandoned Judaism for another faith would continue to be a Jew, although not 'a good Jew'.[68] Since 1945 the problem of defining 'Jewishness' has become even more difficult, as the role of religion has declined amongst Jews, and 'national consciousness' has grown. Whereas in the past Jews may have considered themselves Jewish simply by virture of their religion, there are now many Jews who consider themselves to be Jewish on an ethnic basis, without reference to religious affiliation.[69] Since Israel adopted the 'Law of Return' in 1950, which declares that 'every Jew has the right to come to this country as an immigrant',[70] it has become necessary to establish more definitively who is a Jew. This issue provoked a constitutional crisis in Israel in the 1969 case of *Shalit* v. *Minister of Interior*.[71] The petitioner sought leave to register his minor children as being of Jewish nationality in Israel's population register, even though, as the offspring of a Jewish father and an agnostic mother of non-Jewish parentage, the children were not Jews according to Jewish religious law. At issue was whether Jewish religious affiliation need still be regarded as a necessary element to being Jewish. By a majority of five to four, the High Court held that a registration officer in the Ministry of Interior could not question the declaration of persons as to their affiliation with a certain nation, as distinct from their affiliation with a certain religion. The Court's decision caused a furore throughout Israel, and resulted in 1970 in an amendment of the Law of Return and the Population Registry Law, which defined a Jew as 'a person who was born of a Jewish mother or has become converted to Judaism and who is not a member of another religion'.[72] Israeli law therefore now defines 'Jewishness' in terms of affiliation with the Jewish religion, even though such affiliation has declined in importance with many Jews.

The Han Chinese are another ethnic group which does not fit the usual objective criteria. Amongst the Han Chinese population there are numerous social attributes which are normally associated with ethnic differences. Amongst other things, the various regional groups of Han Chinese possess differing physical characteristics and speak different languages.

---

[68] Nathan Feinberg 'The Recognition of the Jewish People in International Law' (1948) 18–19. The comments of the Chief Rabbi should be contrasted to the decision of *Rufeisen* v. *Minister of Interior* (1962) 16(4) PD 2428, in which the High Court of Israel found that a Jew who had converted to Christianity and joined the Carmelite Order was not a Jew for the purpose of obtaining Israeli nationality under Israel's Law of Return (1950) 4 LSI 114.

[69] Akzin, 261.

[70] (1950) 4 LSI 114.

[71] (1969) 23(2) PD 477.

[72] (1970) 24 LSI 28.

Nevertheless, because political unification occurred in China in 221 BC a common civilization was able to develop throughout the entire country. This civilization became highly refined and sophisticated, while remaining for centuries geographically isolated from other civilizations of comparable importance. This monolithic civilization has exerted a powerful, unifying influence on the Han Chinese, and has produced among them a sense of cultural unity.[73]

The problem of attempting to define a 'nation' is compounded by difficulties relating to the subjective element of the definition. A particular nation exists as a politically significant unit only when the group is conscious of being a separate and distinct group. If this consciousness is lacking, the ethnic group remains no more than an academic classification, without political significance. The existence of a particular nation is thus in large part a subjective phenomenon, and it therefore becomes virtually impossible to formulate a precise definition of the 'nation', as each nation differentiates itself on the basis of criteria which that nation chooses to regard as important, rather than by established and universally applicable criteria.[74] The criteria by which ethnic groups choose to identify themselves, moreover, may vary not only from group to group, but also within one group over a period of time. The fluid and changeable nature of this subjective element can be seen in the case of the Palestinian people. Originally there was no separate ethnic group known as 'Palestinians'. In 1919 Amir Faysal of the Hijaz wrote to the Supreme Council of the Paris Peace Conference that the 'Arabs ... expect the powers to think of them as one potential people'.[75] In 1947, when the General Assembly adopted Resolution 181(II) dividing the Palestine mandate into two independent states, it referred simply to the 'Jewish state' and the 'Arab state', with no reference to 'Palestinians'. Arabs residing in the Palestine Mandate at this time spoke of being 'a part of the Arab nation'.[76] They shared the same language, belonged to the same culture, and adhered to the same religions as other Arabs, yet there developed a consciousness amongst Arab inhabitants and refugees from the former Palestine Mandate which has not only resulted in the emergence of a new national identity, the Palestinian people, but one which has been recognized by the General Assembly.[77]

[73] Fung Yu-lan *A Short History of Chinese Philosophy* (1948) 181, 188–90, 323. Sun-Yat Sen regarded the Chinese as a unique form of nation, referring to them as a 'race-nation': Cobban, 222. For a discussion of the elusive nature of 'Irishness' see Nathaniel Berman 'Nationalism Legal and Linguistic: The Teachings of European Jurisprudence' (1992) 1571–2.

[74] Inis L. Claude, Jr. *National Minorities* (1955) 2.

[75] 'Amir Faysal's Memorandum to the Supreme Council at the Paris Peace Conference' 1 Jan. 1919 in J. C. Hurwitz (ed.) *Diplomacy in the Near and Middle East: A Documentary Record*, Vol. 2 (1956) 39.

[76] Ronen, 86. See also 'Amir Faysal's Memorandum' in the preceding fn.: 'In Palestine the enormous majority of the people are Arabs': 39.

[77] Resolution 2672C(XXV) of 8 Dec. 1970.

A change of consciousness amongst the population of East Bengal similarly resulted in a new awareness of that population as a separate nation. At the time of the partition of the Indian subcontinent into the separate states of India and Pakistan, most East Pakistanis had identified themselves essentially in religious terms, and therefore sought to align themselves with their co-religionists in the Muslim state of Pakistan. Twenty-two years later, however, their perception of themselves had undergone a radical transformation, focusing on the ethnic and cultural differences between themselves and the population of West Pakistan rather than on their common religious beliefs.[78]

As the subjective element of self-consciousness amongst a particular ethnic group determines the content of the objective criteria by which that group defines itself, it is impossible to formulate a single, universal definition of the 'nation'. Some commentators have attempted to get around this problem by asserting that the existence of a nation depends uniquely on the presence of the subjective element of self-consciousness, without the need for any additional objective criteria. Ernest Renan, for example, argued that: 'Man is not a slave either to his race, language or religion, nor to the course of the waterways or the location of mountain ranges. Any large concentration of men, of sound mind and stout heart, may forge a consciousness which will call forth the nation.'[79]

However, if national consciousness were the sole criterion for determining ethnic affinity there would be no way of verifying whether such consciousness in one individual actually corresponded with the criteria held by the group to be essential identifying characteristics of that group. This was the problem facing the Permanent Court of International Justice in the case of *Rights of Minorities in Upper Silesia (Minority Schools).*[80] In order to avoid that problem, states which require their citizens to be identified by ethnic affinity generally give consideration to objective factors when assessing whether any link exists between an individual and the ethnic group with which that individual claims identity.[81] For example, Article 6 of the *Bundesvertriebenegesetz* (Federal Law for Expellees), adopted in 1953 by the Federal Republic of Germany, included in its definition of an 'ethnic German' an objective as well as a subjective element: an ethnic German was one who 'acknowledged the German nation'. This was the subjective element. The objective element was the additional requirement that such acknowledgement be corroborated by factors such as birth, language, up-

---

[78] Nanda (1972) 329. The word 'Bangladesh' means 'the Bengali nation': *id.*, 324.

[79] 'Qu'est-ce qu'une Nation?' 176 (author's translation).

[80] (1928) PCIJ Reports, Series A, No. 15, 4. See Chapter 3, pp. 52–3 for a discussion of this case.

[81] Akzin, 260. Amongst those states which require or used to require their citizens to be identified by ethnic affinity are Belgium, Cyprus, Finland, Israel, Romania, Sri Lanka, the former Soviet Union, and the former Yugoslavia: *id.*, 260.

bringing, and culture.[82] Thus, the subjective element, although absolutely essential to the definition of a 'nation', is in itself insufficient. Objective criteria are also necessary. Yet the presence of a subjective element makes it impossible to formulate standard objective criteria. This leads to an impasse. Attempts to define the 'nation' in any precise and generally applicable manner are thus doomed to failure.

Another problem which arises from an ethnic interpretation of the term 'peoples' involves the issue of human rights. The following passage from Brossard illustrates the way in which self-determination would operate for those who equate 'peoples' with ethnic groups:

From another point of view, the population of Québec presently consists of a minority of 20 per cent of Québec residents whose mother tongue is English rather than French. In pure logic, this minority should not be permitted to participate in the exercise of the right of self-determination by the people of Québec in their capacity as the 'French-Canadian nation', because they belong to the English-Canadian people.[83]

In other words, defining a 'people' as an ethnic group means that those who do not belong to that particular group will be excluded from participating in the process of determining the political status of the polity.[84] However, in the two International Human Rights Covenants self-determination has been declared to be a human right.[85] Under Article 1(3) of the United Nations Charter, human rights must be promoted and encouraged 'without

---

[82] G. Goodwin-Gill *International Law and the Movement of Persons Between States* (1978) 18. The law on the status of 'nationalities' in Romania, on the other hand, is completely subjective in nature, providing that 'each citizen is authorized to establish his own nationality. Any interference by any authority in this matter is prohibited and the official organs are obliged to accept the citizen's declaration'. This was also the situation in the former Czechoslovakia: Capotorti, 15.

[83] Brossard, 160 (author's translation). It should be noted that Brossard himself does not advocate that the English minority in Québec be excluded from any exercise of self-determination concerning Québec. But the argument that various racial groups were separate peoples has been used in order to justify apartheid. A South African representataive to the United Nations said in 1967 that 'South Africa's policy of autonomous development is designed to benefit all the nations of South Africa. The purpose is to maintain the self-determination of all her peoples, on a basis of equal human dignity . . . The ultimate aim of South Africa's policy is, therefore, the creation of separate, independent and self-respecting communities which will be free from the more serious prejudices, frictions and struggles which are bound to arise under any policy of attempted forceful integration of the different nations or population groups': GAOR XII, A/6688, 11 Aug. 1967, Annex 7.

[84] Ethnic Russians were excluded from the presidential and parliamentary elections held in Estonia on 20 Sep. 1992: Keesing's *Record of World Events* (1992) Vol. 38, 39110. See also Andrea J. Hanneman 'Independence and Group Rights in the Baltics: A Double Minority Problem' (1995).

[85] Art. 1, International Covenant on Civil and Political Rights (1976) 999 UNTS 171, 173; Art. 1, International Covenant on Economic, Social and Cultural Rights (1976) 993 UNTS 3, 5. See pp. 66–9 of Chapter 4 for a detailed discussion of Art. 1 of the International Human Rights Covenants.

distinction as to race, sex, language or religion'. Article 1(3) of the Charter embodies the principle of equality before the law. This principle, as Lauterpacht points out, 'is in a substantial sense the most fundamental of the rights of man'.[86] An exercise of self-determination which discriminated on the basis of ethnicity would therefore contravene Article 1(3) of the United Nations Charter.

Past derogations from the principle of equality between ethnic groups have been made, not to grant any ethnic group a special advantage, but to ensure that equality of fact exists between groups, which equality of law alone cannot always achieve. When the Permanent Court of International Justice, in *Minority Schools in Albania*,[87] ruled that the Greek minority in Albania could continue to maintain Greek private schools in spite of an Albanian law ordering all private schools closed, it emphasized that its ruling was not designed to grant special privileges to the Greek minority, but rather to ensure a continued equality of fact between the majority and the minority.[88] Capotorti emphasizes that 'no individual should be placed at a disadvantage merely because he is a member of a particular ethnic, religious, or linguistic group'.[89] Similarly, no individual should gain an advantage on such grounds. Yet this is precisely what is sought by those who argue that ethnic groups are 'peoples'. Ethnic self-determination cannot be a human right because it permits the exercise of self-determination on a discriminatory basis, granting it arbitrarily only to those who belong to a particular ethnic group and excluding all others.

6. MINORITIES

Since the Paris Peace Conference of 1919 there have been repeated attempts to define 'peoples' and 'minorities' as two separate and distinct concepts. This has occurred because only 'peoples' are entitled to self-determination. The creation of the minorities treaties regime was, in one respect, an attempt by the Allies to prevent those ethnic groups which had been separated from their respective nation-states as a result of the Conference from claiming a right to self-determination by categorizing them as minorities.[90]

Attempts to keep the concept of peoples separate from that of minorities continued after the War, as can be seen in international instruments such as

---

[86] Sir Hersch Lauterpacht *An International Bill of the Rights of Man* (1945) 115.
[87] (1935) PCIJ Reports, Series A/B, No. 64, 4. See Chapter 3, pp. 54–5 for a discussion of this case.
[88] *Id.*, 19.
[89] Capotorti, 98.
[90] See Chapter 3, pp. 37–9 for a more detailed discussion of this point.

the International Covenant on Civil and Political Rights[91] and the Helsinki Declaration.[92] Article 1 of the International Covenant grants 'peoples' the right to self-determination and Article 27 protects the rights of 'minorities'. Article 1 seeks to ensure the development of a 'people' in all spheres—political, economic, social, and cultural, whereas Article 27 simply protects the members of minorities from being denied the right to enjoy their own culture, practise their own religion, or use their own language.[93] A minority is not entitled under Article 27 to any right of self-determination. It cannot determine its own political status, unlike a people under Article 1.

This same dichotomy between 'peoples' and 'minorities' is evident in the Helsinki Declaration. Paragraph 4 of Principle VII provides protection for 'national minorities'. Principle VIII grants 'peoples' a right of self-determination. Minorities cannot invoke the right of self-determination under Principle VIII. This is evident from the reference contained in Principle VIII that self-determination can occur only 'in conformity with the purposes and principles of the Charter of the United Nations and with the relevant norms of international law, including those relating to territorial integrity of States'.[94] In other words, the principle was designed so that it could not be used 'to bring about the dissolution of federated states comprised of peoples of different nationalities or other minorities'.[95]

In spite of these efforts to separate the concept of a 'people' from that of a 'minority', and to grant only the former a right of self-determination, many ethnic groups which are minorities also identify themselves as peoples and claim a right to self-determination. As Thornberry points out, minorities 'appropriate the vocabulary of self-determination whether governments or scholars approve or not'.[96] This occurs because many ethnic groups seek to determine their own political status and therefore claim to be a people entitled to self-determination. Moreover, if a 'people' can be defined as a 'nation', then ethnic groups may be able to claim to be a people, because the various definitions of a 'minority' do not differ significantly from those of a 'nation' or 'nationality'.

One of the earliest legal definitions of a 'minority' was provided by the Permanent Court in the *Greco-Bulgarian Communities* case.[97] The Court defined a minority as a group characterized by attributes of race, religion, language, and tradition and which was possessed of 'a sentiment of solidarity', having as its goal the preservation of the enumerated attributes of the

---

[91] (1976) 999 UNTS 171.   [92] (1975) 14 ILM 1292.

[93] Antonio Cassese 'The Self-Determination of Peoples' in Louis Henkin (ed.) *The International Bill of Rights* (1981) 96.

[94] Para. 2, Principle VIII, (1975) ILM 1295.

[95] Harold S. Russell 'The Helsinki Declaration: Brobdingnag or Lilliput?' (1976) 270.

[96] Patrick Thornberry 'Self-Determination, Minorities, Human Rights: A Review of International Instruments' (1989) 868.

[97] (1930) PCIJ Reports, Series B, No. 17, 4.

group.[98] In 1954 a minority was defined by the Sub-Commission on the Prevention of Discrimination and Protection of Minorities as follows: 'the term minority shall include only those non-dominant groups in the population which possess and wish to preserve ethnic, religious or linguistic traditions or characteristics markedly different from those of the rest of the population.'[99]

A definition which has obtained wide currency was that formulated by Capotorti in 1979. Capotori described a minority as:

a group numerically inferior to the rest of the population of a State, in a non-dominant position, whose members—being nationals of the State—possess ethnic, religious or linguistic characteristics differing from those of the rest of the population and show, if only implicitly, a sense of solidarity, directed towards preserving their culture, traditions, religion or language.[100]

Each of these definitions elaborates a set of objective criteria by which the minority may be identified and distinguished. They also all specify that there must be a subjective element of awareness by the minority of its own distinct identity and a desire by the minority to preserve that identity. These features of the definition of a minority are precisely those which define a nation. The definitions of both a minority and a nation enumerate objective criteria to identify and define the respective groups. Both definitions likewise require that the respective group possess a subjective awareness of, and a desire to maintain, its separate identity. The two definitions are therefore essentially consistent with each other.[101] Azcarate, the Director of the Minorities Questions Section of the League of Nations, came to the conclusion that the terms 'nationality' and 'minority' were, in the last resort, 'one and the same', and that the primary distinguishing characteristics of both were language and culture.[102] This was also the conclusion of Brownlie, who has declared that 'the heterogeneous terminology which has been used over the years—the references to "nationalities", "peoples", "minorities", and "indigenous peoples"—involves essentially the same idea.'[103] As the concept of 'minorities' may be equated to that of 'nations', the question of whether minorities are entitled to self-determination

---

[98] *Id.*, 21. See p. 52, Chapter 3 for the full text of the definition.

[99] ECOSOC OR. 18th Sess. Supp. No. 7. Commission on Human Rights. Report of 10th Sess., 23 Feb.–16 Apr. 1954, p. 48, para. 420.

[100] Capotorti, 96. Another good definition of a minority was put forward by Jules Deschênes in 1986, which closely parallels that of Capotorti. See Deschênes 'Qu'est-ce qu'une Minorité?' (1986) 291.

[101] The only real difference between the two concepts is that 'minority' is a comparative term, whereas 'nation' is not: James Crawford 'The Rights of Peoples: "Peoples" or "Governments"?' (1988) 60–1.

[102] P. de Azcarate *League of Nations and National Minorities* (1945) 5.

[103] Brownlie, 5. See also Martti Koskenniemi 'National Self-Determination Today: Problems of Legal Theory and Practice' (1994) 260.

on this basis simply rephrases the question of whether 'nations' constitute 'peoples'.[104]

Since only 'peoples' are entitled to self-determination in contemporary international law, minorities must demonstrate that they are 'peoples' in order to qualify for self-determination. Some commentators have asserted that minorities do indeed constitute 'peoples'. Ermacora, for example, after pointing out that both 'peoples' and 'minorities' occupy a specific territory and possess cultural or religious characteristics, concludes that 'minorities also can be considered holders to the right of self-determination. Minorities must be considered as people'.[105] This was also the finding of the Badinter Arbitration Commission's Opinion No. 2 of 11 January 1992.[106] The issue facing the Commission was whether the Serbian minorities of Croatia and Bosnia-Herzegovina had a right of self-determination. If they did, then they would be a people, since only peoples had a right of self-determination.[107] Although the Commission did not explicitly state that the Serbian minorities were peoples, this was necessarily implicit in its finding, because it applied Article 1 of the International Human Rights Covenants to them, holding that they had a right to self-determination. That right was, however, severely circumscribed: although Article 1 specified that a people were entitled, *inter alia*, 'freely [to] determine their political status',[108] the Commission declared that 'the right of self-determination must not involve changes to existing frontiers'.[109] It further declared that the right of self-determination in Article 1 of the International Human Rights Convenants 'serves to safeguard human rights'.[110] In the case of the Serbian minorities of Croatia and Bosnia-Herzegovina, this simply meant that individual members had the right to choose the ethnic, religious, or linguistic group to which they wished to belong.[111] Thus, although the Badinter Arbitration Commission equated the concept of minorities to that of peoples, this did not mean that those groups thereby obtained the collective right freely to determine their own political status. They were certainly not entitled to determine their own political status through secession, which was precisely their political goal; the right of self-determination for such peoples was

---

[104] See *supra*, pp. 154–67.

[105] Felix Ermacora 'The Protection of Minorities Before the United Nations' (1983) 327.

[106] (1992) 31 ILM 1497.

[107] The Serbian minorities in Croatia and Bosnia-Herzegovina comprised at that time approximately 11.5 and 32 per cent of the total population of those states respectively: Marc Weller 'The International Response to the Dissolution of the Socialist Federal Republic of Yugoslavia' (1992) 569.

[108] The International Covenant on Economic, Social and Cultural Rights, Art. 1, para. 1 (1976) 993 UNTS 3, 5; The International Covenant on Civil and Political Rights, Art. 1, para. 1 (1976) 999 UNTS 171, 173.

[109] (1992) 31 ILM 1497, 1498.

[110] *Id.*

[111] *Id.*

instead reduced by the Commission to little more than the protection already accorded to minorities by international law.[112]

Another proposed theory on the relationship of minorities to peoples is that of the 'right of reversion'. One prominent proponent of this theory is Buchheit, according to whom minorities are not *ipso facto* peoples, but do possess 'a right of reversion to self-determination' and therefore constitute 'potential peoples'.[113] The right of reversion is said to apply whenever a minority suffers oppression, in which case the minority attains the status of a people and may exercise a right of self-determination. Such a right of reversion was first articulated in the *Aalands Islands* case. The Commission of Rapporteurs qualified its declaration that minorities were not entitled to self-determination by noting that a minority would 'in the last resort' be permitted to separate from one state and join another in the event of oppression where the state lacked 'either the will or the power to enact and apply just and effective guarantees' of religious, linguistic, and social free-dom.[114] In other words, a minority in such circumstances can act as a people in order to determine its own political status by virtue of the right of reversion. The right of reversion appears again in Resolution 2625(XXV), which prohibits any action which would dismember or impair the territorial integrity of a state conducting itself 'in compliance with the principle of equal rights and self-determination of peoples . . . and thus possessed of a government representing the whole people belonging to the territory with-out distinction as to race, creed or colour'. The right of reversion arises whenever any part of a state's population is not represented in its govern-ment, in which case that part of the population, having been denied self-determination, may be recognized as a separate people with a right of self-determination. An example of this right of reversion, in Buchheit's opinion, was Bangladesh. The underlying justification for the secession of Bangladesh from Pakistan and its subsequent recognition as an independ-ent state could only be found, he argues, in the appalling savagery of the Pakistani army in East Pakistan, which triggered the right of reversion for the Bengalis.[115]

[112] Weller, 592. The Commission also speculated that the right of self-determination could imply a further right to choose one's nationality. Provision was first made for the right to choose one's nationality in the minorities treaties of the inter-war period. At that time, however, the right was considered to be a right of minorities, rather than a right of peoples. The minorities treaties specified that those who opted for a nationality other than that of the state within which they resided were required to move to the state whose nationality they had chosen within 12 months. Opinion No. 2 requires no such relocation. This would have been unworkable in practice. No state could have tolerated having between 10 and 30% of its inhabitants owing allegiance to and seeking protection from a neighbouring hostile state.

[113] Lee C. Buchheit *Secession* (1978) 72.

[114] *The Aaland Islands Question: Report Submitted to the Council of the League of Nations by the Commission of Rapporteurs* (1921) League Doc. B7.21/68/106, 28. See pp. 32–7 of Chapter 3 for a detailed discussion of this case.

[115] Buchheit, 213. See Chapter 8, pp. 189–92 for a discussion of Bangladesh.

7. INDIGENOUS POPULATIONS

One group which does not fall easily into any current legal category is that of indigenous populations. Although indigenous populations were originally considered by writers such as Vittoria, Grotius, Pufendorf, and Vattel to be distinct political entities with territorial rights,[116] their status was considerably eroded during the nineteenth century.[117] By the twentieth century they were no longer considered as peoples at all. In 1926 it was held in *Cayuga Indians (Great Britain)* v. *United States* that North American Indian tribes were 'not a legal unit in international law. The American Indians have never been so regarded.'[118] Two years later, in the *Island of Palmas* case, the Permanent Court of International Justice declared that agreements with 'native princes or chiefs' of indigenous populations did not create 'rights and obligations such as may, in international law, arise out of treaties'.[119] Again, in *Legal Status of Eastern Greenland*, the Permanent Court noted that the indigenous population of Greenland could not acquire sovereignty by conquest.[120]

In more recent years, indigenous populations have been recognized in international law as minorities. The case of *Lovelace* v. *Canada* exemplifies such recognition.[121] Lovelace was a Canadian Indian woman who lost her Indian status and consequent right to live on a reservation upon marrying a non-Indian, pursuant to section 12(1)(b) of Canada's Indian Act.[122] She petitioned the United Nations Human Rights Committee for redress. The Committee found that section 12(1)(b) of the Indian Act contravened Article 27 of the International Covenant on Civil and Political Rights. The Committee did not discuss whether the Indian band to which Lovelace belonged was properly categorized as a minority but clearly assumed it was, since it did not consider any other articles of the Covenant.[123] In two other cases involving indigenous persons, *Kitok* v. *Sweden*[124] and *Ominayak and the Lubicon Lake Band* v. *Canada*,[125] the Human Rights Committee also found that issues raised by the petitioners were governed by Article 27 rather than under Article 1 of the Covenant. Implicit in these findings was

---

[116] Howard R. Berman 'Are Indigenous Populations Entitled to International Juridical Personality?' (1985) 190.

[117] Crawford 'Aboriginal Self-Government in Canada' (1988) 19.

[118] (1926) 6 RIAA 173, 176.

[119] (1928) 2 RIAA 829, 858. See also *Johnson* v. *McIntosh* 21 US (8 Wheat.) 543, 578 (1823) (Marshall CJ).

[120] (1933) PLIJ Reports, Series A/B, No. 53, 22, 47.

[121] UN Doc. CCPR/C/DR(XII)/R6/24 (31 July 1983).

[122] (1970) RSC c.I-6.

[123] Thornberry, 882. For a detailed account of the Lovelace case see Anne F. Bayevsky 'The Human Rights Committee and the Case of Sandra Lovelace' (1982).

[124] UN Doc. A/43/40 (1988).

[125] UN Doc. A/45/40, Vol. II, App. A (1990).

the assumption that the petitioners were members of a minority rather than members of a people.[126]

Despite these findings of the Human Rights Committee, many indigenous populations maintain that they are not 'minorities' but 'peoples'. The Six Nations Confederacy, for example, petitioned the League of Nations for membership in 1923, and the United Nations in 1977.[127] Although unsuccessful in both instances, the persistence of the Confederacy in making such claims demonstrates an enduring conviction about its status as a people.[128] Indigenous populations claim to be 'peoples' because either: (1) they satisfy the generally accepted definition of a people and should therefore be recognized as such, or (2) they constitute a *sui generis* category.

The proposition that indigenous populations are peoples because they satisfy the generally accepted definition of a people is usually advanced on the basis that indigenous populations constitute 'nations'. Clinebell and Thomson declare that 'native nations' possess religions, languages, customs, and values of their own, which they seek to maintain in order to preserve their existence. Native nations therefore fulfill the requirements of a people.[129] Berman notes that indigenous populations 'consist of distinct populations, historically have inhabited defined territories, speak languages and maintain cultural and spiritual traditions decidedly their own', and therefore concludes that they 'thoroughly meet the criteria' of being a people.[130] Implicit in these definitions of indigenous peoples is the assumption that 'nations' and 'peoples' are one and the same. Yet, as has already been seen, there are serious problems involved in defining peoples as 'nations'.[131]

Indigenous populations also argue that they are unlike other 'nations' or 'minorities' as understood in international law, and constitute a *sui generis* category which is entitled to self-determination. In the United States the

[126] In *Micmaq Tribal Society* v. *Canada* GAOR A/39/40 (1984), the Human Rights Committee declared inadmissable an allegation by the Grand Captain of the Society that the Canadian Government was violating the Society's right to self-determination. The Commitee held that the petitioner had not proven that he was authorized to act on behalf of the Society, and further that he had not demonstrated that he personally was the victim of any violation. For a detailed discussion of the *Micmaq* case see Mary Ellen Turpel 'Indigenous Peoples' Rights of Political Participation and Self-Determination: Recent International Legal Developments and the Continuing Struggle for Recognition' (1992).

[127] Judith L. Andress and James E. Falkowski 'Self-Determination: Indians and the United Nations—the Anomalous Status of America's "Domestic Dependent Nations"' (1980) 97.

[128] In deference to such claims, Deschênes deliberately excluded indigenous populations from his study of minorities: Deschênes, 260–2.

[129] John Howard Clinebell and Jim Thomson 'Sovereignty and Self-Determination: The Rights of Native Americans Under International Law' (1977–78) 710.

[130] Berman, 192. See also Darlene M. Johnston 'The Quest of the Six Nations Confederacy for Self-Determination' (1986) 26; Louise Mandell 'Indian Nations: Not Minorities' (1986); Russel Lawrence Barsh 'Indigenous Peoples in the 1990s: From Object to Subject of International Law?' (1994).

[131] See *supra*, pp. 154–67.

special status of indigenous populations was recognized from the earliest times of European settlement.[132] Although not treated as independent states, indigenous populations were recognized as having sufficient independent legal existence to enter into treaties and to be accorded the status of 'dependent nations'. This peculiar status was delineated by Chief Justice Marshall in the Supreme Court decision of *Cherokee Nation* v. *Georgia*.[133] Marshall CJ acknowledged that the Cherokee nation had been recognized by the US Government as a 'state', i.e. 'as a distinct political society, separated from others, capable of managing its own affairs and governing itself'.[134] However, he went on to deny that the Cherokee nation was a 'foreign state': its territory belonged ultimately to the United States. The Indians themselves were 'in a state of pupilage; their relation to the United States resembles that of a ward to his guardian'.[135] Although under the protection of the United States, indigenous populations did not cease to be separate political entities, as Marshall CJ emphatically declared the following year in *Worcester* v. *Georgia*.[136] 'The Indian nations', he stated, 'had always been considered as distinct, independent political communities, retaining their original natural rights, as the undisputed possessors of the soil, from time immemorial.'[137]

These cases represent the highwater mark in recognition by the United States that indigenous populations possessed a separate and distinct political status. Yet they also underscore the highly anomalous nature of this status, because although they recognize that indigenous populations possess a considerable degree of political independence *vis-à-vis* the American federal and state governments, they deny to indigenous populations any political status whatever with respect to any other states.

The peculiar political status of indigenous populations in the United States was subsequently reduced in scope. A clause inserted in the Indian Appropriation Act of 3 March 1871 declared that no Indian nation was henceforth to be recognized as an entity with which the United States could contract by treaty.[138] This provision led the Supreme Court to declare, in *DeCoteau* v. *District County Court*,[139] that 'after 1871, the tribes were no longer regarded as sovereign nations'.[140] Cases such as *Oliphant* v. *Suquamish Tribe*[141] and *United States* v. *Wheeler*[142] have further established that the current political position of indigenous populations in the United States is that of 'dependent nations subject to the will of the United States government'.[143]

---

[132] Kelly, 267.   [133] 30 US (5 Pet.) 1 (1831).   [134] *Id.*, 16.
[135] *Id.*, 16–17.   [136] 31 US (6 Pet.) 515 (1832).
[137] *Id.*, 559.   [138] 16 Stat. 544; Rev. Stat. § 2079.
[139] 420 US 425 (1975).   [140] *Id.*, 432.
[141] 98 S. Ct. 1011 (1978).
[142] 98 S. Ct. 1079 (1978).   [143] Clinebell and Thomson, 683.

Indigenous populations took the view that these later decisions of the US Supreme Court took away from them rights which they possessed by virtue of being indigenous peoples. The right of self-determination, they assert, was not *granted* to them by Marshall CJ in *Cherokee Nation* v. *Georgia*; rather, he simply confirmed that indigenous populations possessed a pre-existing right to self-determination by virtue of being a people.[144] International law, they argue, had already recognized their status as a people when *Cherokee Nation* v. *Georgia* was decided.[145] Such claims to pre-existing rights, however, have been rejected by a number of commentators. Green argues that whatever international law may once have said about indigenous peoples, current claims 'to such concepts as sovereignty, title to territory or self-determination all depend on international law as it now exists, regardless of the origin of such concepts'.[146] As a result of dicta in *Legal Status of Eastern Greenland*,[147] Green asserts that claims to self-determination can no longer be made by indigenous groups at international law.[148] Crawford also rejects the argument of pre-existing rights, observing that a 'related feature of late-nineteenth century international law was its tendency to reject earlier legal doctrines'.[149] He refers specifically to the notions of the protected or dependent state and of legal personality for native tribes as doctrines which were so rejected.[150]

Nevertheless there have been recent moves at the international level towards recognizing indigenous populations as 'peoples'. The Martinez Cobo Report[151] represents one such effort. The Report was commissioned in 1971 by the Sub-Commission on the Prevention of Discrimination and the Protection of Minorities to study the problem of discrimination against indigenous populations, and completed in 1983. The Report declared that 'self-determination, in its many forms, must be recognised as the basic precondition for the enjoyment by indigenous peoples of their fundamental rights and the determination of their own future'.[152] It went on to clarify that self-determination 'constitutes the exercise of free choice by indigenous peoples'.[153] The specific content of the principle was to be created by indigenous peoples themselves, but was not to include a right of secession.[154]

---

[144] Berman, 190.
[145] See *supra*, pp. 173–4.
[146] L. C. Green 'Aboriginal Peoples, International Law and the Canadian Charter of Rights and Freedoms' (1983) 340.
[147] (1933) PCIJ Reports, Series A/B, No. 53, 47. See *supra*, p. 172.
[148] Green, 340.
[149] Crawford 'Aboriginal Self-Government in Canada' (1988) 19.
[150] *Id.*, 19.
[151] UN Doc. E/Cn.4/Sub.2/1983/21/Add.8.
[152] *Id.*, para. 580.
[153] *Id.*, para. 581. For a more detailed discussion of the Martinez Cobo Report see Russel Lawrence Barsh 'Indigenous Peoples: An Emerging Object of International Law' (1986) 373.
[154] *Id.*, para. 581.

Indigenous populations have also been recognized as peoples by the International Labour Conference.[155] In 1989 a' committee of experts convened by the ILO recommended, in view of the claims to self-determination being made by indigenous populations, that substantial changes be made to Convention No. 107, which dealt with the rights of indigenous and tribal peoples. The committee concluded that the aim of the Convention, which sought to promote integration for indigenous populations, 'no longer reflected current thinking' and that indigenous populations should be allowed 'as much control as possible over their own economic, social and cultural development'.[156] These new aims were incorporated into ILO Convention No. 169, entitled 'The Convention Concerning Indigenous and Tribal Peoples in Independent Countries'.[157] The Convention was adopted in June 1989 by the International Labour Conference at its seventy-sixth session. Article 1, paragraph 1 defined indigenous or tribal populations as 'peoples'. Article 7 declared that:

The peoples concerned shall have the right to decide their own priorities for the process of development as it affects their lives, beliefs, institutions and spiritual well-being and the lands they occupy or otherwise use, and to exercise control, to the extent possible, over their own economic, social and cultural development. In addition, they shall participate in the formulation, implementation and evaluation of plans and programmes for national and regional development which may affect them directly.[158]

The Convention took care not to sanction secession. The Preamble recognized the aspirations of indigenous peoples only 'within the framework of the States in which they live'.[159] Moreover, Article 1(3) qualified the definition of indigenous or tribal peoples set out in Article 1(1) by providing that it should not be construed 'as having any implications as regards the rights which may attach to the term under international law'.[160]

The most recent international instrument to deal with indigenous populations is the Declaration on the Rights of Indigenous Peoples,[161] which was agreed upon at first reading by the members of the United Nations Working Group but has yet to be adopted by the General Assembly. The draft Declaration sets out a wide range of rights to be accorded to indigenous populations, which are specifically recognized by the draft declaration to be 'peoples'.[162] Amongst the rights accorded to indigenous

---

[155] Russel Lawrence Barsh 'Revision of ILO Convention No. 107' (1987) 756; Catherine J. Iorns 'Indigenous Peoples and Self-Determination: Challenging State Sovereignty' (1992) 263–4.

[156] ILO Doc. APPL/MER/107/1986/D7 at 32.

[157] (1989) 28 ILM 1382.

[158] *Id.*, 1386.

[159] *Id.*, 1384.

[160] *Id.*, 1385.

[161] UN Doc. E/CN.4/Sub. 2/1992/33.   [162] Preamble, para. 1 *et seq.*

peoples is the right of self-determination. Operative paragraph 1 of the Draft Declaration states that: 'Indigenous peoples have the right of self-determination, in accordance with international law by virtue of which they may freely determine their political status and institutions and freely pursue their economic, social and cultural development. An integral part of this is the right to autonomy and self-government'. By explicitly declaring that indigenous populations are peoples and that they are entitled to self-determination, the draft declaration extends the rights of indigenous populations much further than preceding instruments. Operative paragraph 1 both reflects and extends the language used for Article 1 of the International Human Rights Covenants by declaring that indigenous peoples 'may freely determine their own political status and institutions'. However, the right to self-determination contained in the draft declaration is limited by inclusion of the reference to a 'right of autonomy'; this makes it clear that self-determination does not include secession or the establishment of a separate nation-state, and must rather occur within the framework of the existing state. Operative paragraphs 25 to 28, which set out the rights of indigenous populations both to participate in the government of the state and to establish autonomous indigenous institutions, reinforce this assumption that indigenous rights can only be exercised within the framework of existing states.[163]

These recent international instruments have created a situation in which indigenous populations can be characterized neither as minorities nor as peoples. Although the instruments speak in terms of 'peoples' and use language which evokes the principle of self-determination, in the final analysis they do not grant that which is accorded to 'peoples' by Article 1 of the International Human Rights Covenants and by Resolutions 1514(XV) and 2625(XXV), namely the right freely to determine their own political status. They purport to recognize indigenous populations as 'peoples', while refusing to allow them to determine their own political status.

8. CONCLUSION

In the post-war period the concept of the 'people' emerged as a distinct entity in international law. Kelsen argued that the references to 'peoples' contained in the Charter were simply references to states; this interpretation was not accepted. Instead, the concept of a 'people' was recognized as being distinct from that of a state. This interpretation has been confirmed by subsequent international instruments, which have indicated that it is the 'people' rather than the state which possesses the right of self-

---

[163] Christian Tomuschat 'Self-Determination in a Post-Colonial World' in Christian Tomuschat (ed.) *Modern Law of Self-Determination* (1993) 12–15.

determination. Resolution 2625(XXV) goes so far as to indicate that this right of peoples is in fact opposable to states, declaring that self-determination is a right of 'all peoples' and a duty upon 'every State'.

Some states argue that the right of peoples to self-determination does not directly affect independent states because it applies only to non-self-governing territories. Although the process of decolonization certainly constitutes one aspect of self-determination, it is evident, both from a textual analysis of major international instruments and from a review of United Nations practice, that the term 'people' cannot be limited to the populations of non-self-governing territories. International instruments and United Nations practice both clearly indicate that self-determination also applies to the populations of independent states.

The representative government theory of self-determination recognizes that the term 'people' applies to the populations of both non-self-governing territories and independent states. Nevertheless, the 'people' to whom the state owes a duty under the representative government theory is the entire population of the state. According to Western states, the duty owed by the state is to ensure the periodic exercise of popular sovereignty, which results in a representative government. According to Third World states, on the other hand, the duty owed by the state is merely to ensure that the government does not exclude any part of the population by virtue of their race, creed, or colour.

Diverse ethnic groups within a single state do not usually consider themselves to be a single 'people', nor do they behave in a way which reveals a single 'will of the majority'. On the contrary, such groups frequently form separate and distinct elements within the state and seek to determine their own political status. The notion that ethnic groups could be defined as 'peoples' finds some support in the *travaux préparatoires* of the United Nations Charter. Moreover, in its first fifteen years the General Assembly agreed on a number of occasions to divide non-self-governing territories into separate states in order to accommodate the nationalist aspirations of various ethnic groups within those territories. Although this approach to self-determination was abandoned with the adoption of Resolution 1514(XV), the General Assembly has nevertheless continued to refer to certain specific ethnic groups as 'peoples'. Even the principal resolutions of the General Assembly relating to self-determination describe 'people' in language which implies ethnic affiliation. The admission into the United Nations of states created by specific ethnic groups, such as Bangladesh, may also constitute implicit recognition of ethnic groups as 'peoples'.

On the other hand, equating ethnic groups with 'peoples' raises fundamental problems in international law. First of all, it is extraordinarily difficult to define a 'people' in ethnic terms, given the subjective nature of the concept. The situation is further complicated by the fact that ethnic minorities and indigenous populations also claim to be peoples. However, when self-determination becomes associated with the right of particular ethnic groups to determine their own political status, it ceases to be a human right because it becomes discriminatory in nature. It is highly unlikely that this was the intention when self-determination was included in the International Human Rights Covenants, or when it was referred to as a 'right' in Resolution 1514(XV) and Resolution 2625(XXV). Classifying ethnic groups as peoples also raises the issue of secession, since such groups may wish to determine their own political status by forming a separate nation-state of their own. The question of secession is discussed in the following Chapter.

8

Secession

1. INTRODUCTION

The Charter of the United Nations and several other international instruments refer to the concept of self-determination in terms of its relationship to 'peoples'. Self-determination in international law is the process whereby 'peoples' are entitled to determine their own political status. However, self-determination also necessarily involves territorial considerations of one sort or another. A claim to self-determination is usually not only a claim by a people to determine their own political status, but also represents a claim to territory.[1] If ethnic groups are defined as peoples, the territorial dismemberment of existing states could ensue if such groups decided to form their own nation-states. This Chapter examines territorial integrity and the question of secession with respect to both non-self-governing territories and independent states.

2. THE PRINCIPLE OF TERRITORIAL INTEGRITY

One of the fundamental attributes of statehood is that a state exercises exclusive control over its own territory.[2] Territorial sovereignty, according to Judge Huber, 'involves the exclusive right to display the activities of a State'.[3] Respecting other states' territorial integrity is considered a primary means of maintaining peace and stability in the international community.[4] The principle of territorial integrity was enshrined in Article 10 of the Covenant of the League of Nations, and again in Article 2(4) of the Charter

---

[1] S. K. Panter-Brick 'The Right to Self-Determination: Its Application to Nigeria' (1968) 263.

[2] See e.g. Art. 1, 1933 Montevideo Convention (1936) 165 LNTS 19, 25.

[3] *Island of Palmas* case (1928) 1 RIAA 829, 839, *per* Judge Huber. The comments of de la Pradelle, in his submission on behalf of France in *Nationality Decrees in Tunis and Morocco* (1923) PCIJ Reports, Series B, No. 4 should also be noted. De la Pradelle stated that '. . . territory is neither an object nor a substance; it is a framework. What sort of framework? The framework within which the public power is exercised . . . territory as such must not be considered, it must be regarded as the external, ostensible sign of the sphere within which the public power of the state is exercised': *id.*, Series C, No. 2, 106, 108.

[4] Eisuke Suzuki 'Self-Determination and World Public Order: Community Response to Territorial Separation' (1976) 783.

of the United Nations. It is one of the most fundamental and well established principles of international law.

Secession is the antithesis of territorial integrity. It occurs when part of an independent state or a non-self-governing territory separates itself from the whole in order to become an independent state.[5] Ethnic self-determination implies the possibility of secession, because if an ethnic group is defined as a people then it has the right to determine its own political status. In exercising this right a group may decide to secede from the state of which it is part in order to form its own nation-state. Ethnic self-determination thus represents a threat to the continued existence of states, and has as a result been largely repudiated by the international community. The United Nations and international organizations such as the Organization of African Unity discourage secession and seek to maintain territorial integrity in both independent states and non-self-governing territories. Self-determination is therefore generally defined in terms of territorial criteria; Paragraph 6 of Resolution 1514(XV), which bluntly prohibits secession, provides a good example.[6]

3. THE UNITED NATIONS CHARTER

Article 2(4) of the United Nations Charter prohibits member states from using or threatening force against the territorial integrity or political independence of any state. This injunction applies only as between states. Secession, by contrast, usually occurs within the confines of a single state, and therefore does not fall within the jurisdiction of Article 2(4). References to self-determination in Articles 1(2) and 55 of the Charter do not indicate whether secession is a part of self-determination. Two differing interpretations may be found in the *travaux*. On the one hand, it was emphasized that the principle of self-determination 'corresponded closely to the will and desires of peoples everywhere'.[7] On the other hand, 'it was stated that the principle conformed to the purposes of the Charter only insofar as it implied the right of self-government and not the right of secession'.[8] The first interpretation takes as its starting point the concept of 'peoples', and therefore appears implicitly to allow for the possibility of secession. The second

---

[5] Compare the definitions of secession offered by Lee C. Buchheit *Secession* (1978) 13; James Crawford *The Creation of States in International Law* (1979) 247; Daniel Turp 'Le Droit de Sécession en Droit International Public' (1982) 26; and Greg Craven 'Of Federalism, Succession, Canada and Quebec' (1991) 232. Irredentism involves cases in which a seceding element seeks, not to become independent, but to be associated with or integrated into another state, usually because of an ethnic affinity with that state. Irredentism is discussed in Chapter 9.

[6] See Chapter 4, pp. 70–1 for a detailed discussion of Resolution 1514(XV).

[7] (1945) 6 UNCIO 296.   [8] *Id.*, 296.

interpretation focuses primarily upon states, and explicitly excludes the possibility of secession. The *travaux* therefore do not clarify whether secession is part of self-determination.

Neither do Resolutions 1514(XV) or Resolution 2625(XXV) clarify the matter. Both claim to interpret authoritatively and conclusively the provisions of the Charter relating to self-determination and territorial integrity.[9] However, their provisions are mutually contradictory with regard to territorial integrity. Paragraph 6 of Resolution 1514(XV) absolutely and categorically prohibits any action 'aimed at the partial or total disruption of the national unity and the territorial integrity of a country'. Since that prohibition is not limited to other states or inter-state activities, secession is prohibited whether it results from the actions of another state or from internal conflict. Moreover, paragraph 6 declares that such action is 'incompatible with the principles and purposes of the Charter', although the prohibition against violating territorial integrity contained in Article 2(4) of the Charter applies only to states and inter-state activities.

Paragraph 8 of Resolution 2625(XXV) prohibits states from engaging in 'any action aimed at the partial or total disruption of the national unity and territorial integrity of any other State or country'; it does not prohibit secession resulting from internal conflict. Indeed, paragraph 7, by linking territorial integrity to representative government, appears to allow part of a state's population to secede if that part of the population is not represented in the government of the state. In other words, according to the provisions of Resolution 2625(XXV), only states are prevented from engaging in activities which may cause secession. The population, or part of the population, of any individual state is not prevented from doing so in certain circumstances.

This conflict between the provisions of Resolution 1514(XV) and those of Resolution 2625(XXV) can be resolved by narrowing the ambit of Resolution 1514(XV). If the provisions of Resolution 1514(XV) are limited to non-self-governing territories, the inconsistencies between the two Resolutions, and between Resolution 1514 and Article 2(4) of the Charter, are eliminated. Textual analysis of the two Resolutions allows for such an interpretation. Paragraph 6 of Resolution 1514(XV) prohibits disruption to the

---

[9] Para. 7 of Resolution 1514(XV) charges all states to 'observe faithfully and strictly the provisions of the Charter of the United Nations, the Universal Declaration of Human Rights and the present Declaration', thereby putting itself 'on a par' with the Charter and the Universal Declaration: Crawford, 357. Resolution 2625(XXV) represents the culmination of a project initiated by the General Assembly in 1962 to undertake a study of the principles of international law 'in accordance with the Charter with a view to their progressive development and codification, so as to secure their more effective application': Resolution 1815(XVII) of 18 Dec. 1962. Resolution 2625(XXV) was adopted unanimously by the General Assembly, and its provisions are said to be 'acknowledged by all to be principles of the Charter': Robert Rosenstock 'The Declaration of Principles of International Law Concerning Friendly Relations: A Survey' (1971) 715.

territorial integrity of a 'country'. The term 'country' could be read expansively to include both states and non-self-governing territories. However, the paragraph would then conflict with both Article 2(4) of the Charter, which refers only to states, and paragraph 7 of Resolution 2625(XXV), which appears to permit secession in certain circumstances to a part of the population of 'sovereign and independent States'. In order to achieve consistency with both Article 2(4) and paragraph 7 of Resolution 2625(XXV), the word 'country' should therefore be interpreted as referring only to non-self-governing territories. The same narrow interpretation of 'country' may apply to paragraph 8 of Resolution 2625(XXV). Paragraph 8 declares that states shall refrain from disrupting the territorial integrity of 'any other State or country'. The reference to a 'country' must therefore be taken to mean an entity other than a state, i.e. a non-self-governing territory.[10]

If Resolution 1514(XV) is interpreted in this way, then paragraph 6 of Resolution 1514(XV) and paragraphs 7 and 8 of Resolution 2625(XXV), read conjunctively, produce the following results: (1) no state may disrupt the territorial integrity either of another state or of a non-self-governing territory (paragraph 8 of Resolution 2625(XXV) and paragraph 6 of Resolution 1514(XV)); (2) secession caused by part of a population is prohibited in non-self-governing territories (paragraph 6 of Resolution 1514(XV)); and (3) secession caused by part of a population is permissible in certain circumstances in states (paragraph 7 of Resolution 2625(XXV)). These three aspects of secession are discussed below.

4. SECESSION AND NON-SELF-GOVERNING TERRITORIES

Since the adoption of Resolution 1514(XV) in 1960, the General Assembly has for the most part insisted on the maintenance of territorial integrity in non-self-governing entities, in accordance with the provisions of paragraph 6.[11] The General Assembly has even in some cases forced an administering power to reverse a decision to detach parts from a non-self-governing territory in order to maintain the territorial integrity of that entity.[12] How-

---

[10] Apart from textual analysis, it can also be argued that Resolution 1514(XV) should be limited to non-self-governing territories by virtue of its historical context. As Buchheit points out, when 'the context of a particular pronouncement so clearly refers to decolonization . . . , regardless of how broad the terminology or the intentions of some of the draftsmen, a cautious reader must assume it to have limited import. For purposes of this discussion, this latter category will include, for example, the General Assembly's 1960 Declaration on the Granting of Independence to Colonial Countries and Peoples . . .': Buchheit, 20.

[11] See Chapter 7, pp. 157–60 for a discussion of General Assembly practice with respect to non-self-governing territories.

[12] The case of the British Indian Ocean Territory is one example. This comprised 4 groups of islands, which were detached by the United Kingdom in 1965 from the British colonies of Mauritius and the Seychelles. The General Assembly opposed this action as being contrary to

ever, some administering states have challenged the view that self-determination in non-self-governing territories must, as a matter of international law, occur within the established territorial boundaries of the non-self-governing entity. The dispute between the General Assembly and France over the island of Mayotte is a good example.

Mayotte forms part of the Comoro Archipelago, which lies northwest of the Malagasy Republic. Before independence the Comoro Archipelago was a French overseas territory, comprising the islands of Grande-Comore, Anjouan, Moheli, and Mayotte. The population of Mayotte was predominantly Christian, whereas the population of the other islands was predominantly Muslim.[13] In 1972 a movement for independence gained popular support in the Muslim islands of the Comoro Archipelago; the Comorian Local Assembly declared itself in favour of independence, but the representatives of Mayotte voted against it.[14] On 14 December 1973 the General Assembly adopted Resolution 3161(XXVII), the first paragraph of which affirmed the 'inalienable right of the people of the Comoro Archipelago to self-determination and independence'. Paragraph 4 asserted the 'unity and territorial integrity of the Comoro Archipelago', and in paragraph 5 the General Assembly requested the French Government, as the administering power, 'to ensure that the unity and territorial integrity of the Comoro Archipelago are preserved'. Resolution 3291(XXIX) of 13 December 1974 repeated this language virtually word for word. A plebiscite was held in the Comoro Archipelago on 22 December 1974: 94.56 per cent were in favour of independence. On the island of Mayotte, however, only 36.18 per cent were in favour.[15] The French National Assembly passed a law on 3 July 1975 declaring that the Comoro Archipelago would be granted independence after a constitution had been prepared; each individual island would be required to adopt the constitution and it would apply only to the islands which had accepted it.

On 6 July 1975 the Comoros Assembly unilaterally declared the independence of the Comoro Archipelago within its colonial frontiers, despite opposition from the representatives of Mayotte.[16] The new state requested membership in the United Nations, which was granted by General Assembly Resolution 3385(XXX) of 12 November 1975. This Resolution reaffirmed 'the necessity of respecting the unity and territorial integrity of the

para. 6 of Resolution 1514(XV): General Assembly Resolutions 2066(XX) of 16 Dec. 1965, 2232(XXI) of 20 Dec. 1966, 2357(XXII) of 19 Dec. 1967, and 2430(XXIII) of 18 Dec. 1968. The United Kingdom eventually agreed to return 3 of the island groups to the Seychelles prior to its independence in 1976: J. Robert Maguire 'The Decolonization of Belize: Self-Determination *v.* Territorial Integrity' (1982) 864, fn. 91.

[13] Michla Pomerance *Self-Determination in Law and Practice* (1982) 98, fn. 182.
[14] David Rouzié 'Bulletin de Jurisprudence: Note' (1976) 394.
[15] Hector Gros Espiell *The Right to Self-Determination: Implementation of United Nations Resolutions* (UN Study E/CN.4/Sub.2/405/Rev.1) (1980) 47.
[16] Rouzié, 395.

Comoro Archipelago, composed of the islands of Anjouan, Grande-Comore, Mayotte and Moheli'. France responded by adopting a law on 31 December 1975 which declared that the islands of Anjouan, Grande-Comore, and Moheli were no longer part of the French Republic, but that the inhabitants of Mayotte would be consulted as to whether they wished to become part of the independent state of the Comoros or to remain part of the French Republic. On 6 February 1976 France used its veto to prevent the Security Council from adopting a resolution on the subject. Two days later a referendum was held in Mayotte, in which 99.4 per cent of the populace voted to remain part of France.[17] The General Assembly then adopted Resolution 31/4 of 21 October 1976, paragraph 1 of which condemned and declared 'null and void' the referendum of 8 February 1976. Paragraph 2 condemned the presence of France in Mayotte, which was said to constitute 'a violation of the national unity, territorial integrity and sovereignty of the independent Republic of the Comoros'. Paragraph 3 called upon the Government of France to withdrew immediately from the 'Comorian island of Mayotte', which was described as 'an integral part of the independent Republic of the Comoros'. Since Resolution 31/4, the General Assembly has adopted a resolution each year on the 'Question of the Comorian Island of Mayotte'; these reaffirm the unity and territorial integrity of the Comoros and call upon France to return Mayotte to the Comoros. France refuses to do so.

France takes the position that the frontiers of non-self-governing territories are not immutable, and argues that paragraph 6 cannot prohibit those frontiers from being altered if that is the expressed desire of the population concerned. France has pointed out that paragraph 6 does not reflect the terms of Articles 73 and 74 of the Charter, which nowhere state that the territorial integrity of a non-self-governing territory must be preserved. Article 73 does provide that administering states must recognize as paramount the interests of the inhabitants of non-self-governing territories and must take due account of the political aspirations of the peoples involved. By separating Mayotte from the Comoros, France argues, it has satisfied the political aspirations of the inhabitants of both Mayotte and the other islands of the Comoros. This would not have been achieved had the territorial integrity of the Comoros been preserved.[18]

Those states in the General Assembly which seek the incorporation of

---

[17] Pomerance, 98, fn. 178.

[18] France also invokes Art. 53(3) of its constitution, which prohibits any cession, exchange, or addition of territory 'without the consent of the populations concerned': Albert P. Blaustein and Gisbert H. Flanz (eds.) *Constitutions of the Countries of the World* Binder V, (1989) 'France' 38. National law, of course, cannot be put forward as a reason for not complying with international obligations. See Art. 27 of the 1969 Vienna Convention on the Law of Treaties and ILC Draft Articles on State Responsibility, Part I, Art. 4 and Part II, Art. 6 bis (3). France must therefore show that para. 6 of Resolution 1514(XV) does not constitute a binding obligation at international law.

Mayotte into the Comoros consider that paragraph 6 has become a part of international law, and that its provisions therefore cannot be ignored. The law on non-self-governing territories, it is argued, has continually developed and expanded since the Charter, so that Articles 73 and 74 alone no longer represent the current state of the law. This was expressly recognized by the International Court of Justice in the *Namibia* case, when it discussed 'the subsequent development of international law in regard to non-self-governing territories'.[19] The Court noted in particular the important role played by Resolution 1514(XV) in this development, stating that the Resolution 'embraces all peoples and territories which "have not yet attained independence"'.[20] Paragraph 6 therefore represents the current state of the law and must be obeyed. The General Assembly confirmed this position in Resolution 34/91 of 12 December 1979: paragraph 1 reaffirmed that the territorial integrity of a 'colonial territory' must be respected 'at the time of its accession to independence'.

However, the assertion by the General Assembly that paragraph 6 constitutes law, so that non-self-governing territories can in no circumstances be subdivided, has been weakened by the fact that the General Assembly itself has not been entirely consistent in this regard. In the case of the Gilbert and Ellice Islands, the facts were similar to those of Mayotte and the Comoros. The Gilbert and Ellice Islands comprised a single non-self-governing territory. Most of the inhabitants of the Gilbert Islands were Micronesian in origin, whereas those of the Ellice Islands were Polynesian. The Ellice Islanders voted by over 90 per cent to separate from the Gilbert Islands, and acceded to independence in 1978 as the state of Tuvalu. The Gilbert Islands subsequently received their independence in 1979 as the state of Kiribati.[21] The General Assembly in this case, unlike that of Mayotte, acquiesced in the division of a non-self-governing territory into two independent states.[22]

Micronesia is another example of a non-self-governing territory whose territorial integrity was not preserved upon independence. As a strategic Trust Territory, Micronesia fell within the jurisdiction of the Security Council rather than the General Assembly by virtue of Article 83 of the Charter. The territory had been administered by the United States, which was obliged under the terms of Article 76(b) of the Charter to promote the development of self-government or independence amongst the inhabitants. This was to be done in accordance with 'the freely expressed wishes of the

[19] *Legal Consequences for States of the Continued Presence of South Africa in Namibia (South West Africa) notwithstanding Security Council Resolution 276 (1970)* Advisory Opinion, ICJ Reports, 1971, p. 16, 31. See pp. 84–6 Chapter 4 for a detailed discussion of this case.
[20] *Id.*, 31.
[21] Pomerance, 19, 86, fn. 105.
[22] GA Consensus, 32/407, 28 Nov. 1977.

peoples concerned'. The population of Micronesia was composed of at least two ethnic groups. The majority of the population in the Northern Marianas were Chamorros, who spoke a different language and were ethnically and culturally distinct from the population in the other Micronesian Islands, known as Carolinians. Amongst the Carolinians there was a further subdivision: the Marshallese claimed that they constituted a separate group from other Carolinians.[23]

When negotiations began in October 1969 for a change of status for Micronesia, there was a single negotiating team for the entire Micronesian Trust Territory. The United States initially ignored requests from the Marianas for separate negotiations. However, in December 1972 the United States did enter into such negotiations, and in 1976 a covenant establishing Commonwealth status for the Northern Marianas Islands was agreed upon.[24] Meanwhile, in 1974 and 1975 respectively, the Marshall Islands and Palau also demanded and received separate negotiations with the United States, while negotiations continued with the remaining islands of Micronesia. In 1986 a Compact of Free Association was concluded with the Federated States of Micronesia, the Marshall Islands, and Palau.[25] The terms of the Compact were accepted by Micronesia and the Marshall Islands, which became members of the United Nations on 17 September 1991.[26] Palau also entered into a Compact of Free Association with the United States and became an independent state on 1 October 1994,[27] and a member of the United Nations on 15 December 1994.[28]

The Soviet Union criticized the United States for not promoting the independence of Micronesia and for encouraging parochialism which led to the division of the Trust Territory, contrary to paragraph 6 of Resolution 1514(XV).[29] In response, the United States argued that the separation of the Trust Territory and the final status of each of the entities thereby created were the result of freely expressed choices by the islanders.[30] Given the cultural diversity of the area it was, according to the United States, neither surprising nor unnatural that the islanders should wish to establish separate entities. The United States argued that it had done no more than respect 'the freely expressed wishes of the peoples concerned', as required by Article 76(b). However, the US clearly breached the terms of paragraph 6 of Resolution 1514(XV) in the course of these events.

[23] Naomi Hirayasu 'The Process of Self-Determination and Micronesia's Future Political Status Under International Law' (1987) 489, 500.

[24] *Id.*, 498–500.   [25] *Id.*, 495–6.

[26] Micronesia and the Marshall Islands were admitted to the United Nations pursuant to GA Resolutions 46/2 and 46/3.   [27] Keesing's *Record of World Events* (1994) Vol. 40, 40236.

[28] Palau was admitted to the UN pursuant to GA Resolution 49/63.

[29] John F. Murphy 'Self-Determination: United States Perspectives' in Yonah Alexander and Robert A. Friedlander (eds.) *Self-Determination: National, Regional and Global Dimensions* (1980) 52.

[30] Hirayasu, 522.

An inflexible and dogmatic insistence on territorial integrity in all cases reduces a 'people' to no more than the sum of those who happen to inhabit a given non-self-governing territory; such a 'people' may include various ethnic or religious groups which have little or nothing in common with each other, and whose relationship is characterized by mutual antipathy and distrust. To insist that such groups coexist within a single political unit simply ensures ongoing instability. The General Assembly condemned colonialism because it deprived colonial peoples of the right to control their own political destiny and subjected them to domination by another people; yet by insisting on territorial integrity in all cases the General Assembly has failed to solve this problem, because some ethnic groups within newly independent states will still be subject to political domination by alien forces, although that domination will be by a powerful local group rather than by an imperial power. However, this situation is now largely moot, since very few non-self-governing territories remain in existence.

5. SECESSION AND INDEPENDENT STATES

Resolution 2625(XXV) appears to sanction secession in the case of sovereign and independent states if part of a state's population is not represented in the state's government. Paragraph 7 makes the territorial integrity of a state contingent upon the existence of a 'government representing the whole people', in the absence of which secession is permitted for that part of the population which is not represented in the government.

There is considerable debate about the scope of paragraph 7. Some commentators maintain that it is so narrowly worded as to provide very little real basis for secession. Pomerance, for example, points out 'the racial context in which the requirement of "representative" appears'.[31] Hannum notes the 'limited requirement of non-discrimination only on the grounds of race, creed or colour'.[32] According to such authors, secession would only be legitimate when a state's government was unrepresentative on these narrow grounds: overtly racist regimes would therefore be the only governments to qualify as unrepresentative.[33] Lack of representation on ethnic grounds would not qualify.

Other commentators have interpreted paragraph 7 much more broadly. Buchheit sees it simply as a component of a larger theory based on the premise that oppression legitimizes secession:

---

[31] Pomerance, 39.

[32] Hurst Hannum *Autonomy, Sovereignty and Self-Determination* (1990) 473.

[33] Antonio Cassese 'Political Self-Determination: Old Concepts and New Developments' in Antonio Cassese (ed.) *UN Law/Fundamental Rights* (1979) 145.

international law recognizes a continuum of remedies ranging from protection of individual rights to minority rights, and ending with secession as the ultimate remedy. At a certain point, the severity of a State's treatment of its minorities becomes a matter of international concern. This concern may be evidenced by an international demand for guarantees of minority rights (which is as far as the League was willing to go) or suggestions of regional autonomy, economic independence, and so on; or it may finally involve an international legitimation of a right to secessionist self-determination, as a self-help remedy by the aggrieved group (which seems to have been the approach of the General Assembly in its 1970 declaration).[34]

To advocates of this more extensive 'oppression theory', paragraph 7 represents only one aspect of a wider rationale for secession. Therefore, even if the criteria of paragraph 7 are not strictly satisfied, secession will still be legitimate if there have been other serious violations of fundamental human rights. This expansive 'oppression theory' has been advocated by a number of authors,[35] and has been used to justify the secession of Bangladesh from Pakistan.[36] Given the rapid and widespread recognition of Bangladesh as an independent state following its secession from Pakistan in 1971, it is important to establish the legal basis upon which Bangladesh's emergence into statehood occurred.

Before the secession of Bangladesh, Pakistan had a total population of some 130 million people, of whom 75 million lived in East Pakistan.[37] West Pakistan was comprised of various ethnic groups, including Punjabis, Pathans, Sindhis, and Baluchis, whereas East Pakistan was overwhelmingly Bengali.[38] Although the two regions shared a common religious faith, they had very little else in common. The ethnic origins, language, and culture of the Bengalis were all markedly different from those of Pakistanis in the West.[39] East Pakistan had long been dominated, both politically and economically, by West Pakistan. This led to a sense of considerable disaffection in the East, and eventually resulted in demands by an East Pakistani nationalist organization, the Awami League, for the creation of an autonomous East Pakistan within a federal and highly decentralized framework. In December 1970 a general election was held to elect a Constituent Assembly. The Awami League had campaigned on the basis of a 'Six-Point Program', which had as its goals the establishment of a decentralized federal system and the transformation of East Pakistan into a highly autonomous

---

[34] Buchheit, 222.

[35] See, for example, Suzuki, 807; Umozurike O. Umoruzike *Self-Determination in International Law* (1972) 199; Onyeonoro S. Kamenu 'Secession and the Right of Self-Determination: An OAU Dilemma' (1974) 361; Ved P. Nanda 'Self-Determination Under International Law: Validity of Claims to Secede' (1981) 278; Buchheit, 222.

[36] Buchheit, 212, 213; Ved P. Nanda 'The Tragic Tale of Two Cities—Islamabad (West Pakistan) and Dacca (East Pakistan)' (1972) 328.

[37] M. K. Nawaz 'Bangla Desh and International Law' (1971) 252.

[38] Buchheit, 201.   [39] Nawaz, 252.

region. West Pakistani leaders opposed the Awami League's Six-Point Program, fearing that this would have a destabilizing effect on the ethnically heterogeneous West. The Awami League insisted that its Program form the basis of the new constitution. In the election the Awami League obtained an outright majority, winning 167 of the 313 seats in the Assembly.[40]

The election results provoked a crisis within Pakistan. On 1 March 1971 President Yahya Khan announced that the convening of the Assembly would be indefinitely postponed; violent demonstrations erupted throughout East Pakistan. The Awami League promoted a campaign of non-cooperation and civil disobedience against Pakistani authorities; the Pakistani military, drawn mainly from West Pakistan, then embarked on a policy of widespread and brutal suppression throughout East Pakistan. This involved the arrest, torture, and killing of Awami League activists, students, professional and business men, and other potential leaders of the Bengalis; the extirpation of the Bengali Hindu community (some 20 per cent of the East Pakistani population); the indiscriminate killing of civilians, including women and children; the raping of women, the destruction of towns and villages, and the looting of property: all on a vast scale.[41] According to Nawaz, some one million people were killed between March and December 1971.[42] The International Commission of Jurists, although unwilling to estimate the exact number of persons killed, nevertheless confirmed that they could 'be numbered in tens of thousands, and probably in hundreds of thousands'.[43] It further noted that some ten million East Pakistani refugees had fled to India by December 1971.[44]

During this period the Awami League established a provisional government in exile in India. On 10 April 1971 the League proclaimed the independence of Bangladesh 'in due fulfilment of the legitimate right of self-determination of the people of Bangladesh'.[45] An East Pakistani guerilla organization known as the Mukti Bahini was formed, for which India supplied arms and provided sanctuary. Border incidents between Indian and Pakistani troops became increasingly frequent, and the situation was further exacerbated by the enormous number of refugees fleeing from East Pakistan to India. On 21 November 1971 the Mukti Bahini launched an offensive which greatly intensified fighting in East Pakistan, and on 23 November 1971 President Yahya Khan declared a state of emergency. On 3 December 1971 Pakistani fighter aircraft attacked Indian airfields, and war broke out between the two states. India then recognized Bangladesh as

[40] Suzuki, 805.
[41] The International Commission of Jurists 'East Pakistan Staff Study' (1972) 8 *International Commission of Jurists Review* 23, 26–34; Buchheit, 206; Nawaz, 252.
[42] Nawaz, 254.
[43] The International Commission of Jurists, 33.
[44] *Id.*, 58.
[45] Bangladesh Proclamation of Independence (1972) 11 *International Legal Materials* 119.

an independent state. India also succeeded in establishing an air and sea blockade of Pakistani forces in the East, which resulted in their capitulation within two weeks.[46] As a result of the war Bangladesh was able to secede from Pakistan and to secure its independence as a separate state. It was quickly recognized by a majority of the world's states,[47] and was admitted as a member state of the United Nations in 1974.[48]

The recognition of Bangladesh as an independent state by the United Nations indicates that the 'oppression theory' may indeed represent a valid basis for secession: but what actually constitutes 'oppression', however, is far from clear. There have been a number of attempts to define oppression which is sufficient to legitimize secession. Nanda sets out the following criteria:

The test to determine severe deprivation of a group's human rights involves an examination of the extent to which it suffers 'subjugation, domination and exploitation', and the correlative extent to which its individual members are deprived of the opportunity to participate in the value processes of a body politic because of their group identification.[49]

Kamenu proposes a somewhat different test:

on the basis of hard empirical evidence, the members of the seceding group could no longer live in peace and security, or fulfil their legitimate individual aspirations, within the larger political community . . . However, for this rationale to be plausible it must be demonstrated that all other political arrangements capable of ensuring the aggrieved group a measure of self-determination short of outright independence have been exhausted or repudiated by the dominant majority.[50]

These examples demonstrate that the parameters of oppression required to legitimize secession have yet to be definitively established. It is clear, however, that those parameters extend far beyond the strict confines of paragraph 7 of Resolution 2625(XXV).

Whatever the exact parameters of the oppression theory, there is inherent within the theory a problem which renders it unrealizable in most cases: the prohibition against outside intervention. Paragraph 8 of Resolution 2625(XXV) forbids states from undertaking any action 'aimed at the partial or total disruption of the national unity or territorial integrity of any other State or country'. This principle of non-intervention was strongly emphasized by the International Court of Justice in the *Nicaragua*

---

[46] Buchheit, 207.

[47] Crawford, 115.

[48] GA Resolution 3203(XXIX) of 17 Sep. 1974.

[49] Nanda (1981) 278. Nanda was quoting from the Preamble of the Declaration of Friendly Relations, which provides, *inter alia*, as follows: 'The General Assembly . . . [was] convinced that the subjection of peoples to alien subjugation, domination and exploitation constitutes a major obstacle to the promotion of international peace and security.'

[50] Kamenu, 361.

case.[51] However, without outside intervention it is unlikely that part of a state's population will be able to secede, given that they will ordinarily be struggling against an enemy force superior in both numbers and military might. Bangladesh certainly could not have attained independence without Indian intervention.[52] Paragraph 8 results in a situation whereby an oppressed part of a state's population may be legally entitled to secede, but is in fact unable to do so because the outside assistance necessary to effect a successful secession has been declared illegal.

The 'oppression theory' has also been criticized on the basis that it does not accommodate the desires of ethnic groups to create their own nation-states. The prerequisite for secession underpinning the 'oppression theory' is not ethnic differentiation but oppression.[53] It was the fact of oppression, rather than the fact that the Bengalis were linguistically, ethnically, and culturally different from other Pakistanis, which ultimately justified the creation of Bangladesh as a separate and independent state under the oppression theory. Many ethnic groups find this an unsatisfactory basis upon which to justify secession. A people is entitled to control its own political destiny, it is argued, not only in states in which there is oppression, but also in democratic and non-discriminatory states.[54] Ethnic groups maintain that the right of self-determination should rest, not on the existence or otherwise of oppression, but 'upon the urge to be governed by those like oneself; it is unconcerned with the relative merits of the alien rule because, as in the colonial context, the mere fact of alien domination is the basis of complaint'.[55]

Secession on the basis of ethnic criteria could be justified by the 'internal theory', which maintains that secession is not a matter of international law at all, but solely of domestic concern. The theory is based on the well established principle of non-interference. The principle is set out in Article 2(4) and 2(7) of the United Nations Charter. Article 2(4) prohibits 'the threat or use of force against the territorial integrity or political independence of any state'. Article 2(7) prohibits the United Nations from intervening 'in matters which are essentially within the domestic jurisdiction of any state'. The import of these paragraphs is twofold: on the one hand international law ensures that states are entitled not to have their territorial integ-

---

[51] *Military and Paramilitary Activities in and against Nicaragua* (*Nicaragua* v. *USA*) Merits, Judgment, ICJ Reports 1986, p. 14 at 108.

[52] Crawford, 115.

[53] Kamenu, 361.

[54] This point is made by Brossard, who complains that the Québecois are deprived of the option of secession by the terms of para. 7 of Resolution 2625(XXV) because they enjoy representation in the Government of Canada: Jacques Brossard 'Le Droit du Peuple Québecois de Disposer de lui-même au Regard du Droit International' (1977) 15 *Canadian Yearbook of International Law* 107.

[55] Buchheit, 223.

rity subverted by other states, but on the other hand it offers no protection against subversion within the state itself, because this is outside the jurisdiction of international law. There is no rule of international law which forbids the territorial division of a state, either following peaceful change or as a result of civil conflict.[56] Consequently, those declarations against secession which appear in international instruments or in General Assembly resolutions must be limited to cases of intervention by a third-party state.[57] They cannot be used to establish that secession within a state is illegal, because this is outside the jurisdiction of international law. Any attempt so to argue would be a logical absurdity: it would mean that the seceding entity, by disobeying the prohibition, would be acting illegally at international law, and hence would be a subject of international law—the very object which the prohibition seeks to deny.[58] It follows that 'secession is neither legal nor illegal in international law, but is a legally neutral act, the consequences of which are, or may be, regulated internationally'.[59]

Only if the declaratory (rather than the constitutive) theory of recognition governs secession will that process constitute a neutral act at international law.[60] This is because under the *constitutive* theory the act of recognition is determinative of the seceding entity's status. Under this theory secession cannot be a neutral act at international law, because recognition in the international domain is required before statehood can be attained. Under the *declaratory* theory of recognition, on the other hand, the act of recognition merely acknowledges that a seceding entity has attained statehood; it is not determinative of that status. Secession is a neutral act at international law under that theory, because the attainment of statehood requires no act on the part of other states. It follows that the internal theory cannot be well founded if recognition is constitutive, because recognition at international law by other states is essential to becoming a state. However, the internal theory will be well founded if recognition

---

[56] Crawford, 266; Buchheit, 221; Suzuki, 807, 808; Quincy Wright 'United States Intervention in the Lebanon' (1959) 121; Note 'The Logic of Secession' (1980) 809.

[57] For references to the statements of individual states with regard to self-determination and secession in the *travaux préparatoires* to the International Human Rights Covenants, see Antonio Cassese 'The Self-Determination of Peoples' in Louis Henkin (ed.) *The International Bill of Rights* (1981) 423, fn. 28. For references to such statements in the *travaux préparatoires* to the Helsinki Declaration, see Harold S. Russell 'The Helsinki Declaration: Brobdingnag or Lilliput?' (1976) 269–70; Cassese (1979) 165, fn. 24.

[58] Crawford, 267.

[59] *Id.*, 268.

[60] Attempts to secede will not be neutral at international law if the territory claimed was acquired by an illegal act, because good title cannot be obtained by illegal means: S. K. N. Blay 'Self-Determination Versus Territorial Integrity in Decolonization' (1986) 457, fn. 77. The forcible annexation by the Soviet Union of the Baltic States illustrates this principle: many states did not recognize that annexation, and therefore the desire expressed by the populations of those territories to secede from the Soviet Union remained a matter of international law: Crawford, 419–20.

is declaratory, because in that case a seceding entity can attain statehood without international recognition.

The International Court of Justice, in the case *Reparation For Injuries Suffered in the Service of the United Nations*, appeared to endorse the constitutive theory when it declared that a majority of states 'had the power, in conformity with international law, to bring into being an entity possessing objective international personality, and not merely personality recognised by them alone, together with capacity to bring international claims.'[61] Although the 'entity' referred to by the Court was not a state but an international organization, Wright has argued that the declaration of the Court is equally applicable to states, in that it simply sets out the position of customary international law, under which 'the status of entities subject to international law is determined by general recognition'.[62] The Court's declaration, however, should not be understood as an endorsement of the constitutive theory. The Court had drawn a clear distinction between the United Nations and states.[63] Given that it was the United Nations whose status was being determined in this particular case, and given the clear distinction made by the Court between that organization and states, the Court's declaration should be interpreted narrowly. The 'entity' referred to in the Court's statement should be taken to mean only the United Nations; it certainly should not be understood as an endorsement of the constitutive theory.

There is clear judicial authority in support of the declaratory theory in the case of *Deutsche Continental Gas Gesellschaft* v. *The Polish State*.[64] The German-Polish Arbitral Tribunal, in discussing the existence of the new state of Poland, held that 'the recognition of a State is not constitutive but merely declaratory. The State exists by itself and the recognition is nothing else than a declaration of this existence, recognized by the States from which it emanates'.[65] In affirming the declaratory theory the Arbitral Tribunal was able to avoid a number of fundamental problems associated with the constitutive theory. If the determination of a state's international status depends upon its recognition by other states, the legal existence of that state would be relative to its relationships with other states; in other words, a state would not have any absolute existence in international law.[66] Under the constitutive theory international law itself would be reduced to 'a system of imperfect communications' whereby 'every rule of international law would be the subject of, in effect, an "automatic reservation" with respect to every State'.[67] Moreover, if recognition were constitutive in nature recog-

---

[61] Advisory Opinion, ICJ Reports 1949, p. 174, 185.
[62] Quincy Wright 'Recognition and Self-Determination' (1954) 32.
[63] ICJ Reports 1949, p. 174 at 179.
[64] (1929) 5 AD No. 5.
[65] *Id.*   [66] Crawford, 19.   [67] *Id.*, 18.

nition itself could never be invalid or void. If this were so, recognition could be used as an alternative form of intervention.[68] Recognition should not therefore be seen as constitutive of a state's status in international law, but should be understood simply as a political act which is 'independent of the existence of the new State as a full subject of international law'.[69] Acceptance of the declaratory theory as the correct approach to the issue of recognition necessarily implies acceptance of the internal theory with regard to secession.

Many of the issues discussed above came to the fore when Biafra attempted to secede from Nigeria. Both the 'oppression theory' and the 'internal theory' were put forward as justification for Biafra's secession. The recognition of Biafra by a small number of states raised the issue of whether Biafra had in fact become an independent state in international law. There was also the question of whether the Biafrans were a 'people', and if so, by what understanding of the term 'people'.

Nigeria was a British colony which attained independence on 1 October 1960. It is the most densely populated country in Africa. In 1968 it had a population numbering some 56 million. This population was composed of three major ethnic groups: the Hausa-Fulani in the North, the Yoruba in the West, and the Ibo in the East.[70] The Hausa-Fulani were overwhelmingly Muslim, the Ibo predominantly Christian, and the Yoruba an approximately equal mixture of Muslims and Christians.[71] There were also some 250 smaller ethnic groups within the country, of differing languages, cultures, and religions.[72]

As a colony, Nigeria was ruled as a tri-regional federal structure. This arrangement, with Northern, Western, and Eastern Regions, was continued after independence, with a fourth Region—the Mid-Western—created in 1963.[73] This division intensified the ethnic, cultural, linguistic, and religious differences which already existed between the various ethnic groups. Each political party represented only the interests of its own ethnic region.[74] During the first five years of independence these political parties were unable to work together. There were frequent threats to secede from all the regions, but particularly from the North and the West. By the end of 1965 Nigeria was on the brink of political chaos.

On 15 January 1966 the Government was overthrown in a military coup by a group of officers seeking to establish national unity and to end governmental corruption. Although they proclaimed a policy of national unity, the

---

[68] *Id.*, 19.   [69] *Id.*, 20.
[70] M. G. Kaladharan Nayer 'Self-Determination Beyond the Colonial Context: Biafra in Retrospect' (1975) 322.
[71] Buchheit, 162.
[72] Nayer, 322.
[73] *Id.*, 322.
[74] K. W. J. Post 'Is There A Case For Biafra?' (1968) 31.

officers who effected the coup were all Ibos, whereas most of those killed during the coup were Northerners, a fact which sat very ill in the North.[75] Major-General Aguiyi Ironsi, who assumed the leadership of the new Government, declared that the root cause of Nigeria's problems was 'a rigid adherence to "regionalism"'. He attempted to remedy this situation with the 'Unification Decree' of 24 May 1966, which would have abolished the regions and replaced them with a centralized unitary system.[76] The North considered this to be a ploy by the Ibos to dominate the country, and on 29 July 1966 officers from the North carried out a second coup. Lieutenant-Colonel Yabuku Gowon became the new head of state. Gowon's initial plan was to re-establish the dominance of the North over the rest of the country, or else to effect the secession of the North. In the meantime, ethnic tensions throughout the country intensified. In September and October 1966 widespread rioting in the North resulted in the massacre or expulsion of many thousands of Easterners.[77]

After coming to power Gowon's position changed radically: he became committed to the idea of a united Nigeria, and by November 1966 was publicly advocating 'the continued existence of Nigeria as one political and economic unit'.[78] The East, on the other hand, was deeply aggrieved at the treatment of Easterners in the North, and became alienated from the entire process of constitutional reform. Nevertheless, negotiations for constitutional reform continued throughout this turbulent period. In an effort to reconcile the East, Gowon entered into direct negotiations with Lieutenant-Colonel Odumegwu Ojukwu, the Governor of the Eastern Region, in January 1967. Initially it appeared that the two sides had reached agreement about key issues of constitutional reform, but within a month each was making totally different assertions about the terms of the agreement. According to Gowon, it had been agreed that a strong central government was necessary. Ojukwu maintained that a loose federal arrangement had been envisaged, under which each region would have full control over its internal affairs and would have a right of veto of any policy decisions made by the central government. The two men subsequently accused each other of deliberately contravening the agreement.[79]

---

[75] K. W. J. Post 'Is There A Case For Biafra?' (1968), 29.

[76] Buchheit, 165.

[77] According to Panter-Brick, approximately 10,000 Easterners were killed: 262, fn. 5. Post set the figure much higher, declaring that as many as 40,000 Easterners had been killed, and over one million expelled from the North: 32. The Biafran authorities themselves claimed that 30,000 Easterners were 'known to have been killed': 'Proclamation of the Republic of Biafra' (1967) 6 ILM 665, 668.

[78] Buchheit, 167.

[79] John R. Wood 'Secession: A Comparative Analytical Framework' (1981) 129; Buchheit, 167.

Thereafter the situation steadily deteriorated. In April 1967 the Eastern Region refused to remit funds to the Federal Government.[80] On 27 May 1967 the Federal Government unilaterally redefined Nigeria's regions, creating a new state of Lagos and dividing the Northern Region into six new states, the West into two, and the East into three.[81] The Eastern Region immediately declared the Government's action unconstitutional. On the same day a joint session of the Eastern Region's Consultative Assembly and the Advisory Committee of Chiefs and Elders adopted a resolution directing Ojukwu 'to declare at the earliest practicable date Eastern Nigeria a free, sovereign and independent state by the name and title of the Republic of Biafra'.[82] On 30 May the Republic of Biafra declared its independence. On 6 July 1967 the Federal Government announced that it would undertake military action to reincorporate the Eastern Region into Nigeria.[83] A military and economic blockade was imposed on Biafra, and Gowon predicted a 'short, surgical police action'.[84] Instead, a prolonged and devastating civil war ensued. The Eastern Region was a traditional importer of food; as a result of the blockade Biafra became unable to feed its population, and many thousands of civilians died of starvation.[85] After intense combat lasting thirty months, Biafran authorities surrendered to the Nigerian armed forces on 12 January 1970, bringing to an end their attempt to secede.

The conflict in Nigeria illustrates the problems surrounding the proper meaning of self-determination. Nigeria maintained that the right of self-determination was simply that of decolonization in a non-self-governing territory, and that once this had occurred the territorial integrity of the emergent independent state was inviolable. Biafra, on the other hand, asserted that the right of self-determination was available to any people with a grievance, and that it included the right to secede.[86] In support of its position Biafra argued the 'oppression theory'. The Proclamation of the Republic of Biafra[87] detailed the political injustices suffered by the Eastern Region, and underscored the slaughter or expulsion of the many thousands of Easterners from the Northern Region in the previous year.[88] Moreover, in its appeal to the United Nations in December 1967, Biafra charged the

---

[80] Francis Wodie 'La Sécession du Biafra et le Droit International Public' (1969) 1022.

[81] Post, 130.

[82] 'Proclamation of the Republic of Biafra' (1967) 6 ILM 665, 678.

[83] Wodie, 1022.

[84] Nayer, 323.

[85] *Id.*, 323. According to a medical survey of the International Red Cross it was estimated that, by December 1968, 10,000 people were dying of starvation each day in unoccupied Biafra, and 4,000 each day in occupied Biafra: 323.

[86] Panter-Brick, 263.

[87] (1967) 6 ILM 665.   [88] *Id.*, 665 *et seq.*

Federal Government of Nigeria with genocide and alleged that it had engaged in deliberate and continuous contraventions of the United Nations Charter provisions on human rights.[89]

During its brief existence Biafra was recognized by five states.[90] Tanzania was the first, eleven months after Biafra's declaration of independence. Tanzania invoked the 'oppression theory' as its primary reason for recognizing Biafra. Tanzania's Minister of State for Foreign Affairs, Chedid Mgonja, noted that 30,000 Easterners had been killed by other Nigerians. The fears of the Easterners which led them to create their own state were therefore real and their action was justified. 'Only by this act of recognition', Mgonja declared, 'can Tanzania remain true to her conviction that the purpose of Society is the service to man'.[91] Gabon recognized Biafra on the basis that its people were fighting 'for the right of existence recognized to every human being'.[92]

The United Nations did not accept Biafra's argument that it should be recognized on the basis of the 'oppression theory'. In December 1967 the United Nations refused to consider Biafra's charges of genocide and human rights abuses against Nigeria.[93] Three years later, on 9 January 1970, the Secretary-General reiterated that the United Nations could not act with respect to the Biafran situation unless Nigeria itself raised the matter at the United Nations.[94] The position of the United Nations, according to the Secretary-General, was that the Nigerian–Biafran war was 'purely an internal problem'.[95] This was also the position of the Organization of African Unity. In the OAU Resolution on the Situation in Nigeria in 1967[96] the Organization, after reiterating its 'condemnation of secession in any Member States', went on to recognize that the situation in Nigeria was 'an internal affair the solution of which is primarily the responsibility of Nigerians themselves'.[97] By treating the Biafran situation as an internal affair the United Nations and the Organization of African Unity were in effect confirming that the question of secession was not a matter which came within the competence of international law. Moreover, although both the Secretary-General of the United Nations and the Head of the OAU made

---

[89] Nanda (1981) 273.

[90] The 5 were Tanzania, Gabon, the Ivory Coast, Zambia, and Haiti: David A. Ijalaye 'Was "Biafra" At Any Time a State in International Law?' (1971) 554.

[91] Suzuki, 804.

[92] *Id.*, 804.

[93] Nanda (1981) 273.

[94] Suzuki, 803, 804.

[95] UN Press Release No. SG/SM 1062 (29 Jan. 1969). This was also the position adopted by the United Nations with respect to the secession of Katanga from the Congo in 1960. Although UN troops intervened in the Congo, the Secretary-General emphasized that the role of these troops was simply to counter external agression from Belgium, and not to suppress an internal secession: Buchheit, 145.

[96] AHG/Res.51(IV) (1967) 6 ILM 1243.   [97] *Id.*, 1243.

statements which insisted on the territorial integrity of member states, the subsequent admission of Bangladesh into the United Nations demonstrates that these statements did not reflect international law. International law was better reflected by the leader of Biafra, General Ojukwu, who argued that territorial integrity would fall within the OAU Charter only 'if one member state attempts to enlarge its territory at the expense of another member state, but certainly not in respect of the emergence of new states arising from the disintegration of a member state'.[98]

Although Biafra was recognized by five states it never managed to attain statehood in international law because Biafra never fulfilled the minimum requirements for statehood due to the ongoing conflict over its territory. In such circumstances recognition is considered inappropriate. As Brierly points out, recognition is premature 'so long as a real struggle is proceeding'.[99]

Biafra had claimed that self-determination should be interpreted so as to allow secession for any 'people with a grievance'.[100] However, there was doubt as to whether the population of Biafra constituted a people. Panter-Brick argued that the Eastern Region, whose frontiers had been drawn up during the colonial era, was no less an artificial creation than Nigeria, and consequently Biafra's claim that its population represented a people was erroneous.[101] A large number of Ibos lived outside the Eastern Region,[102] and within Biafra itself Ibos represented only 64 per cent of the total population.[103] Ethnic minorities of Efiks, Ijaws, Ibibios, and Arrangos comprised the remainder of the population;[104] these groups had as little in common with the Ibos as with other Nigerian ethnic groups.[105] However, the massacre and expulsion of Easterners in the Northern Region had indiscriminately included both Ibos and non-Ibos, so that all Easterners faced a common enemy.[106] Moreover, the vast majority of Biafrans, whether Ibo or non-Ibo, clearly supported the secession, as indicated by the willingness of the entire populace to endure thirty months of famine, disease, and fierce civil war in an attempt to achieve independence.[107] The internal theory of secession does not make the legitimacy of a particular secession contingent upon the ethnic homogeneity of the seceding territory's population, even though most attempts at secession are made by groups which are more ethnically homogeneous than was the case in Biafra.

---

[98] Suzuki, 802.

[99] James Leslie Brierly *The Law of Nations* (1963) 138. See also Ijalaye 556–9; Crawford 265.

[100] See *supra*, p. 197.

[101] Panter-Brick, 263.

[102] Buchheit, 175.

[103] *Id.*, 173.

[104] Wodie, 1028.

[105] Buchheit, 173; Panter-Brick, 263.   [106] Buchheit, 174.   [107] *Id.*, 174.

6. THE DISINTEGRATION OF YUGOSLAVIA

The facts relating to the disintegration of Yugoslavia were discussed in Chapter 5.[108] A significant legal problem involved the nature of Yugosalvia's disintegration: should it be characterized as a process of secession, or a process of dissolution? If secession, then only the entities seceding from Yugoslavia would require recognition because the original state would retain its international personality. On the other hand, if dissolution had occurred then all the successor states, including what remained of Yugoslavia itself, would require recognition because the original state would have ceased to exist. Yugoslavia argued that secession had occurred; Slovenia, Croatia, Bosnia-Herzegovina, and Macedonia argued that it was dissolution.

The nature of the dissolution was considered by the Badinter Arbitration Commission in its Opinion No. 1, handed down on 7 December 1991.[109] The Commission noted that four of Yugoslavia's six constituent republics had indicated a desire for independence. It considered the composition and workings of the essential political organs of the Yugoslav Federation, and concluded that they no longer met the criteria of participation and representativeness inherent in a federal state. Finally, it observed that armed conflict had arisen between the elements of the Federation and that neither the authorities of the Federation nor those of the Republics seemed able to enforce cease-fire agreements. For these reasons the Commission concluded that Yugoslavia was in the process of dissolution.[110] In Opinion No. 8 of 4 July 1992 the Commission found that the process of dissolution was complete and that the Socialist Federal Republic of Yugoslavia no longer existed.[111]

It is questionable whether the reasons cited by the Badinter Commission in Opinion No. 1 in fact establish that dissolution, rather than secession, took place in Yugoslavia. Secession occurs when an element of a previously unified territorial unit separates itself from that unit to become an independent state in its own right.[112] The corollary of secession is that the unit from which a seceding element has separated itself, although truncated by the loss of a part of its population and territory, retains its former identity and international personality. The facts surrounding the declarations of independence of the four constituent Republics indicate that their actions conform much more closely to secession than to dissolution. The four Republics did not separate from Yugoslavia at one point in time or in one act. Nor was there any agreement amongst them comparable to the Alma Ata Declaration signed by the constituent Republics of the Soviet Union,

---

[108] See Chapter 5, pp. 113–22.   [109] (1992) 31 ILM 1494.
[110] *Id*, 1497.   [111] (1992) 31 ILM 1521, 1523.   [112] See *supra*, p. 181.

which agreed that with the establishment of separate states the Soviet Union would cease to exist.[113] On the contrary, declarations of independence were made in the context of independence from the pre-existing Yugoslav Federation. Croatia and Slovenia were the first two Republics to declare their independence, on 25 June 1991. At that point Croatia and Slovenia themselves appeared to recognize that they were engaged in secession from Yugoslavia. In its Declaration of Independence, Slovenia noted, that it had attempted to obtain the peaceful dissolution of Yugoslavia before unilaterally proclaiming its own sovereignty and independence.[114] The new Croatian Constitution declared that: 'The right to peoples' sovereignty guarantees the Croatian nation the right to secession, to the creation of their independent state, to joining forces with other nations and states, as well as the right to manage economic, legal and political relations in its own state.'[115]

The subsequent declarations of independence by Macedonia and Bosnia-Herzegovina, on 9 September 1991 and 16 October 1991, were also made in the context of secession from Yugoslavia rather than in the context of a dissolution of the entire state.[116] Yugoslavia has constantly asserted its continuing identity as a state. The fact that Yugoslavia retained only 40 per cent of its original territory and 45 per cent of its original population is not in itself conclusive of dissolution.[117] As Crawford points out, 'acquisition or loss of territory does not *per se* affect the continuity of the State. This may be so even where the territory acquired or lost is substantially greater in area than the original or remaining State territory.'[118] The same considerations, according to Crawford, apply to changes in population, as such changes are 'concomitants of territorial changes'.[119] Pakistan provides a good example of state continuity in such circumstances: although Pakistan lost the entire eastern part of its territory and approximately 57 per cent of its population when Bangladesh seceded, it nevertheless retained its identity and continuity as a state.[120]

However, it was not simply the reduction of Yugoslavia from six to two constituent Republics which led the Commission to conclude that Yugoslavia was in a state of dissolution: great emphasis was also placed on the fact that Yugoslavia's federal organs of government no longer met the criteria of participation and representativeness necessary in a federal state. In

---

[113] Alma Ata Declaration, Art. 5 (1992) 31 ILM 148, 149.

[114] Roland Rich 'Recognition of States: The Collapse of Yugoslavia and the Soviet Union' (1993) 39

[115] Ben Bagwell 'Yugoslavian Constitutional Questions: Self-Determination and Secession of Member Republics' (1991) 513.

[116] See Chapter 5, pp. 116–17.

[117] Yehuda Z. Blum 'UN Membership of the "New" Yugoslavia: Continuity or Break?' (1992) 833.

[118] Crawford, 303.   [119] *Id.*, 405.   [120] See *supra*, pp. 189–91.

Opinion No. 8 the Commission again referred to the constitutional arrangements of the two remaining constituent Republics of Yugoslavia. The fact
that Serbia and Montenegro had adopted a new constitution on 27 April
1992 was, in the Commission's opinion, evidence that a new state had been
constituted, reinforcing the finding that the previous state of Yugoslavia
was no longer in existence.[121]

In Opinion No. 1 the Badinter Commission specifically stated that its
conclusion would be based on principles of international law,[122] yet no
authority was cited by the Commission to justify its proposition that an
examination of government organs is an established principle of international law for determining whether secession or dissolution has occurred.
Neither was any authority cited for the proposition in Opinion No. 8 that a
change in constitution signifies the dissolution of an existing, truncated
state. Not only did the Commission fail to cite authority, it also failed to
take into consideration those authorities and precedents which were inconsistent with its arguments. Crawford, for example, maintains that changes in
the constitution and form of government of a state do not affect the continuity of that state.[123] Moreover, the Sixth (Legal) Committee of the General
Assembly held that a change in the Indian constitution did not indicate the
extinction of that state. When British India, an original member of the
United Nations, became independent in 1947 and was partitioned into the
two states of India and Pakistan, the Sixth (Legal) Committee held that
India should retain its seat in the United Nations. The Committee declared:
'As a general rule, it is in accordance with principle to assume that a State
which is a member of the United Nations does not cease to be a member
from the mere fact that its constitution or frontiers have been modified'.[124]
It therefore appears that neither a change of frontiers nor a change in
constitution is indicative of the extinction of a state.

Neither are the participation and representativeness of a state's government necessarily indicative of that state's continued existence or otherwise,
because when part of the territory and population of a state separates itself
from that state this will always affect participation and representation in
that state's government, particularly in a federal structure. The secession
of Biafra from Nigeria certainly affected the nature and functioning of
Nigeria's federal government, yet this was never seen as a ground for
asserting that the state of Nigeria itself was in the process of dissolution.[125]
Similarly, in Cyprus, where constitutional provisions were designed to
create a political balance between Greek and Turkish Cypriots, and therefore required the participation of both ethnic communities, the refusal of

---

[121] (1992) 31 ILM 1521, 1523.   [122] *Id.*, 1494–5.
[123] Crawford, 405.
[124] UN GAOR 6th Comm., 2d Sess., 43d mtg. at 38 (1947).
[125] See *supra*, pp. 195–9, for a discussion of the Biafran secession.

Turkish Cypriots to participate in the government of Cyprus has never been cited as a ground for asserting that the state of Cyprus no longer exists.[126]

The Badinter Commission cited the civil conflict in Yugoslavia and the inability of the authorities of both the Federation and the constituent republics to enforce respect for ceasefire agreements as its final reason for concluding that Yugoslavia was in the process of dissolution. However, civil conflict is not necessarily indicative of dissolution. When Biafra and Bangladesh attempted to secede from their respective states, civil conflict resulted between those seeking to secede and those seeking to preserve the territorial integrity of the state. The fact of civil conflict itself, however, was not interpreted as indicating that Nigeria or Pakistan were in the process of dissolution; rather, it was understood in each case that an attempt at secession was taking place, and that the violence was a consequence of that attempt. In such circumstances, given the principle of territorial integrity, a state presumably possesses the right to defend itself against internal attempts to dismember it.[127] Even when a government does not represent the whole people as required by paragraph 7 of Resolution 2625(XXV), this does not mean that the state itself ceases to exist, but simply that its territorial integrity can no longer be guaranteed, so that secession by those not represented in the government becomes permissible.

It therefore appears that the disintegration of Yugoslavia should properly be characterized as a matter of secession by four of Yugoslavia's six republics, rather than a dissolution of the state. Nevertheless, the finding of the Badinter Commission in Opinion No. 1 was subsequently approved by both the Security Council and the General Assembly, which adopted resolutions declaring that the former state of Yugoslavia had ceased to exist.[128]

The finding of the Badinter Commission that the state of Yugoslavia was in a process of dissolution was certainly of great benefit to the European Community as it sought to regulate the civil conflict there and to formulate a basis for settlement amongst the entities emerging out of the dissolution. According to that finding of dissolution, none of the successor states could legitimately claim to be the continuation of the previous state. There was therefore no ongoing state which could accuse the European Community of intervention in its internal affairs when the Community proceeded to recognize breakaway entities as separate and independent states. The Community could also recognize these new entities without appearing to endorse secession. Finally, the European Community was able to deal with all the

---

[126] See Chapter 9, pp. 222–9, for a discussion of the situation in Cyprus.
[127] Marc Weller 'The International Response to the Dissolution of the Socialist Federal Republic of Yugoslavia' (1992) 572.
[128] See Chapter 5, p. 122.

Yugoslav successor states from a position of strength, in that it was able to impose conditions on all of them as a prerequisite to recognition.

As already observed, there are two theories of recognition: the constitutive theory and the declaratory theory.[129] The constitutive theory posits that statehood is only achieved when an entity has been recognized by the international community. Recognition is therefore a legal act because it produces legal effects. The declaratory theory, on the other hand, holds that recognition is simply a *post hoc* acknowledgement of a state which has already fulfilled the legal criteria for statehood.[130] Recognition is therefore not in itself a legal act, but a political act.[131] Because recognition under the declaratory theory is essentially a political act, it is permissible for one state to make its recognition of another state contingent upon conditions which go beyond the minimum legal criteria for statehood, and which do not in themselves constitute legal criteria, being merely of a political nature. However, political conditions attached to recognition are of course dependent on the fulfilment of the legal criteria for statehood. If the traditional minimum legal criteria for statehood are not satisfied, and recognition occurs upon some other basis, then recognition is not declaratory but constitutive in nature.

When the European Community set out its conditions for recognition of the successor states to Yugoslavia in the two Declarations of 16 December 1991, it was motivated by two considerations. It sought, first, to maintain the validity of the declaratory theory of recognition, whereby minimum legal criteria had to be met before a state could be recognized. This is indicated in the Declaration on the 'Guidelines on the Recognition of New States in Eastern Europe and the Soviet Union', which stated that recognition was to be 'subject to the normal standards of international practice'.[132] This reference to the normal standards of international practice made 'statehood, in its orthodox sense, a precondition for recognition'.[133] By appending to the minimum legal criteria for statehood certain additional conditions for recognition, however, the European Community sought, as its second objective, to use recognition to re-establish peace in the region and to arrive at a political settlement. The additional conditions were clearly not part of the

---

[129] See *supra*, pp. 193–5.

[130] Art. 1 of the 1933 Montevideo Convention (1936) 165 LNTS 19, 25, is generally accepted as setting out the minimum legal criteria for statehood. Art. 1 declares that 'The State as a person of international law should possess the following qualifications: a) a permanent population; b) a defined territory; c) government; and d) capacity to enter into relations with other states'.

[131] As Jean Charpentier points out, an 'act of recognition is political in that it is not an act which a state is bound to perform but rather one which issues from the state's free will . . .': 'Les Déclarations des Douze sur la Reconnaissance des Nouveaux Etats' (1992) 350 (author's translation).

[132] (1992) 31 ILM 1486, 1487.

[133] Colin Warbrick 'Recognition of States' (1992) 478.

minimum legal criteria, but were political in nature.[134] The inclusion of political conditions was certainly permissible under the declaratory theory, provided that they were in addition to the traditional legal criteria necessary for statehood.

In its Declaration on Yugoslavia, the European Community specified that all applications for recognition from the successor states to Yugoslavia would first be submitted to the Badinter Arbitration Commission for its advice.[135] Bosnia-Herzegovina, Croatia, Macedonia, and Slovenia applied for recognition, and their applications were considered by the Commission in Opinions Nos. 4 to 7. The Commission found that Macedonia and Slovenia satisfied the criteria for recognition laid down by the European Community.[136] It also found that Croatia would qualify for recognition if its Constitution included a provision for the 'special status' of minorities, as provided for in the draft Convention of 4 November 1991.[137] The Commission recommended that Bosnia-Herzegovina should not be recognized because the will of all its peoples for independence had not yet been fully established. It noted, however, that this finding could be reviewed if a referendum were held.[138] A referendum on the question of independence was held in Bosnia-Herzegovina on 1 March 1992; it was largely ignored by the Serbs, who constituted some 32 per cent of Bosnia-Herzegovina's population. (The remainder, including some Croats and Muslims, presumably did not vote either.) Consequently only 63 per cent of the total electorate voted. Nevertheless, 99.4 per cent of those who voted indicated that they were in favour of independence.[139]

The Badinter Commission handed down its Opinions Nos. 4 to 7 on 11 January 1992. On 15 January 1992 the member states of the European Community recognized Slovenia and Croatia.[140] They also recognized Bosnia-Herzegovina on 7 April 1992 following the referendum. The United States recognized Slovenia, Croatia, and Bosnia-Herzegovina on 7 April 1992. Macedonia, on the other hand, remained unrecognized by both the European Community and the United States, as a result of Greece's objections to the name of Macedonia.[141] The European Community had indicated in its Declaration on the 'Guidelines on the Recognition of New States in Eastern Europe and the Soviet Union' that recognition was to be 'subject to the normal standards of international practice'.[142] Of the three

---

[134] Weller (1992) 588. Charpentier was also of the opinion that the additional conditions were simply political in nature: 347.
[135] (1992) 31 ILM 1485, 1486.
[136] Opinions No. 6 (1992) 31 ILM 1507, and No. 7 (1992) 31 ILM 1512, respectively.
[137] Opinion No. 5, *id*. 1503–5.
[138] Opinion No. 4, *id*. 1501–3.
[139] Keesing's *Record of World Events* (1992) Vol. 38, 38832.
[140] Germany recognized Slovenia and Croatia on 23 Dec. 1991: Warbrick, 478.
[141] See Chapter 5, p. 119.   [142] (1992) 31 ILM 1486, 1487.

successor states recognized by the member states of the European Community, however, only Slovenia complied with the legal criteria set out in Article 1 of the Montevideo Convention. When Croatia was recognized by the member states of the European Community, its government had no control over approximately one-third of its territory.[143] This territory was occupied and controlled by Croatian Serbs, who had set up their own separate Republic of Krajina and were engaged in civil conflict with Croatian forces.[144] The situation in Bosnia-Herzegovina was even worse. Immediately following the referendum on independence, fighting had broken out between Bosnian Serbs, on one hand, and Bosnian Muslims and Croats on the other. The Bosnian Serbs had already declared their own separate Serbian Republic of Bosnia-Herzegovina on 9 January 1992, and rapidly occupied approximately 70 per cent of the territory of Bosnia-Herzegovina.[145] Neither Croatia nor Bosnia-Herzegovina had a government capable of exercising sovereignty over large parts of their putative population or territory. Therefore neither entity met the legal criteria of statehood as set out in Article 1 of the Montevideo Convention. Nevertheless, both entities were recognized as states by both the European Community and the United States. Although the member states of the European Community were at liberty, under the declaratory theory, to impose specific political conditions in return for recognition, such conditions had to be in addition to the minimum legal criteria of statehood, since only by fulfilment of those criteria could a new state come into existence. Yet Croatia and Bosnia-Herzegovina were recognized even though they had not fulfilled the minimum legal criteria for statehood. The criteria for recognition set out in the two Declarations of 16 December 1991 were thus not additional to but replaced the minimum legal criteria. In other words, the conditions for recognition set out by the European Community became the measure of statehood for Croatia and Bosnia-Herzegovina.[146] The European Community was in effect attempting to use recognition in a constitutive rather than a declaratory sense.[147] The European Community thus 'moved away from

---

[143] Rich, 56.

[144] Weller, 585.

[145] Keesing's *Record of World Events* (1992) Vol. 38, 38704, 38832–3.

[146] This approach was also reflected in Opinions Nos. 4 and 5. In Opinion No. 1 (1992) 31 ILM 1494, at 1495, the Commission noted that 'the effects of recognition by other States are purely declaratory'. It then endorsed the traditional minimum legal criteria for statehood by declaring that 'the State is commonly defined as a community which consists of a territory and a population subject to an organized political authority; that such a State is characterized by sovereignty'. However, in Opinions Nos. 4 and 5 the Commission made no mention of these criteria when determining whether Bosnia-Herzegovina or Croatia had fulfilled the requirements for statehood.

[147] The European Community also acted in a constitutive manner when it adopted a policy of insisting that the internal boundaries of the constituent republics be maintained as the frontiers of the new states, rather than recognizing as an integral part of a new state only the

the process of recognition as the formal acceptance of a fact to a process based on value judgments and through which the international community tries to create a fact'.[148]

One of the great benefits of relying upon the minimum legal criteria for statehood as the basis upon which to extend recognition had been that this common standard provided 'a way of maintaining consistency as well as a defence against doubtful claims'.[149] The abandonment of this measure of statehood renders both the question of statehood itself and the process of recognition much less certain and predictable.[150] The response of the international community to the events in Yugoslavia has done much to weaken the principle of territorial integrity and to encourage the notion that self-determination can be achieved through secession from an independent and sovereign state. The findings of the Badinter Commission in Opinions Nos. 1 and 8 that dissolution rather than secession had occurred in Yugoslavia are highly questionable. The purported dissolution of Yugoslavia occurred as a result of the actions of specific elements within the Yugoslav population, which unilaterally affected the breakup of the state by establishing separate entities of their own. These entities were recognized as independent states, even though in some cases they did not fulfil the traditional minimum legal criteria of statehood. A precedent has thus been established whereby a separate state can be unilaterally created by a constituent unit of an existing sovereign state, and recognized as such by the international community even though it has not fulfilled the traditional legal criteria for statehood.

7. AUTONOMY

Autonomy involves self-government for a specific part of the population of a state, within which it may be established on either a territorial or a personal basis.[151] Autonomy appears to be able to satisfy the aspirations of particular ethnic groups while preserving the territorial integrity and sovereignty of the state, and is therefore often suggested as a means of resolving

territory and population which were under the effective control of that state's government. The policy of the European Community in this regard is discussed in detail in Chapter 9 below, pp. 236–7.

[148] Rich, 56.   [149] *Id.*, 55.

[150] Macedonia provides a good example of the way in which recognition has become a capricious and expedient exercise. Although Macedonia satisfied both the minimum legal criteria of statehood set out in Article 1 of the Montevideo Convention and the additional conditions set out in the two Declarations of 16 December 1991, it remained unrecognized by the member states of the European Community and the United States solely on the basis that a member of the European Community had objected to its name: Rich, 56.

[151] Yoram Dinstein 'Autonomy' in Yoram Dinstein (ed.) *Models of Autonomy* (1981) 291–2.

the conflict between demands for ethnic self-determination and the principle of the territorial integrity of states. Some jurists have argued that it should be considered as an alternative form of self-determination at international law. Hannum, for example, equates autonomy with what he calls 'less-than-sovereign self-determination', which he asserts is no less than 'a new principle of international law'.[152] According to Hannum, the principle 'can be discerned in the interstices of contemporary definitions of sovereignty, self-determination and the human rights of individuals and groups'.[153] It also appears in the draft Declaration on the Rights of Indigenous Peoples.[154] The Declaration refers to indigenous populations as 'peoples' and specifically declares in operative paragraph 1 that indigenous peoples have the right of self-determination. However, this right is restricted to autonomy and self-government. Under the Declaration, self-determination for an indigenous people must occur within an existing state. It amounts, in other words, to 'less-than-sovereign self-determination'.

Some jurists contend that autonomy is not a principle of international law but a matter which falls within the domestic jurisdiction of a state. Crawford, for example, maintains that a grant of autonomy can only have consequences in international law if 'it is in some way internationally binding on the central authorities'.[155] State practice also demonstrates that much of the international community has not recognized autonomy as an acceptable form of self-determination. Many states are extremely reluctant to grant any form of autonomy to sections of their populations, and consider that proposals for decentralization lead inevitably to 'Balkanization'.[156] Given the absence of express language in international instruments, and the hostile attitude of many states, autonomy within an independent state cannot be part of self-determination for the purposes of international law. In international law autonomy is a legally neutral act. A state is under no international obligation either to introduce or to maintain a regime of autonomy within its own territory. A state which does do so implements an internal arrangement at its own discretion.

8. CONCLUSION

The question of secession remains one of the most controversial aspects of self-determination. With regard to non-self-governing territories, secession

---

[152] Hannum, 469, 473.   [153] *Id.*, 473.
[154] UN Doc. E/CN.4/Sub.2/1991/33. See Chapter 7, pp. 176–7, for a more detailed discussion of the draft Declaration.
[155] Crawford, 211.
[156] Buchheit, 104. See also Allen Buchanan 'Federalism, Secession and the Morality of Inclusion' (1995).

has been strictly prohibited by paragraph 6 of Resolution 1514(XV), whose effect precludes ethnic groups within non-self-governing territories from being considered as 'peoples'. Such groups, being unable to secede, cannot freely determine their own political status and therefore cannot be 'peoples'. Thus the term 'people', insofar as it relates to non-self-governing territories, can only refer to the entire population of that territory. This can create situations in which distinctive groups within non-self-governing territories are forced into political arrangements which they do not desire and which do not allow them to control their own political affairs. In order to prevent this, some administrative powers, such as the United States and France, have rejected a strict application of paragraph 6 and permitted division of non-self-governing or trust territories under their administration.

With regard to independent states, international law permits secession as a legal remedy in certain circumstances. Paragraph 7 of Resolution 2625(XXV) links the maintenance of territorial integrity to the existence of a government which represents 'the whole people belonging to the territory without distinction as to race, creed or colour'. The implication is that secession is permissible in cases where the government does not represent 'the whole people'. Secession may also be permitted by virtue of the 'oppression theory' when part of a population suffers gross oppression; in these circumstances secession is permitted primarily to prevent the abuse of human rights.

Apart from situations involving oppression or non-representation in government, secession may be permissible by virtue of the 'internal theory', under which secession, occurring as it does within the territory of a single state, is considered not to fall within the jurisdiction of international law. An act of secession therefore cannot be characterized in international law as either legal or illegal: it is simply a political act. Although secession may be political rather than legal in nature, the emergence of a new state nevertheless produces legal consequences on the international plane. This raises issues relating to the nature of recognition: because a seceding entity becomes a state by satisfying established international law criteria, recognition by other states should be simply declaratory of the fact that the entity has satisfied the legal criteria of statehood.

However, these principles of international law were not observed by the international community with regard to the disintegration of Yugoslavia. Recognition was used as a means of 'constituting' states out of the emerging successor entities to Yugoslavia, even though in some cases those entities had not satisfied the legal criteria of statehood. The international community thus appeared to endorse the dissolution of an independent state. This has led various jurists to speculate about the international law basis upon which self-determination may culminate in the dissolution of an existing independent state and the creation of other states in its place. Weller, for example, disregarded the finding of the Badinter Commission that Yugoslavia was in a process of dissolution, and concluded that the events in Yugoslavia and the response of the international community demonstrated 'a right of secession' based on the right of self-determination. This right of secession could lawfully be applied 'to those inhabiting a region whose territorial limits had previously been defined by an autonomous government and administration'.[157] Rich also analysed the disintegration of Yugoslavia in terms of secession, and concluded, 'on the very narrowest view', that 'a constituent unit of a federal state in Europe, if it is acting on the basis of the view of its people expressed in a referendum and if it undertakes to abide by the sort of conditions set in the EC Guidelines, has a right to independence'.[158] The disintegration of Yugoslavia and the emergence of the successor states were also justified in terms of ethnic self-determination.[159] As Rich points out, if ethnic self-determination is the legal basis for secession, then the principle could hardly be restricted to ethnic groups organized within constituent units of federal states.[160] Such a principle would apply to all ethnic groups, whether or not located within federal states.

All of these formulations of a 'right of secession' assume that secession falls within the jurisdiction of international law. However, as has been seen, this is not the case. Secession is a domestic matter, and therefore a legally neutral act in international law. As secession does not fall within the jurisdiction of international law, attempts to secede do not constitute acts of self-determination in the legal sense. Although secession produces consequences in international law when a new state is formed, the act of secession itself is essentially political rather than legal in nature. As a political act, secession cannot be characterized by legal formulations. It will occur as a result of political exigencies which cannot be subjected to legal analysis or legal definition.

---

[157] Weller, 606.   [158] Rich, 57.
[159] See, for example, the statement of the Croatian Constitution in this regard, *supra*, p. 201.
[160] Rich, 61.

9

Irredentism

1. INTRODUCTION

Secession within a state does not generally fall within the jurisdiction of international law. An ethnic group in one state is at liberty, from the standpoint of international law, to secede and form its own nation-state. However, ethnic groups often comprise inhabitants of more than one state. Irredentism involves self-determination by members of a single ethnic group who inhabit more than one state. Irredentist claims may arise in a number of ways. A state may lay claim to territory of another state or non-self-governing territory on the basis that the inhabitants of that territory are of the same ethnic stock as the population of the claimant state. Or, an ethnic group may seek to secede from one state in order to join another with which it shares an ethnic affinity. The population of a non-self-governing territory may seek integration with a neighbouring state of the same ethnic stock upon decolonization. Irredentist claims necessarily involve more than one state, and are therefore governed by international law. In this Chapter their legal status is examined.

2. IRREDENTISM AND TERRITORIAL INTEGRITY: THE CASE OF SOMALIA

As has been seen, the principle of territorial integrity is one of the most fundamental and well established principles of international law. Article 2(4) of the Charter of the United Nations prohibits states from using force or the threat of force against 'the territorial integrity or political independence of any state'. International law therefore clearly prevents one state from making irredentist territorial claims against another. Nevertheless, such claims are made, and are justified on the basis of the will of the populations involved.

A good example is the ongoing demand by the Somali Democratic Republic for the unification of all Somali people within a single 'Greater Somalia'. The territories comprising the Horn of Africa are populated almost exclusively by ethnic Somalis. In the late nineteenth century the United Kingdom, France, and Italy established protectorates over these territories, which became known as British Somaliland, French Somaliland,

and Italian Somaliland respectively. South of Italian Somaliland, the British established the colony of British East Africa, which subsequently became the colony of Kenya. A considerable number of Somali nomads lived in the northern part of Kenya. From 1924 onwards this area, known as the Northern Frontier District, was administered as a separate unit within Kenya.[1] In the 1890s Ethiopia embarked upon a policy of expansion into Somali-inhabited areas, and as a result came into conflict with Italy. The Italians were defeated by the Ethiopians at Adowa in 1896, and were forced to cede part of their territory, the Ogaden, to Ethiopia. The British also made a formal cession to Ethiopia at this time of territories known as the Haud and the Reserved Area. All the ceded territories were inhabited by ethnic Somalis.[2]

During the Second World War British troops occupied Italian Somaliland, as well as the Ogaden, the Haud, and the Reserved Area which had been under Italian rule since 1936 when Italy had conquered Ethiopia. By the end of the Second World War Somali nationalism had developed considerably, and in the early 1950s there was a strong desire amongst Somalis for unification. Ernest Bevin, the British Foreign Secretary, had proposed in 1946 that all the occupied lands be joined with British Somaliland into a single trust territory.[3] This proposal did not meet with the approval of Ethiopia, which demanded the return of its territory. The United Kingdom did return the occupied territories, by an agreement with Ethiopia dated 29 November 1954.[4] This caused widespread unrest and rioting amongst Somalis.[5]

Somali demands for the unification of Somali-inhabited territories initially received support from the first two All African Peoples Conferences, held in 1958 and 1960. The first Conference endorsed a restructuring of territorial boundaries in Africa to enable ethnic groups to inhabit a single state. The second Conference went further, adopting a resolution which specifically sanctioned 'the Somali struggle for independence and for the unity which will give birth to a greater Somalia'.[6] The first step in this process was achieved when the Trust Territory of Somalia (formerly Italian Somaliland) and British Somalia both attained independence in 1960, and shortly thereafter united to form the Republic of Somalia.[7] The Constitution of the new Republic declared in Article 6 that 'the Somali Republic

---

[1]   Lee C. Buchheit *Secession* (1978) 178, 182.
[2]   *Id.*, 178.
[3]   A. Rigo Sureda *The Evolution of the Right of Self-Determination* (1973) 207.
[4]   Buchheit, 180.
[5]   Note 'The Logic of Secession' (1980) 821.
[6]   Eisuke Suzuki 'Self-Determination and World Public Order: Community Response to Territorial Separation' (1976) 839.
[7]   Rigo Sureda, 204. See also General Assembly Resolution 289(IV) of 21 Nov. 1949.

shall promote, by legal and peaceful means, the union of Somali territories'.[8]

The emergence of the independent and united Somali state encouraged Somalis in the Northern Frontier District to seek unification with the new Republic. A delegation from the Northern Frontier District petitioned the British Government at the Kenya Constitutional Conference in 1962 for the incorporation of the District into the Somali Republic. A Commission of Inquiry was sent to the District to ascertain public opinion; it found that 87 per cent of the population desired secession from Kenya and amalgamation with the Somali Republic.[9] Kenya and Ethiopia both objected strongly to any dismemberment of Kenyan territory. Eventually the United Kingdom decided not to separate the Northern Frontier District from Kenya, which attained independence on 12 December 1963. In response, the Somali Republic broke off diplomatic relations with the United Kingdom.[10] The return of Somali-populated territories to Ethiopia and the refusal to cede the Northern frontier territory to Somalia provoked frustration amongst nationalist Somalis. The Somali Republic resorted to armed conflict against Ethiopia and Kenya in an attempt to redress the two situations. In Kenya, Somali tribesmen conducted guerilla activities, with the support of the Somali Republic, from 1963 to 1967.[11] An inconclusive conflict between the Somali Republic and Ethiopia occurred in February and March of 1964.

The relationship between Ethiopia and the Somali Republic remained tense as a result of their rival claims to French Somaliland. French Somaliland had common borders with both Ethiopia and the Somali Republic, and its population was evenly divided between Issas, a Somali tribe, and Afars, an Ethiopian group.[12] With the growth of Somali nationalism the Issas sought unification with other Somalis. The French countered Issa demands for unification by playing on Afar fears of Somali domination. Meanwhile, both Ethiopia and the Somali Republic laid claim to French Somaliland on the basis that it had a population akin to their own and had once belonged to them.[13] In 1967 the General Assembly adopted Resolu-

---

[8] Albert P. Blaustein and Gisbert H. Flanz (eds.) *Constitutions of the Countries of the Modern World*, Binder 11, 'Somalia', l971. The present Constitution of the Somali Democratic Republic contains a similar provision in Art. 16, which provides as follows: 'The Somali Democratic Republic adopting peaceful and legal means shall support the liberation of Somali territories under colonial occupation and shall encourage the unity of the Somali people through their free will': Blaustein and Flanz, Binder 11, 'Somali Democratic Republic', 1990. Cf. the Constitution of Ireland, which proclaims in Art. 2 that the 'national territory consists of the whole island of Ireland, its islands and the territorial seas': *Id.*, Binder VII, 'Ireland', 1990.
[9] Rigo Sureda, 206.
[10] Buchheit, 183.
[11] *Id.*, 184.
[12] Thomas M. Franck and Paul Hoffman 'The Right of Self-Determination in Very Small Places' (1975-76) 352.   [13] Rigo Sureda, 210.

tion 2356(XXII), which called upon France 'to create the political conditions necessary for accelerating the implementation of the right of the people to self-determination and independence'. France indicated that it would be willing to grant independence to the colony provided that its independence and territorial integrity were guaranteed. In 1975 the General Assembly adopted Resolution 3480(XXX), which called upon 'all States to renounce forthwith any and all claims to the Territory and to declare null and void any and all acts asserting such claims'. This resolution also directed France 'to grant immediate and unconditional independence' to French Somaliland. Ethiopia and the Somali Democratic Republic[14] both indicated that they would renounce their territorial claims to French Somaliland. The Somali renunciation, however, was equivocal: the Somali Foreign Minister stated that France was occupying part of Somali territory, and that the Somali Government held to its objective of unifying the Somali people.[15] Ethiopia declared that it would never countenance a union between French Somaliland and the Somali Democratic Republic.[16] In June 1977 French Somaliland received its independence and became the state of Djibouti; it was admitted into the United Nations in September 1977.[17]

Support for the unification of all Somali-inhabited territories by the All African Peoples Conference ended in 1963. At the Addis Ababa Conference, the policy of calling for the readjustment of political boundaries was abandoned, and a new policy was adopted which was founded on respect for the territorial integrity of existing political entities. This new policy was embodied in Articles II and III of the Charter of the Organization of African Unity. The following year the OAU adopted its 'Resolution on Border Disputes' which confirmed that the borders of an African state, on the day of its independence, were to remain as they had been before independence.[18]

Despite its isolated position on this issue, the Somali Democratic Republic has never given up its claims to Somali-inhabited territories. Article 16 of its current Constitution calls on the Republic to 'encourage the unity of the Somali people' and to 'support the liberation of Somali territories under colonial occupation'.[19] This reference to 'Somali territories under colonial occupation' illustrates the Somali contention that, with respect to Somali-inhabited territories, Ethiopia and Kenya are as much colonial powers as were the United Kingdom and Italy.[20] The Somali Democratic Republic

---

[14] Following a coup in 1969, the name of the Somali Republic was changed to the Somali Democratic Republic.

[15] Franck and Hoffman, 356.

[16] *Id.*, 357.

[17] James Crawford *The Creation of States in International Law* (1979) 377, fn. 72; GA Resolution 32/1 of 20 Sep. 1977.

[18] This resolution was opposed by Morocco and the Somali Republic: Buchheit, 186, fn. 142.

[19] See page 213, fn. 8 *supra* for the text of Article 16.   [20] Rigo Sureda, 209.

argues that the cession of Somali territory to Ethiopia by the United Kingdom and Italy was invalid for two reasons: (1) the colonial powers lacked
the competence to effect the cession of territories which they were pledged
to protect, and (2) the cessions had been made without the knowledge or
consent of the Somali inhabitants.[21] The Somali Democratic Republic further argues that Ethiopia and Kenya are obliged by international law to
recognize and respect the right of peoples to self-determination, which
means that they must allow Somalis in the disputed areas to exercise their
right to self-determination in a plebiscite.[22] Ethiopia and Kenya reject these
arguments. Ethiopia argues that the territories in question were validly
ceded to it, while Kenya argues that its northern region has always been an
integral part of the territory of Kenya. Both Ethiopia and Kenya deny that
the right of self-determination is applicable to independent states, and that
it involves any right of secession of a part of a state's territory.[23]

The ongoing campaign of the Somali Democratic Republic for the unification of all Somali-inhabited territories has not received much support
from the international community.[24] The Somalis do not possess a strong
case in international law. Their best argument is that the cessions of territory to Ethiopia by the United Kingdom and Italy were invalid because
those states were not entitled to cede territory which they had pledged to
protect. If this were the case, Ethiopia would then not hold valid title to the
ceded territory. However, the frontiers of the British and Italian Somali
protectorates were never clearly defined.[25] Although the British and Italians did make territorial withdrawals after Adowa, the territory which they
actually ceded to Ethiopia was unclear. Given this state of uncertainty, as
Blum points out, international law may sanction the existing situation of
fact in order to preserve peace and stability, 'even if the origins of such
situations are not free from doubt'.[26] Moreover, the Somali invocation of
self-determination for all Somali people conflicts with the principle of territorial integrity. The position of international law in such cases is that the
territorial integrity of existing states must be preserved. Article 2(4) of the
Charter of the United Nations prohibits states from engaging either in
threats or in the actual use of force against the territorial integrity of any
other state. Resolution 2625(XXV) goes even further: paragraph 8 prohibits states from undertaking 'any action' aimed at disrupting the territorial
integrity of another 'State or country'. The Somali Democratic Republic's
attempts to achieve Somali unification are therefore without doubt contrary
to international law, despite the fact that the overwhelming majority of
Somalis living both in Ethiopia and in Kenya would rather belong to the

[21] *Id.*, 208.   [22] Buchheit, 185.   [23] *Id.*, 185, 186.
[24] Rigo Sureda, 208; Buchheit, 186.
[25] Buchheit, 178, 179.
[26] Yehuda Z. Blum *Historic Titles in International Law* (1965) 4; see also Crawford, 418–20.

Somali Democratic Republic than to their current respective states. However, when claims for ethnic self-determination transcend national frontiers international law manifestly rejects them, and upholds instead the territorial integrity of the state.

3. IRREDENTISM AND STATE CONCURRENCE: THE CASE OF GERMANY

When an irredentist claim threatens the territorial integrity of another state, international law protects the territorial integrity of the state. Ethnic groups straddling national frontiers therefore cannot normally achieve self-determination by unifying the entire group within one nation-state. Such unification can, however, occur if the states involved agree. The unification of the 'two Germanys' is an example of state concurrence. While the issue of the 'two Germanys' in the post-war period was extremely complicated and involved many aspects of international law, irredentism is relevant because the German Federal Republic consistently sought to reunite the entire German population within one state.

Following Germany's unconditional surrender on 8 May 1945, the Allies divided the country into four zones of occupation. Each zone was administered by one of the four Allied Powers. Berlin was divided into four sectors under the joint control of the Four Powers.[27] The Allies had originally agreed at the Potsdam Conference of July—August 1945 that Germany would remain a single economic unit and that political development would be allowed to occur uniformly throughout the occupation zones.[28] However, this proved impossible because of wide-ranging differences and increasing tension between the Soviet Union on the one hand and the three Western states on the other. The onset of the Cold War precluded the signing of any formal peace treaty between Germany and the Four Allied Powers. Eventually the three Western states decided to establish a democratic German state in the territories which they occupied. In 1949 they terminated military rule and granted a measure of sovereignty to the newly created 'Federal Republic of Germany', while retaining supreme authority to revoke or alter any legislative or administrative decisions in the three western zones of occupation.[29] The Federal Republic of Germany was proclaimed on 23 May

---

[27] Art. 13, 'Declaration Regarding the Defeat of Germany and the Assumption of Supreme Authority With Respect to Germany', 5 June 1945 (1950) 68 UNTS 187, 200; 'Agreement Regarding Amendments to the Protocol of 12 September 1944 on the Zones of Occupation in Germany and the Administration of "Greater Berlin"', 26 July 1945 (1956) 227 UNTS 297.

[28] Arthur S. Banks (ed.) *Political Handbook of the World* (1990) 231.

[29] Agreements on Germany, 8 Apr. 1949 (1952) 140 UNTS 196. See especially Art. 1 of the 'Agreed Memorandum Regarding the Principles Governing Exercise of Powers and Responsibilities of US-UK-French Governments Following Establishment of German Federal Republic' at 200. The powers retained by the three Western states were set out in the 'Occupation Statute Defining the Powers To Be Retained By The Occupation Authorities' at 202–7.

1949, after its constitution was approved on 8 May 1949 in a specially elected parliamentary assembly. On 7 October 1949 the Communist state of the 'German Democratic Republic' was created in the Soviet zone of occupation.[30]

On 26 May 1952 the 'Convention on Relations Between the Three Powers and the Federal Republic of Germany' was signed.[31] Article 1(1) terminated the occupation by the three Western Powers of the Federal Republic.[32] Article 1(2) declared that the Federal Republic would have 'the full authority of a sovereign State over its internal and external affairs'.[33] Certain rights were nevertheless reserved to the Three Powers, the most important of which was contained in Article 2. Article 2 declared that the international situation had 'so far prevented the reunification of Germany and the conclusion of a peace settlement'.[34] In view of this, the Three Powers would 'retain the rights and the responsibilities, heretofore exercised or held by them, relating to Berlin and to Germany as a whole, including the re-unification of Germany and a peace settlement'.[35] In other words, any agreement or arrangement to unify Germany would require the participation and concurrence of the three Western Powers.[36] In Article 7(2) the three Powers committed themselves to work for the reunification of Germany.[37]

The Federal Republic of Germany was itself constitutionally bound to seek reunification. The Preamble of the constitution, or 'Basic Law',[38] of the Federal Republic stated that German reunification was the ultimate aim of the Federal Republic. The first sentence of the Preamble declared that the 'German People' were 'animated by the resolve to preserve their national and political unity'.[39] The second sentence emphasized that, in enacting the Basic Law, the German People 'also acted on behalf of those Germans to whom participation was denied'.[40] The third sentence, which came to be known as the 'reunification commandment', addressed the issue of German reunification most directly.[41] It declared that the 'entire German people are called upon to achieve in free self-determination the unity and freedom of Germany'.[42] The irredentist claim of the Federal Republic on the German Democratic Republic was also reflected in Article 116 of the Basic Law.

---

[30] Banks (ed.) 231.   [31] (1959) 331 UNTS 327.   [32] *Id.*, 328.

[33] *Id.*, 328.

[34] *Id.*, 328.

[35] *Id.*, 328–9.

[36] Andrea Kupfer 'International Agreements: Treaty on the Final Settlement with Respect to Germany' (1991) 228.

[37] (1959) 331 UNTS 327, 334.

[38] The name 'Basic Law' (*Grundgesetz*) was intended to emphasize its provisional character: Gregory V. S. McCurdy 'German Reunification: Historical and Legal Roots of Germany's Rapid Progress Towards Unity' (1990) 257.

[39] Blaustein and Flanz (eds.) Binder V 'Federal Republic of Germany' (1985) 43.

[40] *Id.*, 43.   [41] McCurdy, 259.   [42] Blaustein and Flanz (eds.) 43.

This defined as a citizen of the Federal Republic any person 'who possesses German nationality or who has been accepted in the territory of the German Reich as at 31 December 1937 as a refugee or expellee of German stock or as the spouse or descendant of such person'.[43] Citizenship of the Federal Republic was thus extended to include German nationals in the German Democratic Republic.

The Federal Constitutional Court of the Federal Republic had occasion to pronounce at length on the issue of reunification in the *Communist Party* case of 1956.[44] Although the Court found that the Preamble of the Basic Law had a 'mainly political significance' and was a 'political manifesto', the Preamble also had a 'legal content'.[45] 'The Preamble', the Court declared, 'implies a legal duty for all political state organs of the Federal Republic to work toward German unity with all their powers, ... and to make the worthiness of this goal the standard by which they judge their action'.[46] This prevented the Federal Government from undertaking any action which would 'legally impede reunification or make it practically impossible'.[47] However, it remained the responsibility of the Federal Government to decide which 'path to reunification' was 'politically correct and expedient'.[48] Moreover, the legal duty to seek reunification did not require the Federal Government to engage in any 'specific actions for the purpose of reunifying Germany'.[49]

On 21 December 1972 the Federal Republic concluded a treaty with the German Democratic Republic, known as the 'Treaty on the Basis of Relations Between the Federal Republic of Germany and the German Democratic Republic'.[50] The Preamble set out its aims. It noted that the signatories sought 'to render a contribution to detente and security in Europe', and more specifically, 'to create the conditions for co-operation between the Federal Republic of Germany and the German Democratic Republic for the benefit of the people in the two German States'.[51] In Article 3 of the Treaty the Federal Republic and the German Democratic Republic reaffirmed 'the inviolability now and in the future of the frontier existing between them', and undertook 'to respect each other's territorial integrity'.[52] Article 4 declared that neither state could 'represent the other in the international sphere or act on its behalf'.[53] Article 6 further declared that 'the sovereign jurisdiction of each of the two States is confined to its

---

[43] Blaustein and Flanz (eds.), 89.
[44] Judgment of 17 Aug. 1956, Bundesverfassungsgericht, W. Ger., 5 BVerfGE 85. (The passages cited below were translated by Gregory V. S. McCurdy: *op. cit.* page 266.)
[45] *Id.*, 127.
[46] *Id.*, 127.
[47] *Id.*, 128.
[48] *Id.*, 128.
[49] *Id.*, 127, 128.
[50] (1973) 12 ILM 16.   [51] *Id.*, 16.   [52] *Id.*, 16.   [53] *Id.*, 17.

own territory. They respect each other's independence and autonomy in their internal and external affairs.'[54]

The constitutionality of this treaty was immediately challenged in the Federal Constitutional Court by the Bavarian State Government, which alleged that the treaty was incompatible with the terms of the reunification commandment. In the *Intra-German Treaty* case[55] the Court found that the Treaty did in fact comply with the terms of the Basic Law. The Court noted that the Federal Government was required by the Basic Law to formulate policies which would lead to reunification. However, the Federal Government itself must determine which methods would best promote that goal. It was not the role of the Court 'to criticize or express its opinion on the policy's chances for success'.[56] While the Court reaffirmed its right to intervene and to declare unconstitutional any act of the Federal Government which resulted in the surrender of its legal claim to reunification,[57] it found that this particular Treaty could be 'interpreted in such a manner that it does not contradict any provisions of the Basic Law'.[58] The Treaty did not 'purport to be a permanent solution to the German question'[59] and did not amount to a recognition of the German Democratic Republic.[60]

Although the Federal Constitutional Court held that it did not constitute recognition of the German Democratic Republic, the Treaty nevertheless resulted in the admission of the German Democratic Republic as a member state of the United Nations in 1973,[61] and its widespread recognition by the international community as a separate state.[62] The position of the German Democratic Republic as a separate sovereign state was further consolidated by the Helsinki Declaration of 1975.[63] Principle III of the Declaration declared that the participating states regarded as 'inviolable' the frontiers of all the states of Europe. The participating states would consequently 'refrain from any demand for, or act of, seizure and usurpation of part or all of the territory of any participating State'.[64] On the other hand, Principle I noted that the participating states considered that their frontiers could 'be

---

[54] *Id.*, 17.

[55] Judgment of 31 July 1973, Bundesverfassungsgericht, W. Ger., 36 BVerfGE 1. (The passages from the Court's decision which are cited below were translated by Gregory V. S. McCurdy: McCurdy *op. cit.* pages 270–1.)

[56] *Id.*, 18.

[57] *Id.*, 18, 19.

[58] *Id.*, 20.

[59] *Id.*, 20.

[60] *Id.*, 23. Trade between the two states remained on an intra-German rather than an international level. For a discussion of the intra-state nature of trade between the two German states see Franziska Tschofen and Christian Hausmaninger 'Legal Aspects of East and West Germany's Relationship with the European Economic Community After the Collapse of the Berlin Wall' (1990) 653–5.

[61] GA Resolution 3050(XXVII) of 18 Sep. 1973. The Federal Republic of Germany was also admitted as a member state by virtue of this resolution.

[62] Crawford, 273.   [63] (1975) 14 ILM 1293.   [64] *Id.*, 1294.

changed in accordance with international law, by peaceful means and by agreement'.[65] The Federal Republic relied on this Principle, and on Principle VIII relating to Equal Rights and Self-Determination of Peoples,[66] in support of its position that the future reunification of the two German states had not been foreclosed by the provisions of the Declaration.[67]

Reunification became a real possibility in 1989 when a serious political crisis developed in the German Democratic Republic. The conservative Communist Government of Erich Honnecker had refused to follow the lead of the Soviet Union in introducing liberalizing policies in the German Democratic Republic. This provoked considerable dissatisfaction throughout the country, and there was a massive exodus of East Germans to the Federal Republic.[68] In October 1989 Gorbachev publicly called for reform in the Democratic Republic. Gorbachev's statements prompted further demonstrations against the regime, and this, coupled with the mass exodus from the country, led on 8 November 1989 to the resignation of the Honnecker Government. A more liberal Communist regime under Egon Krenz was installed. The Krenz Government opened the borders between the two German states in an attempt to halt the mass exodus, but the flow of Germans from East to West continued unabated.[69]

The new regime removed the Communist Party's monopoly on power from the Constitution on 1 December 1989, permitting the establishment of other political parties. Over a dozen were formed, including several major parties which were simply counterparts of the political parties of the Federal Republic.[70] In the election of 18 March 1990 the Christian Democratic Union (CDU), which had promoted a policy of rapid reunification, received 40.9 per cent of the vote. Together with two other conservative parties, which between them obtained 11.6 per cent of the vote, the CDU was able to form a coalition government and work towards reunification with the Federal Republic.[71] A poll taken immediately prior to the election indicated that 82 per cent of West Germans and 91 per cent of East Germans supported reunification.[72]

The process of reunification at the constitutional level was accomplished by means of Article 23 of the Basic Law. Article 23 enumerated the states of the Federal Republic to which the Basic Law applied. It then declared that in 'other parts of Germany' the Basic Law would 'be put into force on

---

[65] (1975) 14 ILM, 1294.

[66] *Id.*, 1295. Principle VIII is reproduced in Chapter 5, p. 99.

[67] Harold S. Russell 'The Helsinki Declaration: Brobdingnag or Lilliput?' (1976) 269.

[68] This exodus was facilitated by Hungary's decision, on 11 Sep. 1989, to open its border with Austria: Kupfer, 229, fn. 15.

[69] *Id.*, 287.

[70] *Id.*, 289.

[71] *Id.*, 282, fn. 150.

[72] *Id.*, 297, fn. 246.

their accession'.[73] In the *Intra-German Treaty* case the Federal Constitutional Court declared that Article 23 was to be widely construed and that its provisions extended to the German Democratic Republic.[74] Under Article 23 the German Democratic Republic could therefore be incorporated into the Federal Republic. This procedure had been followed in 1956 when Saarland was reincorporated into the Federal Republic.

At the international level, reunification was achieved when the two states signed the 'Unification Treaty'[75] on 31 August 1990. The Treaty was ratified by the parliaments of the two states. Under its terms, the two states would become one single country on 3 October 1990.[76] This single country would be the Federal Republic of Germany. Reunification also required the consent of the Four Occupying Powers, which had maintained their rights on the issue. The United States, the United Kingdom, and France retained 'the rights and the responsibilities' relating, *inter alia*, to 'the re-unification of Germany' by virtue of Article 2 of the Convention on Relations Between the Three Powers and the Federal Republic of Germany.[77] Under the terms of Article 7(2) of the 1952 Convention the United States, the United Kingdom, and France were bound to promote reunification.[78] The Soviet Union had similarly retained rights with regard to the reunification of the German Democratic Republic, by virtue of Article 5 of the Treaty Concerning Relations Between the Union of Soviet Socialist Republics and the German Democratic Republic.[79] When reunification became a real possibility in late 1989 the Soviet Union initially opposed the idea, but by January 1990 that opposition had ceased.[80] On 12 September 1990 the two German states and the Four Occupying Powers signed the Treaty on the Final Settlement with Respect to Germany.[81] The Treaty officially ended the occupation of Germany and eliminated the external obstacles to German unification. In Article 7(1) the Four Occupying Powers terminated all of their rights and responsibilities relating to Berlin and to Germany as a whole.[82] Article 7(2) declared that 'united Germany shall have accordingly full sovereignty over its internal and external affairs'.[83] The two German states became united as the Federal Republic of Germany on 3 October 1990.

---

[73] Blaustein and Flanz (eds.) 50.

[74] Judgment of 31 July 1973, Bundesverfassungsgericht, W. Ger., 36 BVerfGE 1, 28. This citation is taken from Jutta Brunnée 'The Reunification of Germany: Comments on a Legal Maze' (1990).

[75] *Vertrag zwischen der Bundesrepublik Deutschland und der Deutschen Demokratischen Republik über die Herstellung der Einheit Deutschlands (Einigungsvertrag)*, BGBl. II. 1246.

[76] Burkhard Bastuck 'Unity, Law, and Freedom: Legal Aspects of the Process and Results of German Unification' (1991) 257.

[77] 26 May 1952, (1959) 331 UNTS 327, 328-330.

[78] *Id.*, 334.

[79] 20 Sep. 1955, (1956) 226 UNTS 208, 210.

[80] McCurdy, 312.

[81] (1990) 29 ILM 1186. The Treaty is commonly referred to as the Two-Plus-Four Agreement: Kupfer, 227.   [82] (1990) 29 ILM 1186, 1191.   [83] *Id.*, 1191.

No violation of international law occurred when the Federal Republic of Germany made good its irredentist claim on the German Democratic Republic. German reunification did not involve the partial or forced dismemberment of any state by another state, nor did it pit the will of a state against that of part of its population. The reunification of Germany thus differed considerably from the proposed unification of ethnic Somalis: it took place only after an election in the German Democratic Republic in which a large majority of the electorate indicated its desire for reunification. Resolution 2625(XXV), paragraph 4, permits the implementation of self-determination through 'integration with an independent state', which is what occurred when the German Democratic Republic became a part of the Federal Republic of Germany. Moreover, reunification took place with the concurrence of both states. States are at liberty in international law to effect a partial or total merger of their territory if they so desire.[84] Principle I of the Helsinki Declaration specifically declares that frontiers can 'be changed, in accordance with international law, by peaceful means and by agreement'.[85] The integration of the German Democratic Republic into the Federal Republic took place with the concurrence of both the state and a large majority of its population.

4. IRREDENTISM AND DISSIDENT MINORITIES: THE CASE OF CYPRUS

Cyprus offered a very complicated example of irredentism, involving competing interpretations of self-determination. The majority supported a view of self-determination which permitted union with a neighbouring kin-state; the minority, a different ethnic group, supported an interpretation which prevented such a union.

The population of Cyprus includes both ethnic Greeks and ethnic Turks; the former make up some 80 per cent of the island's population, the latter 18 per cent.[86] The island is located forty-four miles from Turkey and 600 miles from the Greek mainland.[87] In 1878 the United Kingdom, by virtue of the Convention of Defensive Alliance, obtained from the Ottoman Empire the right to occupy and administer Cyprus.[88] In return the United Kingdom agreed to protect the Ottoman Empire from further territorial expansion by Russia. When the Ottoman Empire became an ally of the Central Powers in

---

[84] Crawford, 288; Sam Blay 'Self-Determination: A Reassessment in the Post-Communist World' (1994) 305–6.
[85] (1975) 14 ILM 1292, 1294.
[86] Marios L. Evriviades 'The Legal Dimension of the Cyprus Conflict' (1975) 228.
[87] Suzanne Palmer 'The Turkish Republic of Northern Cyprus: Should the United States Recognize It as an Independent State?' (1986) 423–4.
[88] 153 CTS 67.

1914 the United Kingdom renounced the Treaty and annexed the island. British sovereignty over Cyprus was subsequently recognized by Turkey and Greece in the Treaty of Lausanne of 1923.[89] In 1925 the island was declared a British colony, and retained this status until 1960 when it became independent.[90]

The emergence of an independent Greek state in 1830 prompted the growth of a powerful irredentist movement amongst ethnic Greeks both inside and outside Greece. This movement was known as *enosis*, and its object was the union of all Greek-speaking peoples within a single state. In the nineteenth century *enosis* exerted a powerful influence on ethnic Greeks throughout the entire Mediterranean region. It was an important factor in the Greek decision to invade the Turkish mainland in 1921, which resulted in a disastrous defeat for the Greek forces and the expulsion of thousands of ethnic Greeks from Turkey.[91]

Enosis was a firmly established political goal of the Greek Cypriots when the British assumed administrative control of Cyprus in 1878. The British occupation of the island was welcomed by the Greek Cypriots, who believed that it would eventually lead to union with Greece, as had been the case in respect of the Ionian Islands. Throughout the British occupation of Cyprus *enosis* (also referred to as 'self-determination-union') remained the dominant political goal of the Greek Cypriots.[92] However, *enosis* was opposed by Turkish Cypriots, who sought either a maintenance of the status quo or union with Turkey. When self-determination for Cyprus became an issue in the United Nations in the 1950s Turkish Cypriots began to advocate partition of the island.[93]

The issue of self-determination for Cyprus was first brought before the United Nations by Greece in 1954. The Greek Government raised the issue in order to promote *enosis* on behalf of the Greek Cypriot population, and to appeal to public opinion within Greece itself.[94] Greece was unable to persuade the General Assembly to adopt a resolution calling for the exercise of the right of self-determination for the people of Cyprus, but it did manage to get the Assembly to include the issue of Cyprus on its agenda, in spite of British objections that this violated Article 2(7) of the Charter.[95] The General Assembly adopted three resolutions on the question of Cy-

---

[89] Art. 20, (1924) 28 LNTS 12, 25.

[90] Palmer, 424, fn. 10.

[91] Zaim M. Necatigil *The Cyprus Question and the Turkish Position in International Law* (1993) 29–30. For a discussion of the exchange of populations which occurred at the conclusion of this conflict see Chapter 3, fn. 41.

[92] Evriviades, 230–1. A plebiscite held in 1950 amongst Greek Cypriots indicated that 95.7% of them favoured *enosis*: Rigo Sureda, 142, fn. 25.

[93] Evriviades, 231.

[94] Stephen G. Xydis 'The UN General Assembly as an Instrument of Greek Policy: Cyprus, 1954-58' (1968) 142.   [95] Evriviades, 231.

prus, so that Cyprus ceased to be an affair internal to the United Kingdom and became instead an international question.[96] This in turn led to tripartite negotiations involving the United Kingdom, Greece, and Turkey.

Greece's original position was that a plebiscite should be held in Cyprus, under the supervision of the United Nations, in order to ascertain the political wishes of the population as a whole;[97] according to Greece this would constitute a valid exercise of the right of self-determination. Turkey and the United Kingdom opposed the Greek proposal on the basis that it was simply a Greek ploy to annex Cyprus.[98] Turkey argued that the Greek proposal for a single plebiscite would not constitute self-determination for the Turkish Cypriots, but would actually be a denial of self-determination for them.[99] Turkey maintained that there were in fact two 'peoples' inhabiting Cyprus, and that there should consequently be a separate exercise of self-determination for each group.[100] The United Kingdom concurred with the Turkish position, indicating that the principle of self-determination might indeed be applied separately to the two communities, with the possible result of the island's partition.[101]

Greece was anxious to avoid partition of Cyprus. In light of the British and Turkish positions it abandoned its proposal for a single plebiscite, which would undoubtedly have led to union with Greece, and proposed instead independence for the island as a whole; Turkey and the United Kingdom both agreed to this proposal. By 1959 the United Kingdom, Greece, and Turkey had agreed on the basic structure of the constitution for Cyprus.[102] This agreement was incorporated into the Constitution of Cyprus,[103] the Treaty of Alliance,[104] and the Treaty of Guarantee,[105] which entered into force on 16 August 1960 when Cyprus became an independent state. Greece, Turkey, the United Kingdom, and Cyprus were signatories to the two treaties. No Cypriot representatives participated in the preparation of either the Constitution or the two treaties.[106]

The Treaties of Guarantee and of Alliance were given 'constitutional force' by Article 181 of the Constitution, and were included as annexes to the Constitution.[107] In Article I of the Treaty of Guarantee Cyprus

---

[96] Xydis, 142–3. GA Resolution 814(IX) of 17 Dec. 1954 merely stated that the Assembly did not consider it appropriate to adopt a resolution concerning Cyprus at that time. GA Resolutions 1013(XI) of 26 Feb. 1957 and 1289(XIII) of 5 Dec. 1958 both expressed the Assembly's hope that a solution could be found to the Cyprus question.

[97] Rigo Sureda, 68.

[98] Xydis, 157.

[99] Rigo Sureda, 70.

[100] Xydis, 157.

[101] Evriviades, 234–5.

[102] Palmer, 430.

[103] Blaustein and Flanz (eds.) (1972) 'Cyprus' 71.

[104] (1961) 397 UNTS 287.

[105] (1960) 382 UNTS 3.   [106] Palmer, 431.   [107] Blaustein and Flanz (eds.) 71.

undertook 'to ensure the maintenance of its independence, territorial integrity and security, as well as respect for its Constitution'.[108] It further undertook 'not to participate, in whole or in part, in any political or economic union with any State whatsoever', and agreed to prohibit 'any activity likely to promote, directly or indirectly, either union with any other State or partition of the island'.[109] Article IV provided that in the event of a breach of the provisions of the Treaty the three guarantor states were to consult. together to determine the measures appropriate to ensure compliance. If 'common or concerted action' were not possible, each of the guarantor states reserved the right under Article IV 'to take action with the sole aim of re-establishing the state of affairs created by the present treaty'.[110] The Treaty of Alliance was a defensive agreement whereby the parties undertook in Article II 'to resist any attack or aggression, direct or indirect, directed against the independence or the territorial integrity of the Republic of Cyprus'.[111]

The Constitution was designed to create a political balance of power between the two ethnic communities, and to protect the rights of Turkish Cypriots.[112] It contained 199 articles. Forty-eight of these were declared to be unalterable,[113] including Article 1. This provided for a presidential regime, in which the President would be Greek and the Vice-President Turkish, each to be elected by their respective communities.[114] Article 123 was another unalterable article, and provided in subsection 1 that 70 per cent of civil service posts were to be filled by Greeks, and 30 per cent by Turks.[115]

Although the Constitution was designed to create a political balance between the two communities and to safeguard the rights of the minority community, the effective functioning of the new state depended ultimately on the goodwill and co-operation of the two Cypriot communities. However, goodwill existed in neither Cypriot community, whose interrelationship was characterized by mutual distrust and hostility. In the years preceding independence this mutual hostility periodically flared into intercommunal violence. The adoption of the Constitution did very little to improve the situation. Greek Cypriots felt aggrieved that *enosis* had been denied them and that a constitution formulated by others had been imposed upon them. The democratic principle of majority rule had, in their opinion, been traduced by the provisions of the Constitution, which granted Turkish Cypriots representation disproportionate to their numbers. Turkish Cypri-

---

[108] *Id.*, 81.
[109] *Id.*, 81.
[110] *Id.*, 82.
[111] *Id.*, 83.
[112] Palmer, 430.
[113] Constitution Art. 182, Blaustein and Flanz (eds.), 72, 86–7.
[114] *Id.*, 1.
[115] *Id.*, 48.

ots, on the other hand, continued to fear political domination by the Greek Cypriots. To prevent this they clung rigidly to the terms of the Constitution, but their strict legalism succeeded only in exacerbating tensions between the two communities.[116]

Serious intercommunal disputes developed in the first years of the Republic's existence. When the President proposed in 1963 to enact thirteen questionable constitutional amendments, intercommunal fighting broke out on the island.[117] When order had been restored by the United Nations peace-keeping forces[118] the Turkish Cypriot community refused to participate in government, which was thereafter composed solely of Greek Cypriots.[119] This Government purported to enact the thirteen constitutional amendments.[120] Shortly afterwards, Greek Cypriot forces attacked areas occupied by Turkish Cypriots, and Turkey intervened with air attacks against the Greek Cypriots. Turkey's action was condemned by the Security Council,[121] and the Greek Cypriot Government took the opportunity to denounce unilaterally the Treaty of Alliance, declaring that the Turkish bombing constituted a material breach.[122] The Cypriot denunciation was not recognized either by Turkey or by the United Kingdom, while Greece remained silent on the issue. Greece had itself acted in contravention of the Treaty of Alliance by clandestinely stationing some 10,000 troops in Cyprus. When Turkish Cypriot villages were yet again attacked by Greek Cypriot forces in 1967, Turkey demanded that all Greek troops be immediately withdrawn from the island, threatening invasion if this were not done. After intensive negotiations Greek troops were withdrawn and the crisis was defused. As a result of these events the Turkish Cypriot community decided, in December 1967, to set up the 'Provisional Cyprus Turkish Administration', under which the Turkish Cypriot community established its own legislature, executive council, and judiciary.[123]

In 1974 another crisis occurred when the Greek Cypriot Government was overthrown in a coup, and replaced on 15 July by a regime which advocated *enosis*. The coup had been orchestrated by Greek army officers stationed in Cyprus pursuant to Article IV of the Treaty of Alliance.[124] Turkey viewed

[116] Evriviades, 242.

[117] Palmer, 434.

[118] The UN forces were deployed pursuant to Security Council Resolution 186 (1964). A detailed account of the role of the peace-keeping force may be found in John Theodorides 'The United Nations Peace Keeping Force in Cyprus (UNFICYP)' (1982).

[119] Although the Constitution of Cyprus required the participation of both communities in government, the Supreme Court of Cyprus held, in *Attorney-General* v. *Mustafa Ibrihim* (1964) 48 ILR 6, that the doctrine of necessity applied in order to enable essential services of the state, and in particular the administration of justice, to continue to function.

[120] Evriviades, 248.

[121] SC Resolution 193 (1964).

[122] Evriviades, 259.

[123] Necatigil, 61, 62.   [124] Blaustein and Flanz (eds.) 83.

the coup as the first step towards the union of Cyprus with Greece, and thus a breach of the 1960 Agreements. Turkish troops invaded Cyprus on 20 July 1974; Turkey claimed that this action was justified by Article IV of the Treaty of Guarantee.[125] The Security Council responded to the invasion by adopting Resolution 353, which called for an immediate cease-fire and the withdrawal of all foreign troops. A cease-fire did take place several days after the invasion, but Turkish troops remained in Cyprus. Turkey demanded that Cyprus become a federation with separate Greek and Turkish autonomous zones. Each zone would be governed by its own administration. The Turkish zone would comprise the northern part of the island, occupying approximately 35 per cent of the island's total territory.[126] In January 1975 Greek and Turkish Cypriots agreed to negotiate a constitutional settlement based on a federated state. On 13 February 1975 the Turkish Cypriots proclaimed, as an interim measure, the Turkish Federated State of Cyprus. On 8 June 1975 the constitution of this entity was approved in a referendum by a margin of 99.4 per cent.[127] Negotiations between Greek and Turkish Cypriots for a federated state, meanwhile, remained deadlocked for the next eight years.

On 15 November 1983 the Legislative Assembly of the Turkish Federated State of Cyprus unanimously proclaimed the creation of the Turkish Republic of Northern Cyprus, thereby seceding from the Republic of Cyprus. The proclamation emphasized that the creation of this new state was the fulfilment of the right of self-determination. Turkey recognized the Turkish Republic of Northern Cyprus on the day that it was proclaimed.[128] The Security Council, on the other hand, adopted Resolution 541 (1983), which deplored the 'purported secession'. It declared legally invalid the partition of Cyprus, and called upon states not to recognize the new entity.[129] The constitution of the new state was approved in a referendum of the Turkish Republic of Northern Cyprus held in May 1985 by a margin of 70 per cent of the electorate.[130]

The irredentist desire of Greek Cypriots for *enosis* with Greece has dominated political affairs in Cyprus since the nineteenth century. This in turn has engendered Turkish Cypriot separatism. The goals of Greek Cypriot irredentism and Turkish Cypriot separation are totally irreconcilable, yet the proponents of each justify their position by reference to self-

---

[125] Palmer, 438. See *supra*, pp. 224–5, on the terms of the Treaty of Guarantee. The Supreme Court of Cyprus held, in *Liasi and Others* v. *Attorney-General* (1975) 12 JSC 1889, at 1904, that the coup had resulted in 'the constitutional order' being 'temporarily overthrown'.

[126] Evriviades, 263; Palmer, 439.

[127] Necatigil, xxii.

[128] *Id.*, xxv.

[129] To date no state other than Turkey has recognized the Turkish Republic of Northern Cyprus: Palmer, 443; Necatigil, 320–2.

[130] Necatigil, xxvii.

determination. Before independence Greek Cypriots had argued that Cyprus was entitled to self-determination on the basis that it was a non-self-governing territory. Self-determination would be achieved, in the opinion of the Greek Cypriots, by ascertaining and putting into effect the will of the majority. Should the majority decide for union with Greece, this would constitute self-determination, since Resolution 742(VIII) of 27 November 1953 had provided that a non-self-governing territory could become self-governing either through independence or through association with another state. The Greek Cypriots argued that the Turkish Cypriots were not entitled to a separate exercise of self-determination because they were simply an ethnic minority. This minority, in accordance with democratic principles, would have to submit to the will of the majority. The attainment of independence in 1960 did not satisfy the Greek Cypriot community because *enosis*, rather than independence, was their goal. Independence was seen as having been imposed by outside powers. Even after the attainment of independence the Greek Cypriot community continued to call for self-determination based on the will of the majority. In December 1983, for example, the Greek Cypriot Permanent Representative of Cyprus to the United Nations expressed his belief that the Turkish Cypriots did not possess a separate right of self-determination. To assert that they did was a distortion of the principle of self-determination as embodied in Resolution 1514(XV), which was 'to be exercised by a people as a whole, and not on the basis of factional, religious, communal or ethnic criteria'.[131] If the right of self-determination could be exercised by every ethnic group within a state, he argued, 'it would dismember every state and nation on the face of this earth, including Turkey'.[132]

The Turkish Cypriots claimed entitlement to a separate exercise of the right to self-determination, on the basis that they constituted a distinct community characterized by distinctive traditions, language, religion, and political aspirations. They were not a minority but a people, and as such were entitled to self-determination. According to Turkish Cypriots, the attainment of independence in 1960 was a joint exercise of the right to self-determination by the two peoples of Cyprus.[133] However, the assumption of governmental control by the Greek Cypriots in 1963 was an attempt by the Greek Cypriots to deny the existence of the Turkish Cypriots as a separate people. Paragraph 7 of Resolution 2625(XXV) permitted secession when part of a population was not represented in its government. The Turkish Cypriots were therefore entitled to secede. The Constitution of the Turkish Republic of Northern Cyprus underscored the assertion that the Turkish Cypriots were a separate people entitled to a separate exercise of

[131] Security Council, S/PV 2503 of 15 December 1983, 12.
[132] SC, S/PV 2454 of 15 June 1983, 10.
[133] Necatigil, 222.

self-determination by declaring that the new state had been created in fulfilment of the right of self-determination.[134]

Greek Cypriots argue that self-determination in Cyprus should be understood as the right of the majority within a given political unit to exercise its political will. Turkish Cypriots, on the other hand, argue that self-determination is the right of an ethnic group to determine its own political status. Self-determination has not been allowed to take place in Cyprus in either of these two ways. Neither Greek nor Turkish Cypriots have been permitted to effect self-determination as they understand it: the Greek Cypriots have been prevented from uniting Cyprus to Greece, and the Turkish Cypriots have been prevented from establishing a *de jure* state of their own.

5. IRREDENTISM AND EMERGING STATES: THE CASE OF YUGOSLAVIA

Irredentism was one of the most important issues in the ethnic conflict between Serbs and Croats in Croatia, and amongst Serbs, Croats, and Muslims in Bosnia-Herzegovina. It lay at the heart of the struggle in the former Yugoslavia to determine who would control what territory, and where the boundaries of the new states should be.

When the European Community realized in the latter half of 1991 that Yugoslavia would not survive as a single, unified state, it adopted a policy of insisting that the internal boundaries of Yugoslavia's constituent republics constitute the frontiers of the new successor states.[135] There was to be no adjustment of those internal boundaries to reflect more closely the geographical distribution of the various ethnic groups. Yugoslavia's major ethnic groups were for the most part already geographically divided into particular constituent republics. However, within Croatia there was a significant Serb minority, comprising some 11.5 per cent of the population.[136] Moreover, within Bosnia-Herzegovina no single ethnic group predominated, but three groups were intermingled, with Muslims comprising 43 per cent of the population, Serbs 32 per cent, and Croats 18 per cent.[137]

The disintegration of Yugoslavia was largely due to the inability of its ethnic groups to co-operate with each other. Ethnic hatred had marred Yugoslavia's history from its inception as a state in 1919. During the inter-war years the more numerous Serbs established political hegemony over

---

[134] See *supra*, p. 227.

[135] See Chapter 5, pp. 115–22, for a detailed discussion of this policy of the European Community.

[136] Marc Weller 'The International Response to the Dissolution of the Socialist Federal Republic of Yugoslavia' (1992) 569.

[137] *Id.*, 569.

the other ethnic groups in Yugoslavia. This was particularly resented by the Croats. When Yugoslavia was invaded by Germany and Italy in 1941 many Croats sided with the occupying forces. An independent Croatian state was established, governed by the Ustase, a Croatian Fascist party. Croatia annexed Bosnia-Herzegovina, and declared that the new state would have two religions, Roman Catholicism and Islam. Croatia was to be purged of 'alien' elements, which included Serbs, Jews, and gypsies. The policy of the Ustase with regard to the Serbs was to exterminate a third of the population, to deport another third, and to convert the remainder. It is estimated that during the period of Ustase rule between 350,000 and 750,000 Serbs were killed. At the Nuremburg trials the Ustase policy towards the Serbs was found to constitute genocide.[138]

When Croatia and Bosnia-Herzegovina declared independence, fear of renewed persecution arose amongst their respective Serb populations. The declarations of independence provoked insurrections amongst the Serbs of both Croatia and Bosnia-Herzegovina, each unwilling to become an ethnic minority within an independent Croatia or Bosnia-Herzegovina.[139] The Serbs of Croatia and of Bosnia-Herzegovina wanted those areas of Croatia and Bosnia-Herzegovina which were populated mainly by Serbs to become part of Serbia. Their insurrections were supported by the Yugoslav Army, which was mainly Serb in composition. Serbia maintained that the regions of Croatia and Bosnia-Herzegovina which were inhabited mainly by Serbs were entitled to unite with Serbia.[140] Slobodan Milosevic, the President of Serbia, declared in August 1991 that Croatia was at liberty to withdraw from Yugoslavia if it so desired, but that it could not take with it 'a part of

---

[138] Richard F. Iglar 'The Constitutional Crisis in Yugoslavia and the International Law of Self-Determination: Slovenia's and Croatia's Right to Secede' (1992) 235, fn. 169; Ben Bagwell 'Yugoslavian Constitutional Questions: Self-Determination and Secession of Member Republics' (1991) 493, fn. 24.

[139] Thus, when Croatia was about to be recognized by the European Community, the Serbs of Croatia proclaimed the independence, on 19 Dec. 1991, of the 'Serbian Republic of Krajina', which comprised approximately one-third of Croatia's territory. Similarly, when the EC and the USA recognized Bosnia-Herzegovina on 7 Apr. 1992, the 'Assembly of the Serbian People in Bosnia-Herzegovina' declared on the same day the independence of the 'Serbian Republic of Bosnia-Herzegovina', which comprised approximately half of Bosnia-Herzegovina's territory: Roland Rich 'Recognition of States: The Collapse of Yugoslavia and the Soviet Union' (1993) 61–2.

[140] At the same time, however, Serbia has denied this right to the 2 m. ethnic Albanians who inhabit the autonomous province of Kosovo within Serbia, and who constitute more than 90% of the population of that province. In October 1990 the Kosovo Legislative Assembly declared Kosovo to be a 'sovereign and independent state', and in May 1992 secession from Serbia was overwhelmingly approved in an unofficial referendum. Albania recognized Kosovo as an independent state and reserved the right to 'help' the Albanians of Kosovo. But Serbia will not countenance the secession of Kosovo, with which it has strong historical and cultural ties. It has adopted increasingly repressive measures against the Albanian population, and has revoked the autonomous status of the province: Keesing's *Record of World Events* (1991) Vol. 37, 38375; (1992) Vol. 38, 39150.

the Serbian people'. 'The right of self-determination', he added, 'equally belongs to the Serbian people.'[141] Serbia declared that it would agree to the dissolution of Yugoslavia only if the borders of the constituent republics were redrawn to include all Serbs within a single state.[142] On 28 December 1991 Serbia announced that a smaller Yugoslavia would be reconstituted, to include all Serb-inhabited territories. The new Federation would comprise Serbia, Montenegro, and the Serbian enclaves within Croatia and Bosnia-Herzegovina.[143] This was unacceptable to both Croatia and Bosnia-Herzegovina. Croatia refused to accept the secession of its Serb-populated regions and declared that the question of border revision had nothing to do with self-determination, but rather with the territorial aggrandizement of Serbia at Croatia's expense.[144] The President of Bosnia-Herzegovina, Alija Izebegovic, likewise declared that secession by Bosnian Serbs would not be tolerated, and added that any attempt to divide Bosnia-Herzegovina would 'lead to civil war'.[145] In its Declaration on the 'Guidelines on the Recognition of New States in Eastern Europe and in the Soviet Union',[146] issued on 16 December 1991, the European Community also explicitly indicated that Serbia's plan to incorporate the Serbian enclaves of Croatia and Bosnia-Herzegovina into a reconstituted Yugoslavia was contrary to the policy of the European Community. The Declaration called for 'respect for the inviolability of all frontiers' and added that entities which were 'the result of aggression' would not be recognized.[147]

It was in this context that Serbia submitted two questions to the Badinter Commission on 20 November 1991. Serbia sought to ascertain from the Commission whether 'the Serbian population in Croatia and Bosnia-Herzegovina, as one of the constituent peoples of Yugoslavia, have the right to self-determination',[148] and whether 'the internal boundaries between Croatia and Serbia and between Bosnia-Herzegovina and Serbia (can) be regarded as frontiers in terms of public international law'.[149] The Commission responded to these two questions in Opinions Nos. 2 and 3, handed down on 11 January 1992. In Opinion No. 2 the Commission held, as has already been seen, that insofar as the Serbian populations of Croatia and Bosnia-Herzegovina were entitled to self-determination, that right did

---

[141] Nicolas Rothwell 'Croats, Serbs to Exchange Prisoners' *Weekend Australian* 7 Aug. 1991, 15.

[142] 'EC Peace Bid Scuttled by Serbs' *Sydney Morning Herald* 6 Aug. 1991, 1, 8.

[143] 'Serbs Announce Plan for a New, Smaller Yugoslavia' *Sydney Morning Herald* 28 Dec. 1991, 11.

[144] Tim Judah 'Croatia Powerless to Halt Serbian Expansion' *The Australian* 7 Aug. 1991, 6; Tim Judah and Dessa Trevisson 'Yugoslav Talks Fail to Curb Fighting' *id*. 23 Aug. 1991, 10.

[145] Noel Malcolm 'Uneasy Microcosm of the Fractured Balkans' *id*. 22 Oct. 1991, 13.

[146] (1992) 31 ILM 1486.

[147] *Id.*, 1486, 1487.

[148] Opinion No. 2 (1992) 31 ILM 1497, 1498.

[149] Opinion No. 3, *id*. 1499, 1499.

'not involve changes to existing frontiers at the time of independence'.[150]
The Commission elaborated upon this point in Opinion No. 3, where it
found that the internal frontiers of the constituent republics must be maintained as the frontiers of the emerging successor states, both as a matter of
Yugoslav constitutional law and as a matter of international law.

With regard to Yugoslav constitutional law, the Commission relied on
Article 5 of the 1974 Constitution, which declared in paragraph 2 that the
'territory of a Republic may not be altered without the consent of that
Republic', and in paragraph 4 that 'the frontiers of the Socialist Federal
Republic of Yugoslavia may not be altered without the consent of all
Republics and Autonomous Provinces'.[151] The Commission concluded that
'the second and fourth paragraphs of Article 5 of the Constitution of the
SFRY stipulated that the Republics' territories and boundaries could not be
altered without their consent'.[152] However, the constitutional aspects of the
question were not quite as straightforward as the Commission made out. In
addition to Article 5, the Constitution contained another very important
provision related to the establishment of boundaries: Principle I of the
Basic Principles (Introductory Part). Principle I read, *inter alia*, as follows:

The nations of Yugoslavia, proceeding from the right of every nation to self-
determination, including the right to secession, on the basis of their will freely
expressed in the common struggle of all nations and nationalities in the National
Liberation War and Socialist Revolution, and in conformity with their historic
aspirations, aware that further consolidation of their brotherhood and unity is in the
common interest, have, together with the nationalities with which they live, united
in a federal republic of free and equal nations and nationalities and founded a
socialist federal community of working people—the Socialist Federal Republic of
Yugoslavia . . .[153]

The phrase 'proceeding from the right of every nation to self-
determination, including the right of secession' seems to indicate that there
may indeed be a constitutional right of secession.[154] However, even if this is
so, that right of secession does not inhere in the constituent republics of
Yugoslavia, but rather in the 'nations' of Yugoslavia, since Principle I refers
not to Yugoslavia's constituent republics but to its nations. As Hondius
points out, the constituent republics were not parties to the union of Yugoslavia, but simply results of that union, which was effected by Yugoslavia's
nations.[155] The primacy of the nations in Yugoslavia is emphasized in Prin-

---

[150] Opinion No. 3, 1497–8. Opinion No. 2 is discussed in detail in Chapter 7, pp. 170–1.
[151] Blaustein and Flanz (eds.) 'Yugoslavia' (1986) 29, 48.
[152] (1992) 31 ILM 1499, 1500.
[153] Blaustein and Flanz (eds.) 'Yugoslavia' (1986) 29.
[154] Bagwell, 515.
[155] Frits W. Hondius *The Yugoslav Community of Nations* (1968) 250. The boundaries of
Yugoslavia's constituent republics, moreover, have been a matter of dispute amongst the

ciple I by the fact that it links both the unification of the state and its potential dismemberment to the *nations*, while making no reference to the constituent *republics*. A plausible argument can therefore be made that it should be the Serbian, Croatian, and Muslim nations which determine the boundaries of Serbia, Croatia, and Bosnia-Herzegovina in the event of Yugoslavia's dissolution, rather than the constituent republics within which those nations, or parts of those nations, happen to reside. This argument was rejected by Bothe and Schmidt on the basis that constitutional considerations of this sort were no longer relevant, given that Yugoslavia was in the process of dissolution and therefore the provisions of its constitution were no longer applicable.[156] However, if the Badinter Commission thought that constitutional considerations were no longer relevant, it presumably would have said so in Opinion No. 3. By referring to Article 5, paragraphs 2 and 4 of the Constitution as a justification for its finding, it indicated that constitutional matters were of continuing relevance. Yet, astonishingly, the Commission made no reference to Principle I.

In addition to constitutional considerations, the Commission based its finding in Opinion No. 3 on what it referred to as 'principles and rules of public international law',[157] relying specifically on the principle of *uti possidetis*. That principle was originally developed in Central and South America in the early nineteenth century. It was defined by the Swiss Federal Council in its 1922 arbitral award between Columbia and Venezuela:

When the Spanish colonies of Central and South America proclaimed their independence, they adopted a principle of constitutional and international law to which they gave the name of *uti possidetis juris* of 1810, the purpose of which was to declare that the limits of the newly established Republics would be the borders of the Spanish provinces which they had replaced.[158]

In other words, the principle of *uti possidetis* was developed to delimit the frontiers of independent states upon decolonization. The principle ensured that the frontiers of a non-self-governing territory remained constant when that territory became an independent state. Although the principle was originally developed to address the question of frontiers when decolonization occurred, the Badinter Commission asserted in Opinion No. 3 that the principle had developed beyond the colonial context and was now 'recognized as a general principle'.[159] In support of this proposition the

'nations' of Yugoslavia since its inception as a federal socialist state. In 1945 there was a serious internal dispute within the Praesidium of the Yugoslav Communist Party over the frontiers between the constituent republics: *id.*, 139, 271.

[156] Michael Bothe and Christian Schmidt 'Sur Quelques Questions de Succession Posées par la Dissolution de l'URSS et Celle de la Yougoslavie' (1992) 825–6.

[157] (1992) 31 ILM 1499.

[158] *Columbia* v. *Venezuela* (1922) 1 RIAA 223, 228 (author's translation).

[159] (1992) 31 ILM 1499, 1500.

Commission cited the *Case Concerning the Frontier Dispute (Burkina Faso/ Republic of Mali)*.[160] In this case the International Court of Justice, discussing the principle of *uti possidetis*, declared as follows:

Nevertheless the principle is not a special rule which pertains solely to one specific system of international law. It is a general principle, which is logically connected with the phenomenon of the obtaining of independence, wherever it occurs. Its obvious purpose is to prevent the independence and stability of new States being endangered by fratricidal struggles ...[161]

The Commission relied upon this statement to make use of the principle with regard to the situation in Yugoslavia. As a result, it found that as a matter of international law the borders of the constituent republics became international frontiers upon Yugoslavia's dissolution. However, it is doubtful that the International Court had intended by this statement to extend the principle of *uti possidetis* beyond the colonial context. The *Frontier Dispute* case concerned two African states. The disputed frontier had been inherited by the two states from the colonial period, and they had agreed that the resolution of their dispute must be 'based on respect for the principle of the intangibility of frontiers inherited from colonization'.[162] This agreement between the parties prompted the Court to refer to the principle of *uti possidetis*. The Court specifically noted that the principle was 'a firmly established principle of international law where decolonization is concerned'.[163] In other words, the principle applied to situations of decolonization. The Court observed that the principle had first been used in Spanish America, where decolonization had first occurred.[164] At this point the Court said: 'the principle is not a special principle which applies to one system of international law.'[165] That is to say, it was not a principle confined to decolonization in South America. It was thus unlike asylum, for example, which the International Court had found could exist 'between certain Latin-American states only'.[166] By contrast *uti possidetis* was 'a general principle ... connected to the obtaining of independence wherever it occurs'.[167] However, 'the obtaining of independence wherever it occurs' must be read in the light of the Court's previous statement that *uti possidetis* was 'a firmly established principle of law where decolonization is concerned'.[168] The Court was saying, in other words, that *uti possidetis* applied as a general principle of international law to all cases of

---

[160] Judgment, ICJ Report 1986, 554.   [161] *Id.*, 565.
[162] *Id.*, 564.
[163] *Id.*, 565.
[164] *Id.*, 565.
[165] *Id.*, 565.
[166] *Asylum Case (Columbia/Peru)* Judgment, ICJ Reports 1950, p. 266 at 277.
[167] *Case Concerning the Frontier Dispute (Burkina Faso/Republic of Mali)* Judgment, ICJ Reports 1986, p. 554 at 565.   [168] *Id.*, 565.

decolonization, wherever they occurred in the world. It was not saying that the principle applied outside the context of decolonization. The Court's statement in the *Frontier Dispute* case therefore cannot be taken as authority for the proposition that the principle of *uti possidetis* can be used in a context other than that of decolonization.[169]

Applying the principle of *uti possidetis* to the internal boundaries of a sovereign and independent state is also highly questionable from a jurisdictional standpoint. The maintenance or alteration of internal boundaries within an independent state is a matter which falls within the domestic jurisdiction of that state; it does not fall within the jurisdiction of international law. International law did not apply to the Yugoslav situation until the entities emerging from its dissolution qualified as subjects of international law. However, when the Commission handed down its Opinion No. 3 on 11 January 1992 none of the successor states had yet been recognized by the international community. Croatia and Bosnia-Herzegovina had not even satisfied the minimum legal criteria which the Badinter Commission had declared in Opinion No. 1 to be necessary for statehood.[170] Croatia and Bosnia-Herzegovina were not subjects of international law, and therefore the principle of *uti possidetis* did not apply to their borders. Secession and dissolution, as already noted, are neither legal nor illegal in international law, but legally neutral.[171] The process of secession or dissolution does not fall within the jurisdiction of international law, so the principles and rules of international law cannot be used to regulate its progress or outcome. That regulation must be achieved by the parties themselves, and will include the working out of new boundaries for the successor states. Only when the

[169] Other recent cases in which the principle of *uti possidetis* has been invoked have also confined its application to situations involving decolonization. In the case of *Delimitation of the Maritime Boundary Between Guinea and Guinea-Bissau* (Arbitration Tribunal Award of 14 Feb. 1985) (1986) 25 ILM 251, the Tribunal held, at p. 271, that the principle of *uti possidetis* was binding upon the disputants as their boundary had been established during the colonial period and had therefore been inherited by the successor states. In the case of *Land, Island and Maritime Frontier Dispute (El Salvador/Honduras: Nicaragua Intervening)* International Court of Justice, Communiqué No. 92/22, 11 Sep. 1992, the Chamber of the International Court of Justice noted that the parties had agreed that the principle of *uti possidetis* would be the basis for resolving their dispute. The Chamber declared, at p. 9, that 'the essence of the agreed principle is its primary aim of securing respect for the territorial boundaries at the time of independence, and its application has resulted in colonial administrative boundaries being transformed into international frontiers'. The principle of *uti possidetis* was also discussed at some length by Judge Abijola in his Separate Opinion in the case of *Territorial Dispute (Libyan Arab Jamahiriya/Chad)* Judgment, ICJ Reports 1994, p. 6, at pp. 83–92. Although Judge Abijola was of the opinion that *uti possidetis* should apply in all situations involving decoloniation, he made no mention of the principle being applied in any other context.

[170] In Opinion No. 1 the Commission had noted, at p. 1495, that 'the State is commonly defined as a community which consists of a territory and a population subject to an organized political authority; that such a State is characterized by sovereignty'. Croatia and Bosnia-Herzegovina, however, did not exercise sovereignty over large parts of their territory and population: see fn. 139 *supra*.

[171] Crawford, 268. See Chapter 8, pp. 192–3, for a detailed discussion of this point.

process of secession or dissolution is complete does international law become relevant, when the successor entities qualify as states by virtue of having fulfilled the traditional minimum legal criteria of statehood set out in Article 1 of the 1933 Montevideo Convention.[172] Recognition follows, as an acknowledgement by other states that the new entity has fulfilled the requirements of international law for statehood.[173]

Croatia and Bosnia-Herzegovina were recognized as states by the European Community and the United States even though they had not yet satisfied the traditional minimum legal existence for statehood. As there was a real and ongoing struggle over large parts of the territories of both Croatia and Bosnia-Herzegovina, that recognition by the international community was premature and inappropriate.[174] The international community sought to use recognition in a constitutive rather than a declaratory sense. By transforming the internal boundaries of Croatia and Bosnia-Herzegovina into international frontiers through recognition, the international community attempted to define the territorial limits of the successor states, and thereby to discourage the various ethnic groups within those states from engaging in further conflict over those territories. As the International Court of Justice had said in the *Frontier Dispute* case, the purpose of the principle of *uti possidetis* was 'to prevent the independence and stability of new States being endangered by fratricidal struggles'.[175] However, neither international law nor the actions of the international community can force ethnic groups to live together in harmony or prevent 'fratricidal conflict' simply by decreeing that boundaries will not be altered and forcing those groups to cohabit within a single state.[176] If the mutual antipathy of Serbs, Croatians, and Muslims made it impossible for them to live together within Yugoslavia, it is unlikely that they will coexist happily within a successor state.[177] Attempts to maintain internal boundaries through the application of *uti possidetis* and early recognition are thus unrealistic and unworkable, as well as bad law.

Early recognition of Croatia and Bosnia-Herzegovina by the international community also precluded the possibility of a political settlement based upon a readjustment of boundaries to reflect more closely the ethnic

---

[172] (1936) 165 LNTS 19, 25.   [173] See Chapter 8, pp. 193–5.

[174] See Chapter 8, p. 199.

[175] *Case Concerning the Frontier Dispute (Burkina Faso/Republic of Mali)* Judgment, ICJ Reports 1986, p. 554, at 565.

[176] It is as though one were to decree marriage to be indissoluble, and then assume that this would eliminate marital discord between antagonistic spouses.

[177] As Adeno Addis points out, the formation of such states simply reproduces ethnic conflict at a 'smaller level, rather than solving it. It would be like dividing up a crystal. When a crystal is cut into smaller pieces, those small pieces reproduce the same (molecular) structure as the original: the size, not the structure, has changed': 'Individualism, Communitarianism and the Rights of Ethnic Minorities' (1992) 626. See also Hurst Hannum 'Rethinking Self-Determination' (1993) 54–6.

distribution in the region and thereby to create states which were ethnically more homogeneous. Having recognized Croatia and Bosnia-Herzegovina as states, the international community was forced to consider solutions to the ethnic conflict in Croatia and Bosnia-Herzegovina only within the framework of the existing frontiers, even though it was clear that the groups within those frontiers were unable to co-exist peacefully. In Croatia the minority Serbs have simply been driven out. In Bosnia-Herzegovina the state has effectively been partitioned by the warring factions into two separate entities, although the territorial integrity of the state has been formally preserved.[178]

6. CONCLUSION

Ethnic self-determination is irredentist in nature when it involves an attempt by an ethnic group to create a nation-state whose boundaries will transcend existing state borders. Irredentist claims to self-determination, unlike secessionist claims, involve more than one state and so come within the jurisdiction of international law. The examples considered above show how international law has regulated irredentist claims. Where irredentist claims are concerned, the state retains the supreme and decisive role in international law. The case of Somalia demonstrates that there is no legal basis for irredentist claims founded solely on ethnic affinity between the population of a claimant state and the inhabitants of the territory claimed. Such claims violate the principle of territorial integrity and are clearly contrary to Article 2(4) of the United Nations Charter and paragraph 8 of Resolution 2625(XXV). Claims for union on the basis of common ethnicity will succeed in international law only if the concurrence of the state itself is obtained. International law permits the partial or total merger of two states if the states themselves so agree, as was the case in the reunification of Germany.

The unification of two states whose populations are essentially of the same ethnic stock may not be possible if one of those states has a substantial ethnic minority which opposes union. The case of Cyprus illustrates this. Although a large majority of Cypriots were ethnic Greeks and desired political union with Greece, their attempt to do so was thwarted by the Turkish Cypriots, who formed a significant minority in Cyprus and were part of the much larger Turkish nation, which was also opposed to the union of Cyprus and Greece. The existence of a significant ethnic minority within a particular state is therefore a factor which complicates the irredentist union of two states.

[178] See Chapter 5, pp. 120–1.

Problems of an irredentist nature may also arise when a state disintegrates as a result of ethnic conflict, as in Yugoslavia. The finding of the Badinter Commission that in such circumstances the internal boundaries of the constituent units of the former state must be maintained as the external frontiers of the new states did not resolve the problem of ethnic conflict which had led to the disintegration of the state in the first place. It would have been far better to avoid irredentist problems by allowing the frontiers to be readjusted so as to separate hostile ethnic groups.

10

Historical Title

1. INTRODUCTION

Ethnic claims to self-determination challenge the principle of territorial integrity. An ethnic group seeking self-determination, by definition, threatens the territorial integrity and the boundaries of the state or states involved.

Territorial claims based on historical title also pit the principle of territorial integrity against the concept of self-determination. The issue of historical title arises whenever a state claims that territory belonged to it in the past and should be returned in order to restore the territorial integrity of the claimant state. In cases of historical title, claimant states argue that the principle of territorial integrity is more important than self-determination for the population of the territory claimed. Such claimants demand the return of the territory whether or not its inhabitants share a common language and culture with the population of the claimant state, and whether or not they desire to be part of that state. This Chapter examines the relationship of self-determination to territorial claims based on historical title.

2. RESOLUTION 1514(XV)

Since the Second World War a number of states have laid claim to territories which they allege to have been detached from them as a result of colonization. As legal justification for such claims paragraph 6 of Resolution 1514(XV) has been cited. Paragraph 6 provides that any attempt 'aimed at the partial or total disruption of the national unity and the territorial integrity of a country is incompatible with the purposes and principles of the Charter'. This paragraph, it is argued, applies to situations in which the territorial integrity of a state has been disrupted as a result of colonization, so that a return of the territory in question simply restores the state to its original condition. This means that the inhabitants of a territory claimed on the basis of historical title are precluded from exercising a right of self-determination, because the only political status available to them is integration with the claimant state. Although paragraph 2 of Resolution 1514(XV) provides that 'all peoples have the right to self-determination', in

cases of historical title paragraph 6 would pre-empt paragraph 2. The territory claimed in such cases must revert to the claimant state without the
inhabitants of that territory being permitted to determine their political
status.

Many states reject this interpretation, arguing that paragraph 6 cannot be
read to justify territorial claims. The purpose of paragraph 6, they contend,
was simply 'to ensure that acts of self-determination occur within the established boundaries of colonies, rather than within sub-regions'.[1] This is the
position, for example, of the United Kingdom. The United Kingdom has
pointed out that the use of the word 'attempt' in paragraph 6 connotes
future action, and that paragraph 6 cannot therefore be construed to justify
territorial redress for past actions. Its aim is rather to protect 'colonial
territories or countries which have recently become independent against
attempts to divide them . . . at a time when they are least able to defend
themselves'.[2] This interpretation makes paragraph 6 subordinate to paragraph 2, so that the right of self-determination remains available to the
inhabitants of all non-self-governing territories without exception.

Although the British interpretation may more accurately reflect the
grammatical sense of paragraph 6, a number of states adhered to the opposite interpretation from the time when Resolution 1514(XV) was originally
adopted.[3] During the drafting of paragraph 6, for example, Guatemala
proposed that a sentence be added to the effect that the principle of self-
determination should not 'impair the right of territorial integrity of any
state or its right to the recovery of territory'.[4] However, that proposal was
never put to the vote. Guatemala withdrew its amendment on the grounds
that claims based on historical title were already fully protected by the
wording of paragraph 6 as it then stood.[5] That withdrawal may have had
more to do with the fact that Guatemala was unwilling to face the prospect
of defeat for its proposed amendment. Guatemala had already attempted
unsuccessfully to introduce a similar clause into the provisions of Chapter
XII of the United Nations Charter. That proposal would have had the effect
of preventing the Trusteeship System from applying to any territory in
dispute between states members of the United Nations; it was decisively
defeated.[6]

---

[1] Thomas M. Franck and Paul Hoffman 'The Right of Self-Determination in Very Small
Places' (1975–76) 370.

[2] A/AC.109/PV 284.

[3] A. Rigo Sureda *The Evolution of the Right of Self-Determination* (1973) 185.

[4] 15 UN GAOR Annex 2 (Agenda Item 87) at 7, UN Doc. A/L 325 (1960). See also the
statement of Jordan in this regard: 15 UN GAOR 1946th plen. mtg.) at 1268, UN Doc. A/PV
946 (1960).

[5] Iran, Afghanistan, Indonesia, and Morocco supported Guatemala's interpretation of para.
6 but, like Guatemala, maintained that the current wording of para. 6 already adequately
covered such situations: Miguel Antonio Sanchez 'Self-Determination and the Falkland Islands Dispute' (1982) 567–8.   [6] (1945) 10 UNCIO 463, 465, 476, 485.

3. THE WESTERN SAHARA CASE

The proper interpretation of paragraph 6 came up before the International Court of Justice in the *Western Sahara* case of 1975.[7] Morocco and Mauritania both claimed the territory of the Western Sahara, a former Spanish colony, on the basis of historical title. The Court was called upon to determine, *inter alia*, the legal ties between the Western Sahara and the two claimant states. The Court found that there were no 'legal ties of such a nature as might affect the application of Resolution 1514(XV) in the decolonization of Western Sahara and, in particular, of the principle of self-determination through the free and genuine expression of the will of the peoples of the Territory'.[8] The Court was therefore able to resolve the case without having to pronounce on either the correct meaning of paragraph 6 or its relationship to paragraph 2. Judge Petren, in his Separate Opinion, summed up the attitude of the Court towards the issue of territorial claims based on historical title, and the relationship of such claims to the right of self-determination, when he declared that the problem fell 'within an as yet inadequately explored area of contemporary international law' which was 'not yet considered ripe for submission to the Court'.[9]

Although the Court reached no definitive conclusions on the meaning or scope of paragraph 6, the individual opinions of various members of the Court indicated a clear preference for the primacy of the right of self-determination. Judge Nagendra Singh declared that:

the consultation of the people of the territory awaiting decolonization is an inescapable imperative whether the method followed on decolonization is integration or association or independence . . . Thus even if integration of territory was demanded by an interested State, as in this case, it could not be had without ascertaining the freely expressed will of the people—the very *sine qua non* of all decolonization.[10]

Judge Dillard was even more emphatic:

It is for the people to determine the destiny of the territory and not the territory the destiny of the people. Viewed in this perspective it becomes almost self-evident that the existence of ancient 'legal ties' of the kind described in the Opinion, while they may influence some of the projected procedures for decolonization, can have only a tangential effect in the ultimate choices available to the people.[11]

[7] Advisory Opinion, ICJ Reports 1975, p. 12. See pp. 85–6 of Chapter 4 for a general discussion of this case.

[8] ICJ Reports 1975, p. 12 at 68.

[9] *Id.*, 110.

[10] ICJ Reports 1975, p. 12 at 81. Judge *ad hoc* Boni reached the same conclusion: 'If the General Assembly had before it an advisory opinion of the Court declaring that there were ties of sovereignty between Morocco and certain areas of Western Sahara, it would have been obliged to consult the inhabitants of the region on the different options provided for in Resolution 1514(XV)': *id.*, 174.

[11] *Id.*, 122. For an analysis of Judge Dillard's position see Rosalyn Higgins 'Judge Dillard and the Right to Self-Determination' (1983).

Judge Castro likewise supported the primacy of self-determination. He argued that the ties of a claimant state to a former territory were subject to intertemporal changes in the law. Consequently, ties which may have existed under a previous regime of international law would be superseded by the current law relating to self-determination, which had established a new legal regime with respect to non-self-governing territories. Under this new legal regime 'the Administering Power . . . has a duty to recognize the principle that the interests of the inhabitants of the territory are paramount'.[12] These individual opinions add considerable weight to the view that the Court did not in fact accept the proposition that territorial claims based on historical title should preclude the process of self-determination.[13]

4. UNITED NATIONS PRACTICE

The United Nations has dealt with disputes involving self-determination and historical title on a number of occasions. However, it has established no consistent policy as to whether self-determination or historical title should take precedence in conflicting claims.

The issue arose in 1975 with regard to the Indonesian invasion and subsequent annexation of East Timor. East Timor had been a Portuguese colony since the sixteenth century. In 1960 it was designated as a non-self-governing territory by the General Assembly.[14] The three major political parties of East Timor had widely differing political agendas for the territory, which ranged from the attainment of independent statehood to the incorporation of the territory into Indonesia.[15] Civil war broke out in 1975, following the withdrawal of Portuguese authorities. A unilateral declaration of independence was made by one political party on 28 November 1975; two days later another party proclaimed the integration of East Timor into Indonesia.[16] On 7 December 1975 Indonesian troops invaded East Timor and the territory was incorporated into Indonesia. Indonesia justified its invasion and annexation of East Timor on the basis, *inter alia*, of histori-

[12] ICJ Reports 1975, p. 12 at 169.

[13] Commentators who support the view that the Court favoured the supremacy of self-determination include Thomas M. Franck 'The Stealing of the Sahara' (1976) 711; Malcolm Shaw 'The Western Sahara Case' (1978) 149; James Crawford *The Creation of States in International Law* (1979) 380; and S. K. N. Blay 'Self-Determination *Versus* Territorial Integrity in Decolonisation' (1986) 463. For an opposite interpretation of the Court's finding see Alejandro Schwed 'Territorial Claims as a Limitation to the Right of Self-Determination in the Context of the Falkland Islands Dispute' 458; and Miguel Antonio Sanchez, 577.

[14] GA 1542(XV) of 15 Dec. 1960.

[15] Kwaw Nyameke Blay 'Self-Determination Versus Territorial Integrity in Decolonization Revisited' (1985) 395.

[16] Jean-Pierre L. Fonteyne 'The Portuguese Timor Gap Litigation Before the International Court of Justice: A Brief Appraisal of Australia's Position' (1991) 172.

cal title. It argued that East Timor had been part of the precolonial state of Indonesia, and should therefore revert to it upon the termination of its non-self-governing status. Indonesia claimed that by invading East Timor it was merely reclaiming its own territory. It also argued that there was an ethnic and cultural affinity between the people of East Timor and those of Indonesian West Timor, as well as a territorial contiguity between East Timor and the surrounding Indonesian islands.[17]

Portugal, in its capacity as the Administering Power of East Timor, referred the matter to the United Nations. On 12 December 1975 the General Assembly condemned the invasion and affirmed the right of the people of East Timor to self-determination.[18] The Security Council reiterated the declaration of the General Assembly on 22 December 1975 in Resolution 384 (1975). A second resolution of the Security Council, adopted in April 1976,[19] called upon Indonesia to withdraw its troops, and again emphasized the right to self-determination of the people of East Timor. The General Assembly adopted a resolution on East Timor every year from 1976 to 1982, all of which condemned Indonesia's presence in East Timor and reaffirmed the right of self-determination for the people of East Timor.[20] However, support dwindled from year to year, and since 1983 the question of East Timor has not been put before the General Assembly.[21]

The question of whether self-determination or historical title should take precedence was overshadowed in the case of East Timor by Indonesia's use of force, which was clearly contrary to international law and condemned as such both by the Security Council and the General Assembly, both of whom emphasized that the people of East Timor were entitled to exercise a right of self-determination. In the *East Timor* case, the International Court of Justice confirmed that East Timor remained a non-self-governing territory whose people retained the right of self-determination.[22]

The General Assembly also had occasion to consider the relationship of self-determination to historical title in relation to Belize.[23] Guatemala had long claimed that Belize was an integral part of its territory, a claim made on the basis of historical title, and specifically on the principle of *uti possidetis*.[24] Guatemala claimed that the territory had originally been ad-

---

[17] Blay (1986) 456.   [18] GA Resolution 3485(XXX).

[19] SC Resolution 389 (1986).

[20] GA Resolutions 31/53 of 1 Dec. 1976, 32/34 of 28 Nov. 1977, 33/39 of 13 Dec. 1978, and 34/40 of 21 Nov. 1979, 35/27 of 11 Nov. 1980, 36/50 of 24 Nov. 1981, and 37/30 of 23 Nov. 1982.

[21] Fonteyne, 172.

[22] *East Timor (Portugal* v. *Australia)* Judgment, ICJ Reports 1995, p. 90 at 103. See pp. 88–90, Chapter 4 for a detailed discussion of the *East Timor* case.

[23] Belize was originally known as British Honduras. In 1973 the House of Representatives and the Senate of British Honduras enacted legislation to change the name to Belize: Franck and Hoffman, 358, fn. 121.

[24] It was this claim to Belize which prompted Guatemala to propose an amendment to para. 6 of Resolution 1514(XV) which would have ensured that territorial claims based on historical

ministered as part of the former Spanish province of Guatemala.[25] Although there was evidence that the northern part of Belize had once been under the jurisdiction of the Spanish province of Yucatan, there was no evidence that the southern part had ever been under the jurisdiction of the province of Guatemala.[26] Moreover, Guatemala's reliance on the principle of *uti possidetis* erroneously assumed that the principle was one of general application. In fact the principle applied only to those states which were former Spanish provinces, and therefore could not be used as a basis for determining the disposition of territory between a state party to the principle and one which was not.[27] Guatemala's claim to Belize also depended upon the proper interpretation of the Anglo-Guatemalan Treaty of 1859.[28] That treaty was intended to resolve Guatemala's claim to Belize, which intention was thwarted by a dispute as to its interpretation. Guatemala maintained that the entire treaty had been rendered null and void because the United Kingdom had breached Article 7, which obliged the United Kingdom to build a road from the Atlantic coast to the Guatemalan border.[29] This the United Kingdom failed to do. Construction of the road, according to Guatemala, was the consideration for an agreement to cede territory, provided for in Article 1.[30] According to the United Kingdom, the Treaty was not one of territorial cession at all, but one which established the boundaries between sovereign territories. Moreover, the United Kingdom pointed out that even if the Treaty were one of territorial cession, Guatemala would first have to prove legitimate title to the territory in question, which it had not done.[31]

In 1964 the United Kingdom granted Belize full internal self-government, and announced that it would grant the colony independence in due course.[32] This was unacceptable to Guatemala, which declared that any change in the status of Belize must await the prior settlement of Guatemala's territorial claim. Guatemala's representative to the United Nations declared that Guatemala would otherwise be compelled to resort to force. The General Assembly at first sought to accommodate Guatemala's claim, and postponed any decision on the status of Belize until Guatemala and the

---

title would take precedence over the right of self-determination. See *supra*, p. 240, for a discussion of Guatemala's proposed amendment.

[25] Blay (1986) 458–9.

[26] J. Robert Maguire 'The Decolonization of Belize: Self-Determination v. Territorial Integrity' (1982) 853–4.

[27] *Id.*, 853. See Chapter 9, pp. 233–6, for a discussion of the principle of *uti possidetis*.

[28] Wycke-Aycinena Treaty, 30 Apr. 1859, 120 CTS 371.

[29] *Id.*, 377.

[30] Maguire, 854–5.

[31] *Id.*, 854–5.

[32] Blay (1986) 459.

United Kingdom had reached some settlement on the issue.[33] However, it became increasingly apparent that the positions of Guatemala and the United Kingdom were irreconcilable, and that no settlement would be reached. Guatemala's refusal to allow any change in the status of Belize until its own claim had first been settled meant that the status of Belize as a non-self-governing territory would be perpetuated indefinitely.[34] The General Assembly therefore decided to resolve the dispute itself. It adopted Resolution 35/20 of 11 November 1980, whereby Belize would become 'an independent State before the end of 1981'. In adopting this Resolution the General Assembly gave precedence to self-determination rather than historical title. The Resolution made no reference to Guatemala's claim. On 21 September 1980 Belize became an independent state, and was admitted to the United Nations on 25 September 1980; Guatemala formally protested, but took no other action.[35]

In the cases of both Belize and East Timor the United Nations rejected the argument that a territorial claim based on historical title could oust the right of self-determination. However, the United Nations has indicated in a number of other cases that historical title can oust the right of self-determination, for example in the cases of Gibraltar and the Falkland Islands.

Gibraltar was ceded to the United Kingdom by Spain in the Treaty of Utrecht of 1713.[36] Article X of the treaty declared that Spain would yield to the United Kingdom 'the full and entire propriety [*sic*] of the town and castle of Gibraltar, together with the port, fortifications and forts thereunto belonging'.[37] It also stipulated that, should the United Kingdom by any means 'alienate' Gibraltar, 'the preference of having the same shall always be given to the Crown of Spain before any others'.[38] Spain maintains that Article X creates a right of retrocession which, because it predates the development of the right of self-determination, must take precedence over that right, and must therefore apply to Gibraltar. Gibraltar cannot attain independence through exercising a right of self-determination, but must simply revert to Spain by virtue of Article X. This reversionary right under Article X is, according to Spain, reinforced by paragraph 6 of Resolution 1514(XV).

---

[33] The first 5 Resolutions of the GA reflect this stance: Resolutions 3432(XXX) of 8 Dec. 1975; 31/50 of 1 Dec. 1976; 32/32 of 28 Nov. 1977; 33/36 of 13 Dec. 1978; and 34/38 of 21 Nov. 1979.

[34] Maguire, 856–7.

[35] *Id.*, 858. Belize was admitted to the UN by Resolution 36/3 of 25 Sep. 1981. Guatemala was the only state to vote against the Resolution: Resolutions and Decisions Adopted By the General Assembly During the First Part of Its Thirty-Sixth Session (From 15 Sep. to 18 Dec. 1981) UN Press Release GA 6546, 4 Jan. 1982, 1–2.

[36] 28 CTS 325.   [37] *Id.*, 330.   [38] *Id.*, 331.

The United Kingdom, on the other hand, has argued that paragraph 2 of Resolution 1514(XV) is paramount. This means that the inhabitants of Gibraltar must be given the right freely to determine their own political status. The right of self-determination is superior to that of historical title in modern international law, and so the reversionary right of Spain contained in Article X has been supplanted by the right of the Gibraltareans to determine their own political status. In support of this proposition, the United Kingdom relies on Article 73 of the Charter, which enjoins administering powers to recognize that the interests of the inhabitants of non-self-governing territories are 'paramount'. Consequently, the United Kingdom has refused to transfer Gibraltar to Spain unless its population agrees, which it has not done. The United Kingdom held a referendum in Gibraltar on 10 September 1967 to ascertain whether its inhabitants wished to retain their association with the United Kingdom or to accept Spanish sovereignty: the result was a vote of 12,138 in favour of continued association with the United Kingdom, and forty-four against.[39]

Spain contends that the population of Gibraltar does not have the right to determine its own political status. Article X gave Spain a preference 'before any others', and therefore its reversionary right must prevail, since the words 'any others' include the Gibraltareans themselves.[40] Moreover, even if paragraph 2 of Resolution 1514(XV) takes precedence over paragraph 6, Article X of the Treaty and paragraph 6 are not supplanted by paragraph 2 in this particular case because the Gibraltareans, according to Spain, do not qualify as a 'people' under paragraph 2, and are therefore not entitled to exercise the right to self-determination. Spain argues that the Gibraltareans are an 'artificial population' because they were brought in by the British to settle Gibraltar after the original inhabitants were expelled.[41] The Gibraltareans have 'no roots in the territory',[42] and consequently the necessary 'identity' does not exist between inhabitants and territory which goes to make up a true people.[43] In response, the United Kingdom has noted that the inhabitants of Gibraltar are the descendants of a population which has resided in the territory longer than any previous Spanish population. Spanish rule in Gibraltar began in 1494 when the Moors were expelled, and ended in 1713 when the territory was ceded to the United Kingdom. That period is shorter than the ensuing period since 1713.[44]

[39] Franck and Hoffman, 373.

[40] Blay (1986) 469.

[41] J. E. S. Fawcett 'Gibraltar: The Legal Issues' (1967) 249. The Gibraltareans are 'an integrated mixture of Maltese, Italians, Jews and other Mediterranean peoples': Franck and Hoffman, 376.

[42] Michla Pomerance *Self-Determination in Law and Practice* (1982) 21.

[43] Rigo Sureda, 192. See also Simon J. Lincoln 'The Legal Status of Gibraltar: Whose Rock Is It Anyway?' (1994) 310.

[44] Franck and Hoffman, 376.

In 1965 the General Assembly adopted Resolution 2070(XX), which instructed the United Kingdom and Spain to undertake negotiations concerning Gibraltar. In 1966 the General Assembly adopted Resolution 2231(XXI), which called upon the United Kingdom and Spain to continue negotiations for the 'decolonization of Gibraltar'. Resolution 2231(XXI) indicated that the United Kingdom and Spain were to negotiate the future status of Gibraltar 'taking into account the interests of the people of the Territory', but neither resolution mentioned the right of the inhabitants of Gibraltar to self-determination. Resolution 2353(XXII), which the General Assembly adopted in December 1967 following the September referendum in Gibraltar, manifestly subordinated the claim by the inhabitants of Gibraltar to self-determination to the territorial claim of Spain. The Resolution repudiated the September referendum and noted that 'any colonial situation which partially or completely destroys the national unity and territorial integrity of a country is incompatible with the purposes and principles of the Charter of the United Nations, and specifically with paragraph 6 of General Assembly resolution 1514(XV)'. Significantly, the Resolution did not refer to the 'people of the Territory', as had Resolution 2231(XXI), but only to the 'population', whose interests were simply to be 'safeguarded'.

If Resolution 2353(XXII) stood for the proposition that territorial claims by historical title were to be included within the ambit of paragraph 6, and further that paragraph 6 was to pre-empt paragraph 2, then the continued validity of this proposition must be considered in the light of the General Assembly's subsequent action with respect to Belize, as reflected in Resolution 35/20. The two Resolutions are not necessarily contradictory. Resolution 35/20 may simply have reflected the General Assembly's conclusion that Guatemala did not have a legitimate territorial claim to Belize. If this were the case, there would be no conflict between Resolution 2353(XXII) and Resolution 35/20. Resolution 2353(XXII) would then establish the general principle that claims to territory based on a legitimate historical title supersede the right to self-determination. Resolution 35/20 would merely represent an instance in which the claim to historical title was found by the General Assembly not to be legitimate. On the other hand, the General Assembly may have sought to establish in Resolution 35/20 the principle that the right of self-determination must take precedence over all territorial claims based on historical title. It would then be immaterial whether Guatemala had a legitimate territorial claim to Belize, because the right of self-determination would oust even legitimate claims. The general proposition contained in Resolution 35/20 must then be considered to have superseded the general proposition in Resolution 2353(XXV). A third interpretation is possible: Resolution 2353(XXII) may stand for the proposition that the inhabitants of Gibraltar were not a 'people', and therefore not entitled to self-determination under paragraph 2. Resolution 2353(XXII) could then be reconciled with Resolution 35/20 on the basis that, although self-determination will oust a territorial claim based on historical title, it will do so only if the inhabitants of the territory are a 'people'. If not there is no question of self-determination, and a territorial claim based on historical title need not conflict with a claim for self-determination. Article 73 of the United Nations Charter refers to both 'peoples' and 'inhabitants'. It has been argued that two different words were used in order to distinguish between two different types of population. Blay, for example, asserts that the term 'people' refers to the 'indigenous population' of a territory, and that 'inhabitants' refers to 'all residents of the territory, including migrant settlers'. Only 'peoples', according to Blay, are entitled to self-determination.[45]

The dispute over the Falkland Islands also involves the issue of whether the population of a colony may be denied the right of self-determination on the ground that it is not a 'people'. The Falkland Islands are located some 350 miles from the Argentinian mainland.[46] East Falkland was first settled by the French in 1764. In 1766 France sold the territory to Spain, which established a settlement there. Meanwhile, the British established a settlement in West Falkland in 1765. The British settlement was abandoned in 1774 on grounds of economy, although a metal plaque was left at the site of the settlement, proclaiming the Falkland Islands to be 'the sole right and property of His Most Sacred Majesty George the Third'.[47] However, the Spaniards effectively administered all the Falkland Islands until 1810. At this time a revolt against Spain was gaining ground in Argentina, and in 1811 the Governor of Montevideo ordered the Spanish colony in the Falklands to be abandoned.[48]

Argentina proclaimed its independence from Spain in 1810,[49] and in 1820 it claimed sovereignty over the Falkland Islands. A governor was sent there and an Argentinian settlement established. In 1831 the governor seized two American vessels which were violating Argentinian fishing regulations; an American warship in the area responded by attacking the Argentinian settlement, which was largely destroyed.[50] In 1833 two British warships arrived and proclaimed British sovereignty over the islands. The remaining Argentinian settlers departed, and over the next decade a British settlement was established, which has been continuously maintained.[51] Argentina

---

[45] Blay (1986) 465.

[46] D. W. Greig 'Sovereignty and the Falkland Islands Crisis' (1983) 59.

[47] *Id.*, 30.

[48] Lowell S. Gustafson *The Sovereignty Dispute Over the Falkland (Malvinas) Islands* (1988) 21.

[49] Franck and Hoffman, 382.

[50] Gustafson, 24.

[51] *Id.*, 25–6.

has regularly objected to British occupation of the islands, officially protesting in 1841, 1849, 1884, 1888, 1908, 1927, 1933, 1946, and yearly thereafter in the United Nations.[52]

Argentina claims the Falkland Islands on the basis of historical title, and asserts that it obtained title to them by virtue of the principle of *uti possidetis*. As title to the Falkland Islands predates the development of the right of self-determination, and as Argentina has been a persistent objector to British occupation of the islands, Argentina argues that its claim to the Falklands takes precedence over any competing claim based on self-determination. Argentina also invokes paragraph 6 of Resolution 1514(XV) as justification for the reintegration of the islands with Argentina. It argues that the current population of the Falklands, which is overwhelmingly of British origin, is not entitled to self-determination because it is a 'settler population' which replaced the legitimate population of Argentinian inhabitants.[53] The current population, according to Argentina, does not have a 'legitimate relationship' with the territory.[54]

The United Kingdom argues that it has maintained sovereignty over the Falkland Islands from the time of its original settlement there in the eighteenth century. The United Kingdom also points out that, even if title to the islands were determined on the basis of the principle of *uti possidetis*, the successor of Spain to the Falkland Islands should be Uruguay rather than Argentina, since the Spanish settlement on the Falkland Islands was ordered to withdraw by Montevideo, rather than by Buenos Aires.[55] In any event, according to the United Kingdom, territorial claims are subject to the universal and overriding principle of self-determination; it is therefore the prerogative of the Falkland Islanders to determine their own political status. This the Islanders have done. In 1964 the Falklands Legislative Council informed the United Nations Special Committee of the desire of the Falkland Islanders to retain and strengthen their links with the United Kingdom. In 1980 the Islanders reiterated this desire and repudiated the suggestion that sovereignty over the Falklands be transferred to Argentina.[56]

The General Assembly's approach to the Falkland Islands dispute has been similar to its approach with regard to Gibraltar. The Assembly adopted its first resolution on the Falkland Islands on 16 December 1965.

---

[52] *Id.*, 34.

[53] Franck and Hoffman, 381.

[54] Sanchez, 563. The Falkland Islands are inhabited by approximately 2,000 people, but Argentina has never argued that the Falkland Islanders should not be granted the right to self-determination on the basis that they constitute such a small population. As Franck and Hoffman point out, 'infinitesimal smallness has never been seen as a reason to deny self-determination to a population': 383.

[55] Greig, 59.

[56] *Id.*, 47.

Resolution 2065(XX) declared in its Preamble that Resolution 1514(XV) had been 'prompted by the cherished aim of bringing to an end everywhere colonialism in all its forms, one of which covers the case of the Falkland Islands (Malvinas)'. It went on to urge the United Kingdom and Argentina to negotiate a settlement to their dispute over sovereignty of the Falkland Islands. The Resolution did not mention any right of self-determination for the Falkland Islanders, noting only that the two negotiating states were to bear in mind 'the interests of the population'. Eight years later the General Assembly adopted Resolution 3160(XXVII) of 14 December 1973. This specified that 'the way to put an end to this colonial situation is the peaceful solution of the conflict of sovereignty between the Governments of Argentina and the United Kingdom with regard to the aforementioned islands'. The Resolution urged the two states to negotiate a 'peaceful solution of the conflict of sovereignty between them concerning the Falkland Islands . . . in order to put an end to the colonial situation'. Again the parties were simply urged to bear in mind 'the interests of the population of the Falkland Islands (Malvinas)'. Resolution 31/49 of 1 December 1976 repeated statements made in the two previous Resolutions, and urged the parties to expedite negotiations. Following the Anglo-Argentinian conflict over the Falklands in 1982, the General Assembly adopted a series of resolutions urging the United Kingdom and Argentina to resume negotiations in order to resolve their dispute over the Falklands.[57]

The General Assembly resolutions relating to the Falklands call for a solution to the dispute over sovereignty without taking into account the wishes of the inhabitants of the islands, other than in a subordinate way. The wording of these resolutions reveals that the solution envisaged by the General Assembly involves the transfer of sovereignty to Argentina. In the cases of both Gibraltar and the Falkland Islands, the Assembly has decided that the territories in question should be returned to the claimant states, without the inhabitants of those territories being permitted to exercise the right of self-determination.

The General Assembly's position with regard to the Falkland Islands appears to have been reached, as in the case of Gibraltar, largely on the basis that the Falkland Islanders are a 'settler population' occupying territory for a colonial power. Not being 'indigenous' to the territory they cannot be considered as a 'people', and are therefore not entitled to self-determination as provided in paragraph 2 of Resolution 1514(XV). The language of the Falklands resolutions confirms this interpretation. The word 'population', rather than 'people', is consistently used to describe the Falkland Islanders, who are granted no right of consultation on the

---

[57] Resolutions 37/9 of 4 Nov. 1982; 38/12 of 16 Nov. 1983; 39/6 of 1 Nov. 1984; 40/21 of 27 Nov. 1985; 41/40 of 25 Nov. 1986; 42/19 of 17 Nov. 1987; and 43/25 of 17 Nov. 1988.

political future of the islands. The resolutions state only that the 'interests', not the wishes, of the 'population' are to be borne in mind when their future is being determined.

But, if 'indigenousness' is now being used by the General Assembly as a criterion to determine whether a population is entitled to self-determination, it has never been defined by the General Assembly, nor has it been applied by the Assembly in any consistent manner. With regard to Gibraltar, the General Assembly concluded that 250 years of habitation was insufficient to establish the indigenous character of the territory's inhabitants.[58] Yet the General Assembly refused to draw any distinction based on indigenousness between the native Fijian and immigrant Indian communities, insisting that independence should be attained on the basis of 'one man, one vote'.[59] Nor did the Assembly take into account the notion of indigenousness in the case of Belize. Forty per cent of the population of Belize was made up of Guatemalan Mayan Indians, the remaining 60 per cent had come to Belize from neighbouring Caribbean islands.[60] Yet when Guatemala attempted to argue that this 60 per cent of Belize's population were non-indigenous to the territory, the General Assembly not only made no mention of this issue but, in Resolution 35/20 of 11 November 1980, reaffirmed 'the inalienable right of the people of Belize to self-determination, independence and territorial integrity'. If 'indigenousness' has been a factor in the General Assembly's decisions with regard to self-determination, it has been applied by the Assembly in a highly selective and far from uniform manner. However, the Assembly has never explicitly indicated that it does take 'indigenousness' into consideration in deciding whether a particular population is a people with a right of self-determination.

Neither have the pronouncements of the International Court of Justice done much to clarify the matter. The Court indicated in the *Namibia* case[61] that the populations of all non-self-governing territories are entitled to self-determination, stating that the development of international law with regard to non-self-governing territories 'made the principle of self-determination applicable to all of them'.[62] By virtue of this declaration the inhabitants of all non-self-governing territories would be considered as 'peoples', since they are all entitled to self-determination. However, the Court also noted, in the *Western Sahara* case,[63] that in those instances when

---

[58] See *supra*, p. 246.

[59] Pomerance, 21. See GA Resolutions 1951(XVIII) of 11 Dec. 1963; 2068(XX) of 16 Dec. 1965; 2185(XXI) of 12 Dec. 1966; and 2350(XXII) of 19 Dec. 1967.

[60] Sanchez, 580.

[61] *Legal Consequences for States of the Continued Presence of South Africa in Namibia (South West Africa) notwithstanding Security Council Resolution 276 (1970)* Advisory Opinion, ICJ Reports 1971, p. 16.

[62] *Id.*, 31.   [63] Advisory Opinion, ICJ Reports 1975, p. 12.

the General Assembly has dispensed with the requirement of consulting the inhabitants of a non-self-governing territory, it has done so on the ground, *inter alia*, 'that a certain population did not constitute a people entitled to self-determination'.[64] In other words, not all inhabitants of non-self-governing territories necessarily constitute 'peoples'. It is difficult to reconcile these two statements by the Court.

The *travaux préparatoires* of Article 73 are somewhat more enlightening. There is no indication anywhere in the *travaux* that those drafting Article 73 had any intention of establishing a dichotomy between 'peoples' and 'inhabitants'.[65] The absence of any discussion on the matter would seem to indicate that no such dichotomy was envisaged, and that the words 'peoples' and 'inhabitants' are synonyms. If this is indeed the case, then there is no basis for distinguishing between populations which are, and those which are not, 'peoples' on the basis of indigenousness.

5. COLONIAL ENCLAVES

There are those who argue that the General Assembly's policy of promoting the integration of Gibraltar with Spain and the Falklands with Argentina has nothing to do with indigenousness, but reflects the policy of the Assembly with regard to 'colonial enclaves'. According to this theory, colonial enclaves represent a special category of territories not subject to the principle of self-determination. Crawford defines colonial enclaves as: 'minute territories which approximate, in the geographical sense, to "enclaves" of the claimant State, which are ethnically and economically parasitic upon or derivative of that State, and which cannot be said in any legitimate sense to constitute separate territorial units.'[66] Goa, Ifni and Walvis Bay are often cited as examples of colonial enclaves.

Goa is located on the Arabian seaboard of India and was a Portuguese colony. In 1962 India invaded and annexed Goa, declaring that it was both historically and legally part of India's territory. India argued that Goa belonged to India not only because it was geographically an enclave within Indian territory, but also because the history, culture, language, and traditions of the Goans linked them to the surrounding Indian population.[67] A majority of the members of the Security Council came to the conclusion that India had violated Article 2(4) of the Charter, but nevertheless took no action against India.[68] The annexation subsequently came to be

---

[64] Advisory Opinion, 33.

[65] (1945) 3 UNCIO 548–9, 609–14; (1945) 10 UNCIO 421–716.

[66] Crawford, 384. For a critique of Crawford's theory of colonial enclaves see D. W. Greig 'Reflections on the Role of Consent' (1992) 155–7.

[67] Blay (1986) 466.   [68] *Id.*, 466.

regarded 'as an acceptable instance of the retrocession of a colonial enclave'.[69]

Ifni provides another example of the retrocession of a colonial enclave. It was a Spanish colony, and lies on the Atlantic coast of Morocco. It covered an area of 1,500 square miles and had a population of 50,000 persons.[70] Unlike Goa, the General Assembly acted to endorse the retrocession of Ifni to Morocco before it occurred.[71] The actual transfer took place in 1969, under the terms of the Treaty of Fez, by which Spain agreed to cede the territory to Morocco.[72] The transfer was subsequently approved by the General Assembly.[73]

A third example of a colonial enclave is Walvis Bay, a South African possession of 434 square miles, located on Namibia's Atlantic coast.[74] Walvis Bay is the only deep-water port on the Namibian coastline, and is therefore of vital economic significance to Namibia. Namibia has no claim to Walvis Bay on the basis of historical title, unlike India and Morocco with respect to Goa and Ifni. Walvis Bay became a British possession in 1878, and was annexed to the Cape of Good Hope in 1884. The surrounding territory of what became South West Africa, and ultimately Namibia, was claimed by the Germans in 1884.[75] Walvis Bay, being a part of the Cape Colony, subsequently became part of the Cape Province upon Union in 1910, and a part of the Republic of South Africa in 1961. The territory of South West Africa, on the other hand, became a South African mandate, and eventually attained independence. Although Namibia has never had any historical basis for laying claim to Walvis Bay, the General Assembly has nevertheless repeatedly indicated that Walvis Bay must be considered as part of Namibia's territory. Resolution 32/9 of 4 November 1977 declared Walvis Bay to be 'a part of Namibia, with which it is inextricably linked by geographical, historical, economic, cultural and ethnic bonds'. The Security Council likewise declared, in Resolution 432 (1978), that the territorial integrity of Namibia required 'the reintegration of Walvis Bay within its territory'. These Resolutions demonstrate that the colonial enclave exception to self-determination is not based on historical title. Namibia has no claim to Walvis Bay on the basis of historical title. India's claim to Goa on the basis of historical title was also tenuous, given that the Indian subcontinent had never been politically united prior to the twentieth cen-

---

[69] Maguire, 870.

[70] Blay (1986) 467.

[71] See GA Resolutions 2072(XX) of 16 Dec. 1965; 2229(XXI) of 20 Dec. 1966: 2354(XXII) of 19 Dec. 1967: and 2428(XXIII) of 18 Dec. 1968.

[72] 4 Jan. 1969, Morocco–Spain, 1969 Boletin Oficial Estato (Spain) R. 1053 (1969); Blay (1986) 467.

[73] 24 UN GAOR C.4 (Agenda Item 23) at 293, UN Doc. A/C.4/Sr.1865 (1969).

[74] Blay (1986) 467.

[75] Lynn Berat *Walvis Bay* (1990) 4.

tury.[76] A colonial enclave situation can therefore occur quite apart from considerations of historical title.

The primary basis for determining that a territory is a colonial enclave appears to be either that it constitutes an integral part of the surrounding state,[77] or that it cannot be said to constitute a separate territorial unit.[78] However, the Falkland Islands cannot be considered to be a colonial enclave on either of these criteria. The Falkland Islands are some 350 miles from the Argentinian mainland, and therefore lack the element of territorial unity which characterized the relationship of Goa, Ifni, and Walvis Bay to their surrounding claimant states.[79] Crawford excludes the Falkland Islands from the category of colonial enclaves by stating that such a category 'would not include island territories—which are by definition not enclaves'.[80] Crawford also states that a colonial enclave should be composed of a population which is ethnically 'derivative' of the claimant state,[81] and which 'acquiesces in the annexation' of the enclave by the surrounding state.[82] On that basis it is doubtful that Gibraltar could be considered a colonial enclave, as its population, unlike that of Goa and Ifni,[83] is ethnically dissimilar to the population of the surrounding state, and it has indicated emphatically that it opposes the annexation of Gibraltar to Spain.[84] The General Assembly could not therefore have endorsed the integration of Gibraltar with Spain and that of the Falkland Islands with Argentina on the basis that they were colonial enclaves.

6. CONCLUSION

The relationship between territorial claims to non-self-governing territories based on historical title and the right of self-determination of the peoples of those territories remains unsettled and ill defined in international law. Paragraph 6 of Resolution 1514(XV) is the purported legal basis for claims

---

[76] Maguire, 870, fn. 114; Blay, 466, fn. 118.
[77] Blay (1986) 467.
[78] Crawford, 384.
[79] Greig, 61.
[80] Crawford, 384.
[81] *Id.*, 384.
[82] *Id.*, 118.
[83] A 1950 Portuguese census of Goa found that there were 800 Europeans in Goa, for the most part transient administrators, and 316 persons of mixed descent. The rest of the population of 650,000 were officially described as Indians: Greig, 61, fn. 52. In 1969 Ifni's population of between 40,000 and 50,000 was comprised of some 10,000 Europeans. The rest of the population were indigenous Arabs: Keesing's *Contemporary Archives* (1969–1970) Vol. 17, 23146. In 1976 there were in Walvis Bay 10,100 Whites, 4,200 Coloureds, 12,947 Africans and 1 Asian: Berat, 64, fn. 110.
[84] There is some evidence to suggest that the Goans might not have acquiesced in India's annexation had a plebiscite been held: Quincy Wright 'The Goa Incident' (1962) 627, fn. 32.

based on historical title, but little guidance can be obtained from the Resolution because the meaning and scope of paragraph 6, and the relationship of paragraph 6 to paragraph 2, are matters of ongoing dispute. This uncertainty leaves open the question of whether historical title takes precedence over self-determination, or vice versa.

The practice of the General Assembly with regard to claims based on historical title has been inconsistent. In those cases which have come before it the General Assembly has sometimes decided in favour of the territorial claim and sometimes in favour of self-determination. No underlying rationale has been offered by the Assembly for these apparently contradictory determinations.

The International Court of Justice, in the *Western Sahara* case,[85] dealt very cautiously with the issue of historical title and its relationship to self-determination. The Court did not pronounce definitively on the relationship of historical title to self-determination in the *Western Sahara* case, as historical title was found not to be applicable to the particular facts of that case. Nevertheless, various individual judges of the Court expressed opinions which appear to endorse the view that self-determination should take precedence over claims based on historical title. The relationship between self-determination and historical title, however, remains to be decided in a definitive manner.

[85] Advisory Opinion, ICJ Reports 1975, p. 12.

Epilogue

At its most fundamental level self-determination is the process whereby a people freely determines its own political status. However, the manner in which a people may validly do so has been defined in widely divergent ways. In Western Europe and the United States self-determination has generally been understood to constitute the process by which a population within a given state periodically elects a representative government. In Central and Eastern Europe self-determination has been linked to ethnicity and has therefore been thought to occur whenever an ethnic group formed a nation-state of its own. In the Third World the concept has been equated with decolonization, so that self-determination would take place whenever a non-self-governing territory attained independence and became a state in its own right.

Before the Second World War, these various theories of self-determination amounted to little more than political objectives in the international sphere. They did not generally form part of international law. This situation changed after the war when self-determination was written into the Charter of the United Nations and other major international instruments. But the extent to which self-determination has become a legal right has still not been definitively established, because the term 'people' has never been defined in any precise manner, and because international practice with regard to self-determination has been inconsistent. Although de-colonization has been universally accepted as an integral part of the law of self-determination, the legal status of other aspects of self-determination remains unclear. The theory that self-determination entails representative government is widely acknowledged by Western states and by the majority of the former Soviet bloc states. However, this understanding of self-determination is not accepted as a part of international law by many states in the Third World. The status of ethnic self-determination remains even more uncertain. Although it is widely claimed as a legal right by many ethnic groups throughout the world, it is not accepted as such by most states.

Ethnic self-determination does not fit easily into the system of international law. The theory of ethnic self-determination elevates the ethnic group to a position of supreme importance.[1] The goal of ethnic self-determination is to create a 'nation-sate' for the ethnic group, whose role will be to serve the ends of that group. International law, by contrast, is essentially

---

[1] As Lord Acton has observed, 'Nationality is founded on the perpetual supremacy of the collective will, to which the unity of the nation is a necessary condition, to which every other influence must defer and against which no obligation enjoys authority, and all resistance is tyrannical': 'Nationality' (1967) 148.

a system of interstate relations,[2] and the traditional valucs of international law 'have been state values—state autonomy and benefits to the state *qua* state'.[3] The primacy of the state in international law has meant that a state's population has been considered simply as an attribute of that state.[4] The traditional primacy of the state in international law is therefore fundamentally at odds with claims of ethnic groups seeking self-determination, because such groups in effect seek to subordinate the position of the state to that of the group. This tension is most clearly manifest with regard to questions of territorial integrity and transboundary territorial claims.

One response of international law to the problems of ethnic self-determination has been to categorize ethnic groups as 'minorities' and to extend to the members of such minorities guarantees of cultural, linguistic, and religious freedoms, but to deny them the right of self-determination. It was thought that this would ensure the preservation and protection of the ethnic group while maintaining the primacy and territorial integrity of the state. Granting the members of such groups the freedom to enjoy their own culture, use their own language, and practise their own religion would also have the effect of guaranteeing equality and non-discrimination to all persons within the state.

Ethnic groups, however, are not satisfied with the status of ethnic minority. Inspired by nationalism, such groups consider themselves to be 'peoples', and as such claim a right of self-determination. The goal of such groups is to create separate nation-states of their own. However, because the *raison d'être* of the nation-state is to serve the ends of the ethnic group which formed it, it follows that there can be no place within such a state for other ethnic groups. Such groups are seen as anomalous and alien elements within the state, and as a result intolerance and discrimination are often directed against them by the majority.[5] Nation-states are a testimony to the inability of ethnic groups to coexist and to work together.

Yet despite the essentially negative character of ethnic self-determination, it may in some instances be the only way of resolving ethnic conflict. Ethnic groups may be divided by such profound cultural and religious differences, or hold such intense animosity towards each other, or be so

---

[2] James Crawford 'The Rights of Peoples: Some Conclusions' in James Crawford (ed.) *The Rights of Peoples* (1988) 174.

[3] Louis Henkin 'Law and Politics in International Relations: State and Human Values' (1990) 190–1.

[4] Art. 1, Montevideo Convention (1936) 165 LNTS 19, at p. 26, provides an example of this orientation.

[5] As Pierre Trudeau points out, 'a state that defines its function essentially in terms of ethnic or religious attributes inevitably becomes chauvinistic and intolerant. Nationalists . . . are politically reactionary because they are led to define the common good as a function of an ethnic group or religious ideal rather than in terms of "all the people" regardless of individual characteristics': 'Against Nationalism' (1990) 60. See also Alexis Heraclides 'Secession, Self-Determination and Nonintervention: In Quest of a Normative Symbiosis' (1991) 410.

blinded by nationalism, that coexistence within a single state is simply not possible. In such circumstances the creation of nation-states may in fact be the only way of resolving ongoing and intractable political and social strife between such groups. Therefore international law, while not encouraging the creation of nation-states, must allow for the inability of ethnic groups to coexist within a single state. The law does not currently achieve this with regard to non-self-governing territories. Paragraph 6 of Resolution 1514(XV) prohibits the total or partial dismemberment of non-self-governing territories upon attaining independence. Since the adoption of Resolution 1514(XV) in 1960, the General Assembly has largely abandoned its pragmatic approach of dividing non-self-governing territories into separate states in cases of ethnic incompatibility, and has insisted that the territorial integrity of such territories be maintained at all costs, even though this has led in some cases to bitter ethnic conflict. The International Court of Justice has reinforced this stance by affirming that the principle of *uti possidetis* has become a general principle of international law for the purposes of decolonization. With regard to independent states, however, international law does provide for ethnic incompatibility. It does so in two possible ways. First, the law will permit secession as a legal remedy when an ethnic group has suffered gross oppression. An oppressed ethnic group will be entitled to create a nation-state of its own in order to escape oppression. Secondly, ethnic groups may create nation-states of their own in circumstances other than that of gross oppression if international law considers secession to be a matter of domestic jurisdiction. This means that international law neither sanctions nor prohibits secession within a particular state. Ethnic self-determination is simply a political act which occurs outside the jurisdiction of international law and is not governed by its principles.

The political approach to claims of ethnic self-determination does not work when such claims transcend national boundaries. In such circumstances international law protects the territorial integrity of a state against irredentist claims. This can give rise to ethnic tensions both within and between the states in question, which international law can only address through recourse to minority rights provisions.

The problem of ethnic incompatibility may also arise when a state makes a territorial claim based on historical title to an adjoining non-self-governing territory whose population does not share the same ethnic, cultural, or linguistic attributes as the population of the claimant state. When such claims arise, it remains unclear whether the inhabitants of those territories will be considered as 'peoples' entitled to exercise a right of self-determination, and whether the exercise of that right of self-determination will take precedence over a competing territorial claim based on historical title.

International law does not deal adequately with many of the problems associated with self-determination. However, as this book has shown, the very nature of self-determination renders it less than amenable to the prescriptive processes of the law. The concept of self-determination remains elusive, and defies all attempts to generalize its characterization. Moreover, its implementation usually creates as many problems as it solves—including, paradoxically, further claims to self-determination.

Bibliography

Acton, Lord 'Nationality' 131 *Essays in the Liberal Tradition of History* Chicago: University of Chicago Press, 1967

Addis, Adeno 'Individualism, Communitarianism and the Rights of Ethnic Minorities' (1992) 67 *Notre Dame Law Review* 615

Akehurst, Michael *A Modern Introduction to International Law* (6th edn.) London: Allen and Unwin, 1987

Akzin, Benjamin 'Who Is a Jew? A Hard Case' (1970) 5 *Israel Law Review* 259

Andress, Judith L. and Falkowski, James 'Self-Determination: Indians and the United Nations—the Anomalous Status of America's 'Domestic Dependent Nations' (1980) 8 *American Indian Law Review* 97

Arangio-Ruiz, Gaetano 'The Normative Role of the General Assembly of the United Nations and the Declaration of Principles of Friendly Relations' (1972) 137 *Recueil des Cours de l'Académie de Droit International* (Vol. III) 419

Arieli, Yehoshua *Individualism and Nationalism in American Ideology* Cambridge, Mass.: Harvard University Press, 1964

Asher, Robert E., Katschnig, Walter M., Brown, William Adams, Jr., Green, James Frederick, Sady, Emil J., and Associates *The United Nations and Promotion of the General Welfare* Washington: Brookings Institution, 1957

Azcarate, P. de *The League of Nations and National Minorities* Washington: Carnegie Endowment For International Peace, 1945

Bagwell, Ben 'Yugoslavian Constitutional Questions: Self-Determination and Secession of Member Republics' (1991) 21 *Georgia Journal of International and Comparative Law* 489

Baker, Ray Stannard and Dodd, William F. (eds.) *The Public Papers of Woodrow Wilson: The New Democracy, 1913–1917*, Vol. 2 Harper & Brothers, Kraus Reprint Co., 1970

Baker, Ray Stannard and Dodd, William F. (eds.) *The Public Papers of Woodrow Wilson: War and Peace, 1917–1919*, Vols. 1 and 2 New York: Harper & Brothers; Kraus Reprint Co., 1970

Ball, M. Margaret *Post-War German-Austrian Relations* Stanford: Stanford University Press, 1937

Banks, Arthur S. (ed.) *Political Handbook of the World: 1990* New York: CSA Publications, 1990

Barros, James *The Aland Islands Question* New Haven: Yale University Press, 1968

Barsh, Russel Lawrence 'Indigenous Peoples: An Emerging Object of International Law' (1986) 80 *American Journal of International Law* 369

Barsh, Russel Lawrence 'Revision of ILO Convention No. 107' (1987) 81 *American Journal of International Law* 756

Barsh, Russel Lawrence 'Indigenous Peoples in the 1990s: From Object to Subject of International Law?' (1994) 7 *Harvard Human Rights Journal* 33

Bastuck, Burkhard 'Unity, Law, and Freedom: Legal Aspects of the Process and Results of German Unification' (1991) 25 *International Lawyer* 251

Bayevsky, Anne F. 'The Human Rights Committee and the Case of Sandra Lovelace' (1982) 20 *Canadian Yearbook of International Law* 244

Bengoetxea, Joxerramon 'Nationalism and Self-Determination: the Basque Case' 133 William Twining (ed.) *Issues of Self-Determination* Aberdeen: Aberdeen University Press, 1991.

Bennett, T. W. and Peart, N. S. 'The Ingwavuma Land Deal: A Case Study of Self-Determination' (1986) 6 *Boston College Third World Law Journal* 23

Bentwich, Norman and Martin, Andrew *A Commentary on the Charter of the United Nations* London: Routledge & Regan Paul, 1950

Berat, Lynn *Walvis Bay* New Haven: Yale University Press, 1990

Berman, Howard R. 'Are Indigenous Populations Entitled to International Juridical Personality?' (1985) 79 *American Society of International Law Proceedings* 189

Berman, Nathaniel 'Sovereignty in Abeyance: Self-Determination and International Law' (1988) 7 *Wisconsin International Law Journal* 51

Berman, Nathaniel 'A Perilous Ambivalence: Nationalist Desire, Legal Autonomy, and the Limits of the Interwar Framework' (1992) 33 *Harvard International Law Journal* 353

Berman, Nathaniel 'Nationalism Legal and Linguistic: The Teachings of European Jurisprudence' (1992) 24 *New York University Journal of International Law and Politics* 1515

Birch, Anthony H. 'Minority Nationalist Movements and Theories of Political Integration' (1977) 30 *World Politics* 326

Blay, Kwaw Nyameke 'Self-Determination Versus Territorial Integrity in Decolonization Revisited' (1985) 25 *Indian Journal of International Law* 386

Blay, S. K. N. 'Self-Determination Versus Territorial Integrity in Decolonization' (1986) *New York University Journal of International Law and Policy* 441

Blay, Sam 'Self-Determination: A Reassessment in the Post-Communist World' (1994) 22 *Denver Journal of International Law and Policy* 275

Blum, Yehuda Z. *Historic Titles in International Law* The Hague: Martinus Nijhoff, 1965

Blum, Yehuda Z. 'Reflections on the Changing Concept of Self-Determination' (1975) 10 *Israel Law Review* 509

Blum, Yehuda Z. 'UN Membership of the "New" Yugoslavia: Continuity or Break?' (1992) 86 *American Journal of International Law* 830

Bothe, Michael and Schmidt, Christian 'Sur Quelques Questions de Succession Posées par la Dissolution de l'URSS et Celle de la Yougoslavie' (1992) 96 *Revue Générale de Droit International Public* 811

Bowett, D. W. 'Self-Determination and Political Rights in the Developing Countries' (1966) 60 *American Society of International Law Proceedings* 129

Brand, Jack *The National Movement in Scotland* London: Routledge & Kegan Paul, 1978

Breuilly, John *Nationalism and the State* Manchester: Manchester University Press, 1982

Brierly, James Leslie *The Law of Nations* (6th edn.) Oxford: Oxford University Press, 1963

Brossard, Jacques 'Le Droit du Peuple Québecois de Disposer de lui-même au regard du Droit International' (1977) 15 *Canadian Yearbook of International Law* 84

Brossard, Jacques 'Le Droit du Peuple Québecois, à l'Autodétermination et à l'Indépendance' (1977) 8 *Etudes Internationales* 151

Brown, Jonathan (ed.) *Australian Practice in International Law 1984–1985* Public International Law Seminar, University of NSW, Sydney, 1986

Brown, Philip Marshall 'Self-Determination in Central Europe' (1920) 14 *American Journal of International Law* 235

Brown, Philip Marshall 'The Mandate Over Armenia' (1920) 14 *American Journal of International Law* 396.

Brown, Philip Marshall 'The Aaland Islands Question' (1921) 15 *American Journal of International Law* 268

Brownlie, I. *Basic Documents in African Affairs* Oxford: Clarendon Press, 1971

Brownlie, Ian 'The Rights of Peoples in Modern International Law' 1 James Crawford (ed.) *The Rights of Peoples* Oxford: Clarendon Press, 1988

Bruegel, J.-W. 'A Neglected Field: The Protection of Minorities' (1971) 4 *Revue des Droits de l'Homme* 413

Brunnée, Jutta 'The Reunification of Germany: Comments on a Legal Maze' (1990) 13 *Dalhousie Law Journal* 725

Buchanan, Allen 'Self-Determination and the Right to Secede' (1991) 45 *Journal of International Affairs* 347

Buchanan, Allen 'Federalism, Secession and the Morality of Inclusion' (1995) 32 *Arizona Law Review* 53

Buchheit, Lee C. *Secession* New Haven: Yale University Press, 1978

Butt Philip, Alan *The Welsh Question* Cardiff: University of Wales Press, 1975

Calvaré, Louis *Le Droit International Public Positif*, Vol. 1 Paris: Editions A. Pedone, 1951

Capotorti, Francesco 'Les Développements Possibles de la Protection Internationale des Minorités' (1986) 27 *Cahiers de Droit* 239

Capotorti, Francesco *Study on the Rights of Persons Belonging to Ethnic, Religious and Linguistic Minorities* (UN Study E/CN.4/Sub.2/384/Rev.1) New York: United Nations, 1979

Carey, T. 'Self-Determination in the Post-Colonial Era: The Case of Québec' (1977) *ASILS International Law Journal* 55

Carr, E. H. (Chairman) *Nationalism* (A Report by a Study Group of Members of the Royal Institute of International Affairs) London: Frank Cass, 1939

Carr, Edward Hallett *The Bolshevik Revolution 1917–1923*, Vol. 1 London: Macmillan, 1960

Carter, Michael S. 'Ethnic Minority Groups and Self-Determination: The Case of the Basques' (1986) 20 *Columbia Journal of Law and Social Problems* 55

Cassese, Antonio 'The Helsinki Declaration and Self-Determination' 83 Thomas Buergenthal (ed.) *Human Rights, International Law and the Helsinki Accord* Monclair, New Jersey: Allanheld, Osmun & Co., 1977

Cassese, Antonio 'Political Self-Determination: Old Concepts and New Developments' 137 Cassese (ed.) *UN Law/Fundamental Rights* Alphen aan den Rijn: Sijthoff & Noordhoff, 1979

Cassese, Antonio 'The Self-Determination of Peoples' 92 Louis Henkin (ed.) *The International Bill of Rights* New York: Columbia University Press, 1981

Cassese, Antonio *Self-Determination of Peoples* Cambridge: Cambridge University Press, 1995

Charpentier, Jean 'Les Déclarations des Douze sur la Reconnaissance des Nouveaux Etats' (1992) 96 *Revue Générale de Droit International Public* 343

Chinkin, C. M. 'The Merits of Portugal's Claim Against Australia' (1992) 15 *University of New South Wales Law Journal* 423

Choudhury, G. W. 'Dismemberment of Pakistan, 1971: Its International Implications' (1974) 18 *Orbis* 179

Chowdhuri, R. N. *International Mandates and Trusteeship Systems* The Hague: Martinus Nijhoff, 1955

Claude, Inis L., Jr. 'Domestic Jurisdiction and Colonialism' 121 Martin Kilson (ed.) *New States in the Modern World* Cambridge, Mass.: Harvard University Press, 1975

Claude, Inis L., Jr. *National Minorities* Cambridge, Mass.: Harvard University Press, 1955

Clinebell, John Howard and Thomson, Jim 'Sovereignty and Self-Determination: The Rights of Native Americans under International Law' (1977–78) 27 *Buffalo Law Review* 669

Cobbah, Josiah A. M. 'Toward a Geography of Peace in Africa: Redefining Sub-State Self-Determination Rights' 70 R. L. Johnston, David B. Knight, and Eleonore Kofman (eds.) *Nationalism, Self-Determination and Political Geography* London: Croom Helm, 1988

Cobban, Alfred *The National State and National Self-Determination* New York: Thomas Y. Crowell, 1969

Coleman, James S. 'Tradition and Nationalism in Tropical Africa' 3 Martin Kilson (ed.) *New States in the Modern World* Cambridge, Mass.: Harvard University Press, 1975

Connor, Walker 'The Politics of Ethnonationalism' (1973) 27 *Journal of International Affairs* 2

Corbeil, Pierre and Montambault, André 'Secession and Independence for Québec: How Legitimate?' 181 Ralph R. Premdas, S. W. R. de A. Samarasinghe, and Alan B. Anderson (eds.) *Secessionist Movements in Comparative Perspective* London: Pinter, 1990

Craven, Greg 'Of Federalism, Secession, Canada and Québec' (1991) 14 *Dalhousie Law Journal* 231

Crawford, James *The Creation of States in International Law* Oxford: Clarendon Press, 1979

Crawford, James 'Aboriginal Self-Government in Canada' Unpublished Research Report for the Canadian Bar Association, Committee on Native Justice, January 1988

Crawford, James 'The Rights of Peoples: Some Conclusions' 159 James Crawford (ed.) *The Rights of Peoples* Oxford: Clarendon Press, 1988

Crawford, James 'The Rights of Peoples: "Peoples" or "Governments"?' 55 James Crawford (ed.) *The Rights of Peoples* Oxford: Clarendon Press, 1988

Crèvecoeur, Hector St John de (Michel Guillaume St Jean de Crévecoeur) *Letters From An American Farmer* New York: New American Library of World Literature, 1963

Critescu, Aureliu *The Right to Self-Determination: Historical and Current Development on the Basis of United Nations Instruments* (UN Study E/CN.4/Sub.2/404/Rev.1) New York: United Nations, 1981

Das Gupta, Jyotirinda 'Ethnicity, Language Demands, and National Development in India' 466 Nathan Glazer and Daniel P. Moynihan (eds.) *Ethnicity* Cambridge, Mass.: Harvard University Press, 1975

Davidson, Eugene *The Trial of the Germans* New York: Collier Books, 1966

de Silva, K. M. 'Separatism in Sri Lanka: The 'Traditional Homelands' of the Tamils' 32 Ralph R. Premdas, S. W. R. de A. Samarasinghe, and Alan Anderson (eds.) *Secessionist Movements in Comparative Perspective* London: Pinter, 1990

Deschènes, Jules 'Qu'est-ce qu'une Minorité?' (1986) 27 *Cahiers de Droit* 255

DeVries, Henry P. and Galston, Nina M. (eds.) *Materials for the French Legal System* New York: Columbia University, 1969

Dijk, P. van 'The Final Act of Helsinki: Basis for a Pan-European System?' (1980) 11 *Netherlands Yearbook of International Law* 97

Dinstein, Yoram 'Collective Human Rights of Peoples and Minorities' (1976) 25 *International and Comparative Law Quarterly* 102

Dinstein, Yoram 'Autonomy' 291 Yoram Dinstein (ed.) *Models of Autonomy* New Brunswick, New Jersey: Transaction Books, 1981

Djonovich, Duson J. (ed.) *United Nations Resolutions* Series I Resolutions Adopted by the General Assembly, Dobbs Ferry; New York: Oceana Publications, 1973 (Vol. II), 1974 (Vols. VIII and X), and 1978 (Vol. XIV)

Dore, Isaak I. *The International Mandate System and Namibia* Boulder: Westview Press, 1985

Dorn, Walter, Jr. van 'The Concept of Free Association: An End to the Trust Territory of the Pacific Islands' (1987) 5 *Boston University International Law Journal* 213

Dyke, Vernon van 'Self-Determination and Minority Rights' (1969) 13 *International Studies Quarterly* 223

Eagleton, Clyde 'Self-Determination in the United Nations' (1953) 47 *American Journal of International Law* 88

Emerson, Rupert *From Empire to Nation* Cambridge, Mass.: Harvard University Press, 1962

Emerson, Rupert 'Self-Determination' (1971) 65 *American Journal of International Law* 459

Ermacora, Felix 'The Protection of Minorities Before the United Nations' (1983) IV *Recueil des Cours de l'Académie de Droit International* (Vol. 182) 247

Evans, Ifor L. 'The Protection of Minorities' (1923–24) 4 *British Yearbook of International Law* 95

Evriviades, Marios L. 'The Legal Dimension of the Cyprus Conflict' (1975) 10 *Texas International Law Journal* 227

Fawcett, J. E. S. 'Security Council Resolutions on Rhodesia' (1965–66) 41 *British Yearbook of International Law* 103

Fawcett, J. E. S. 'Gibraltar: The Legal Issues' (1967) 43 *International Affairs* 236

Feinberg, Nathan 'The Recognition of the Jewish People in International Law' (1948) *Jewish Yearbook of International Law* 1

Fonteyne, Jean-Pierre L. 'The Portuguese Timor Gap Litigation Before the International Court of Justice: A Brief Appraisal of Australia's Position' (1991) 45 *Australian Journal of International Affairs* 170

Ford, Paul Leicester (ed.) *The Works of Thomas Jefferson* Vol. 3 New York: G. P. Putnam's Sons, 1904

Franck, Thomas M. 'The Stealing of the Sahara' (1976) 70 *American Journal of International Law* 694

Franck, Thomas M. 'Dulce et Decorum Est: The Strategic Role of Legal Principles in the Falklands War' (1983) 77 *American Journal of International Law* 109

Franck, Thomas 'The Emerging Right to Democratic Governance' (1992) 86 *American Journal of International Law* 46

Franck, Thomas M. and Hoffman, Paul 'The Right of Self-Determination in Very Small Places' (1975–76) 8 *New York University Journal of International Law and Politics* 331.

Fung Yu-lan *A Short History of Chinese Philosophy* London: Collier-Macmillan, 1948

Gill, T. D. *South West Africa and the Sacred Trust* The Hague: T. M. C. Asser Institute, 1984

Gittleman, Richard 'The African Charter on Human and Peoples' Rights: A Legal Analysis' (1982) 22 *Virginia Journal of International Law* 667

Goodrich, Leland M., Hambro, Edvard, and Simons, Anne Patricia *Charter of the United Nations* (3rd edn.) New York: Columbia University Press, 1969

Goodwin-Gill, G. *International Law and the Movement of Persons Between States* Oxford: Clarendon Press, 1978

Gowlland-Debbas, Vera *Collective Responses to Illegal Acts in International Law* Dordrecht: Martinus Nijhoff, 1990

Green, L. C. 'Protection of Minorities in the League of Nations and in the United Nations' 180 Allan Gottlieb (ed.) *Human Rights, Federalism and Minorities* Toronto: Canadian Institute of International Affairs, 1970

Green, L. C. 'Aboriginal Peoples, International Law and the Canadian Charter of Rights and Freedoms' (1983) 61 *Canadian Bar Review* 339

Gregory, Charles Noble 'The Neutralization of the Aaland Islands' (1923) 17 *American Journal of International Law* 63

Greig, D. W. 'Sovereignty and the Falkland Islands Crisis' (1983) 8 *Australian Yearbook of International Law* 20

Greig, D. W. 'Reflections on the Role of Consent' (1992) 12 *Australian Yearbook of International Law* 125

Gros Espiell, Hector *The Right to Self-Determination: Implementation of United Nations Resolutions* (UN Study E/CN.4/Sub.2/405/Rev.1) New York: United Nations, 1980

Grzybowski, Kazimierz *Soviet Public International Law* Leiden: A. W. Sijthoff, 1970

Gustafson, Lowell S. *The Sovereignty Dipute Over the Falkland (Malvinas) Islands* New York: Oxford University Press, 1988

Hanneman, Andrea J. 'Independence and Group Rights in the Baltics: A Double Minority Problem' (1995) 35 *Virginia Journal of International Law* 485

Hannum, Hurst *Autonomy, Sovereignty and Self-Determination* Philadelphia: University of Pennsylvania Press, 1990

Hannum, Hurst 'Rethinking Self-Determination' (1993) 34 *Virginia Journal of International Law* 2

Harvie, Christopher *Scotland and Nationalism* London: George Allen & Unwin, 1977.

Hauser, Rita E. 'International Protection of Minorities and the Right of Self-Determination' (1971) 1 *Israel Yearbook on Human Rights* 92

Hayes, Carlton J. H. *Nationalism: A Religion* New York: Macmillan, 1960

Heater, Derek *National Self-Determination* New York: St Martin's Press, 1994

Henkin, Louis 'Law and Politics in International Relations: State and Human Values' (1990) 44 *Journal of International Affairs* 183

Heraclides, Alexis 'Secession, Self-Determination and Nonintervention: In Quest of a Normative Symbiosis' (1991) 45 *Journal of International Affairs* 399

Hertz, Frederick *Nationality in History and Politics* London: Kegan Paul, Trench, Trubner & Co., 1944

Heyking, Baron 'The International Protection of Minorities: the Achilles' Heel of the League of Nations' (1927) 13 *Transactions of the Grotius Society* 31

Higgins, Rosalyn *The Development of International Law Through the Political Organs of the United Nations* London: Oxford University Press, 1963

Higgins, Rosalyn 'Judge Dillard and the Right to Self-Determination' (1983) 23 *Virginia Journal of International Law* 387

Himmer, Susan E. 'The Achievement of Independence in the Baltic States and Its Justifications' (1992) 6 *Emory International Law Review* 253

Hirayasu, Naomi 'The Process of Self-Determination and Micronesia's Future Political Status Under International Law' (1987) 9 *University of Hawaii Law Review* 487

Hitler, Adolf *Mein Kampf* Boston: Houghton Mifflin Co., 1943

Hondius, Frits W. *The Yugoslav Community of Nations* The Hague: Mouton & Co. N.V., 1968

Humphrey, John P. 'Preventing Discrimination and Positive Protection for Minorities: Aspects of International Law' (1986) 27 *Cahiers de Droit* 23

Hurewitz, J. C. (ed.) *Diplomacy in the Near and Middle East: A Documentary Record*, Vol. 2 New York: Octagon Books, 1956

Iglar, Richard F. 'The Constitutional Crisis in Yugoslavia and the International Law of Self-Determination: Slovenia's and Croatia's Right to Secede' (1992) 15 *Boston College International and Comparative Law Review* 213

Ijalaye, David A. 'Was "Biafra" At Any Time a State in International Law?' (1971) 65 *American Journal of International Law* 551

International Commission of Jurists 'East Pakistan Staff Study' (1972) 8 *International Commission of Jurists Review* 23

Iorns, Catherine J. 'Indigenous Peoples and Self-Determination: Challenging State Sovereignty' (1992) 24 *Case Western Reserve Journal of International Law* 199

Jayawickrama, Nihal 'The Right of Self-Determination: A Time for Reinvention and Renewal' (1993) 57 *Saskatchewan Law Journal* 1

Jennings, Sir Ivor *The Approach to Self-Government* Cambridge: Cambridge University Press, 1956

Johnson, Harold S. *Self-Determination Within the Community of Nations* Leyden: A. W. Sijthoff, 1967

Johnston, Darlene M. 'The Quest of the Six Nations Confederacy for Self-Determination' (1986) 44 *University of Toronto Faculty of Law Review* 1

Jones, Mary Gardiner 'National Minorities: A Case Study in International Protection' (1949) *Law and Contemporary Problems* 599

Kaeckenbeeck, George *The International Experiment in Upper Silesia* London: Oxford University Press, 1942

Kamenu, Onyeonoro S. 'Secession and the Right of Self-Determination: An OAU Dilemma' (1974) 12 *Journal of Modern African Studies* 355

Kaur, Satpul 'Self-Determination in International Law' (1970) 10 *Indian Journal of International Law* 479

Kedourie, Elie *Nationalism* London: Hutchinson University Press, 1960

Kelly, Joseph B. 'National Minorities in International Law' (1973) 3 *Denver Journal of International Law and Policy* 253

Kelsen, Hans *The Law of the United Nations* London: Stevens & Sons, 1951

Kertesz, G. A. *Documents in the Political History of the European Continent* Oxford: Clarendon Press, 1968

Kilson, Martin (ed.) *New States in the Modern World* Cambridge, Mass.: Harvard University Press, 1975

Kohn, Hans *Prophets and Peoples* New York: Macmillan, 1952

Kohn, Hans *The Idea of Nationalism* New York: Macmillan, 1961

Koskenniemi, Martti 'National Self-Determination Today: Problems of Legal Theory and Practice' (1994) 43 *International and Comparative Law Quarterly* 241

Kunz, Josef L. 'The Future of the International Law for the Protection of Minorities' (1945) 39 *American Journal of International Law* 89

Kunz, Josef L. 'Chapter XI of the United Nations Charter in Action' (1954) 48 *American Journal of International Law* 103

Kunz, Josef L. 'The Present Status of the International Law for the Protection of Minorities' (1954) 48 *American Journal of International Law* 282

Kupfer, Andrea 'International Agreements: Treaty on the Final Settlement with Respect to Germany' (1991) 32 *Harvard International Law Journal* 227

Lachs, Manfred 'Some Reflections on the Problem of Self-Determination' (1957) 4 *Review of Contemporary Law* 60

Ladas, Stephen P. *The Exchange of Minorities* New York: Macmillan, 1932

Lansing, Robert 'Self-Determination' *Saturday Evening Post* 9 Apr. 1921, 6

Lauterpacht, Sir Hersch *An International Bill of the Rights of Man* New York: Columbia University Press, 1945

Lemarchand, René 'The Limits of Self-Determination: The Case of the Katanga Secession' (1962) 56 *American Political Science Review* 404

Lenin, V. I. *Selected Works* Vols. 1 and 2 London: Lawrence & Wishart, 1947

Lenin, V. I. 'Socialism and War' 221 Alfred Zimmern (ed.) *Modern Political Doctrines* London: Oxford University Press, 1939

Lenin, V. I. *The Right of Nations to Self-Determination* Moscow: Foreign Language Publishing House, 1950

Levin, D. B. 'The Principle of Self-Determination of Nations in International Law' (1962) *Soviet Yearbook of International Law* 45

Levkov, Ilya 'Self-Determination in Soviet Politics' 133 Yonah Alexander and Robert A. Friedlander (eds.) *Self-Determination: National, Regional and Global Dimensions* Boulder, Colorado: Westview Press, 1980

Lincoln, Simon J. 'The Legal Status of Gibraltar: Whose Rock Is It Anyway?' (1994) 18 *Fordham International Law Journal* 285

Lloyd George, David *The Truth About the Peace Treaties* Vol. 1 London: Victor Gollancz, 1938

Locke, John *Two Treatises of Government* Cambridge: Cambridge University Press, 1970

Low, Alfred D. *Lenin on the Question of Nationality* New York: Bookman Associates, 1958

Luxemburg, Rosa *The National Question* New York: Monthly Review Press, 1976

Macartney, C. A. *National States and National Minorities* New York: Russell & Russell, 1934

McCurdy, Gregory V. S. 'German Reunification: Historical and Legal Roots of Germany's Rapid Progress Towards Unity' (1990) 22 *New York University Journal of International Law and Politics* 253

McGoldrick, Dominic 'Canadian Indians, Cultural Rights and the Human Rights Committee' (1991) 40 *International and Comparative Law Quarterly* 658

MacMillan, C. Michael 'Language Issues and Nationalism in Québec' (1987) 14 *Review of Studies in Nationalism* 229

Magnes, Judah L. *Russia and Germany at Brest-Litovsk* New York: Rand School of Social Science, 1919

Maguire, J. Robert 'The Decolonization of Belize: Self-Determination v. Territorial Integrity' (1982) 22 *Virginia Journal of International Law* 849

Mandell, Louise 'Indian Nations: Not Minorities' (1986) 27 *Cahiers de Droit* 101

Mandelstam, André 'La Protection des Minorités' (1923) 1 *Recueil des Cours de l'Académie de Droit International* 362

Mazrui, Ali A. *The African Condition* London: Cambridge University Press, 1980

Meissner, Boris 'The Right of Self-Determination After Helsinki and Its Significance for the Baltic Nations' (1981) 13 *Case Western Reserve Journal of International Law* 375

Mercer, John *Scotland: The Devolution of Power* London: John Calder, 1978

Mill, John Stuart *Considerations on Representative Government* London: Parker, Son, and Bourn, West Strand, 1861

Miller, David Hunter *The Drafting of the Covenant* Vols. 1 and 2 New York: G. P. Putnam's Sons, 1928

Minogue, K. R. *Nationalism* London: Batsford, 1967

Modeen, Tore *The International Protection of National Minorities in Europe* Abo: Abo Akademi, 1969

Modeen, Tore 'The Situation of the Finland-Swedish Population in the Light of International, Constitutional and Administrative Law' (1970) 16 *McGill Law Journal* 121

Montesquieu *De l'Esprit des Lois* Paris: Editions Sociales, 1969

Morris, C. R. and Morris, M. *A History of Political Ideas* London: Christophers, 1924

Morrow, Ian F. D. *The Peace Settlement in the German Polish Borderlands* London: Oxford University Press, 1936

Muggeridge, Malcolm *The Thirties* London: Collins, 1967

Murphy, Alexander B. 'Evoking Regionalism in Linguistically Divided Belgium' 135 David B. Knight and Elinore Kofman (eds.) *Nationalism, Self-Determination and Political Geography* London: Croom Helm, 1988

Murphy, John F. 'Self-Determination: United States Perspectives' 43 Yonah Alexander and Robert A. Friedlander (eds.) *Self-Determination: National, Regional and Global Dimensions* Boulder, Colorado: Westview Press, 1980

Nanda, Ved P. 'Self-Determination in International Law: The Tragic Tale of Two Cities—Islamabad (West Pakistan) and Dacca (East Pakistan)' (1972) 66 *American Journal of International Law* 321

Nanda, Ved P. 'Self-Determination Under International Law: Validity of Claims to Secede' (1981) 13 *Case Western Reserve Journal of International Law* 257

Nawaz, M. K. 'The Meaning and Range of the Principle of Self-Determination' (1965) *Duke University Law Journal* 82

Nawaz, M. K. 'Bangla Desh and International Law' (1971) 11 *Indian Journal of International Law* 251

Nayar, M. G. Kaladharan 'Self-Determination Beyond the Colonial Context: Biafra in Retrospect' (1975) 10 *Texas International Law Journal* 321

Necatigil, Zaim M. *The Cyprus Question and the Turkish Position in International Law* (2nd edn.) Oxford: Oxford University Press, 1993

Nkala, Jericho *The United Nations, International Law and the Rhodesian Independence Crisis* Oxford: Clarendon Press, 1985

Note 'The Logic of Secession' (1980) 89 *Yale Law Journal* 802

Nye, Joseph S. 'Nationalism, Statesmen, and the Size of African States' 158 Martin Kilson (ed.) *New States in the Modern World* Cambridge, Mass.: Harvard University Press, 1975

O'Connor 'The Politics of Ethnonationalism' (1973) 27 *Journal of International Affairs* 2

Ofuatey-Kodjoe, W. *The Principle of Self-Determination in International Law* New York: Nellen, 1977

Padelford, Norman J. and Andersson, K. Gosta A. 'The Aaland Islands Question' (1939) 33 *American Journal of International Law* 465

Palmer, Suzanne 'The Turkish Republic of Northern Cyprus: Should the United States Recognize It as an Independent State?' (1986) 4 *Boston University International Law Journal* 423

Panter-Brick, S. K. 'The Right to Self-Determination: Its Application to Nigeria' (1968) 44 *International Affairs* 254

Patterson, Frank Allen (ed.) *The Works of John Milton* Vol. 5 New York: Columbia University Press, 1932

Pechota, Vratislav 'The Development of the Covenant on Civil and Political Rights' 32 Louis Henkin (ed.) *The International Bill of Rights* New York: Columbia University Press, 1981

Pellet, Alain 'The Opinions of the Badinter Arbitration Committee: A Second

Breath for the Self-Determination of Peoples' (1992) 3 *European Journal of International Law* 178

Petersen, William 'On the Subnations of Western Europe' 177 Nathan Glazer and Daniel P. Moynihan (eds.) *Ethnicity* Cambridge, Mass.: Harvard University Press, 1975

Pi-Sunyer, Oriol 'Catalan Nationalism' 254 Edward A. Teryakian and Ronald Rogowski (eds.) *New Nationalisms in the Developed West* Boston: Allen & Unwin, 1985

Pipes, Richard *The Formation of the Soviet Union* Cambridge, Mass.: Harvard University Press, 1964 (revised edn.)

Pipes, Richard 'Nationality Problems in the Soviet Union' 453 Nathan Glazer and Daniel P. Moynihan (eds.) *Ethnicity* Cambridge, Mass.: Harvard University Press, 1975

Pomerance, Michla 'The United States and Self-Determination: Perspectives on the Wilsonian Conception' (1976) 70 *American Journal of International Law* 1

Pomerance, Michla *Self-Determination in Law and Practice* The Hague: Martinus Nijhoff, 1982

Pomerance, Michla 'Self-Determination Today: The Metamorphosis of an Ideal' (1984) 19 *Israel Law Review* 310

Post, K. W. J. 'Is There A Case For Biafra?' (1968) 44 *International Affairs* 26.

Pye, Lucian W. 'China: Ethnic Minorities and National Security' 489 Nathan Glazer and Daniel P. Moynihan (eds.) *Ethnicity* Cambridge, Mass.: Harvard University Press, 1975

Rawkins, Phillip 'Living in the House of Power: Welsh Nationalism and the Dilemma of Antisystem Politics' 294 Edward A. Tiryakian and Ronald Rogowski (eds.) *New Nationalisms of the Developed West* Boston: Allen & Unwin, 1985

Redslob, Robert 'Le Principe des Nationalités' (1931) 37 *Recueil des Cours de l'Académie de Droit International* 5

Reisman, W. Michael 'Coercion and Self-Determination: Construing Charter Article 2(4)' (1984) 78 *American Journal of International Law* 642

Renan, Ernest 'Qu'est-ce qu'une Nation?' 172 *Pages Choisies* Paris: Calmann-Levy

Renard, Ronald D. 'The Karen Rebellion in Burma' 93 Ralph R. Premdas, S. W. R. de A. Samarasinghe, and Alan Anderson (eds.) *Secessionist Movements in Comparative Perspective* London: Pinter, 1990

Renouf, Alan 'The Present Force of the Minorities Treaties' (1950) 28 *Canadian Bar Review* 804

Rich, Roland 'Recognition of States: The Collapse of Yugoslavia and the Soviet Union' (1993) 4 *European Journal of International Law* 36

Rigo Sureda, A. *The Evolution of the Right of Self-Determination* Leiden: A. W. Sijthoff, 1973

Robinson, Jacob 'From Protection of Minorities to Promotion of Human Rights' (1948) *Jewish Yearbook of International Law* 115

Robinson, Jacob 'International Protection of Minorities: A Global View' (1971) 1 *Israel Yearbook on Human Rights* 61

Ronen, Dov *The Quest for Self-Determination* New Haven: Yale University Press, 1979

Rosenstock, Robert 'The Declaration of Principles of International Law Concerning Friendly Relations: A Survey' (1971) 65 *American Journal of International Law* 713

Rosett, Arthur 'Legal Structures for Special Treatment of Minorities in the People's Republic of China' (1991) 66 *Notre Dame Law Review* 1503

Rosting, Helmer 'Protection of Minorities By the League of Nations' (1923) 17 *American Journal of International Law* 641

Rothwell, Nicolas 'The Yeltsin Challenge' *Weekend Australian* 14 Dec. 1991 26

Rousseau, Jean-Jacques *The Social Contract and Discourse on the Origin and Foundation of Inequality Among Mankind* (ed. Lester G. Crocker) New York: Washington Square Press, 1967

Rouzié, David 'Bulletin de Jurisprudence: Note' (1976) 103 *Journal du Droit International* 392

Russell, Harold S. 'The Helsinki Declaration: Brobdingnag or Lilliput?' (1976) 70 *American Journal of International Law* 242

Russell, Ruth B. *A History of the United Nations Charter* Washington: Brookings Institution, 1958

Sabine, George H. *A History of Political Theory* London: George G. Harrap, 1937

Sadler, Robert J. 'The Federal Parliament's Power to Make Laws "With Respect to . . . the People of Any Race . . ."' (1985) 10 *Sydney Law Review* 591

Sagay, Itsejuwa *The Legal Aspects of the Namibian Dispute* Ile Ife, Nigeria: University of Ife Press, 1975

Samarasinghe, S. W. R. de A. 'The Dynamics of Separatism: The Case of Sri Lanka' 48 Ralph R. Premdas, S. W. R. de A. Samarasinghe, and Alan Anderson (eds.) *Secessionist Movements in Comparative Perspective* London: Pinter, 1990

Sanchez, Miguel Antonio 'Self-Determination and the Falkland Islands Dispute' (1982) 21 *Columbia Journal of Transnational Law* 557

Schachter, Oscar 'The Legality of Pro-Democratic Invasion' (1984) 78 *American Journal of International Law* 645

Schoenberg, Harris O. 'Limits of Self-Determination' (1976) 6 *Israel Yearbook on Human Rights* 91

Schwed, Alejandro 'Territorial Claims as a Limitation to the Right of Self-Determination in the Context of the Falkland Islands Dispute' (1982–83) 6 *Fordham International Law Journal* 443

Shafer, Boyd C. *Faces of Nationalism* New York: Harcourt Brace Jovanovich, 1972

Shaheen, Samad *The Communist Theory of National Self-Determination* The Hague: W. Van Hoeve, 1956

Shaw, Malcolm 'The Western Sahara Case' (1978) 49 *British Yearbook of International Law* 19

Sinha, S. Prakash 'Is Self-Determination Passé?' (1973) 12 *Columbia Journal of Transnational Law* 260

Sloan, Blaine 'General Assembly Resolutions Revisited (Forty Years Later)' (1987) 58 *British Yearbook of International Law* 39

Slonim, Solomon *South West Africa and the United Nations: An International Mandate in Dispute* Baltimore: John Hopkins University Press, 1973

Smelser, Ronald M. *The Sudeten Problem, 1933–1938* Folkstone, William Dawson & Sons, 1975

Smith, Anthony D. *Nationalism in the Twentieth Century* Canberra: Australian National University Press, 1979

Smith, Edward Conrad (ed.) *The Constitution of the United States* (11th edn.) New York: Barnes & Noble Books, 1979

Smuts, J. C. *The League of Nations* London: Hodder & Stoughton, 1918

Snyder, Louis L. *The Meaning of Nationalism* Westport, Conn.: Greenwood Press, 1954

Snyder, Louis L. *Varieties of Nationalism: A Comparative Study* New York: Holt, Rinehart and Winston, 1976

Sohn, Louis B. 'Models of Autonomy Within the United Nations Framework' 5 Yoram Dinstein (ed.) *Models of Autonomy* New Brunswick, NJ: Transaction Books, 1981

Sohn, Louis B. 'The Rights of Minorities' 270 Louis Henkin (ed.) *The International Bill of Rights* New York: Columbia University Press, 1981

Stalin, Josef *Marxism and the National and Colonial Question* London: Lawrence & Wishart, 1936

Stalin, Josef 'Reply to the Discussion on National Factors in Party and State Affairs' 269 *Works* Vol. 5 Moscow: Foreign Languages Publishing House, 1953

Starr, Richard F. (ed.) *Yearbook on International Communist Affairs 1991* Stanford: Hoover Institution Press, 1991

Starushenko, G. B. 'Abolition of Colonialism and International Law' 79 G. I. Tunkin (ed.) *Contemporary International Law: Collection of Articles* Moscow: Progress, 1969

Stone, Julius *International Guarantees of Minority Rights* London: Oxford University Press, 1932

Stone, Julius *Regional Guarantees of Minority Rights* New York: MacMillan, 1933

Sutton, Eric (ed. and trans.) *Gustav Streseman: His Diaries, Letters and Papers* Vol. 2 London: Oxford University Press, 1935

Suzuki, Eisuke 'Self-Determination and World Public Order: Community Response to Territorial Separation' (1976) 16 *Virginia Journal of International Law* 779

Tapié, Victor-L. *The Rise and Fall of the Habsburg Monarchy* New York: Praeger, 1971

Taylor, A. J. P. *The Course of German History* London: Methuen, 1961

Temperley, H. W. V. *A History of the Peace Conference of Paris* Vols. I and IV London: Oxford University Press, 1920 and 1921

Theodorides, John 'The United Nations Peace Keeping Force in Cyprus (UNFICYP)' (1982) 31 *International and Comparative Law Quarterly* 765

Thornberry, Patrick *International Law and the Rights of Minorities* Oxford: Clarendon Press, 1991

Thornberry, Patrick 'Is There a Phoenix in the Ashes? International Law and Minority Rights' (1980) 15 *Texas International Law Journal* 421

Thornberry, Patrick 'Self-Determination, Minorities, Human Rights: A Review of International Instruments' (1989) 38 *International and Comparative Law Quarterly* 867

Tomuschat, Christian 'Self-Determination in a Post-Colonial World' 1 Christian

Tomuschat (ed.) *Modern Law of Self-Determination* Dordrecht: Martinus Nijhoff, 1993

Toynbee, Arnold 'Self-Determination' (1925) 244 *The Quarterly Review* 317

Trudeau, Pierre 'Against Nationalism' (1990) 7 *New Perspectives Quarterly* 60

Tschofen, Franziska and Hausmaninger, Christian 'Legal Aspects of East and West Germany's Relationship With the European Economic Community After the Collapse of the Berlin Wall' (1990) 31 *Harvard International Law Journal* 647

Tudjman, Franjo *Nationalism in Contemporary Europe* New York: Columbia University Press, 1981

Tunkin, G. I. *Theory of International Law* Cambridge, Mass.: Harvard University Press, 1974

Turp, Daniel 'Le Droit de Sécession en Droit International Public' (1982) 20 *Canadian Yearbook of International Law* 24

Turpel, Mary Ellen 'Indigenous Peoples' Rights of Political Participation and Self-Determination: Recent International Legal Developments and the Continuing Struggle for Recognition' (1992) 25 *Cornell International Law Journal* 579

Umozurike, Umozurike O. *Self-Determination in International Law* Hamden, Conn.: Archon Books, 1972

Wambaugh, Sarah *Plebiscites Since the World War* Vol. 1 Washington: Carnegie Endowment for International Peace, 1933

Warbrick, Colin 'Current Developments: Public International Law: Recognition of States' (1992) 41 *International and Comparative Law Quarterly* 473

Webb, Keith *The Growth of Nationalism in Scotland* Glasgow: Molindinar Press, 1977

Weill, Georges *L'Eveil des Nationalités* Paris: Felix Alcan, 1930

Weller, Marc 'The International Response to the Dissolution of the Socialist Federal Republic of Yugoslavia' (1992) 86 *American Journal of International Law* 569

Wengler, Wilhelm 'Le Droit de la Libre Disposition des Peuples comme Principe du Droit International' (1957) 10 *Revue Héllenique de Droit International* 26

Wheeler-Bennett, John W. *Brest-Litovsk: The forgotten peace, March 1918* London: MacMillan, 1966

White, Robin C. A. 'Self-Determination: Time for a Re-assessment?' (1981) 28 *Netherlands International Law Review* 147

Wodie, Francis 'La Sécession du Biafra et le Droit International Public' (1969) 73 *Revue Générale de Droit International Public* 1018

Wood, John R. 'Secession: A Comparative Analytical Framework' (1981) 14 *Canadian Journal of Political Science* 107

Woolsey, Theodore S. 'The Rights of Minorities Under the Treaty with Poland' (1920) 14 *American Journal of International Law* 392

Wright, Quincy *Mandates Under the League of Nations* Chicago: University of Chicago Press, 1930

Wright, Quincy 'Recognition and Self-Determination' (1954) 48 *American Journal of International Law* 23

Wright, Quincy 'United States Intervention in the Lebanon' (1959) 53 *American Journal of International Law* 112

Wright, Quincy 'The Goa Incident' (1962) 56 *American Journal of International Law* 617

Xydis, Stephen G. 'The UN General Assembly as an Instrument of Greek Policy: Cyprus 1954–58' (1968) 12 *Journal of Conflict Resolution* 141

Yapou, Eliezer 'The Autonomy That Never Was' 97 Yoram Dinstein (ed.) *Models of Autonomy* New Brunswick, NJ: Transaction Books, 1981

Young, M. Crawford 'Nationalism and Separatism in Africa' 57 Martin Kilson (ed.) *New States in the Modern World* Cambridge, Mass.: Harvard University Press, 1975

Zenushkina, I. *Soviet Nationalities Policy and Bourgeois Historians* Moscow: Progress, 1975

Zimmern, A. *The Third British Empire* (3rd edn.) London: Oxford University Press, 1934

Zimmern, Alfred *The League of Nations and the Rule of Law 1918–1935* London: MacMillan, 1936

Index